History Education
and National Identity
in East Asia

Reference Books in International Education

EDWARD R. BEAUCHAMP, SERIES EDITOR

EDUCATION, CULTURES, AND
ECONOMICS
Dilemmas for Development
edited by Fiona E. Leach and
Angela W. Little

SCHOOLING IN SUB-SAHARAN
AFRICA
*Contemporary Issues and
Future Concerns*
edited by Cynthia Szymanski
Sunal

GENDER ISSUES IN
INTERNATIONAL EDUCATION
Beyond Policy and Practice
edited by Maggie Wilson and
Sheena Erskine

CHINA'S NATIONAL MINORITY
EDUCATION
*Culture, Schooling, and
Development*
edited by Gerard A.
Postiglione

THIRD WORLD EDUCATION
Quality and Equality
edited by Anthony R. Welch

THE ETHNOGRAPHIC EYE
*Interpretive Studies of
Education in China*
edited by Judith Liu, Heidi
Ross, and Donald P. Kelly

TEACHER EDUCATION IN THE
ASIA-PACIFIC REGION
A Comparative Study
edited by Paul Morris and
John Williamson

DISTANT ALLIANCES
*Promoting Education for Girls
and Women in Latin America*
edited by Regina Cortina
and Nelly P. Stromquist

INTENSE YEARS
*How Japanese Adolescents
Balance School, Family, and
Friends*
by Gerald K. LeTendre and
Rebecca Erwin Fukuzawa

JAPANESE MODEL OF SCHOOLING
Comparisons with the U.S.
by Ryoko Tsuneyoshi

COMPETITOR OR ALLY?
*Japan's Role in American
Educational Debates*
edited by Gerald K.
LeTendre

POLITICS OF EDUCATIONAL
INNOVATIONS IN DEVELOPING
COUNTRIES
*An Analysis of Knowledge and
Power*
edited by Nelly P. Stromquist
and Michael L. Basile

EDUCATIONAL RESTRUCTURING IN
THE CONTEXT OF GLOBALIZATION
AND NATIONAL POLICY
edited by Holger Daun

TEACHING IN JAPAN
A Cultural Perspective
by Nobuo K. Shimahara

CIVIC EDUCATION IN THE
ASIA-PACIFIC REGION
*Case Studies across
Six Societies*
edited by John J. Cogan,
Paul Morris, and
Murray Print

HEGEMONIES COMPARED
*State Formation and Chinese
School Politics in Postwar
Singapore and Hong Kong*
by Ting-Hong Wong

PROFESSIONAL DEVELOPMENT OF
SCIENCE TEACHERS
*Local Insights with Lessons for
the Global Community*
edited by Pamela
Fraser-Abder

CONSTRUCTING EDUCATION FOR
DEVELOPMENT
*International Organizations
and Education for All*
by Colette Chabbott

SCHOOL LEADERSHIP AND
ADMINISTRATION
*Adopting a Cultural
Perspective*
edited by Allan Walker and
Clive Dimmock

DEVELOPMENT EDUCATION IN
JAPAN
*A Comparative Analysis of the
Contexts for its Emergence,
and Its Introduction into the
Japanese School System*
by Yuri Ishii

DAUGHTERS OF THE THARU
*Gender, Ethnicity, Religion,
and the Education of Nepali
Girls*
by Mary Ann Maslak

CRISIS AND HOPE
*The Educational Hopscotch of
Latin America*
edited by Stephen J. Ball,
Gustavo E. Fischman, and
Silvina Gvirtz

INSIDE JAPANESE CLASSROOMS
The Heart of Education
by Nancy E. Sato

RE-IMAGINING COMPARATIVE
EDUCATION
*Postfoundational Ideas and
Applications for Critical Times*
edited by Peter Ninnes and
Sonia Mehta

LEARNING THROUGH
COLLABORATIVE RESEARCH
*The Six Nation Education
Research Project*
edited by Noel F. McGinn

QURANIC SCHOOLS
*Agents of Preservation and
Change*
by Helen N. Boyle

HISTORY EDUCATION AND
NATIONAL IDENTITY IN EAST ASIA
edited by Edward Vickers and
Alisa Jones

History Education and National Identity in East Asia

Edited by

Edward Vickers
and Alisa Jones

Routledge
Taylor & Francis Group

NEW YORK AND LONDON

Published in 2005 by
Routledge
Taylor & Francis Group
270 Madison Avenue
New York, NY 10016

Published in Great Britain by
Routledge
Taylor & Francis Group
2 Park Square
Milton Park, Abingdon
Oxon OX14 4RN

10 9 8 7 6 5 4 3 2 1

International Standard Book Number-10: 0-415-94808-8 (Hardcover)
International Standard Book Number-13: 978-0-415-94808-1 (Hardcover)
Library of Congress Card Number 2004025137

Library of Congress Cataloging-in-Publication Data

History education and national identity in East Asia / edited by Edward Vickers and Alisa Jones.--
    1st ed.
        p. cm. -- (Reference books in international education)
    Includes bibliographical references and index.
    ISBN 0-415-94808-8 (hardback : alk. paper)
    1. History--Study and teaching--East Asia. 2. Education--Political aspects--East Asia. I. Vickers, Edward, 1971- II. Jones, Alisa. III. Series.

D16.4.E18H57 2005
907'.1'05--dc22   2004025137

Taylor & Francis Group
is the Academic Division of T&F Informa plc.

Visit the Taylor & Francis Web site at
http://www.taylorandfrancis.com

and the Routledge Web site at
http://www.routledge-ny.com

Contents

Series Preface

This series of scholarly works in comparative and international education has grown well beyond the initial conception of a collection of reference books. Although retaining its original purpose of providing a resource to scholars, students, and a variety of other professionals who need to understand the role played by education in various societies or world regions, it also strives to provide accurate, relevant, and up-to-date information on a wide variety of selected educational issues, problems, and experiments within an international context.

Contributors to this series are well-known scholars who have devoted their professional lives to the study of their specializations. Without exception these men and women possess an intimate understanding of the subject of their research and writing. Without exception they have studied their subject not only in dusty archives, but have lived and traveled widely in their quest for knowledge. In short, they are "experts" in the best sense of that often overused word.

In our increasingly interdependent world, it is now widely understood that it is a matter of military, economic, and environmental survival that we understand better not only what makes other societies tick, but also how others, be they Japanese, Hungarian, South African, or Chilean, attempt to solve the same kinds of educational problems that we face in North America. As the late George Z. F. Bereday wrote more than three decades ago: "[E]ducation is a mirror held against the face of a people. Nations may put on blustering shows of strength to conceal public weakness, erect grand façades to conceal shabby backyards, and profess peace while secretly arming for conquest, but how they take care of their children tells unerringly who they are" (*Comparative Methods in Education*, New York: Holt, Rinehart and Winston, 1964, p. 5).

Perhaps equally important, however, is the valuable perspective that studying another education system (or its problems) provides us in understanding our own system (or its problems). When we step beyond our own limited experience and our commonly held assumptions about schools and learning in order to look back at our system in contrast to another, we see it in a very different light. To learn, for example, how China or Belgium handles the education of a multilingual society; how the French provide for the funding of public education; or how the Japanese control access to their universities enables us to better understand that there are reasonable alternatives to our own familiar way of doing things. Not that we can borrow directly from other societies. Indeed, educational arrangements are inevitably a reflection of deeply embedded political, economic, and cultural factors that are unique to a particular society. But a conscious recognition that there are other ways of doing things can serve to open our minds and provoke our imaginations in ways that can result in new experiments or approaches that we may not have otherwise considered.

Edward R. Beauchamp
University of Hawaii

Acknowledgments

We would like to thank Catherine Bernard and Kimberly Guinta of Routledge in New York for their patience as we struggled to get the manuscript ready for publication. Even in this Internet age, the logistical difficulties involved in drawing together and editing contributions from thirteen people proved daunting. In the end they might have defeated us, had it not been for the last-minute assistance of Warren Lee in rescuing several of the most crucial chapters from electronic limbo.

We would also like to thank some of the people who provided us with advice and encouragement over the almost four years from the inception of this project to the completion of the manuscript. These include Professor Paul Morris, President of the Hong Kong Institute of Education; Professor Anthony Sweeting; Professor Mark Bray and Dr. Peter Cunich of the University of Hong Kong; Professor Ed Beauchamp of the University of Hawaii; and Professor Andy Green of the Institute of Education, University of London. We would also like to thank Shi Guopeng of Beijing's Number 4 Middle School, a mutual friend who first introduced us in late 2000. Lee Chi Hung of Hong Kong's Education and Manpower Bureau and Patrick Wong of the Hong Kong Examinations and Assessment Authority have over the years been of enormous assistance to Edward Vickers and Flora Kan. Ms. Wu Huei-Chun of the Cultural Division of the Taipei Representative Office in London was extremely helpful in many ways, not least in liaising on our behalf with organizations in Taipei, and the staff of National Institute of Compilation and Translation in Taipei were extraordinarily generous in lending assistance and making important materials available to us. Meg Wang of the National Palace Museum in Taipei; Dr. Patricia Huang, former assistant to the Deputy Minister of Culture in the Government of the Republic of China (Taiwan); Dorothy Chen of the National Chi Nan University; and Kevin Chang of Academia Sinica also gave us invaluable assistance in collecting data on history education in Taiwan. Edward Vickers would also like to thank Dr. Germ Janmaat of the Institute of Education, University of London, who read and commented on an earlier version of the introductory chapter, and Professor Hugh Baker of SOAS for his helpful comments on a draft of the Hong Kong chapter.

Our thanks of course go to all of the contributors to this volume for the hard work they have put into preparing their separate chapters. However, we should express our particular gratitude to two contributors: Dr. Peter Cave of the Unversity of Hong Kong and Dr. Stéphane Corcuff of the University of La Rochelle, who also helped in locating other contributors and by giving us very useful feedback on our own contributions.

Lastly, we gratefully acknowledge the permission granted by Elsevier, the publishers of the *International Journal of Educational Research*, to adapt and expand three articles that were originally published in the Winter 2002 issue of that journal. These form the basis of chapter 3 (by Liu, Hung, and Vickers), chapter 9 (by Nozaki), and chapter 10 (by Cave). An earlier version of chapter 5 (by Vickers and Kan) was first published in the Spring 2004 issue of the *American Asian Review*. Chapter 4 (by Stéphane Corcuff) is largely based on an article that was first published in French in a 2001 issue of *Études chinoises*.

Edward Vickers and Alisa Jones

Introduction
History, Nationalism, and the Politics of Memory

EDWARD VICKERS

History education in East Asia is a subject that for many years has generated a great deal of journalistic heat, but upon which only isolated rays of academic light have been shed. The lack of published research on history education and national identity first struck editors of this volume while we were completing Ph.D. dissertations examining the development of history curricula in Hong Kong and the Chinese mainland. The compilation of these studies thus arose from a desire to supply the kind of reference work we would have wished for when pursuing our own doctoral research. That research — and our long experience of living, working, and traveling in Hong Kong, the Chinese mainland, Taiwan, Japan, and elsewhere in the region — brought home the extreme political sensitivity of interpretations of the past in East Asia and, in particular, the ways they are transmitted to high school students. When we ourselves were sixth form students in the late 1980s, the controversy in England over the introduction of the National Curriculum for History had already demonstrated to us the way that the selection and presentation of historical knowledge to students was intimately bound up with perceptions of national identity, with conceptions of the role of education in citizenship formation, and with ideas concerning the nature of history and of how we knew what we knew about the past. A great amount of scholarly ink has been spilled over the years in the course of the debates surrounding the English National Curriculum and the place of history within it (Phillips, 1998). However, the political struggles we later observed over history education in East Asia, in terms of both the extreme positions adopted by the contesting parties and the potentially disturbing implications of these for domestic and international stability, made that English tussle seem, by comparison, about as momentous and alarming as a towel fight at a netball match.

The distortion of accounts of the Second World War in Japanese history textbooks is an issue that has long aroused intense interest both within and beyond East Asia. Ian Buruma's stimulating and readable comparison of memories of

1

the war in Japan and Germany, *Wages of Guilt* (Buruma, 1994), was one of the first accessible works in English to discuss the Japanese textbook controversy in any depth and highlighted the way Germany had gone further than Japan in confronting its record of aggression and genocide. In 2000, Laura Hein and Mark Selden's edited volume, *Censoring History* (Hein and Selden, 2000), brought together essays looking specifically at history textbooks in Germany, Japan, and the United States, again taking memories of war — principally the Second World War, but also the Vietnam War — as its major theme. However, the relative paucity of studies that attempt to set the Japanese controversy in its regional context remains striking (one notable exception being Rose 1998). Recent articles for the *American Asian Review* by Tomoko Hamada, comparing middle school history textbooks in Japan and the People's Republic of China, and by Chunghee Sarah Soh, analyzing the Korean furor over Japanese history textbooks, have begun to remedy this lack (Hamada, 2003; Soh, 2003). We hope this volume will constitute a further contribution to plugging this scholarly gap, especially by broadening the scope of comparison to the East Asian region as a whole. The cases of Hong Kong and Taiwan, in particular, deserve more attention than they have hitherto received, not least for the way in which they highlight the role played by education in exacerbating the tensions and dangers resulting from Beijing's attempt to impose a one-size-fits-all vision of Chineseness on communities from Kashgar to Kaohsiung. Although most of the contributions to the present volume focus on individual societies, this introductory chapter and the historiographical chapter that follows attempt to analyze and explain some of the global, cross-regional, and country-specific factors that have influenced curriculum development in these different states and regions.

The Origins and Scope of the Present Volume

As every Chinese schoolboy knows, printing was one of ancient China's "four great inventions." Meanwhile, in Korea, schoolboys — and girls — can take pride in the fact that it was their people who gave the moveable type printing press to the world. The printed word as technological achievement has in these states been woven into the official historical narrative of national greatness. In practice, printing in premodern times was instrumental not only in the early formation of a common identity among China's educated elite but also in the development of cultural traditions shared across East Asia through the dissemination of Confucian classics, Buddhist scriptures, and much else from Japan to Java and from Taiwan to Tibet. However, the printed word in contemporary East Asia is at least as likely to be the vehicle for expressions of nationalist triumphalism, xenophobic resentment, or straightforward ethnic chauvinism as for the celebration of traditions shared within the region and beyond. Modern print capitalism in East Asia, as elsewhere, has been a powerful force for the formation of imagined communities (Anderson, 1983) but this region's tortured recent past, and its portrayal through various media, has both shaped and been shaped by national communities that have constructed their identities in exceptionally absolute, totalizing, and homogenizing ways. In the hands of political and intellectual elites, history — of wars, of great men, or of great inventions — has tended to stress essential cultural virtues, the primordial and eternal unity of the nation, and the record of conflict and victimhood that has separated "our country" from its enemies. When it comes to national histories, the print medium in East Asia has become part of a message with a vengeance.

Meanwhile, the printing presses of Western academic publishers have been kept busy in recent years by the output of scholars researching the nationalism in the Far East. However, with some notable exceptions, remarkably little attention has been devoted to the role played by history education in schools in reflecting and constructing nationalist visions of the past. Barmé (1999), Befu (1993), Duara (1995), Dikotter (1992, 1997), Unger (1993, 1996), Fogel (2000), and others have analyzed political, popular, and academic discourse in these societies, and their findings — some of which are discussed in more detail below and in chapter 1 — have revealed the salience of often disturbingly extreme nationalist attitudes. Their work has traced the origins of these attitudes to the interactions between indigenous traditions and foreign cultural imports from neo-Darwinist racial essentialism to anti-Western postcolonialist cultural relativism. The contingencies of political history and the consequent rise and fall of particular legitimating ideologies also play their parts. Whatever ideological preoccupations color the view, the importance of visions of the past to the construction of political and cultural identity in East Asia is axiomatic, but what is less clear is the process by which such visions, and the values that they carry, are transmitted from generation to generation. Popular culture, in the form of literature, film, television, print media and, more recently, the Internet, undoubtedly plays a crucial role here and has justly attracted the attention of a number of scholarly and journalistic commentators.

Schools, curricula, and textbooks might also be expected to play a significant part in this process, but these have so far not been the focus of similar interest on the part of academic observers. The reasons for this almost certainly have less to do with the intrinsic importance of the subject matter than with the consequences of the typical division of academic labor within university campuses. The study of school curricula is generally seen as the province of specialists in education, and such specialists are seldom to be found within faculties or departments of history, politics, or Asian studies. Even within education faculties, only a small number of researchers look in detail at school curricula and, across much of East Asia itself, those inclined to approach this field critically may face political constraints in terms of what they can safely write and publish. Meanwhile, Western-based analysts of the history, politics, and culture of East Asia tend to focus overwhelmingly on the writings and pronouncements of prominent intellectuals, artists, and political leaders. These are undoubtedly far more stimulating than the banalities of school history textbooks, but they are by no means necessarily more important or influential. Banality, whether in textbooks, on television, or in the popular press, tends to be more popularly influential than intellectual sophistication — and this is as true of America or Britain as it is of China or Korea. Analyzing the way history has been taught and learned in schools may thus contribute as much as the study of high culture to an understanding of the ways particular visions of the past have come to influence public discourse, and vice versa. The study of history textbooks and official curricula cannot necessarily tell us what people actually believe about their national past (or the pasts of neighboring nations). Nonetheless, it can tell us what those who draft these curricular materials — whether the state or its agencies, textbook publishers, or individual authors — would like children to believe: the kinds of national, local, or global identities considered desirable and appropriate.

The present volume aims to serve as a starting point for such an understanding, by exploring the post-1945 development of history as a school subject in seven East Asian societies: China, Japan, Taiwan, Hong Kong, Singapore, and the two Koreas. It expands upon an earlier collection of essays published in 2003 as a special issue of the *International Journal of Educational Research*, though that collection included no articles on Korea or Singapore and focused primarily on curriculum development over the most recent quarter century. These societies have been chosen because of their shared Confucian educational and historiographical traditions. On these grounds we could — and perhaps should — have also included a chapter on Vietnam, but a line had to be drawn somewhere, and it was decided that Vietnam and the rest of Indochina would be better left to a future volume devoted to history education and identity formation in Southeast Asia. Singapore, on the other hand, as a former British colony populated overwhelmingly by the descendants of Chinese immigrants, suggested interesting comparisons with Hong Kong. Moreover, the Singapore government's attempt to invoke Asian values in support of its neo-authoritarian political model, and to promote these values through the local education system, has aroused considerable interest among governing elites elsewhere in what might be termed "post-Confucian" East Asia.

With the exception of Peter Cave's chapter, which uses data drawn from interviews and classroom observations to compare aspects of the learning and teaching experience in Japanese and English history lessons, the focus here is primarily on published sources, in particular curriculum outlines and textbooks. Official curricular guidelines should always be treated with caution, since they serve as symbols of official intent and are not necessarily reflective of classroom reality. The same could be said of textbooks in some education systems, but the role of the officially recommended textbook in schools throughout East Asia has tended to be far more central than is the case in systems where official regulation of the textbook market is much more limited, where the variety of teaching and learning materials available is consequently larger and where modes of assessment are designed to discourage the rote memorization of authorized texts. Across East Asia, the style of public examinations, the level of official control over textbooks, and a strong and long-standing belief in the need for authoritatively "correct" versions of history have all tended to reinforce the importance attached by both students and teachers to the approved texts (McClelland, 1991).

The extent to which traditional notions of the nature and purpose of history continue to influence official and popular views of the past is an issue that confronts any researcher investigating the historiography of the contemporary Far East. However, despite general acknowledgment of the fact that the states of East Asia share, Confucian heritage, surprisingly little comparative research has been undertaken into the different ways traditional views of the past and its relationship to national identity have been reinterpreted, co-opted, or rejected by modern nationalist historiographies throughout the region. Numerous studies have been undertaken at the country level, but the tendency among specialists on China, Japan, Taiwan, or Korea has been to burrow their way through lonely mountains of national data, only seldom emerging to survey the surrounding landscape. The first two chapters of this volume therefore set out to chart that broader vista, first by way of an overview of worldwide approaches to history and the politics of nation building and then through a closer mapping of the East Asian terrain.

History, the Modern State, and the Politics of Identity

In Europe, the birthplace of the modern nation-state, the open espousal of nationalist presuppositions is no longer as fashionable as it once was, at least in more intellectual circles. In particular, visions of national identity based on ideas of ethno-cultural homogeneity, let alone of common racial descent, have been subjected to systematic scholarly demolition in the decades since the fall of Nazi fascism and the dissolution of European colonial empires. The political and intellectual elites of postwar Europe have consciously sought to discredit the political — and economic — tribalisms of the prewar era, and to a greater or lesser extent subsume these within a vision of a peaceful and united pan-European community characterized by democracy, tolerance, and respect for human rights. That most European-minded of British intellectuals, Eric Hobsbawm, while recognizing that nationalism remains a force to be reckoned with in the contemporary world, suggests that the phenomenon may be past its peak, concluding his analysis of *Nations and Nationalism since 1780* with this observation, "The owl of Minerva which brings wisdom, said Hegel, flies out at dusk. It is a good sign that it is now circling round nations and nationalism" (Hobsbawm, 1992, 192).

However, even in supposedly progressive, twenty-first century multicultural Britain, this feathered friend of liberal internationalism is still more commonly found in the intellectual stratosphere than at ground level. Concluding his study of Victorian English historiography, J. W. Burrow suggests reasons for this as valid today as they were for the England of the Victorians, or for that matter when Burrow was writing in the 1970s:

> The class of purposive and justificatory historical myths of which English Whig histories are a distinguished sub-species is unlikely to be dispelled by any changes in the professional practice and ethics of historians. This is so not only because analysis may be impotent against prejudice, or because even being made to read learned articles in historical journals seems not so incompatible as might have been hoped with continued subscription to some form of political Manichaeanism. It is because, even in the conditions of exasperated tribalism in which such myths flourish most vigorously, the facts appealed to on both sides may be perfectly true: the Apprentice Boys did play a part in the defence of Londonderry. What gives such history its continuing power is not falsehood, or for that matter truth, but the sense of continuing identity, expressed in re-enactments by ritual or riot. The enemy of such myths is not truth but individualism, the dissolving of the sense of collective identities and temporal continuities — a fact which explains and justifies our ambivalence toward them. (1983, 297–298)

While academic historians continue to expose the mythological nature of the nationalist teleologies that characterize much popular history, these myths may remain to some extent necessary to our sense of community and to the cohesion of the societies in which we live.

The consciousness of a shared past is fundamental to the collective identities that underpin the legitimacy of our political institutions — so much so that where a shared past does not exist, it may be felt necessary to try to invent one. (On the politics of myth making, see Brown, 1999).

This applies not only to conventional nation-states but also to other political (or politico-religious) entities that claim our allegiance: the city, the federal state, the church, or a supranational entity such as the European Union. Indeed, Hobsbawm suggests that the antidote to narrow nationalism may lie in the multiplication of levels and forms of identity, so that "being English or Irish or Jewish, or a combination of all these, is only one way in which people describe their identity among the many others which they use for this purpose, as occasion demands" (Hobsbawm, 1992, 192). These communities of identity are each founded upon narratives of a common past, and the tensions and inconsistencies between these narratives might be expected to stimulate greater awareness of their mythological nature and to lessen the potential for unwholesome obsession with any single one. However, a boundary remains between healthy skepticism and a relativistic, ultraindividualistic anomie that, by corroding the legitimacy of shared identities, may undermine the basis of social cohesion.

What, then, determines the currency of nationalistic visions of the past, and the degree of credence attached to these, in popular discourse? Many critics of what is often referred to as nineteenth-century nationalism blame nationalist attitudes for fostering a sense of ethno-cultural superiority, xenophobic paranoia, and intercommunal or international fear and insecurity. School history textbooks have often been seen as instrumental to this process and have frequently attracted international and domestic criticism on these grounds — the Japanese history textbook controversies being only one of the most recent and widely publicized instances of this phenomenon. (It is perhaps worth noting that in the 1920s and early 1930s, it was the Japanese who officially criticized Chinese history textbooks for their virulent anti-Japanese xenophobia. Such criticisms were made in the context of political instability and rising militarism in Japan and efforts to whip up anti-Chinese sentiment among the populace but, as Jones notes in chapter 1, Chinese textbooks of this period were indeed intensely xenophobic.) However, while criticisms of nationalistic or xenophobic history textbooks are often justified and necessary, simply calling for changes in textbook content may be ineffectual because the insecurities that fueled the xenophobia in the first place remain unaddressed. Bickers' observation concerning the British settler community in China 100 years ago could apply equally to other larger, national communities:

> They lacked, in the treaty system, an assured, unassailable future. The stridency of the treaty port propagandists, and the rigidity of the practices which preserved British identity from dilution or deterioration, stemmed from the fundamental insecurity of the improvised settlements in China. (Bickers, 1999, 223)

Education, and history education in particular, is just one of the many practices that a community may deploy to preserve its identity and cohesion from perceived threats. The way in which British schools in Shanghai or Tianjin taught national (British) history may be imagined, though it has yet to be researched. However, the broader point that emerges here is that structures that guarantee or protect political and economic security may be a precondition for a relaxation of the rigidity with which societies cling to narrowly nationalistic visions of their collective identities.

In their comparative study of history textbooks in Japan, Germany, and the United States, Hein and Selden (2000) make a similar point when they argue that it is political factors, rather than any essential cultural differences, that explain the contrast between the ways Germans and Japanese remember the Second World War and choose to transmit these memories to pupils. Implicitly criticizing the theories of anthropologists such as Ruth Benedict (1989), who famously posited a distinction between a Japanese culture of shame and a Western culture of guilt, they write:

> Germans are still divided over how to remember the war, but they have greater incentive than their Japanese counterparts to satisfy neighbouring countries. This is not because the Germans feel guilt whereas the Japanese feel only shame. Nor are Germans more remorseful by nature than the Japanese. Some Germans feel guilt, shame and remorse for their wartime actions as do some Japanese. Others in both countries do not. Rather, larger numbers of Germans than Japanese currently believe that teaching their children positive accounts of Nazism and the war will cost them too much in the future. (Hein and Selden, 2000, 10)

Why do Germans believe this? According to Hein and Selden, this belief has much to do with the way Germany has been integrated politically, economically, and culturally within a wider European community through first the European Economic Community and later the European Union. A German official is quoted as saying, "You cannot preach a European Union and at the same time continue to produce textbooks with all the national prejudices of the nineteenth century" (16). In East Asia, by contrast, Hein and Selden (2000) point out that formidable obstacles remain to any similar Asian Union, the biggest one being "the deep mistrust potential member states feel toward one another." "Without clear incentives for regional reconciliation," they argue, "many Japanese are reluctant to take on the domestic battles inherent in rethinking their World War actions" (18). The experience of prereunification East Germany, where school history textbooks largely ignored the Nazi Holocaust and portrayed Nazism as the product of a bygone bourgeois era, is cited to reinforce the claim that "the contrast between Japan and the Federal Republic of Germany is political rather than cultural" (30).

This argument is convincing as far as it goes, but it leaves us needing to resolve a familiar conundrum: which comes first, the egg of exasperated tribalism or the chicken of the political and cultural forms (including school curricula and textbooks) that manifest and perpetuate it? In postwar Western Europe, the Cold War, along with American encouragement, prompted national leaders to overcome their mutual mistrust and to move toward closer political, military, and economic cooperation on the basis of mutual tolerance and respect for liberal-democratic values a process later extended to post-Communist Eastern Europe. Where political, economic, and military necessity led, culture and curricula eventually, albeit to varying extents, followed, so that today the specter of a German Fourth Reich sending its armies goose-stepping across the continent would seem an unreal, not to say paranoid, phantasm to most Europeans.[1] In East Asia, however, the Cold War led to a complex set of bilateral relationships between the United States and Japan, South Korea, and Taiwan, but the East Asian nations were required to take little or no collective responsibility for their common security, nor were they pressured into embarking on thoroughgoing internal democratic reforms. America's regional dominance protected these states from Russia, China, and North Korea, but it also insulated them from each other and allowed them to rebuild or reinforce internal social cohesion during the postwar period through old-fashioned appeals to naked ethno-nationalist sentiment, without having to confront any seriously adverse consequences in terms of their relations with their neighbors (although Taiwan, as we shall see, has more recently become something of an exception in this regard). The overbearing protection afforded by the American nanny thus allowed regional political elites to play nasty nationalist games without risk of injury; however, since the end of the Cold War, they have found themselves being coaxed and cajoled out of the nursery to face a neighborhood increasingly dominated by the intimidating presence of China. Meanwhile, the process of accommodating China within a stable new order in East Asia is complicated by that state's own troubled infancy. As Hein and Selden point out, "the political legitimacy of the People's Republic of China is built on the national memory of the war of liberation against relentless Japanese savagery" (83). This institutionalization of Sino-Japanese hatred makes it hard to conceive of a Franco-German-style reconciliation between China and Japan. Yet the long-term stability of East Asia requires precisely this kind of reconciliation not only between China and Japan but also between Japan, China, and Korea; China and Taiwan; China and Vietnam; and perhaps even China, Tibet, and India.

Chinese hatred for the Japanese may have been stoked by the Communist regime, especially in recent years as nationalism has displaced Marxism as the defining official ideology, but neither this hatred nor the broader sense of China's historical and cultural identity has been simply invented by the nationalist state. These are sentiments that most Chinese imbibe, almost literally, with their mothers' milk — through folklore handed down by families and local communities that serves to locate individuals, clans, villages, towns, or cities within a wider world. Stories told by state propagandists, or by history textbook authors, are likely to establish only shallow roots in popular consciousness if they fail to relate convincingly to the stories that families and communities tell each other. The power, or weakness, of the nationalist narrative of Chinese history as developed and refined under the Communists derives ultimately from its consonance, or dissonance, with popular folk memory. Folk memories may themselves be as false or distorted as the stories of party propagandists, but they are not simply the imaginative conjurings of political elites.

The case not only of China, but also of Japan and Korea, suggests that the arguments of Western scholars who extrapolate primarily from European examples to construct theories of nationalism as an invented tradition require some qualification. Hobsbawm, the European Marxist, and Gellner, the self-proclaimed Enlightenment liberal, have highlighted the novelty of the modern nineteenth-century nation-state and the role of schools and universities as vehicles for the transmission of the shared national identities that constituted the social glue of these new polities. Schools undoubtedly were designed to perform this function, and frequently did so — but equally failed to do so. No amount of singing the "Marseillaise" or studying the history of the Grand Revolution transformed Vietnamese into Frenchmen, just as learning about the Magna Carta or the 1832 Reform Act did not turn Malays or Chinese into Britons. Where political socialization merely involves a clumsy top-down imposition of obviously alien histories and values, it is unlikely to succeed.

Ernest Gellner recognizes this when he argues that the importance in modern societies of access to the dominant high culture — "a literate codified culture permitting context-free communication, community membership and acceptability" — means that "if there is no congruence between the culture in which [people] are operating and the culture of the surrounding economic, political and educational bureaucracies, then they are in trouble" (Gellner, 1999, 33). In circumstances where a community feels so excluded, people may "automatically" become nationalists. Gellner cites the case of the Estonians, who at the beginning of the nineteenth century "did not even have a name for themselves" but who gradually developed the full paraphernalia of national identity and culture as a result of their sense of exclusion from the high culture of the German, Swedish, and Russian elites. The case of Estonia invites comparison with the more recent development of a sense of national identity in Taiwan and perhaps also of what might be termed a subnational or pseudonational identity among the population of Hong Kong. These examples suggest that Gellner is probably right when he claims that "cultural continuity is contingent and inessential" to the development of nationalism, if this continuity is defined as an ability to trace the cultural distinctiveness of a community back to "primordial" roots (33). In Chapter 4, Stéphane Corcuff forcefully propounds precisely this sort of antiprimordialist view in relation to Taiwan. Nevertheless, if this is valid as a general rule, it may require substantial qualification in the case of East Asian nationalisms more broadly and Chinese nationalism in particular. This is because national identity in China, and to a lesser extent in Japan and Korea, has come to be rooted in a consciousness of distinctive cultural traditions that are, demonstrably, exceptionally ancient. In these cases, premodern high culture did not, as in the case of ancient Greece, simply demarcate the distinction between "those who read Homer (or the Confucian *sishu*) and those who did not" (though this was in each case one of the most important ways of distinguishing between those who were or were not "civilised"). In much of East Asia, this high culture also imparted a sense of shared history and, importantly, of common ancestry, which underpinned the legitimacy of the state (Dikotter, 1992, 1997). These historiographical and genealogical traditions may ultimately have been "invented", just as Estonian or Taiwanese nationalisms have more recently been conjured up apparently "out of thin air," but they were inventions whose artificiality was effectively obscured by the mists of time. Moreover, while in Japan and Korea nationalism may generally have constituted the features of a shared elite culture from which the mass of the agrarian population was largely excluded (as Gellner suggests is typically the case in premodern societies), throughout most of "China proper," these traditions arguably constituted a proto-nationalism that permeated both elite and popular cultures. History, along with genealogy (Dikotter, 1992, 1997; Faure and Liu, 1996; Siu, 1996), was also an important force in the spiritual universe of traditional China, and its principal function — as is discussed further in Chapter 1 — was to explain the rise and fall of ruling dynasties by reference to a set of eternal moral norms embodied in the Chinese classical canon. The ongoing exegesis of these classical texts by the scholarly elite, alongside the currency of bowdlerized versions of many of the stories they contained at the popular level, suggests parallels with the role of the Bible and of ecclesiastical history in premodern Europe. In the case of Europe, Chadwick has argued that ecclesiastical history eventually "begat" secular history and that the child "slowly began to change its father." He also claims that "men of Eastern philosophies and religions paid small heed to [history], neglecting it as a kaleidoscope of trivial little lights which pale before the sight of eternal being and truth."('). One wonders which particular "Eastern philosophies" he had in mind; however, in China, and perhaps to a lesser extent in those states that were part of the "Chinese World Order" (such as Korea, Japan, and Vietnam), history, far from being seen as "trivial", was regarded — at least among educated elites — as the touchstone of state legitimacy. The difference with "the West" lay not in history's absence, but in the way in which it was conceived. History in the traditional Chinese world, far from being the ungrateful child of religion, was its Siamese twin; for the elite, history *was* religion — and the state was both the object of worship and the ultimate source of doctrinal authority (Jenner, 1993).

This traditional obsession with the state, incorporating and reinforced by the deeply rooted practice of ancestor worship (Faure and Liu, 1996; Dikotter, 1992, 1997), perhaps helps to account for the extraordinary receptiveness of East Asian societies to the neo-Darwinist theories of nationalism that were fashionable in Europe during the late nineteenth and early twentieth centuries — just at the time when Chinese, Japanese, and Koreans were attempting to redefine and "modernise" their polities by reference to European precedents. Influenced by Darwinist ideas, they intensified, reinvented, or reimagined — but did not suddenly conjure up out of thin air — forms of nationalism that posited the existence of primordial, homogenous race-nations, their efforts given extra impetus by a laager mentality induced by the menace of Western imperialism. In the process, as Duara has shown, rival visions of history — both indigenous and "Western" — that challenged this primordialist, state-centered master narrative by advocating more liberal, pluralist, or secular alternatives were swept aside (Duara, 1995). The task of "rescuing history from the nation" in China and elsewhere in East Asia was rendered all the more difficult by the early love match between the dominant native tradition of state-centered sacred history and the late nineteenth-century Western emphasis on the primacy of eternal, racially defined national communities. This union spawned a virulent brood of pseudoreligious, racialist nationalisms in China, Japan, and Korea and inspired revised standard versions of the old histories to serve as scripture for the faithful members of these reformed national communities.

Ways of Relating to the Past: A Question of Standards

It is important to emphasise at this point that the cultures and histories of the Far East are not in any fundamental sense incommensurable with those of the rest of the world; the cultural traditions of these communities may have predisposed them to adopt primordialist visions of their national past, but those traditions, however ancient they may be, are themselves the products of history and not of some ineffable "essence" and, as such, are contingent and subject to change. Just as German nationalism, historiography, and history curricula developed differently in East and West Germany in the decades after World War II, so in the People's Republic, Hong Kong, Taiwan, and Singapore visions of the history of China and perceptions of what it means to be Chinese have multiplied and diverged. There may be dominant trends in historical thought and in the way in which national communities construct their own identities but, as we argue in later chapters, in East Asia these dominant discourses — to adopt a fashionable term — have never held the field entirely unchallenged, whether from without or within.

The assumption that these dominant visions should be challenged, both for the health of these communities and for the good of the wider world, is one that informs the contributions to this volume. However, the claim that there are "better" and "worse" ways in which nations can go about constructing their identities historically and teaching history in their schools is itself open to attack, not least from those who may feel that the standards by which such judgments are made are "Western" standards, and thus are by definition inapplicable to non-Western societies. In what we are often told is a "postmodern" world, the relativity of all cultures and standards is often taken as axiomatic. Before proceeding to analyse the different ways in which history can be presented through school curricula and textbooks, it is important to address the issue of cultural relativism, especially since this idea, along with others associated with postmodernist and postcolonialist theory, has in recent years attracted considerable interest in East Asia.

Postmodernism, or the very wide range of ideas associated with it, has inspired much extremely valuable and stimulating research into such areas as the history of culture and into previously neglected fields such as women's history. However, the value of the contribution made by this research, as with historical scholarship of any kind, still implicitly depends upon its potential for improving our understanding of the past. It is the capacity of history to do this at all that has come under attack in recent years from more "fundamentalist", or theoretically oriented postmodernists or poststructuralists. The latter have tended to argue that claims to "truth" on behalf of a particular interpretation of history or a particular culture, political ideology, or religion are all in the final analysis merely screens for a Nietzschean "will to power" (Jenkins, 1991, 1995, 1997; Foucault, 1997). Since "truth" is a mirage, the dominance of any particular set of beliefs at any time is irrelevant to their validity; it is merely a reflection of the power that those who benefit from their acceptance are able to wield over others. The acceptance or rejection of ideas or beliefs is not a matter of rational choice because that would imply a set of standards according to which any choice could be judged to be rational or otherwise, a possibility denied by relativism. Perceptions of "truth" are merely the consequence of an irrational preference — a preference that may be inherited, like one's genes, from predecessors within a cultural tradition, or may be foisted onto an individual or group as a result of unequal power relations (for example, between East Asians and Western "imperialists"). This, at least, is taken to be the usual pattern, since most people are trapped within "'dominant discourses'" that they believe to be "true" — apart from these extreme postmodernists themselves, whose role it is to expose and analyse these discourses for the rest of us. In doing so, they aspire to demonstrate that the list of choices — in narrative accounts of the past, as in political, religious, or moral beliefs — is theoretically endless. At the same time, however, many of them assert that it is desirable (they cannot, if they are consistent, claim to offer a rational explanation as to *why* it is desirable), that we should choose narratives or beliefs that are authentically "ours", while respecting the rights of other groups or individuals to do the same. The view is frequently advanced by its left-leaning Western advocates that postmodernism is fundamentally liberating, since exposing the way in which dominant discourses are rooted in political interests legitimizes struggles on the part of oppressed groups — workers, women, blacks, Asians — to construct "counter-discourses" of their own. However, as Richard Evans (2000) has pointed out, postmodernist relativism can be as "empowering" for neo-fascists as for neo-Marxists; self-styled "antibourgeois" irrationalism can serve right-wing as well as left-wing causes and indeed historically has done just that — both in Europe and in East Asia.

In his book *In Defence of History,* Evans asks rhetorically of one of his avowedly antirationalist critics, "Does he really want to live in a society where the evidence for an argument counts for nothing and the moral (or immoral) force behind its advocacy for everything?" (Evans, 2000, p. 300). The answer is obvious — the principles that the more extreme postmodernists advocate from the security of their ivory towers bear no relation to the principles by which, presumably, they would wish to be tried in court if they happened to be wrongly accused of murder. Gellner similarly concludes his trenchant critique of postmodernism and religious fundamentalism by declaring to the "relativists" that "you provide an excellent account of the manner in which we choose our menu or our wallpaper. As an account of the realities of our world and a guide to conduct, your position is laughable." It may be laughable, at least as a cosy Western parlour-game, but the relativism that postmodernists avow has been thrown back in their faces by an emerging Asian "New Right" from Bombay (or Mumbai) to Beijing. The philosophy of extreme cultural relativism lends a veneer of intellectual respectability to pseudofascist proponents of *Hindutva* in India, just as it does to the new breed of self-styled "postmodernists" in China, who propound a deeply illiberal brand of cultural nationalism. And views of history — or of mythology masquerading as history, or even displacing it in a postmodern world where history and myth are indistinguishable — are fundamental to these political struggles over national identity and cultural exceptionalism. Thus, well-heeled Hindu nationalists in India weave the legends of Lord Ram into a pseudohistorical narrative of the national past to serve their own political ends, while Chinese nationalists invoke history in support of a totalizing and homogenizing vision of the Chinese "race-nation", whose unity and defining characteristics are traced back to immemorial antiquity.

Nevertheless, the relativist critique of rationalism raises serious philosophical issues that could, and indeed have, served as the subject of entire books. Notable among these are the works of the philosopher Alastair MacIntyre, who argues that extreme relativism stems from the inevitable collapse of the Enlightenment project to define the tenets of Reason or Truth scientifically, absolutely, once and for all (MacIntyre, 1985 and, 1990). Thus far he is in agreement with Nietszche and Foucault, and in disagreement with an Enlightenment rationalist such as Gellner. However, according to MacIntyre, reason is not an entirely lost cause, at least not if we see rationality as something internal to traditions of moral and philosophical thought, rather than an eternal absolute above and beyond them. Tradition, for MacIntyre, is moreover neither the solipsistic, self-referential discourse of Foucauldian genealogy, nor a fixed body of custom in the Burkean sense, but instead is (or should be) a living, ongoing debate over how to order the practices of our collective lives in conformity with reason and justice. In other words, traditions embody "continuities of conflict", and thus it should be the ultimate role of education to initiate students into these as active participants rather than merely passive bystanders (MacIntyre, 1985, p. 222). Like the historical philosopher R. G. Collingwood, MacIntyre sees philosophy not as an exercise in rarefied academic abstraction, but as a practical argument over the "good life", whose questions and problems, far from being arrived at arbitrarily, can arise only from the history of the debate itself (Collingwood, 1944, 1994). We cannot aspire to a "perfect theory" — all we can aspire to is "the best theory so far," and any progress toward this is tentative and reversible, rather than a matter of Whiggish certainty (MacIntyre, 1985, p. 277).

Like most contemporary Western philosophers (though unlike some of their eighteenth-century predecessors), MacIntyre has little to say about Eastern philosophy in general, or Confucian philosophy in particular, though he has written on the potential for meaningful conversation between Aristotelians and Confucians (MacIntyre, 1991). However, as is demonstrated in Jones' discussion in chapter 1 of the development of historical thought and practice in East Asia, the same is emphatically not true of thinkers in general, and historians in particular, in modern and contemporary Asia. The business of distinguishing what ideas or practices are, or are not, part of indigenous Chinese, Japanese, or Korean traditions is rendered exceedingly complex by the interpenetration of Western and Asian philosophy and practice over the past century and more. Many have seen this as a symptom of the subjection of Asian minds to Western colonisation, but it can alternatively, and perhaps more convincingly, be viewed as a consequence of Asian attempts to deal with problems of modernisation, state formation, and the maintenance of social cohesion that are the common currency of a world that has been "jointly, if unequally, created" (Hopkins, 2002, p. 2).

The task of charting a course between the Scylla of dependency on the West and the Charybdis of the kind of wholesale rejection of international norms and precedents sometimes advocated by the relativists is one that has preoccupied intellectual and political elites throughout the developing world. In contemporary Asia, the relativists and cultural essentialists may sometimes make the most noise, but there have always been those who advocate more critical attitudes to the indigenous cultural inheritance along with selective borrowing from the West. Collingwood, for example, has been translated into Chinese, and his book *The Idea of History* has featured as a set text for postgraduate students of history education in Beijing. However, studying Collingwood, and thereby learning to view history as a critical craft rather than a body of received knowledge, presumably does not make these students any less authentically Chinese. In India, the eminent historian (and history textbook author), Romila Thapar, was relentlessly pilloried by the Hindu nationalist acolytes of India's BJP administration precisely because she offered a secular, rational, evidence-based account of the early Indian past that exposed their neo-fascist mythologizing for the fraudulent, and dangerous, exercise it is, and she would no doubt dismiss allegations that such an approach marks her as somehow un-Indian (Thapar, 1999). Meanwhile, Li Shenzhi, seen by some as the doyen of Chinese liberals, has drawn a direct parallel between the penchant of the current Beijing regime for appeals to nationalist sentiment and the practices of fascist or totalitarian regimes in Europe and Asia.

Commenting on the massive celebrations organized for China's National Day in 1999, he wrote:

> "Hitler is dead, and Stalin is no longer around. There should be few countries in the world that would seek such a grandiose spectacle. Maybe I am a bit old-fashioned, but I suppose only a man like Kim Jong-il of Korea would have that kind of enthusiasm. ... I have noticed that Jiang Zemin also likes to use Sun Yat-sen's words, 'The currents of the worlds are vast and mighty; those who follow them flourish, while those who go against them perish.' The problem is seeing clearly the currents of the world. Globalization is the current of the world, market economics is the current of the world, democratic politics is the current of the world, and increasing human rights is the current of the world. Those who follow these currents will flourish, and those who go against them will perish." (quoted in Fewsmith, 2001, pp. 222–223).

Li's view of globalisation may be somewhat starry-eyed, but this need not detract from his implication that appeals to nationalist sentiment are potentially as dangerous for China today as they were for Germany in the 1930s, and for similar reasons.

It should be borne in mind that for every Li Shenzhi–style liberal, one is likely to come across at least twenty Beijing taxi drivers who will confess that Hitler (along with Chairman Mao and Margaret Thatcher) is one of their heroes, "because he was a strong leader." However, this only lends all the more urgency to criticisms of the propagation, through state-controlled media as well as through the education system, of an uncritical, unreflective patriotism that prioritises the strength of the state above all else. It may be that a preoccupation with a strong state, or with strong leaders, conceived as the embodiment of a homogenous *volksgemeinschaft* is a tendency reinforced by old habits of thought in China (perhaps in part because, as in Germany before Bismarck, the unity, independence, and strength of the state has in the past so often been a distant ideal), but this does not render such an obsession any less disturbing. Nationalist cultural essentialism may appeal to the tastes and prejudices of many Chinese people, but this does not mean that their choice is therefore value-neutral, like the preference for a particular pattern of wallpaper (to borrow Gellner's analogy).

The dangers of extreme nationalism, and of the distorted views of history upon which such nationalism feeds, are a recurring theme of Chinese and Korean criticisms of Japan, and in particular of the Japanese failure to confront the atrocities committed by Imperial troops during the Pacific War through accounts of that war in school history textbooks. However, it is not nationalism in general, but Japanese nationalism in particular, that Japan's neighbors tend to view as problematic. The parallel drawn by Buruma between Hitler's manipulation of the Munich Olympic Games of 1936 and the way in which the Seoul Olympics of 1988 became an occasion for the whipping up of often hysterical nationalist chauvinism would doubtless be greeted with outrage and incredulity by most Koreans (or by the Chinese, if a similar comparison were to be made between 1936 Munich and 2008 Beijing). After all, Korean nationalism (the argument runs) is a benign force. Koreans are a set-upon people who merely crave their rightful place in the community of nations; Korea is not a threat to her neighbors. Korean nationalism, in other words, is an inoffensive, unthreatening sentiment, because the aggressive and militaristic qualities that characterised wartime Japanese nationalism are simply not among Korea's defining national characteristics. Similar arguments are advanced by apologists for Chinese nationalism, some of whom portray the Chinese as a race innocent of the original sin of aggressive expansionism; the history of foreign invasions forms the basis of a self-justifying nationalist victimology. According to the orthodox nationalist account, foreign aggressors have relentlessly persecuted a China that has "never invaded another country," but that by refraining from aggression has, if anything, become a victim of its own moral superiority. With rare exceptions such as Li Shenzhi, most Chinese and Koreans — young or old — appear blind to any comparisons between their home-grown nationalisms and foreign varieties, a blindness reflected and reinforced by messages conveyed through the media and school curricula.

There is, it should be noted, nothing intrinsically or inevitably Asian about such attitudes; after all, only half a century ago Britain's greatest prime minister penned a triumphalist four-volume tract on the "History of the English-speaking peoples" — a work that owed much to nineteenth-century myths concerning the special historic mission of the Anglo-Saxon race. Nowadays, the mainstream of Western Europe's intellectual and political elites frowns on such ethnocentric triumphalism and sees nationalism as a dangerous virus to be isolated and contained whenever outbreaks occur. However, such outbreaks do continue and in recent years appear to have worsened, as witnessed by the strong showing of the Front Nationale in the French presidential elections of 2002, and of far right and Eurosceptic parties in other recent polls. Northern Ireland, despite the fragile success of the Peace Process, remains riven by sectarian divides that embody contradictory and irreconcilable readings of the Ulster past. Meanwhile, in many of the postcommunist states of Eastern Europe, nationalist historians have reinvented the past — and rewritten school history textbooks — to serve present political ends, often with a breathtaking disregard for what a naïve empiricist might term "the facts." In the case of a country such as the Ukraine, whose past has throughout most of recorded history been so closely interwoven with that of Russia as to render the two so-called "nations" virtually indistinguishable, revisionist accounts that aim to trace the primordial origins of a homogenous Ukrainian ethnic identity have given rise to particularly bizarre fictions (Wilson, 2002).

If nationalist extremism and intolerance remain a threat to the political health of both Asia and Europe, then how can the school curriculum help to innoculate societies against it? On this score, consensus has proved elusive. Debate over the function that formal education can or should play in inculcating the common values necessary to underpin social cohesion — overshadowed for many years in some countries by concerns to make education more directly serve economic ends — has recently resurfaced. The fierce controversy over the right of Muslim French students to wear the *hejab*, or traditional headscarf, has highlighted the way in which France remains, in Alexander's words, almost the "archetype of cultural reproduction" (Alexander, 2000, p. 166). The French education system retains its explicit and unabashed focus on the national goals served by formal schooling — the inculcation of common values of citizenship, general culture and the disciplined mind. In England, by contrast, attempts to define common values or a coherent vision of English citizenship through the school curriculum remain vague and tentative, creating "confusion about the kind of person the state, through its schools, seeks to produce" (ibid., p. 169) — a situation perhaps compounded by the confusion over what constitutes Britishness versus Englishness, Scottishness, or Welshness — let alone Northern Irishness. This, Alexander argues, has led to a situation whereby "at the turn of the century the vacuum or conundrum of identity in England is an open door to political appropriation; the more so as in England education is now more tightly controlled by central government than [in any other of the five countries in Alexander's study]" (ibid., p. 169).

History curricula in England and France reflect this contrast, with the French according greater prominence to a largely triumphalist narrative of national history, while the English curriculum at all levels tends to offer, in place of a coherent narrative, a more fragmented overall picture of the past, focusing in greater depth on particular periods and historical themes (see chapter 10 by Peter Cave). Similarly, the insistent and relentless appeal to patriotism that pervades political and popular rhetoric in the United States is reflected by and transmitted through school history curricula that generally still take the story of American progress as their unifying theme.

In discussions of the different forms of national identity, the distinction is often made between "civic" nationalisms, whereby nationality is seen primarily as a question of subscribing to common values and a shared sense of belonging, and "ethnic" or "ethno-cultural" nationalisms, which regard national identity as an inherited given. The validity of this rather black-and-white dichotomy has been challenged by some scholars, notably Anthony Smith (1999), who argues that all nationalisms ultimately have ethno-cultural origins; others, meanwhile, have sought to refine and qualify the distinction by pointing to how civic and ethnic bases for identity can coexist or overlap with each other and with other powerful sources of identity, such as religion, in complex and contradictory ways. Thus, while official or elite constructions of national identity in Britain and France tend nowadays to be couched more in civic than in ethno-cultural terms (largely due to a need to maintain social cohesion in societies characterised by mass immigration), at a popular level, ethno-cultural markers of identity still exert a powerful hold on the imagination. Meanwhile, in America — the classic example of a "civic nation" — various exclusionary ethno-cultural (or multicultural) subnationalisms persist and proliferate, while the ideals of Protestant Christianity permeate public rhetoric and feature prominently in the nation's founding myth.

Those who place the most emphasis on the civic-ethnic divide often tend to assume that civic nationalism is "good" because it involves a recognition of the constructed nature of identity and tends to be associated with more open and tolerant polities, whereas ethnic nationalism is "bad" because, by definition, it sees national belonging as an exclusive and predetermined attribute. In theory, this argument may have much to recommend it. However, in practice, the American example illustrates that even if a civic ideal of national identity can be divorced from ethnic considerations (a big "*if*"), civic nationalisms themselves can become ramified into elaborate mythologies as fantastic as the inventions of ethnic chauvinists.

The ideological as well as the "factual" content of a school history curriculum — the civic values embodied in its narrative of the national past and the relative emphasis attached to the various ethno-cultural components of the national community — is nonetheless important. Even to the extent that constructing historical narratives may be an exercise in selective myth making, some myths are arguably better than others — and the myths of civic nationalism, insofar as they tend to foster a more inclusive and tolerant vision of citizenship, are perhaps better than ethno-cultural visions that emphasise the cultural, religious, or racial divisions between nation-states, while obscuring or denying diversity within them. However, when it comes to history education, the content is only half of the story. As significant as *what* history is taught is *the way in which* decisions are reached over content selection, and how that content, however selected, is presented to students. Historical knowledge can be presented as an authorised version beyond criticism, or as a living tradition of debate over the past, whose findings are always provisional and open to revision. In other words, process is as important as content, and two processes are involved here: the process of educational debate and curriculum development that determines the content of curricula and the process of historical investigation itself and the extent to which this — rather than merely its results — forms part of the subject matter of history classes.

The curriculum development process, as well as institutions of formal education more broadly, has tended to be portrayed by sociologists as a means whereby society imposes its rules and conventions on the individual. Some, like Durkheim (1961), have seen this exercise in a positive light arguing that formal education in a modern state should serve to inculcate a democratic morality (involving, amongst other things, respect for reason) that cements social solidarity. Others, from Marx to Althusser and Bourdieu, have tended to argue that formal education bolsters and reproduces an unequal and exploitative class structure; for Althusser (1971), schools and universities have taken the place of organized religion as the dominant ideological state apparatuses in modern society, whereas for Bourdieu and Passerson (1990) schools are instruments of symbolic violence, inculcating modes of behaviour and belief that reinforce the existing social order. As Tremlett (2004) has indicated, the problem with this neo-Marxist perspective is that it posits a structure of social determinism that, if true, would also shape the thought of those such as Althusser or Bourdieu, who write as if they are observers situated at a vantage point above and outside the closed system they are describing. The same criticism applies, as was noted above, to Foucault and the postmodernist-relativist scholars, who see discourse as an enclosed and self-regulated system of rules and relationships; their position could be seen as one of cultural, or discursive, determinism.

A subtler, neo-Gramscian vision of hegemony as a negotiated process, rather than as a crudely deterministic and rigid structure of domination, might contribute more to an understanding of curriculum change. However, the way in which many educational scholars have deployed the concept of "hegemony" has tended to reflect less than subtle neo-Marxist assumptions. World System theorists, for example, observing the adoption by developing countries of curricular categories originating in the West (especially America), have seen this as evidence of blind imitation. Thus S. Y. Wong has argued that "The dramatic post–World War II worldwide shift from the traditional history and geography content to a new form of integrated subject matter called 'social studies' is a reflection more of a general change in world social patterns than of internal attributes of national societies. This change is also a response to the transformation of structural dominance among hegemonic powers since World War II in that social studies ... illustrates the extensive influence of the United States in the rest of the world" (cited in Morris, McClelland, and Wong, 1997). Claims of this sort are usually based on a rather superficial analysis both of the processes whereby Western curricular models are adopted and adapted in non-Western contexts and of the content of the resulting curricula themselves. This point is also made by Morris, McClelland, and Wong (1997, p. 27–43):

> The ability to identify prevailing curriculum models that transcend national boundaries does not, of itself, explain curriculum change in any particular country. An adequate explanation would need to account for the internal and external pressures for change, as well as the source of the innovations promoted.

This applies to attempts to explain why, in recent years, a vision of history education as a vehicle for training students in critical thinking skills has aroused interest among curriculum developers in East Asia. The idea that history lessons in schools, in addition to providing students with knowledge of past events, should also initiate them into the craft of the professional historian has gained popularity among history educators in Britain, America, and elsewhere in the West since the 1960s. In part, this has arisen from a perceived need to render a traditionally dry, academic subject more relevant and useful to secondary school pupils in an era of mass education. The emphasis on history as a training in analytical skills rather than as a didactic, moralistic narrative to be memorized and internalised has also tended to be associated more with liberal or left-leaning educators, for whom part of the attraction of the approach lies in its potential for assisting students to critique self-serving historical myths promoted by dominant social elites. The move away from teaching a single, received narrative of the national past and toward a more in-depth, contemporary, and thematic focus involving the use of primary sources has been promoted for its contribution, on the one hand, to developing generic analytical skills and, on the other, to encouraging attitudes of tolerance of diverse views and skepticism toward dominant interpretations of the past. At the same time, the decreasing emphasis on the traditional account of high politics has been accompanied in some systems by efforts to increase the amount of attention devoted to the history of previously neglected or despised groups — women, blacks, Native Americans, or Australian aborigines. In Western contexts, this vision of history education thus sees it as playing a crucial role in the formation of an active, tolerant, democratic citizenry.

However, this is not to imply that such an approach to history education is unproblematic, nor that it has swept all before it in the schools of the democratic West. Even, and perhaps especially, in ostensibly liberal-democratic societies, consensus over the best way to teach history to the young remains elusive. This is not just because conservative or reactionary elements wish to maintain or return to a more traditional, triumphalist narrative of the national past, though many undoubtedly do. In Britain, for example, serious concerns have been voiced, and not only by figures on the right of the political spectrum, over the way in which the focus in recent years on skills at the expense of broad narrative coverage appears to have left many youngsters with an extremely patchy and disconnected knowledge of the national and global past. In 2001, Germany's ambassador to London publicly voiced concerns over the impact that a disproportionate focus by history teachers on the history of Nazi Germany was having on perceptions of his country among English youth (*Economist*, 2001). Meanwhile, as we shall see, the idea that history education can play a role in developing the sort of generic thinking skills that are useful in a globalised knowledge economy, while attractive to politicians and curriculum developers in some parts of East Asia, has proved difficult to reconcile with strongly ingrained notions of the fundamental didactic and moralistic function of history education. The terms of the debate over history education may appear similar in distant corners of the globe, but the outcome of the argument is not dictated by any Western hegemons; rather, it is primarily the product of pressures arising from within the local political, cultural, and social context.

If the school curriculum, and the curriculum for history in particular, is implicated in the construction of a kind of hegemony, then it is what Raymond Williams (1997, p. 112) calls "a lived hegemony" one which "does not just passively exist as a form of dominance" but that "has continually to be renewed, recreated, defended and modified" while also "continually resisted, limited, altered [and] challenged by pressures not all its own." Only when hegemony is seen in these terms does it become possible to envisage any potential for social or cultural change or to explain those changes that have characterised conceptions of the nature of history and the purpose of teaching it in schools in various countries. Thus this book begins from the premise that change — or the lack of it — in history curricula, as in history itself, has to be explained in terms of shifting, complex, and sometimes contradictory political, cultural, and socio-economic factors, rather than by reference to cultural essences or self-replicating hegemonic structures. Dictatorship, democracy, and the exasperated tribalisms or critical-liberal attitudes that underpin or undermine them — whether in Europe, America, or East Asia — have their origins within historical processes, rather than above or beyond them. Barrington Moore (1997, p. 486) perhaps expressed it best:

> The assumption of inertia, that cultural and social continuity do not require explanation, obliterates the fact that both have to be recreated anew in each generation, often with great pain and suffering. To maintain and transmit a value system, human beings are punched, bullied, sent to jail, thrown into concentration camps, cajoled, bribed, made into heroes, encouraged to read newspapers, stood up against a wall and shot, and sometimes even taught sociology. To speak of cultural inertia is to overlook the concrete interests and privileges that are served by indoctrination, education, and the entire complicated process of transmitting culture from one generation to the next.

An Outline of this Volume

The contributors to this volume fully acknowledge that any truly comprehensive study of the influences upon, and impact of, history education in schools would need to take into account a whole range of factors that lie beyond the scope of most of the essays presented here — from the nature and extent of the training that history teachers receive to the ways in which children themselves construct their visions of history (whether through formal study in the classroom, or exposure to extra curricular sources). Although most of the following chapters focus on the official process of curriculum development, this does not imply that we assume a uniform correlation between official curricula and classroom practice, let alone any precise equivalence between the latter and the way in which students, as a result of a whole range of cultural influences, come to perceive the past and their place in it. Nevertheless, as noted above, research on curriculum in East Asia has indicated a relatively high degree of reliance on textbooks among teachers in the classroom and, even more so, among students outside it (Marsh and Morris, 1991). Top-down systems of curriculum development and official mechanisms for the vetting and approval of published teaching materials also ensure that what students read in their textbooks tends to conform closely to official syllabi. This does not mean that teachers or students always and everywhere simply parrot the authorised textbook account, but it does ensure that centrally defined syllabi — and especially examination syllabi — play a crucial role in determining what is taught and learned in history classrooms.

The bulk of this book is devoted to analyses of the development of curricula and textbooks in the various states of East Asia from 1945 to the present day. The end of the Second World War represented, for Asia as for Europe, a huge political watershed, heralding the demise of right-wing militarism in Japan, the rise of Communism (and the resultant Cold War stand-offs on the Korean peninsula and across the Taiwan Strait), and the process of decolonisation (immediate in the case of Japan's colonies, more gradual in the case of Britain's). Nevertheless, it is impossible to understand the development of history education in postwar East Asia without taking into account the shared inheritance of the premodern period, and in particular the influence of Confucian historiography. It is this Confucian heritage that Alisa Jones examines in Chapter 1, as she traces and explains the evolution of East Asia's historiographical traditions in the context of the political and cultural relationships that have shaped the region's past. As her analysis reaches the late nineteenth and early twentieth centuries, she underlines the strength of essentialist ethnocultural nationalisms in the reinvented nation-states of modern East Asia and shows how this affected the early development of history curricula for schools.

In Chapter 2, Jones continues to pursue the theme of nationalism, showing how in China the pre-1949 Kuomintang (KMT) regime and its post-1949 Communist successors, despite many ideological differences, shared similarly ethnocentric, homogenous, and totalising visions of Chinese nationhood. While the doctrine of class struggle and historical materialism came to pervade history textbooks in Mao's China, the assertion that China had always been (and forever would remain) essentially "one" — that national unity was immemorial and inviolable — was a belief that the Communists and their KMT enemies emphatically shared. This denial of diversity applied even — or perhaps especially — to the histories of China's minority nationalities (such as the Tibetans, Mongols, and Uighurs), as it dictated their incorporation within the party's uniform and teleological narrative of the national past. However, Jones' analysis reveals the Byzantine character of the curriculum policymaking process in the People's Republic and the limits to the Party's ability to devise and impose a coherent vision of Chinese history. She argues that this lack of coherence has become increasingly clear in the post-Mao period, due partly to the tensions between a residual attachment to the tenets of Marxist "scientific materialism" on the one hand and the attraction of resurgent Han Chinese nationalism on the other. The latter has encouraged renewed celebration of elements of China's old feudal culture, including many of the Great Men of the traditional historical canon (such as Confucius). At the same time, as Communist ideology has been quietly downplayed, the promotion of patriotism has become the central aim of history syllabi.

Inculcating Chinese patriotism was also one of the main aims of history curricula in Taiwan under the KMT. Following its defeat in China's Civil War, the KMT regime fled to Taiwan, taking its school curriculum with it, as it attempted to turn the island into a 'base for the recovery of the mainland.' For four decades or more, Taiwanese schoolchildren studied a curriculum focused entirely on the history of the central Chinese state and entirely divorced from the Taiwanese context. However, as Mei-Hui Liu, Li-Ching Hung, and Edward Vickers show in chapter 3, this began to change under the leadership of Lee Teng-hui in the 1990s. In the progress of democratisation since the 1980s, syllabi and textbooks on the island change to reflect the popular sense of Taiwan's distinctiveness vis-à-vis the mainland. For the first time, significant teaching time has been allocated to Taiwanese history, and textbooks have acknowledged the relatively recent nature of Chinese settlement, the diversity of Taiwanese society, and the historical importance of both the non-Han aboriginal communities and of foreign influences from the Dutch to the Japanese. However, despite Taiwan's strikingly open political atmosphere, internal divisions and tensions in relations with the Chinese mainland continue to limit the extent to which curriculum developers feel free to confront the controversial issue of "historical identity."

In Chapter 4, Stéphane Corcuff provides a more detailed analysis of the most significant episode in the reform of Taiwan's history curriculum: the move in the mid-1990s to introduce a course in Taiwanese history at junior high (secondary) level in the form of the new *Renshi Taiwan* (knowing taiwan) programme. The authors of the teaching materials for this course (History, Geography, and Society) were for the first time intellectuals recruited from outside a party-state apparatus that under Lee Teng-hui had already started to lose much of its former ideological rigidity. They undertook a reevaluation of the Japanese colonial period, presented Taiwan's ethnic and historical plurality, and helped to nurture a pluralistic vision of national identity among young people. The reaction of conservative intellectuals and politicians — mostly of mainland origin — was one of vociferous outrage. However, proreformist native politicians and intellectuals defended the programme with arguments that reflected a process of introspection regarding the possibility and legitimacy of distinguishing between Taiwanese statehood and Chinese ethnicity. Corcuff argues that the adoption of this programme, in the face of conservative protests, constituted an important step forward in efforts on the part of the elite to foster a sense of Taiwanese national identity. For the first time, students would be taught about the existence of a Taiwanese "community of destiny", before taking courses on China during their second year of high school. China's status in textbook accounts was transformed from that of the motherland for which Taiwanese were supposed to yearn to that of Taiwan's main, but no longer its sole, cultural matrix.

In this respect, the contrast between Taiwan and Hong Kong is striking. As Edward Vickers and Flora Kan show in Chapter 5, local history in Hong Kong, as in Taiwan, was absent from school syllabi until the 1990s. It was necessary to go back as far as the 1960s to find a time when local history was included in the curriculum for senior secondary level, though then it was treated as a subset of British imperial history. However, the 1970s and 1980s witnessed a change in Hong Kong's political situation and, more significantly for any consideration of the treatment of the local past, in local culture and local people's sense of identity. By the 1980s, a sense of 'Hongkongese' identity had emerged, but this was scarcely reflected in the school curriculum. Meanwhile, perhaps more than their counterparts anywhere else in East Asia, curriculum developers in Hong Kong sought to make the subject of history a vehicle for the teaching of critical thinking skills. However, Vickers and Kan argue that attempts to promote a skills-based approach have been largely emasculated by a simultaneous concern, on the part of officials and textbook publishers, to steer clear of all issues liable to cause offense in pro-Beijing circles. The result has been a "Hong Kong history" that emphasises the positive aspects of the region's historical relationship with the motherland, largely ignores or downplays the impact of colonialism, and confines itself otherwise to "safe" topics in economic and social history.

In Singapore too, the account of local history presented to students in their government-commissioned textbooks has tended to paint a somewhat partial picture of the island's past, and one calculated to instill sentiments of patriotism and admiration for the legacy of the ruling People's Action Party (PAP). However, as Goh Chor Boon and Saravanan Gopinathan Goh demonstrate in Chapter 6, history in general and local history in particular for many years occupied a very minor place in Singapore's school curriculum. It was only from the late 1970s onwards, once the city-state had already attained a relatively high level of economic development, that the PAP regime began to focus increasingly on the development of a sentimental sense of Singaporeanness. Since the 1980s, history education has played a central role in schemes aimed at fostering an affective loyalty to a Singaporean nation that both embraces and transcends the ethnic communities that constitute it. The official vision of Singaporean identity has come to be rooted in a notion of Asian values that implies an essentially primordialist view of ethno-cultural divisions, but at the same time sees no contradiction between this and the promotion of an inclusive civic nationalism. Meanwhile, the government has in recent years become concerned to use history education to foster students' critical and analytical skills but, as in Hong Kong, the exercise of such skills has tended to be severely circumscribed by the regime's anxiety to ensure that pupils derive the correct messages from their study of the past.

In Korea, as in Singapore, tensions have developed between ethno-cultural and civic dimensions of identity; however, whereas in Singapore multiple ethnicities are subsumed within a common civic nationalism, in the two Koreas what has historically been viewed as a single ethno-cultural unit has since the 1940s been divided between two antagonistic regimes. As might be expected, the regimes of North and South have used history education and textbooks to portray the national past in radically different ways, designed to bolster their legitimacy and serve their respective political ends. Nonetheless, as Chris Wilson, Danton Ford, and Alisa Jones argue in Chapter 7, underlying these ostensibly diametrically opposing narratives has been a similar absolute and totalizing vision of ethno-cultural Koreanness and a similarly moralising and didactic approach to history education that has only recently begun to show signs of changing in the South. In this respect, and leaving aside the issue of capitalism versus socialism (or *chu'che*), the conceptualization of national identity in the North and South, and of the relationship between identity and history, has in fact shared broad similarities, the main difference between the two Koreas being that each claims to be the sole legitimate heir and representative of the common national heritage.

One of the issues on which both Koreas can agree (up to a point) is their resentment of Japanese colonialism. Of all the states of East Asia, the two Koreas have perhaps been the most vociferous in their criticism of what is seen as Japan's failure to face up to its colonial and wartime past in its school history textbooks. In Chapter 8, Julian Dierkes analyses the development of Japan's postwar history curriculum in the context of global trends, particularly with reference to the World Systems Theory advanced by Meyer and others. He concludes that this theory cannot account for the way in which history curriculum development in Japan has clearly diverged from what the world systems theorists posit as the dominant global discourse in this field and argues that any explanation of the pattern of curriculum change (or the lack of it) in Japan must take full account of the particular political, social, and cultural context there.

Chapter 9, by Yoshiko Nozaki, traces in greater detail the series of Japanese history textbook controversies during the postwar period, and especially since the 1970s, showing how the Liberal Democratic Party, facing growing threats to its political monopoly, has attempted to distract attention from other issues by playing the nationalist card over history education. Nozaki's account also sets the textbook issue in the context of Japan's closed, corporatist, and highly bureaucratic political culture by demonstrating the importance of behind-the-scenes deals between publishers and Education Ministry officials. Her account of Japan's struggles over the portrayal of the wartime past explains the persistent failure to resolve this issue in terms not of any essential cultural peculiarity but primarily by reference to the contingencies of postwar Japanese politics.

Chapter 10, by Peter Cave, presents a very different perspective on Japanese history education, by comparing how schools in Japan and England teach students about their countries' imperial pasts. Cave's analysis highlights significant differences between the styles of pedagogy in these two countries, while noting that many Japanese teachers do in fact go beyond the textbook in their teaching. His findings suggest that, as far as the neglect of imperial history in school curricula is concerned, the singling out of Japan for special criticism may be somewhat unfair. He suggests that part of the problem with Japanese syllabi and textbooks is that by expecting students to study a broad sweep of history chronologically, they leave insufficient space for a comprehensive treatment of any particular topic. If this is to change, not only textbooks, but also examinations and the overall conception of the nature and purpose of history as a school subject will need to be transformed.

Endnotes

1. Fears of Russia, on the other hand, may seem far more real — especially to Eastern Europeans — but Russia's relative economic weakness makes that threat appear, for the present at least, far less imminent than the threat posed by China to the East Asian status quo.

References

Alexander, R. (2000). *Culture and Pedagogy: International Comparisons in Primary Education*. Oxford: Blackwell.
Althusser, L. (1971). *Lenin and Philosophy and Other Essays*. [Trans. B. Brewser]. New York: Monthly Review Press.
Anderson, B. (1983). *Imagined Communities*. London: Verso.
Barmé, G. (1999). *In the Red*. New York: Columbia.
Befu, H. (Ed.). (1993). *Cultural Nationalism in East Asia*. California: Institute of East Asian Studies, Berkeley.
Benedict, R. (1989). *The Chrysanthemum and the Sword*. Boston: Houghton Mifflin.
Bickers, R. (1999). *Britain in China*. Manchester: Manchester University Press.
Bourdieu, P. and Passerson, J. C. (1990). *Reproduction in Education, Society and Culture*, 2nd ed. London: Sage.
Brown, D (1999). *Contemporary Nationalism*. New York and London: Routledge.
Burrow, J. W. (1983). *A Liberal Descent: Victorian Historians and the English Past*. Cambridge: Cambridge University Press.
Buruma, I. (1994). The Wages of Guilt: Memories of War in Germany and Japan. London: Phoenix.
———. (1996), "The Seoul Olympics," in *The Missionary and the Libertine*. London: Faber and Faber, pp. 154–169.
Chadwick, O. (1975). *The Secularization of the European Mind in the Nineteenth Century*. Cambridge: Cambridge University Press.
Collingwood, R. G. (1944). *An Autobiography*. Harmondsworth: Pelican.
———. (1994). *The Idea of History*. Oxford: Oxford University Press.

Cumings, B. (2004). *North Korea: Another Country.* New York: The New Press.

Dikötter, F. (1992). *The Discourse of Race in Modern China.* London: Hurst; Stanford University Press.

Dikötter, F. (Ed.). (1997). *Race and National Identity in China and Japan.* Hong Kong: Hong Kong University Press.

Duara, P. (1995). *Rescuing History from the Nation.* Chicago: University of Chicago Press.

Durkheim, E. (1961). *Moral Education.* New York: Free Press.

Economist. (2001). *History Lessons.* (November 1st, 2001).

Fairbank, J. K. (Ed.) (1968). *The Chinese World Order.* Cambridge, Massachusetts: Harvard University Press.

Faure, D. and Tao Tao Liu. (1996). *Unity and Diversity: Local Cultures and Identities in China.* Hong Kong: Hong Kong University Press.

Fewsmith, J. (2001). *China since Tiananmen.* Cambridge: Cambridge University Press.

Fogel, J. (2000). *The Nanjing Massacre in History and Historiography.* Berkeley: University of California Press.

Foucault, M. (1997). "Nietzsche, genealogy, history," in K. Jenkins, K. (Ed.), *The Postmodern History Reader.* London: Routledge, pp. 124–26.

Gellner, E. (1983). *Nations and Nationalism.* Oxford: Blackwell.

———. (1999). "Adam's Navel: Primordialists versus 'Modernists," in E. Mortimer (Ed.) *People, Nation and State: The Meaning of Ethnicity and Nationalism.* London: I. B. Tauris, pp. 31–35.

Harrell, S. (1996). *Cultural Encounters on China's Ethnic Frontiers.* Hong Kong: Hong Kong University Press.

Hamada, T. (2003). "Constructing a National Memory: A Comparative Analysis of Middle-School History Textbooks from Japan and the PRC," *in The American Asian Review* (Vol. XXI, No. 31, 4), pp. 109–144.

Hein, L. & Selden, M. (2000). *Censoring History: Citizenship and Memory in Japan, Germany and the United States.* New York: M.E. Sharpe.

Hobsbawm, E. *Nations and Nationalism since 1789.* Cambridge: Cambridge University Press.

Hopkins, A. G. (2002). *Globalization in World History.* London: Pimlico.

Jenkins, K. (1991). *Rethinking History.* London: Routledge.

———. (1995). *On "What is History?": From Carr and Elton to Rorty and White.* London: Routledge.

———. (1997). *The Postmodern History Reader.* London: Routledge.

Jenner, W. J. F. (1993). *The Tyranny of History.* London: Penguin.

MacIntyre, A. (1981). *After Virtue: A Study in Moral Theory.* London: Duckworth.

———. (1990). *Three Rival Versions of Moral Enquiry.* London: Duckworth.

———. (1991). "Incommensurability, Truth and the Conversation between Confucians and Aristotelians about the Virtues," in Eliot Deutsch (Ed.) *Culture and Modernity: East-West Philosophic Perspectives.* Honolulu: University of Hawaii Press pp. 104–122.

McClelland, J. (1991). "Curriculum Development in Hong Kong," in C. Marsh and P. Morris (Eds.) *Curriculum Development in East Asia.* London: Falmer.

Moore, B. (1977). *Social Origins of Dictatorship and Democracy.* London: Peregrine.

Morris, P., McClelland, J., and Wong Ping Man. (1997). "Explaining Curriculum Change: Social Studies in Hong Kong." *Comparative Education Review* (February 1997), pp. 27–43.

Phillips, R. (1998). *History Teaching, Nationhood and the State.* London: Cassell.

Rose, Caroline. (1998). *Interpreting History in Sino-Japanese Relations: A Case Study in Political Decision-Making.* London: Routledge.

Siu, H. (1996). "Remade in Hong Kong: Weaving into the Chinese Cultural Tapestry," in D. Faure and Tao Tao Liu (Eds.) *Unity and Diversity: Local Cultures and Identities in China.* Hong Kong: Hong Kong University Press.

Smith, A. (1999). "The Nation: Real or Imagined" in *People, Nation and State: The Meaning of Ethnicity and Nationalism.* London: I. B. Tauris, pp. 36–42.

Soh, C. S. (2003). "Politics of the Victim/Victor Complex: Interpreting South Korea's National Furor over Japanese History Textbooks" in *The American Asian Review* (Vol. XXI31, No. 4), pp. 145–178.

Thapar, R. (1999). "Some Appropriations of the Theory of Aryan Race Relating to the Beginnings of Indian History," in D. Ali (Ed.) *The Uses of the Past.* New Delhi: Oxford University Press.

Tremlett, J. P. (2004). "Writing Education in Taiwan." [Paper presented as part of a series on Taiwan and Western thought]. London: LSE.

Unger, J. (Ed.) (1993). *Using the Past to Serve the Present: Historiography and Politics in Contemporary China*. New York: M. E. Sharpe.

———— (Ed.). (1996). *Chinese Nationalism*. New York: M. E. Sharpe.

Williams, R. (1977). *Marxism and Literature*. Oxford: Oxford University Press.

Wilson, R. (2002). *The Ukrainians: Unexpected Nation,*. 2nd ed. New Haven: Yale University Press.

Zheng, Y. (1999). *Discovering Chinese Nationalism in China*. Cambridge: Cambridge University Press.

1

Shared Legacies, Diverse Evolutions: History, Education, and the State in East Asia

ALISA JONES

The chapters in this volume are chiefly concerned with the ways school history curricula across East Asia have been shaped by politics over the past half-century: by the internal politics of government factions and power elites; by the international political and economic climate; by the politics of education administration, teacher training, curriculum development and textbook production; and by discourses on national identity at all levels of society. Although most of the chapters focus on the contexts in which history curricula have been devised and/or implemented in a single East Asian society, they have been written and organized with a view to providing a comparative perspective across the region. The introduction outlined the rationale underpinning such a comparison, repudiating essentialist conceptions of nations, peoples, and cultures and placing the analysis of history education in East Asia and its relationship to national identity formation squarely within the global political and historical context. This chapter situates our study within the regional context, providing an overview of the relationships between the various states and societies of East Asia and their historical development and looking more specifically at the place and nature of historiography and education across the region prior to 1945, the point at which the present study commences.

Rejecting cultural relativism, the introduction argued that the history and national identity relationship in any society can be legitimately compared and contrasted with each other. It was maintained, nonetheless, that the East Asian societies under consideration here invite and perhaps even require particular comparison — not simply because of their geographical proximity but because they have a long history of intraregional cooperation and conflict that informs contemporary national identities and shapes perceptions of and policies toward neighboring others. Furthermore, they share a Confucian heritage of considerable antiquity. Like any credo, Confucianism has not been a monolithic tradition, handed down from antiquity entirely unmodified by contact with competing philosophies or local religious and cultural beliefs and practices, nor has it been the only dominant ideology in East Asia, having enjoyed varying degrees of influence at different times and in different places (see Elman 2002). There are, however, some key concepts and features of Confucianism that have survived these adaptations, profoundly affecting numerous aspects of political and social life throughout the region. Some of these were identified in the introduction, such as an emphasis on reverence for and obedience to one's elders and betters, veneration of ancestors, and faith in the wisdom and correctness of authorized texts. Perhaps in no sphere, however, have Confucian principles been more influential than in historiography and education. Although, during the late nineteenth and early twentieth centuries, ideas and practices imported from the West catalyzed major intellectual, political, and social changes, including the introduction both of new approaches to historiography and of modern mass education systems, Confucian principles have to a remarkable degree continued to pervade educational thought and practice, particularly in relation to the subject of history. Precisely how these principles have manifested themselves in individual East Asian societies, and corresponded or conflicted with the various political and pedagogical objectives officially ascribed to the history subject over the past half century will be discussed in subsequent chapters. This chapter sets out first to clarify what is meant by Confucian historiography and education and to demonstrate how it was spread to and appropriated by non-Chinese societies. Second, it examines how and why East Asian societies attempted to turn away from Confucian historiography in the late nineteenth century, adopting instead theories, methods, and models developed in Europe and North America. Finally, the evolution of modern education systems and the place of history in the curriculum up to 1945 are discussed. Particular attention is paid throughout to the role of the state in circumscribing what should and should not be publicly remembered, defining what constitutes the nation and the rights and duties of citizenship and determining how this knowledge should be disseminated. Approaches to official and national history, rather than to unofficial, local or global history, and to formal rather than informal education are thus the primary focus here, providing the background against which the contemporary purposes, form, content, and pedagogies of the history subject may be understood.

History, Education, and Confucianism: First Principles

Yi tong wei jian ke zheng yiguan, yi gu wei jian ke zhi xingti

Using bronze as a mirror, one may adjust one's attire; using the past as a mirror, one may know the rise and fall [of empires].

— Emperor Tang Taizong, A.D. 597–649

China's golden age of philosophy was the Warring States period (fifth–third century B.C.), when Zhou suzerainty over the many states of East and Central China was weakened and rival states vied for supremacy. The Confucian school (*rujia*) was one of many to emerge during this time, and its adherents, like their contemporaries, sought to convince Warring States leaders that they alone had the recipe for victory. For Confucians, the key was a comprehensive education, which they maintained was "the way of kings," enabling rulers to wield power through moral, intellectual, and physical superiority and to improve or transform the plebeians and their uncivilized customs (*huamin yisu*) by behavioural example. Although Confucians are normally associated with social and political conservatism, their views were in some ways quite radical, for not only did they advocate rule by role-modelling, benevolence (*ren*), and justice (*yi*) rather than coercion, but they also implicitly defied the principle of heredity by suggesting that the ruler's Mandate of Heaven (*tianming*) could be forfeited through misgovernment and moral turpitude. Mencius even argued that in such cases rebellion and overthrow of the ruler were justified. Confucian thinkers thus redefined the formerly straightforward genealogy of legitimate succession (*zhengtong*) to the throne as predicated on a moral rather than a hereditary mandate. Additionally, they maintained that talented persons (*rencai*) should be appointed to administrative office over the hereditary nobility and that anyone theoretically could become a "superior man" — and thereby fit for kingship — through rigorous mental and moral training.

Confucians insisted, however, that they were anything but radical, and indeed, despite the formal equality suggested by the idea of the self-made king, they by no means challenged the patriarchal social order or its ritualized inequalities and obligations. In fact, they believed that the chaos (*luan*) of their times stemmed directly from self-centered leaders who had cast aside traditional values and practices, forsaking their responsibilities in pursuit of venal pleasure and leading the multitudes astray by their degenerate example. Yet, Confucians did not believe that the future was irretrievably lost. Order and harmony, they asserted, could be restored by returning to the ways of the founders of Zhou and further beyond into antiquity, when sage kings had supposedly created a utopian society and handpicked their successors from among the virtuous and wise rather than passing the mandate to their imperfect progeny. This restoration could be effected through studying the classics: the *Books of Songs* (*Shijing*), *Documents or History* (*Shujing*), *Rites* (*Liji*) and *Changes* (*Yijing*), and the *Spring and Autumn Annals* (*Chunqiu*). According to Confucian analysis, these texts were not the simple explications of rituals and divination (*Liji, Yijing*) or chronicles of past events (*Shujing, Chunqiu*) they may have appeared to be but actually taught eternal social truths and ethical principles. Even the poems in the *Shijing* were thought to be oblique political or social commentaries, providing valuable guides to present action. Through exegesis, the lessons behind the texts could be revealed, and through applying these lessons, the halcyon days of antiquity could be recreated. The past was a mirror (*jian*), a historical lesson teaching morality and social norms by examples,[1] enabling better understanding of the present and preparation for the future. History — albeit in mythological and quasireligious form — was to take center stage in the Confucian project of moral education and social regeneration.

Confucius may have attracted many disciples, but his ideas found little favor with Warring States leaders. Indeed, the state of Qin, which emerged victorious to unify the Warring States as China in 221 B.C., followed a Legalist philosophy that in many respects was fundamentally opposed to Confucianism, endorsing the impunity of the ruler and enforcing social and ideological control through penal laws and proscription of all philosophies other than Legalism and all histories other than that of Qin. This attempt to destroy the past and standardize and control the present and future culminated in the infamous Burning of the Books in 213 B.C. The severity of the Qin regime and its willful violation of social norms and established hierarchies, however, soon alienated both the aristocracy and the populace, and the dynasty fell shortly after its founder's death.

With the incoming Han dynasty (202 B.C.–8 A.D.), Confucianism finally found a ready audience at court where the emperor was not an aristocrat but a truly self-made king, a rebel leader who had been a minor official in the Qin administration and sought to prove himself the legitimate inheritor of the mandate against rival aristocratic clans that seemed to pose as significant a threat to dynastic power as popular unrest and invasion by neighbouring barbarians erupted. An acceptable ethical-ideological veneer was desired for continued rule by harsh laws. Thus began the formal association of moral conduct with political legitimacy, the unfolding of history, the union of ideology and the state, and the tradition of employing scholars rather than aristocrats as government officials.

Confucianism in Action: Education, Historiography, and Political Power

Reject heterodoxies so as to exalt the true learning.

— The Sacred Edict

As Confucianism became entrenched as official orthodoxy, knowledge of the Classics became correspondingly important in determining bureaucratic appointments. By the seventh century, the court had introduced a civil service examination that tested candidates' abilities to memorize and interpret the Classics and their commentaries and to apply the historical precedents therein to analysis of contemporary political issues. The examinations sought not only to select the most talented persons but also to ensure that future officials owed their principal loyalty to the imperial administration and its legitimating ideology rather than to a locale or clan. In the twelfth century, some scholars contended that state-sanctioned Confucianism had lost its way in the quagmire of politics and advocated a return to the true Confucian path of moral rectification. By the fourteenth century, this neo-Confucian philosophy had become state orthodoxy, and the Four Books (Confucius' *Analects* [*Sishu*], *Mencius*, *The Great Learning*, and *The Doctrine of the Mean*) and the commentaries that constituted the neo-Confucian canon were added to the examination curriculum.

Although few could afford the intensive education required for probable examination success, potential for social mobility through Confucian scholarship engendered widespread belief in the value and status of Classical learning. Those possessing such learning were seen to have culture (*you wenhua*) and to be deserving of high status and respect. A quasiformal national curriculum was thus followed not only by aristocrats with personal tutors in elite state-supported schools or private academies but also by the sons (and occasionally the daughters) of families with more limited financial resources in local, clan-run, or charitable schools. The Classics and their exegetical commentaries were obviously far too difficult for young children and the early years were spent studying Chinese-character primers, such as the widely used *Thousand-Character* and *Three-Character Classics* (*Qianziwen* and *Sanzijing*),[2] which were normally written in rhyming tri- or tetra-syllabic couplets to facilitate group chanting and memorization. History was a key component, teaching core Confucian principles of filial piety and loyalty to the ruler through praising and blaming (*baobian*) Great Men of antiquity whose deeds and misdeeds had determined the fate of their states and people, setting precedents for subsequent generations to emulate or shun. More advanced texts consisted of excerpts from the Classics or the Four Books and essays on Confucian themes, such as Zhu Xi's *Elementary Learning* (De Bary and Chaffee 1989). Some texts, however, were apparently designed specifically to transmit historical data, albeit almost solely that concerning emperors and other Great Men, as well as to promote the moral determinist view of history. These potted histories also reflected the genesis of a broader intellectual movement to establish historiography (*shixue*) as a separate discipline from classical exegesis (*jingxue*). Some scholars even attempted to historicize the Classics; as Su Xun (1009–1066) noted, "Without history, the Classics would have no evidence for apportioning praise and blame" (cited in Su 1998, 438). This point was later emphasized more strongly by philosopher-statesmen Wang Yangming (1473–1529) and Zhang Xuecheng (1738–1801), who argued that the Classics were "all history" and thus subject to the same questions regarding their authenticity.

If the Confucian discourse of the past was central to the moral-ideological education of the scholar-gentry, it was still more important to China's rulers as a source of political legitimacy, for it demonstrated how the preceding dynasty had forfeited the ruling mandate through degeneracy and corruption.

Axiomatically, this proved the moral superiority and right to rule of the current regime; although, since new rulers and dynasties were frequently established by murderous conspiracies and military muscle, this in fact merely proved the maxim "victors are kings, the vanquished are bandits" (*chengzhe wei wang, baizhe wei kou*), overlaying might with a veneer of right. To control the past and protect their legitimacy, therefore, China's rulers produced official histories (*zhengshi*) detailing the rise and fall of the previous dynasty. Detailed records of current matters were also kept for an ongoing national history (*guoshi*) on which future histories of the dynasty would be based.[3] These were intended to transmit the wisdom of administrative experience from one generation to the next and also to ensure a favorable review of the present in the future, for among a largely agnostic, secular elite, history was the Last Judgment. Emperors and their courtiers cared how they would be remembered by future historians, and perhaps sometimes even kept their less noble instincts in check, mindful of the damage they might inflict on their posthumous reputations (Jenner 1992, 11).

Initially commissioned from private historians, official histories and national records from the Tang dynasty (618–907) onwards were compiled under the auspices of a government History Bureau by teams of civil servants. Having passed the highest examinations, official historians were thoroughly schooled in Confucian ethics and historiography and, under direct supervision of the Imperial Secretariat, they were also tightly bound to the throne. They were thus constantly compromised as employees of the state, required to serve the emperor and extol his virtues while, as good Confucians, being duty-bound to admonish him should he deviate from the Way. To fulfill their public obligations, defend their own interests in maintaining the status quo, and protect themselves personally from imperial wrath, most historians chose self-censorship when writing for the History Bureau, charting a careful course between truth and appropriate concealment (*hui*) and writing private histories or employing subtle historical analogies when they wished to make unorthodox comments. As the seventeenth-century historian Liu Chenggan declared, "In private history writing, it is permissible to use one's personal views as a basis. When a history is compiled by imperial order, it is necessary to integrate the collective, impartial judgment of the empire. One should not trust his own opinion or indulge in criticism" (cited in Yang 1961, 53). The court was, of course, fully alive to the possibility of challenging regime legitimacy or criticizing current policies through historical narratives. The strategy of control by encouraging orthodoxy could, therefore, easily become one of suppressing heterodoxy, and works of history (and fiction) could be banned and their authors severely punished if seditious intentions were suspected.

Narrating the chain of legitimate succession likewise required considerable dexterity. Although it rarely required much imagination to demonstrate that decadence and corruption had hastened the preceding dynasty's demise, proving the direct, unbroken transmission of the mandate was more complex, since dynastic collapse was often followed by entropic disintegration of central administration and the establishment of multiple independent states, sometimes coexisting, sometimes vying for supremacy. Moreover, many new rulers were non-Confucian barbarian conquerors. Although they usually left China's administrative structure intact and were seen as subject to eventual assimilation (*tonghua*) by China's "superior" culture, how could they have become inheritors of the moral mandate before they were fully Sinicized (*Hanhua*)? Acknowledging these problems, Ouyang Xiu (1007–1072) suggested omitting periods of disunity from the account of the chain of succession (Chan 1984). Restoring or preserving state unity could also, he argued, be a sufficient condition of legitimacy. This permitted the acknowledgment of any strong leader as the legitimate ruler, even a barbarian. Although the concept was deplored by those who argued that only ethnic Chinese (*huaren*) could possess the mandate and who rejected the notion that barbarians could be civilized by Confucian culture (Fincher 1972), many scholar-officials accepted the principle of cultural assimilation. This allowed them to serve the conquest dynasty or the strong but amoral leader with few qualms. Legitimacy, and the loyalty it commanded, in reality no longer resided in the ideal of the virtuous hegemon, but in the continuity of bureaucratic administration. Official history's highest purpose was to narrate the genealogy of the state.

Confucianism on the Move: Education and Historiography in Korea and Japan

Evidence regarding the interactions between the various peoples of East Asia is relatively sparse until well into the first millennium A.D. The earliest extant texts on Korea and Japan were composed by Chinese writers and included in official histories as brief monographs describing the customs and character of neighboring tribes.[4] Nothing is known of how these societies perceived China, themselves, or each other until several centuries later, when the first native histories were written. Although nationalists in Japan and Korea past and present have insisted that they are racially homogeneous peoples with unique cultures that have evolved in a continuous linear progression from the IR mythical ancestors, Amaterasu and Tan'gun, it is clear that Northeast Asians not only share descent from a common genetic stock but that there was a high level of population movement and cultural interaction within the region. Indeed, it has been suggested that in the middle of the first millennium A.D. as much as one third of Japan's population were descendants of recent migrants from the Korean peninsula (Cumings 1997, 31). Similarly, many Koreans originated from northern China and Siberia.

The true extent and direction of early population commingling may be unknown, but the overwhelmingly dominant civilisation in the region clearly developed in east-central China where, as we have seen, a centralized state with a sophisticated literary culture emerged in the third century B.C. This led China to develop a self-image as the Middle Kingdom (*Zhongguo*) of All under Heaven (*tianxia*), apex of a concentric hierarchy of peoples, distinguished by its moral mandate and cultural and technological superiority. According to this Sinocentric worldview, China was surrounded on all sides by barbarian tribes of varying degrees of savagery. In theory, geographical proximity to the core (Chinese civilization) rendered a people less barbaric and more human than those on the periphery in the submissive wastes (*huangfu*) (Dikötter 1992, ch. 1). In practice, pastoral nomads were normally categorized as raw barbarians (*shengfan*), considered less civilized than sedentary agricultural peoples who were known as cooked barbarians (*shoufan*) regardless of geographical location. With China not only culturally but often also militarily dominant, it successfully imposed this vision of the known world on surrounding peoples and enforced a tribute system under which barbarians acknowledged the Chinese emperor as suzerain in return for access to Chinese culture and permission to conduct private trade. The more civilized a state was thought to be, the more often it was permitted to present tribute. From the perspective of the barbarians, admiring of Chinese culture as many of them were, this remained largely a pragmatic exchange — the price of doing business; from the Chinese vantage point, the arrangement confirmed their own moral superiority, for not only did they bountifully bestow their glorious culture on inferior peoples, but the cost of tribute missions was borne by the Chinese imperial coffers.[5]

Inhabitants of the Korean peninsula joined the ranks of China's cooked neighbors at an early juncture. The expansionist Han dynasty established four Chinese commanderies there, providing locals with systematic and sustained exposure to Chinese culture and institutions. The Chinese writing system was soon adopted, and Korean elites quickly began to absorb Chinese thought, although the most influential philosophy during the period of the Three Kingdoms of Koguryô, Paekche, and Silla (second–tenth centuries) was Buddhism, which arrived via China and rapidly took root at all levels of society, dominating spiritual and intellectual life for the next millennium. Confucianism, however, gradually made an impact and, by the time the Three Kingdoms were united as Koryô in 935, it had made sufficient inroads for the court to appoint Confucian advisers. A civil service examination system that assessed candidates' knowledge of the Confucian canon was introduced in the kingdom of Silla in 788 and became firmly established under Koryô in 958, supported, as in China, by a network of state-run schools in which a Confucian curriculum was taught. Access to political power, however, remained limited to the landed and military elites (*yangban*), while commoners (*yangmin*), base people (*ch'ônmin*, a social underclass), and slaves were excluded from public schools and examinations. (Commoners were later admitted.) Thus, for all but the richest commoners, who could afford tutors or private academies, education — if available at all — was provided at home or at the local Buddhist temple.

The rulers of the Three Kingdoms had kept records of their reigns in the chronicle style of the Chinese classic *The Spring and Autumn Annals*, although they did not use historiography to serve Confucian ends; there was, after all, no need for ideological legitimation because both the king and the ruling classes were members of a hereditary aristocracy and Buddhism dominated the spiritual and moral dimensions of contemporary thought. Under Koryô, however, the first court-sponsored histories that moved beyond simple chronicles were written. The first of these was Kim Pusik's (1075–1151) *Historical Record of the Three Kingdoms* (*Samguk sagi*). Kim and his coauthors emphasized Confucian moral determinism, apparently imposing ideology at the expense of data and failing to "include all the facts and legends then known, particularly those that went against their own view of history" (SKT.1, 256). They also criticized the Three Kingdoms' annals for unrefined writing and deficient information, which led to failure to "expose whether the ruler is good or evil, the subjects are loyal or treasonous, the country is at peace or in crisis, the people are orderly or rebellious." Despite adhering closely to Sino-Confucian precepts, the writers displayed a strong conviction that Korea was not simply a minor outpost of Chinese civilisation and, in their preface, emphasized the importance of studying Korean history, lamenting the fact that so many Koryô scholars were well versed in the Chinese Classics and even the dynastic histories, yet knew nothing of their own country (SKT.1, 257).[6] However, not all history during this period was written from a Confucian perspective, nor did the state monopolize the production of historical texts. *The Memorabilia of the Three Kingdoms* (*Samguk yusa*) was written by the monk Iryôn (1206–1289) and included discourses on Buddhist themes as well as other stories not included in *Samguk sagi*. It is also the first extant record of the Tan'gun legend, in which it was claimed that Tan'gun established his court contemporaneously with China's mythical emperor Yao, thereby demonstrating an early assertion not only of independence from China but of equality in terms of political and cultural seniority.

When Koryô fell to Chosôn in 1392, the Buddhist age ended and the Confucian age began — at least, so Chosôn historians would have it (Deuchler 1995, 106; Palais 1996, 5), for they wished to distinguish themselves as better, more authentic Confucians than their predecessors to demonstrate that Koryô had forfeited its mandate through decadence and misrule and that General Yi Sônggye, founder of Chosôn, was the legitimate successor. During the subsequent five centuries of Yi dynastic rule, Chosôn became so devout in its adherence to neo-Confucianism (imported from China in the twelfth century) that it is often asserted that Koreans were not only thoroughly Sinicized but were even more orthodox neo-Confucians than the Chinese (Duncan 2002, 68). This may or may not be accurate. Certainly, the Confucian ideal of meritocratic governance, accepted as it was in principle, was never realized through the elite-monopolized civil service system, in contrast to the situation in China, where men of humble origin did sometimes rise to prominence; and despite efforts by hard-line neo-Confucians, neither Buddhism nor indigenous traditions were ever entirely obliterated even among the elite. Nonetheless, Chosôn vigorously propagated neo-Confucian thought, reestablishing the state school system, which had fallen into disrepair; promoting the neo-Confucian curriculum; slowly suppressing Buddhism; and instituting a code of laws and ritual practices that enshrined Confucianism as a social as well as a political and intellectual orthodoxy (Deuchler 1995). Chosôn also established a cohort of official historians who, like their Chinese counterparts, hovered close to the throne, keeping detailed records for the compilation of an ongoing national history.

Chosôn borrowed heavily from Chinese civilisation and maintained a policy of "deference (*sadae*) to the Great Ming [dynasty]," acknowledging China as the senior state. Yet, it was during the Chosôn period that the Korean phonetic script (*Hangul*) was developed and that an interest in indigenous arts burgeoned. Furthermore, despite occasionally invoking Mencius' doctrine of "using Chinese ways to transform the barbarians" (ostensibly self-deprecating, but more likely intended to legitimize the new, Chinese-style institutions and laws), Korean Confucians did not regard themselves or their state as inferior. Confucianism to them was universal, and Korea a proud and worthy inheritor of this great tradition. In fact, some Chosôn historians consciously bypassed contemporary China, alleging an indigenous ancestral link to Confucius' golden age of early Zhou rule through the legendary Kija, who had supposedly been enfeoffed in "Old Chosôn" by sage-King Wu himself (Deuchler 1995, 107; SKT.1, 183). This assertion of cultural and moral parity with China, like the claim to equivalent historical antiquity in support of which the Tan'gun legend was invoked, grew stronger as Confucianism gradually superseded older ideas, values, institutions, and forms of social organization and came to appear more integral to Korean culture. Indeed, following the conquest of Ming China by Manchu "barbarians," Chosôn apparently regarded itself as the true representative of the neo-Confucian way. For the sake of its own security, however, it continued to acknowledge the Manchu Qing Dynasty as suzerain and barring periodic troubles with marauding Japanese pirates and the devastating 1592–1598 Japanese invasion, Korea remained largely at peace and wholly independent until the late nineteenth century.

Japan's first close encounters with Chinese culture and technologies came via the Korean peninsula, with Chinese writing and Confucianism probably imported from Paekche in the late fourth or early fifth century. While Buddhism, which arrived in Japan a century later (again via China and Korea), rapidly established itself, Confucianism first took an identifiable hold two centuries later when Japan began to feel threatened by its Chinese and Korean neighbours, then uniting or reuniting into powerful states. Confucian thought and institutions appeared to underpin this movement and, in 604, Prince Shótoku drafted a constitution centralizing government under imperial control, although it was only intended to regulate secular matters; spiritual business was left to Buddhism. Envoys were also sent to China, both to enhance Japanese knowledge of Confucianism and its associated techniques of governance and to placate the Middle Kingdom through acknowledgement of Chinese suzerainty. Some historians claim that Shótoku's letters to the Chinese court evince an assertion of Japanese equality in using the superscriptions "The Son of Heaven of the Land of the Rising Sun to the Son of Heaven of the Land of the Setting Sun" and "The Eastern Emperor Greets the Western Emperor." However, Shótoku may simply have been ignorant of the proper procedure for establishing tribute relations (SJT.1, 37).

Over the next four centuries, Confucianism was earnestly studied and promoted, but its influence did not penetrate far beyond the imperial court and had little impact on education and, as in Korea, still less impact on the sociopolitical hierarchy. It did, however, catalyze the development of Japanese historiography and state involvement therein. Shótoku reportedly drafted a national history in 620, and another was apparently commissioned by imperial order in 681. Neither of these survived, and Japan's earliest extant histories are *Records of Ancient Matters* (*Kojiki*), published in 712, and the *Six National Histories* (*Rikkokushi*), the first of which, *Nihon-shoki*, was published in 720. All were compiled by committees commissioned and overseen by the court.

The *Rikkokushi* consciously imitated Chinese histories, although clearly they could not be dynastic because Japan had only one legitimate imperial line (which survives to this day) allegedly descended directly from the mythical divinity Amaterasu; legitimate succession theory was thus applied to reigns or groups of reigns. *Kojiki*, by contrast, freely amalgamated Chinese and Japanese styles and was the first text to use the Japanese vernacular (rendered phonetically in Chinese characters). None of these histories displayed Chinese preoccupations with distributing praise and blame, and in only one of the *Six Histories* did the compilers declare "We know that it is the function of history to ensure that no fault be concealed which might serve as a warning, and that every excellence be published which might illuminate the path of virtue" (Robinson 1961, 218).

During Japan's feudal period, the court lost all but its symbolic authority and power was vested in shóguns who had little taste for effete Confucian learning or things Chinese, focusing on military matters and seeking spiritual and intellectual enlightenment and/or salvation in Buddhism and the native Shintó tradition. Neither official records nor histories were written between the eleventh and sixteenth centuries, but an indigenous, non-Confucian historiography evolved from the vernacular literary tradition (epitomized by *The Tale of*

Genji) established with the introduction of a phonetic Japanese writing system (*kana*). The turn away from China toward indigenous traditions, however, bred no national unity and factional wars raged; during the fourteenth century, there were even two imperial courts, Northern and Southern. Historical tales (*rekishi-monogatari*) written during this period thus sought to exalt one or another clan or court and legitimize their claims to authority. Most notable was Kitabatake Chikafusa, who championed the Southern Court and insisted on Japan's superiority over Confucian China and Buddhist India since Japan had Shintó, the one true creed, and an emperor and people of divine descent inhabiting a chosen "continent" entirely separate from the rest of Asia ([*Jinnó shótóku*] SJT.1, 270–72; Robinson and Beasley 1961, 239–243). Whether such notions of superiority underlay Toyotomi Hideyoshi's 1592 to 1598 campaign to subjugate Korea, intending thence to overrun Ming China, is uncertain. However, the ideas of Kitabatake and like-minded thinkers were to be explicitly coopted by modern nationalists to promote Shintó and imperial worship (*sonnó*) and to justify twentieth-century Japanese imperialism.

The Tokugawa victory at the end of the sixteenth century ended centuries of strife and led to the establishment of a central government at Edo in 1600. The new regime displayed a keen interest in neo-Confucianism and in the past as a source of political legitimacy, useful knowledge, and experience. Numerous histories were commissioned, and official recordkeeping was resumed to transmit the wisdom of the present to posterity. The histories compiled marked an explicit return to Chinese-style, Chinese-language, Confucian moral didacticism. As pronounced in History of Great Japan (*Dai Nihonshi*), "good deeds will serve to inspire men and bad deeds to restrain them, so that rebels and traitors may tremble in fear of history's judgment. The cause of education and the maintenance of social order will thus greatly benefit" (SJT.1, 364).

The "cause of education," not to mention "the maintenance of social order," were major concerns of the Tokugawa regime, which promoted Chinese-language, neo-Confucian scholarship through subsidizing libraries, printing Confucian texts, and supporting Hayashi Razan's famous Confucian Academy (Dore 1965, 17). Schooling for the young, however, remained a mainly private or local fief affair, with the samurai class employing tutors or sending their sons to fief schools. Samurai sons studied both literary culture (*bun*) and military arts (*bu*) to prepare them for their future roles in society as men of virtue, wisdom, taste, physical courage, tactical nous, and honor, who would set an example for the common people to emulate. As in China and Korea, the *bun* curriculum focused on memorisation and recitation, learning Chinese characters from primers, such as the *Three-* and *Thousand-Character Classics*, or Japanese versions thereof, as a foundation for studying the Confucian canon. Perhaps because there was no civil service examination for which to prepare, the curriculum was somewhat more flexible than in China and Korea, and other subjects were also studied. These included history — either the official

Chinese and Japanese histories or digests thereof (Mehl 1998, 53) and the sciences (mathematics, botany, medicine), almost invariably taught through Chinese texts. Only the *bu* curriculum, which was academic as well as practical, sometimes used Japanese texts, since Classical Chinese remained the formal written language of the polity (Dore 1965). Education of commoners was a lesser concern, but the demand for literacy catalyzed the establishment of numerous private schools and, for the poorer commoners, semiformal writing schools (*terakoya*) that focused on the Japanese vernacular. The rapid spread of vernacular literacy that ensued would prove a valuable foundation when Japan turned its attention to political, social, and economic transformation in the late nineteenth century.

Confucianism Challenged: Modernisation and the Western Barbarians

By the end of the eighteenth century, neo-Confucianism had been decreed the state ideology in China, Korea, and Japan, determining the content of most formal education and official historiography. Additionally, all three states had implemented a policy of seclusion, closing their borders both to outsiders and to emigration by their own citizens. It would be wrong, however, to conclude that neo-Confucianism was a monolithic tradition that necessarily engendered intellectual, social, or cultural stasis or that seclusion policies effectively locked each country in rigid isolation. Economic migration, primarily from the southern Chinese provinces of Fujian, Guangdong, and Guangxi to Southeast Asia, which had persisted for many centuries, increased during the late Ming Dynasty despite official prohibition. Following the Manchu invasion, more economic migrants and Ming loyalists also fled the mainland, primarily to those areas under European colonial control, where business opportunities were plentiful. Most famously, Koxinga (Zheng Chenggong) led thousands to Taiwan, where he proceeded to expel Dutch colonists, subdue the indigenous people, and claim the territory as a base from which to restore Ming rule over the mainland. This mass migration continued briskly until the twentieth century, firmly establishing a major ethnic Chinese presence in Southeast Asia. It also led to Taiwan's incorporation into the Chinese empire as a prefecture of Fujian province when the Qing crushed the forces of Koxinga's descendants in 1683.

There was considerably less population movement to and from Korea and Japan, but they were by no means wholly isolated by seclusion. The tributary relationship with China was unaffected, and neighbourly relations between Korea and Japan (K. *kyôrin*) were restored within a decade after the withdrawal of Japanese troops from Korea in 1598. Certain ports remained open both to bilateral trade and to trade with China, and ideas were exchanged along with goods. Philosophical debates between rival neo-Confucian schools in China were thus transported to Korea and Japan, where they were vigorously taken up and developed. Although in all three countries official edicts had technically banned heterodoxy (anything non-Confucian), books that promoted alternative philosophies circulated relatively freely as long as they did not directly challenge neo-Confucianism, subvert the social or political order, or attack the ruling house itself. Abstruse discussions of neo-Confucian metaphysics, therefore, were far from the only current of intellectual activity. Japanese National Learning scholars (*kokugakusha*), for example, took a nativist stance, and although not directly attacking neo-Confucianism or even the prevalence of Chinese learning — indeed, most of them wrote in Classical Chinese — they lamented the relative paucity of indigenous historiography and called for the establishment of an institute of Japanese learning to remedy this deficiency and promote Japanese literature (Beasley and Blacker 1961; SJT.2, ch. 22). Others, such as the practical learning (*sirhak*) scholars in Korea and the New Text school in China, criticized neo-Confucianism as divorced from administrative realities, proposing a return to pragmatic Confucianism and a revision of the civil service examinations to include more questions on relevant political and historical matters. Similar concerns were articulated by Ancient Learning (*kogaku*) advocates in Japan, who felt that the samurai were not applying Confucian precepts to governance and emphasized the importance of using education to cultivate talented persons (*jinzai*). Perhaps the most significant innovation, however, was evidential scholarship (Ch. *kaozhengxue*, J. *kóshó-gaku*, K. *kojûnghak*), which dispensed with the numerous commentaries on the Classics, seeking instead to discover the original meaning in the original texts. This school focused on philology, but more significantly, it sought to raise the status of history to equivalence with the Classics. Both, after all, dealt in truth; the former provided the evidence, the latter explicated its moral import. This approach was reflected in Japanese historiography by an emphasis on facts, which were, according to Tokugawa Tsunaeda, to be "presented as exhaustively as possible. Arbitrary selection and wilful alteration has no place in authentic history" ([*Dai Nihonshi*] SJT.1, 364).

It was not only variations on a Confucian theme that attracted scholarly research, especially in Japan, where there was continued interest in Buddhism and Shintó and also a burgeoning curiosity regarding European learning. Some familiarity with the latter had already developed via China, where Jesuits had for a time been welcomed at the imperial court, teaching mathematics and astronomy. Their works, either originally written in or translated into Chinese, soon found their way to Japan, where they were used as textbooks in some fief schools (Dore 1965, 136). More sustained contact, however, came from Dutch traders at Nagasaki (the Dutch were the only Europeans permitted to land in Japan during the period of seclusion), where local translators and intellectuals began to take an interest in Dutch writings on science, particularly medicine, leading to the formation of a school of "Dutch studies" (*rangaku*) (CHJ.5, 435–438). This would later form the basis of a more broadly conceived foreign studies school, covering all aspects of European arts and sciences.

Things European held far less attraction for the Chinese and Koreans, who were more tightly wedded to the cultural glories of their own civilizations, and especially to neo-Confucianism and the institutions it underpinned. History had shown them, moreover, that foreigners came to Asia to procure spices, silk, tea, porcelain, and other luxury products, not by exchanging them for goods but by paying hard cash; what else, after all, did the pale-faced barbarians have to offer the civilized world? When Europeans and Americans arrived en masse in the mid-nineteenth century to "open" East Asia to international trade, they were rebuffed. The foreign traders did not simply slink away, however, but used the might of their national navies to blast open Asia's closed doors, forcing first China, then Japan, and finally Korea into a succession of humiliating unequal treaties that granted foreigners extraterritoriality and privileged trading rights.

Numerous scholarly tomes have been written about the impact of the West on East Asia's subsequent historical development, many wondering why East Asia, having been so far ahead of Europe for so long, fell so far behind, and why it took foreign invasion to catalyze the transition to modernity. Many commentators have also wondered why Japan adapted so much faster than its neighbors, expanding from a small island state to a vast Asian empire within a century. It is far beyond the scope of this discussion to analyse the causes of Japan's expansion in any detail here. There is some merit, nevertheless, in the somewhat cliché assertion that Japan's long-standing openness to foreign ideas and the less rigid imposition of neo-Confucian orthodoxy in the late Tokugawa period contributed substantially to its adaptability in the face of new challenges. Additionally, many Tokugawa leaders were already conscious of a potential threat from the West (primarily Russia), and with the first attack directed at China in the 1839–1842 Opium War and subsequent demands on Japan to open-or-else, Japan was at least partially prepared for the American warships that enforced the first opening agreement in 1854. More treaties with foreign powers followed, galvanizing a drive to overcome regional and clan loyalties and unite the nation against the foreign threat. This further weakened the already ailing Tokugawa regime and, by 1868, the *bakufu* (as the Tokugawa government was known) had fallen and the Emperor Meiji had been restored to power, bringing to an end seven centuries of shogun rule.

The primary goals of the Meiji Restoration were national enrichment and military strengthening (*fukoku kyóhei*), which the new regime intended to achieve by accelerating the modernisation efforts begun under Tokugawa rule, rejecting "evil customs of the past" and seeking "knowledge ... throughout the world" ([1868 Charter Oath] SJT 2, 137). Within a few years, thoroughgoing institutional reforms based on Western (primarily Prussian) models had been implemented, industrialisation begun, and a modern, mass schooling system legislated. By contrast, Korean and Chinese elites were unwilling, until it was far too late, to countenance reforms that might have made feasible a Japanese-style modernisation program. In China, some leading figures did advocate "self-strengthening" and "using the techniques of the barbarians to control the barbarians," recommending the establishment of schools in which science, military technology and engineering, foreign languages, Western history, and geography could be studied. They also suggested civil service examination reform to give scholars of the new learning access to official posts where they could deploy their skills. However, the reformers were bitterly resisted by conservative leaders and most of the scholar-gentry for whom Confucian learning remained the rock of their legitimacy. Afflicted by official corruption and mismanagement, natural disasters, and domestic rebellions, China was unable to mount an effective defense against foreign encroachment. Korea was similarly resistant to reform, and by the time it began to study the modernising efforts of Japan and China and implement its own self-strengthening program, the former had already emerged as a growing power with expansionist ambitions; indeed, Korea's first unequal treaty was signed not with a European power, but with its former equal (or, in the eyes of many Koreans, inferior), Japan. By the beginning of the twentieth century, Japan had carved out a sphere of influence in Northeast China and had acquired Taiwan as its first colony through the Treaty of Shimonoseki after a resounding victory over China in the war of 1894–1895. In 1905, Korea became a Japanese protectorate, and in 1910 it was annexed as Japan's second colony. Although nationalist revolutionaries overthrew China's Qing dynasty in 1911, ending two millennia of imperial rule, the Republic of China they established was weak and war-torn, as rival groups contended for the ruling mandate. China was thus virtually powerless to resist an increasingly powerful Japan. In 1931, the Japanese invaded Manchuria and established the puppet state of Manchukuo; in 1937, óChina proper was also attacked. Within the next few years, Japanese troops occupied most of the Far East. East Asia was clearly no longer a Sinocentric world.

History and Nationalism in the New World Order

Following the first foreign incursions, there was considerable reluctance even among reformers to adopt anything more from the Western nations than the superior technologies that apparently underpinned their strength. Under slogans such as "Eastern ethics, Western Science," "Chinese learning as the essence, Western learning as the application," and "Western implements, Eastern Way," which presumed that Western techniques could be used with no adverse effects on the natural Confucian order if traditional values were preserved, some foreign technologies were adopted to aid the development of industry, infrastructure, and military defense. Gradually, however, it was realized that this onslaught was unlike barbarian invasions of yore, when nomadic steppes tribes had swept down into the civilized plains, only to be assimilated by the superior Confucian culture they found there. The new invaders clearly had their own powerful ideologies and established political systems, and the technology they wielded was the product of a sophisticated scientific tradition. While the Chinese and Korean governments remained largely unwilling to explore Western ethics or the essence of foreign learning, they did not prevent many individuals from taking a private interest in such matters. Some students traveled to Europe and America to acquire the new learning at the source, and Western works on science, philosophy, history, law, and politics were translated either from the original texts or from Japanese translations thereof. However, by the time China and Korea began to take Western learning seriously, Japan was already well into its reform program, with a booming translation market catering to a vibrant intellectual market. Japan, in fact, was the chief destination for Chinese and Koreans seeking to understand the ways of the West, as well as for radical reformers fleeing oppression at home. Even after Japan had forced Korea into unequal treaties and defeated China in the 1894–1895 war, students and refugees continued to pour into Japan eager to learn how modernisation was to be achieved. Many Western theories and concepts thus arrived in China and Korea filtered through Japanese lenses; one source estimates that in the early twentieth century, as much as three-quarters of all new words in China (for concepts such as *democracy* and *nationalism*) were imported from Japan (CHC.11, 362).

Western history was among the first subjects to attract scholarly attention. This was initially part of an effort to "know the other side as one knows oneself,"[7] to understand how and why those states now encroaching on East Asian soil had evolved, but interest soon developed in Western historiographical theories and methods as universal laws were sought to explain the new international order rationally and scientifically and to justify the changes (or demands for change) being made at home. For many, it was part of an iconoclastic rejection of the traditional culture and ideologies they believed had landed them in their current predicament vis-à-vis the West. It was also a search by nationalist historians for ways to demonstrate to the West (and, perhaps more significantly, to themselves) both the uniqueness of their national traditions and their equivalence with those of the advanced and modern Western powers. Perhaps most importantly, it was an attempt to find solid foundations upon which to construct new national narratives that would resonate not only with the elite but also with the newly imagined national citizens.

Rankean historiography quickly made an impression at the newly established universities in Japan and China and was soon transmitted to Korea through the Japanese colonial project, which sought not merely to conquer but also to modernize. Historians belonging to the school of evidential scholarship were especially attracted to Rankean historiography with its promise to reveal the truth of the past exactly as it was. Many historians concluded that traditional historiography was severely lacking in this regard, for it had ignored vast swaths of history, focusing primarily on the lives of rulers and their acolytes or the rise and fall of dynasties. Too little attention, they argued, had hitherto been paid to economic, social, and cultural history and to questions of cause and effect, weighing of evidence had been inadequate, and the moralizing impulse of Confucian historiography had led many writers to deliberately distort the facts. "This," insisted Japanese historian Shigeno Yasutsugu, "is contrary to the true meaning of history. History only results if the moral lessons — the encouragement of good and the discouragement of evil, the clarification of moral relationships — emerge as a product of a faithful account of the facts" (Numata 1961, 279–280).

In order to present a faithful account of the facts, however, "the facts" had first to be found, generating a frenzy of data collection and compilation. Indeed, in Japan, the Office of Historiography, originally established in 1868 to compile an official national history, was reorganized as the Historiographical Institute of Tokyo Imperial University and was thereafter devoted solely to this purpose.[8] Japanese government ministries also compiled historical documents relating to their own fields and these formed the nucleus of vast archival resources (Mehl 1998, 57). It was soon realized that the facts also had to be evaluated objectively as true or false, and rigorous methods of source criticism were accordingly applied. Traditional reverence for the authority of ancient texts, already challenged by evidential scholarship, thus received a further blow as historians such as China's Gu Jiegang not only looked to primary sources but cast doubt on their authenticity. All texts, Gu maintained, are written after the event and are susceptible to distortion. "We therefore should treat ancient history in the same way as we treat the stories of our own day, for they have all passed from mouth to mouth" ([Gushibian] SCT.2, 184). In so doing, he rejected much of China's ancient history as myth and fabrication. Fortunately for Chinese nationalists, antiquity was salvaged by the new field of archaeology and the discovery of numerous sites that proved scientifically that China did indeed have a sophisticated ancient culture, although not quite of the sort that had once been alleged. This allowed nationalists to assert equivalence and even superiority over, the civilizations of the West in one area at least. Furthermore, evidence of this culture was widespread in many areas inhabited by ethnic minorities, apparently substantiating the claim that these peoples had been assimilated by superior Han Chinese culture and were, therefore, integral constituents of China's national community. (That this ancient culture might have originated elsewhere and been adopted by Han Chinese was a possibility never given serious consideration.)

If scientific theories and methods of investigating, analysing, and explaining the past debunked some traditional mythologies, they aided substantially in the construction of modern ones, not the least of which was the myth of science itself, which filled the vacuum left when Confucian universality was disproved by all-too-real historical experience. Science, to the modernizers, was omnipotent (Ch. wanneng), seen, together with democracy, to have propelled once backward Western civilization to its present position of power. If these barbarous young nations could achieve so much in so short a time, surely science, reasoned reformers, could also restore East Asian states to greatness. Had not Japan — historically an inferior society in the Sinocentric world order — already shown the way? Why then, historians wondered, had China and Korea failed to follow? Many concluded that Confucianism was the obstacle, shackling people's minds in feudal darkness, rendering them blind to the fact that history was not a cyclical process of dynastic rise, decline, and fall, but an evolutionary movement. A new linear history was thus needed to explain the present and show the way to the future. Furthermore, ordinary citizens, maintained thinkers such as Liang Qichao, required an inclusive history with which they could identify and which would inspire them to strive for the nation's survival and prosperity.

Much new historiography accordingly attempted to emphasize social and cultural aspects of the past and to focus on the nation and its people as subjects and agents of history. But what was the nation and who were the people that were to replace the Great Men and dynastic rulers at the heart of the national narrative? Science — or at least the Social Darwinist pseudoscience of race espoused by the likes of Herbert Spencer and Lewis Morgan — came to the rescue, helping to create new mythologies of primordial nations, races, and national peoples that could lend continuity and cohesion to linear narratives of the past. While these new mythologies owed much of their language and structure to foreign discourses of race and the contemporary international order of nation-states, they were not simply foisted onto hitherto innocent, race-blind peoples by European intellectual-cultural imperialism, but built on or merged with preexisting racial and cultural taxonomies (Dikötter 1992, 1997). This mixture of old and new ideas of race, ethnicity, culture, and state coalesced to form the rather nebulous concept of *minzoku* (J.), *minzu* (Ch.), or *minjôk* (K.) — terms encountered throughout this volume — that may be seen as variously connoting "nation," "national people," "race-nation," or "ethne", according to context. Nationalist historians thus wrote teleological histories that provided the veridical evidence to substantiate such theories of primordial peoples and innate, race-based, national qualities. Predictably enough, such histories tended to demonstrate the superiority of the historians' own nations and races, in turn legitimizing territorial claims over minority regions or colonies inhabited by inferior peoples. History, in this view, was a Darwinian struggle between races; only the strongest would survive. Moral determinism had ostensibly been supplanted by biological determinism. Despite these grandiose theories, the transformation of historiography was in practice less obviously dramatic than might be supposed. Many historians continued to take the rise and fall of dynasties as their principal theme and to treat Great Men as the agents of historical change, although the latter were often reevaluated according to whether they had championed or oppressed the national people (as currently defined) and advanced or hindered the nation's development. At the same time, perhaps the most significant step in making new narratives of the past relevant and accessible to the common people was the move away from Classical Chinese to the use of vernacular languages as the medium of historical writing.

History may have become more a professional rather than a state affair in the course of the modernisation process, with historians based in universities and research institutes rather than at the royal court, and historians may also have largely rejected the moral didacticism of traditional historiography in favor of science and objectivity, but this did not mean that they (or any other intellectuals) ceased to believe that they were duty-bound to serve the state (or now the nation) admonishing the ruler (now the government) should he (or it) fail to act in the best interests of the people. While some historians maintained a studied neutrality, many were actively involved in politics, critiquing current policies in the plethora of journals and newspapers now available to an increasingly literate citizenry. Even in Korea, where the Japanese colonial government had initially implemented a repressive military policy (*budan seiji*), a more conciliatory cultural policy (*bunka seiji*) and approach to social and ideological control was subsequently taken, and historians such as Chông Inbo, Mun Ilp'yông, and Ch'oe Namsôn were able to publish both Korean histories and journalistic writings with a proindependence, nationalist slant. Unsurprisingly though, the most explicitly nationalist works were published abroad by Korean exiles such as Sin Ch'aeho and Pak Ûnsik (SKT.2, 316–20).

In Japan and China, meanwhile, many critics felt that reforms based on Western models — hitherto presumed to be the only route to modernity and enhanced world status — had not enabled East Asia to catch up or be treated as equal in the international order. Such sentiments tended to come to the fore particularly after the First World War, which left both the Japanese and the Chinese feeling slighted by the condescending racism displayed by the Western powers as they carved up the postwar world at Versailles. Some concluded that reform had not gone far or fast enough and called for accelerated Westernization; others criticized the embrace of ideas once perceived as universally modern but now seen as simply Western, and thus as a negation of East Asia's rich cultural heritage and unique national identities. For those who saw domestic problems as rooted in social inequalities, and the failure of reform as a product of bureaucratic collusion with big business and foreign powers, Marxism and the Russian Revolution were an inspiration. Marxist historical materialism offered an alternative scientific explanation of the past and a guaranteed future, while the idealized USSR showed how the higher form of modernity — socialism — could be quickly attained in a largely agrarian society with only a small proletariat, bypassing the stage of full capitalism to overtake the Western imperialist powers. That Marx had explicitly excluded East Asia from his model of socioeconomic development, dismissing it (as Hegel had done) as characterized by historical inertia, interminably stuck in an "Asiatic mode of production," however, was clearly problematic for Asia's Marxist historians. How some attempted to resolve this apparent contradiction is discussed in subsequent chapters; for the moment suffice it to say that controversies raged as historians attempted to reconcile intractable historical data to Marxist theory, foreshadowing later struggles in Communist China and North Korea, where the both the data and the ideology would prove rather more malleable and the stakes much higher.

History and the Modern School Curriculum

Japanese Education

Japan had rejected Chinese models and looked toward Europe for a path to national strength and prosperity. When Prussia defeated France in 1871, therefore, Japanese reformers analyzed the source of Prussian power and determined that the success of the nation depended not merely on having an elite corps of talented persons but on educating the general populace. Japan accordingly established, with the 1872 Education Code, a modern education system based on the Prussian model, introducing 16 months of compulsory (but not free) education. By 1890 this had increased to 4 years and, by 1910, to 6, with 98 percent enrollment and 85 percent attendance (CHJ.6, 560). Local authorities were responsible for administration and funding, while the Ministry of Education (MOE) sponsored preservice and in-service teacher training and accreditation. The MOE also issued curriculum guidelines and produced some model textbooks, but most textbook compilation was left in private hands, frequently undertaken by the recently established "normal schools" (the name by which teacher training colleges were and still are known in most of East Asia) and, in the case of history, by the Office of Historiography. Individual teachers or schools were mostly free to select textbooks, although the MOE issued a list of approved editions from which they had the option to select.

Far from implementing an ideologically dogmatic and pedagogically rigid curriculum, at the inception of the new education system, the latest Western pedagogies and theories of child psychology were extremely influential. Child-centered developmental education (*kaihatsu-shugi*), which emphasised the discovery of knowledge and the maximization of individual potential, was championed over the traditional one-size-fits-all spoon-feeding (*chūnyū*) method of memorizing and reciting set texts (Lincicome 1996). This, it was thought, would deliver civilisation and enlightenment (*bunmei kaika*) to the common people and accelerate Japan's progress toward modernity. The subject of history was deemed an important part of the enlightenment process and, influenced by the Rankean views of professional historians, the study of both Japanese and foreign (predominantly European) history was steered away from Confucian concerns toward a focus instead on "facts" (Mehl 1998, 54).

By the 1880s, a reaction against perceived over-Westernization had set in and teacher autonomy, textbook pluralism, and the developmental education project were gradually superseded by a more centralised system that focused on moral training, social conformity, and obeisance to the imperial house. In the revised primary school curriculum of 1881, the subject of moral education (*shushin*) was brought to the fore while science was removed from the list of compulsory subjects. Japanese history remained in the curriculum, but world history was dropped. Rejecting earlier, Rankean views, history was also explicitly required to reinforce the principles taught in moral education (Lincicome 1996, 78–80). School history should not be conflated with professional historical scholarship, it was later stated. The latter was pure history (*junshó shigaku*), the former was applied (*óyó shigaku*); legitimate knowledge for scholars was not necessarily appropriate for the masses. Thus, school students learned that the Japanese Empire was founded in 660 B.C.; university students could be told that this actually occurred about 600 years later (Mehl 1998, 145).

Although experiments in developmental education continued throughout the 1880s, by 1890, the state was asserting tighter control, promoting "emperor worship and love for the nation" (*sonnó aikoku*), and overtly restoring Confucian values to the curriculum. The 1890 Imperial rescript on education famously set out the new (old) goals:

> Ye, Our subjects, be filial to your parents, affectionate to your brothers and sisters; as husbands and wives be harmonious, as friends true; bear yourselves in modesty and moderation; extend your benevolence to all; pursue learning and cultivate arts, and thereby develop intellectual faculties and perfect moral powers; furthermore, advance public good and promote common interests; always respect the Constitution and observe the laws; should emergency arise, offer yourself courageously to the State; and thus guard and maintain the prosperity of Our Imperial Throne coeval with heaven and earth. So shall ye not only be Our good and faithful subjects, but render illustrious the best traditions of your forefathers. (cited in Yamashita 1996, 133)

Moral education accordingly focused increasingly on the state and emperor, teaching the young to be obedient subjects (*komin*) and useful citizens (*kokumin*) through praising and blaming Great Men from Japanese — and occasionally foreign — history and legend (Yamashita 1996).

The revival of the Confucian ethos further enhanced the moralizing function of history, and as Japan's imperial ambitions intensified, domestic unrest grew, criticism of the government became more vocal, and the sensitivity of textbook content correspondingly increased. Thus a textbook that had already been in use for several years was suddenly attacked in 1911 for its ambiguous position on the question of the legitimacy of the fourteenth-century Northern and Southern courts. With no official verdict on this issue from the imperial government, most professional historians had hitherto ignored it. There were simply two courts at one time, and this had been reflected in the school textbooks they drafted. "During the events surrounding ... 1911 [a particularly sensitive time] [.] It was probably just unfortunate then that a zealous teacher publicised the matter at a politica, warning that "if moral principles [are] not clearly set forth and taught in the schools individualistic and nihilistic ideologies could spread unhindered." That such a textbook, which "violated the dignity of the imperial house and destroyed the principles of education," could be authorized by the MOE was not merely shocking but dangerous. Provoked into action, the emperor (a descendant of the Northern court) finally declared for the Southern court, the textbook was revised, erasing the existence of the Northern court, and the author, Kita Sadakichi,[9] was dismissed by the MOE (Mehl 1998, 142–144). Despite this instance of state intervention, professional historians were able to continue debating most questions openly until the war years of the late 1930s, when all dissent was stifled and historians were expected to use the past to serve the present national cause. By contrast, barring another brief flirtation with developmental education in the 1920s, history for children remained until 1945 a means of inculcating the knowledge and values considered necessary to legitimize the national polity (*kokutai*), preserve the national essence (*kokusui*) and create loyal, obedient subjects for whom the highest honor would be pro patria mori.

Colonial Education: Taiwan and Korea

Japan's education policies in its new colonies of Taiwan and Korea were designed both to foster obedience to the colonial masters and to modernise what appeared to an already modernising Japan to be backward societies. Modernisation would serve Japan's interests by providing a broader industrial base for further expansion, but from a Japanese perspective, it would also liberate the local population, both from the shackles of retrograde patterns of thought and from Euro-American imperialism. More importantly, the fruits of modernisation would shatter the Sinocentric worldview of the Taiwanese and Koreans and establish Japan as the model of civilization. It is somewhat ironic then that the pan-Asianism used to justify Japan's conquest of its neighbors was couched in terms of precisely the same archaic, Chinese-derived "same culture" (*dōbun*) from which the Japanese were committed to liberating them. The imperialist project was also legitimized by asserting that East Asian peoples were of the "same race" (*dōshu*), a "yellow" people embroiled in a Darwinian struggle against the "whites" for their rightful position at the apex of the racial hierarchy. In reality, neither Koreans nor Taiwanese Chinese (and certainly not Taiwan's aboriginal peoples) were ever regarded as racially equal to the unique and pure Japanese race imagined by Japanese nationalists, but education could, it was thought, at least turn them into useful Japanese subjects, albeit second-class ones.

Japan's schooling system was accordingly exported to both of its Asian colonies, although in neither was compulsory education introduced until the last years of Japanese rule. During the early years, traditional Confucian academies were mostly left in place since the new Japanese-style primary schools could not be established fast enough to replace them, but they were encouraged to add Japanese language courses to the curriculum and were subject to Japanese inspections and approval. Mission schools, which had flourished in much of Asia since the mid-nineteenth century (normally teaching in the local vernacular and encouraging girls to attend classes), were similarly permitted to continue teaching but banned from providing religious instruction. In Korea, there was also a motley crop of both government and private schools, established from the mid-1890s onwards as part of the "education for the nation" drive, which taught a modern curriculum through the medium of *hangŭl*. While the government schools generally cooperated with the colonial administration, the private schools, warned Korea's governor-general Terauchi Matasake, were nationalist havens where "the desire for independence is propagated and opposition to the Empire is encouraged" (Lee 1963, 97). Many of these schools were closed down.

Hostility toward Japanese education was strong in Korea and, although the Japanese schools offered better facilities and a more modern curriculum, many Koreans chose to attend less well-endowed private academies. Eventually, however, the Japanese schools began to lure more students, for they offered greater access to secondary and tertiary education and lucrative employment opportunities. The Japanese school curriculum in both Korea and Taiwan was a slightly modified version of that in Japan itself, with a primary emphasis on literacy, numeracy, and moral education. Science, Japanese history and geography, and physical education were also taught. In Korea, the Cultural Policy effort to mollify the local populace permitted the reinstatement of Korean history and geography in the primary school curriculum, taught, naturally, from a Japanese imperialist perspective that suggested some measure of historical legitimacy for Japanese claims to Korea (Tsurumi 1977, 171). In Taiwan, by contrast, resistance to Japanese rule was weaker and the transition to Japanese schooling much faster. This was perhaps partly because Taiwanese felt less loyalty toward China's Qing administration, which had often treated them as semibarbarians inhabiting a lonely frontier outpost, providing little public welfare and applying criminal punishments far harsher than those stipulated in the Qing code (Anthony 1993; Boulais 1924). It was perhaps also because the Taiwanese, composed mainly of Hokkien and Hakka Chinese and various aboriginal peoples, had a less powerful sense of shared identity than the Koreans. Thus, although the Taiwanese were well aware of the inequalities between colonizer and colonized and knew that care was taken to prevent locals becoming "educated above their station," protests against the administration were primarily motivated by a desire for "a larger slice of the unevenly divided colonial pie, rather than the destruction of the pie itself" (Tsurumi 1977, 23, 175). The Japanization policy (*kominka*) of the war years, which sought to enhance obedience and loyalty toward the empire through persuading colonials to identify themselves as nominally equal Japanese citizens (complete with Japanese names) was thus bitterly resented in Korea but at least partially welcomed in Taiwan.

Colonial Education: Hong Kong and Southeast Asia

As Vickers (2000, ch. 3) has shown, much writing on colonial education is informed by the overly simplistic assumption — frequently based on little concrete evidence — that colonial powers have always and everywhere used education primarily to reinforce control over their dominions, imposing hegemonic curricula on unfortunate natives in an effort to create cultural dependency and stem resistance to colonial rule. While there is undoubtedly much truth in this view, crude or excessive generalisation may fail to account for the disparate objectives and approaches to native education taken by various colonial powers at different times. As previously stated, Japanese colonial administrations did indeed attach great importance to education as an instrument of political socialisation and economic modernisation, while in Republican China, efforts were made to enforce a Mandarin-language standard national curriculum throughout the country, including the non-Chinese areas that had been conquered by the Qing dynasty and incorporated into the Chinese empire. Some European colonial governments adopted a similar approach, but others paid far less attention to educational matters, leaving responsibility for schooling largely in local or missionary hands. In their East Asian colonies, the British mostly adopted a relatively laissez-faire approach, providing English-language schooling for a select few who were trained to serve in the colonial administration and other literate professions, while leaving the rest to their own devices. Traditional academies and small private schools teaching a Confucian curriculum thus remained the educational mainstay of the overseas Chinese population until the twentieth century.

When the British began to contemplate investing more resources in mass education for their colonial subjects from the late nineteenth century onwards, they did so in part because they sought to provide a foundation for much-needed vocational training and to prepare locals for greater participation in public administration. In addition, they aimed to stifle rising nationalist movements, in particular Chinese nationalism. Nationalism among overseas Chinese populations had become increasingly perceptible since the late nineteenth century, when many Chinese nationalists fled to Hong Kong and Southeast Asia, where they plotted the overthrow of the Manchu Qing Dynasty and campaigned for support among ethnic Chinese communities. Following the 1911 Revolution, overseas Chinese support for and identification with China rather than the Southeast Asian societies where they were domiciled grew rapidly more pronounced. Although British colonial authorities in Malaya, for example, had substantially expanded educational provision, partly with a view to fostering a more united identity among heterogeneous peoples, Chinese communities showed little interest, preferring to keep to themselves and maintain their own schools rather than study in Malay or English alongside other ethnic groups. Overseas Chinese across the region closely followed trends in Republican China and Confucian academies were rapidly transformed into modern schools using textbooks imported from the motherland.

As discussed further in the following chapter, by the 1930s some Republican Chinese textbooks — and history textbooks in particular — were profoundly nationalistic, persistently harping on China's superiority over its neighbors and, in their coverage of the non-Chinese world, bordering on blatant xenophobia. The texts expressed righteous indignation against the European imperial powers that had encroached on China since the nineteenth century, especially against Britain, which had started it all with the Opium War. For the British authorities, as well as for the governments of other Southeast Asian states with significant Chinese populations, this was a worrying trend that might foment discord between Chinese and other indigenous or immigrant populations or incite hostility toward the colonial regime. Chinese schools thus came under closer official scrutiny. In Siam, Chinese schools were increasingly suppressed, while in Indonesia, the Dutch authorities extended state resources to support education of ethnic Chinese and discourage parents from sending their children to schools in China (Purcell 1965, 142–147, 453–456). British colonial administrations adopted a similar approach, offering financial assistance to Chinese schools. In many cases, such aid was refused, because the Chinese were unwilling to accept the corollary of official interference. Interference, however, became seen as unavoidable as fears of Chinese nationalism and the increasing influence of Chinese communism (especially in adult education) impelled the authorities to clamp down. History textbooks imported from China that were deemed particularly objectionable were banned in Malaya in the late 1930s. The publishers, keen to protect their market, compromised and produced overseas editions free from some of the more controversial material. As Purcell (1965) observed, however, this was far from an ideal solution in terms of encouraging ethnic integration and creating Chinese identification with Malaya, for it meant that Straits Chinese continued to learn only about a country in which they did not live and learned nothing about the one in which they did (280). As discussed in Chapters 3, 4, and 5 in this volume, this problem and its relationship to the identity question is one that continued to be highly salient in postwar Hong Kong and Taiwan.

Chinese Education

For China, defeat in the 1894–1895 Sino-Japanese War was a traumatic affair. Not only had its navy been decimated and Taiwan ceded, but Japan had violated the natural Confucian order in which China had been the teacher, the elder brother, the leader, and Japan the student, the younger brother, the led. Seen from this prespective, Japan's victory was not only humiliating, but immoral. Ignominious defeat, however, catalyzed reform; within 10 years, the civil service examinations had been abolished and an MOE was established to coordinate the transition to a modern school system. The new system, based on the Japanese model, introduced subjects such as mathematics and science, deemed necessary for China's modernisation. Physical education was also emphasized to transform the pale, frail literatus into a strong, healthy citizen who could defend his country. However, unlike early Japanese efforts to move completely to a Western curriculum, traditional learning remained paramount in China, with 30 to 50 percent of total class hours allotted to the Classics, self-cultivation (*xiushen*, a moral education class deriving its name from the Japanese *shushin* subject), and history, both Chinese and foreign.

After the 1911 Revolution, education reforms were accelerated in order to serve the nationalist modernisation project and create loyalty to the new state. In 1912 and 1913, new curricula were issued that attempted to provide a more balanced education and, most importantly, eliminate Classics classes, which were deemed overly taxing for children. They were also thought to perpetuate old thinking. Such concepts as "loyalty to the ruler," "respecting Confucius," and the backward ethics of the patriarchal social hierarchy were thus to be replaced by the "bourgeois morality of *liberté, égalité et fraternité*" (Xiong 1999, 79). In fact, new morality remained barely distinguishable from Confucian morality, focusing on "the pristine virtues of filial piety, love, trustworthiness, righteousness and courage, respect, industry and frugality." This it was hoped would "nurture the spirit of altruism and patriotism" among the people (COCP 1912, 63, 69), something that was proving difficult in a mainly clan- and region-oriented society; indeed, Sun Yat-sen advocated marketing patriotism as an extension of clan loyalty (and familial metaphors have remained a prominent feature of Chinese nationalist rhetoric, for example, the image of a "Great Chinese National Family" consisting of the "big brother" Han and the various "little brother" nationalities: Mongols, Tibetans, Uighurs, and others).

History was to play a significant role in Republican citizen-making and teaching new morality. It was to convey social Darwinian concepts such as "the evolution of races" (*minzu jinhua*) and to pay "particular attention to the evolution of political systems and the origins of the Republic" (COCP 1912, 69). History's core purpose was thus to narrate the genealogy of the nation-state, create a strong identification between citizenship and membership of the Chinese nation (*Zhonghua minzu*), and situate China in the global multistate system. What defined membership of the nation and/or citizenry was, however, uncertain, fluctuating between Confucian culture, a Han biological-racial unity, a multiethnic national people of shared descent from the mythical Yellow Emperor (*Huangdi*) (by fortuitous coincidence, defined as precisely those peoples inhabiting the territories of the Qing empire in its expansionist heyday and now claimed, if not controlled by, the Republic), and a political community with protodemocratic aspirations.

By 1917, Tibet and Mongolia had declared independence, and the rest of the Qing empire had effectively split into autonomous regions governed by military strongmen. National policies were, therefore, selectively implemented and inconsistently funded. This did not mean, however, that they were not promulgated, presumably based on the assumption (or hope) that the state would soon be reunified. In the field of education, a group of U.S.-trained scholars who were heavily influenced by John Dewey dominated both higher education institutions and national education policymaking. They understood China's current problems as a product of cultural (and sometimes racial) ennui and debilitation and, like Japanese proponents of "civilization and enlightenment," argued that national salvation lay in profound cultural and ethical transformation (which education reforms had hitherto failed to achieve) as a prerequisite for scientific and social modernisation and the eventual transition to democracy (Keenan 1977; Dikötter 1992).

The 1922 Decree on Reform of the Education System reflected these views and the Deweyan, child- rather than text-centered, education-for-life approach. The stated goals of the new system were to

1. Meet the needs of social progress
2. Develop the spirit of education among the people
3. Develop [the child's] personality
4. Develop citizens' economic potential
5. Emphasize "life education"
6. Facilitate the universalization of education
7. Allow regional flexibility. (COCP 1922, 105)

To meet these disparate demands, a system of 4-year compulsory education was legislated, the curriculum was substantially revised and, for the first time, individual subject curricula were issued, briefly outlining subject-specific teaching goals and providing detailed syllabi that were intended to constitute the basis of teaching and textbooks.

Inspired by professional historiography, archaeology, and a more internationalist ethos, the history curriculum avoided traditional moralizing and stipulated that the subject should describe how "human lives have changed over time," should "awaken [students'] sympathy with all humanity and cultivate a spirit of fraternalism," and should help them to "discover the origins of things so they may understand the true nature of present issues." To elucidate the "common development of human society throughout the world," and "eradicate the narrow conception of dynasties as the basic historical unit." Chinese and non-Chinese history were merged, with Chinese history simply to be "described in added detail" within the "framework of world history" (COH 1923, 14).

The new curricula, however, were followed in few schools beyond the wealthy urban centers. Local education bureaus rarely had the funds or the political will to implement the costly new program. Many teachers were classically trained, and the rural population in particular remained hostile to the new learning which, as in the past, represented attempts by educated elites to "transform the (common) people and change their (crude) customs." Although some individual educators working outside the sphere of formal education, and some local warlords, tried to improve literacy and/or develop genuinely mass education, most people remained illiterate, and many rural schools simply evaded the new regulations, continuing to teach the Confucian canon from ancient character primers.

When the Nationalist Party (Kuomintang [KMT]) reestablished central control in 1927, the liberal experiment ended as efforts were made to centralise education, standardise textbooks, and elevate Sun Yat-sen's socialist-inspired Three Principles of the People (the Nation, People's Rights, People's Livelihood) to the status of official orthodoxy. Throughout its brief rule, the education policy of the KMT was chiefly oriented toward the promotion of modern science (humanities had hitherto been widely favored) on the one hand, and the revival of traditional Confucian values on the other. It was also deeply concerned with inculcating patriotism and loyalty to the party. This combination, it was believed, would provide the knowledge, skills, and mindset necessary for self-defense against the increasingly threatening Japanese and the moral fortitude to see the struggle through. History education was seen as crucial to this project, as it was deemed particularly useful for encouraging national pride and righteous anger at China's past and present humiliations, thereby motivating China's youth to strive for national salvation. As is discussed in more detail in the following chapter, this resulted in an increasingly nationalist curriculum that repudiated the objectivity and global perspective advocated by many earlier historians and educational reformers and steered history back into the warm, familiar embrace of Confucian moral didacticism.

Confucianism, History Education, and National Identity since 1945

The foregoing discussion has offered a whirlwind tour of the continuities and changes within the historiographical and educational traditions of several East Asian societies over the past two millennia. It has also attempted to highlight some key episodes or features of those societies that have been significant in the formation and maintenance of national identities. Inevitably, far more was omitted than included, but it was broadly demonstrated that, across the region, education has long been seen as a means of moral transformation, a path to self-perfection, and a mark of social status. History has been a key factor in the educative process, teaching through analogy and precedent. It has also been an important component in legitimising the state, ruler, political, and social structures and shaping worldviews. Furthermore, the Confucian philosophy that underpinned these conceptions of history and education, and especially the Chinese and Korean civil service examination systems, intensified the close relationship between morality and politics and solidified the role of the state in defining right thinking and action and authorising particular versions of the past. While Confucianism has been shared by peoples across much of East Asia, it was not the only ideology in China, let alone in non-Chinese societies, that retained a strong sense of cultural distinctiveness and political independence even while they borrowed liberally from Chinese civilisation and acknowledged the Middle Kingdom as suzerain. In fact, as Elman (2002) showed, many non-Chinese societies appropriated Confucianism, modifying it and making it part of their own cultural heritage.

In the late nineteenth and twentieth centuries, however, foreign incursions led many to reject Confucianism as outmoded and irrelevant to the modern world. Scientific Western models were vigorously promoted, especially in education, which was seen as the key to national strength and prosperity. Yet, traditional views continued to exert a powerful influence even if they were not explicitly acknowledged. East Asian societies began at this time to reorient their national and international identities and to define themselves less in relation to China than to Japan and the West. Primordialist race- and nation-views also began to feature more prominently in identity discourses. Since World War II, against the global backdrop of the Cold War, East Asia has continued to undergo much trauma with the creation of new states, the destruction of old ones, and the establishment of numerous new and often radical regimes. New identities have been sought to parallel political, economic, and social transformation and regimes across the region have accordingly set about revising their national histories and rewriting the school history curriculum to reflect these goals.

As the remaining chapters will demonstrate, the narratives that have emerged have in many ways been rather less new than their proponents are apt to claim, while many of the glorious national traditions they profess to have preserved are often, if not invented, at least constructed on the basis of questionable evidence. The ideological and pedagogical functions of history have likewise displayed many unacknowledged continuities and changes from the past; while contemporary modes of political socialization may differ in significant respects from the state-ordained Confucianism of the past (especially that of China and Korea), the continuing influence of long-established values and practices is evident in history education across the region. By the same token, pedagogical approaches that value critical thinking need be seen neither as entirely modern innovations, nor as purely alien Western imports; rather, they have precedents not only in the experimental education projects of the early modern period, but in the ancient advocacy of dialogue between teacher and student as the core of learning.

In the following chapters, therefore, we explore post-1945 continuities and changes in relation to both the recent and distant past, analysing in particular how East Asian regimes have attempted to create and transmit authorized historical memories on the basis of which contemporary national identities can be constructed. The rapid economic development of East Asia and the changing balance of power since the end of the Cold War have led to a powerful self-assertion in much of the region, the reembracing of once-rejected traditions and more vocal criticism of the West, which is widely blamed for the evils attendant on capitalist modernisation and globalisation. In this climate, Confucianism has enjoyed something of an official resurrection as a source of Asian identity and a symbol of (superior) Asian values such as frugality, collectivism, and duty to family and nation, which are juxtaposed to the decadent individualism and selfishness of an amoral West. As we shall see, despite the recent emphasis on history as a vehicle for fostering analytical skills, the repackaging and redeployment of Confucianism by state elites in their battle for the hearts and minds of the nation's youth has meant that, across most of East Asia, moral and political didacticism continue to inform both the goals and content of the history subject.

Endnotes

1. This paraphrases Voltaire's oft-quoted dictum, "History is philosophy teaching by examples" from *Essai sur les Moeurs et l'Esprit des Nations*.
2. *Qianziwen* was written during the Southern Dynasties period (420– 589) and *Sanzijing* during the Southern Song Dynasty (1127–1276). They are the most famous of the mnemonic primers and were widely used until Republican times (1911–1949).
3. These included the Diaries of Activity and Repose (*qi ju zhu*) and Records of Current Government (*shi zheng zhi*). They were prepared by chief ministers and their subordinates and were the source for the Daily Records (*rili*), in turn the chief source for the Veritable Records (*shilu*).
4. See SKT.1, 6–13 and SJT.1, 3–13 for extracts from these Chinese works. It is probable that the Chinese had not directly encountered all the peoples of which they wrote but relied on second-hand reports from representatives of other Korean and Japanese communities.
5. For in-depth discussions of the Sinocentric worldview and the tribute system see Fairbank (1968).
6. Ironically, Kim was later criticized by nationalist scholars for overdeference to Chinese histories and ignoring native narratives in omitting to mention that the Tang emperor had lost an eye in an attempted invasion of Koguryô (Shin 2000, 9).
7. "Know the other side as one knows oneself in order to secure victory in all battles" is a well-known saying deriving from *The Art of War* by Sunzi, a military tactician and philosopher of the Warring States period.

8. The Meiji reformers had intended the Office of Historiography to be a state organ for the compilation of a national history that would take up where the Six Histories had left off, but the project was abandoned after criticism from conservatives who saw the moral function of history being undermined, liberals who opposed state involvement in history production, and the National Learning scholars who resented Japanese history being written in Chinese. The Historiographical Institute continues the compilation and publication of historical materials to this day. For a full account see Mehl (1998).

9. It is worth noting that Kita also publicly rejected the homogeneous Japanese race theory, arguing that the evidence showed the "Japanese race" to have evolved from various groups (Morris-Suzuki 1998, 157–158). Yet he was subsequently hired at the Imperial University of Kyoto (1920), suggesting a high degree of academic freedom of expression prevailed at this time.

References

Abbreviations

CHC.1–15   *Cambridge History of China*, vols. 1–15
CHJ.1–6   *Cambridge History of Japan*, vols. 1–6
COCP   Ershi shiji Zhongguo zhongxiaoxue kecheng biaozhun, jiaoxue dagang huibian: kecheng (jiaoxue) jihua juan (Collected twentieth century standard curricula and teaching outlines for Chinese primary and secondary schools: Curriculum.
COH   Ershi shiji Zhongguo zhongxiaoxue kecheng biaozhun, jiaoxue dagang huibian: lishi juan (Collected twentieth century standard curricula and teaching outlines for Chinese primary and secondary schools: History).
SCT.1, SCT.2   *Sources of Chinese Tradition*, Vol. 1, Vol. 2.
SJT.1, SJT.2   *Sources of Japanese Tradition*, Vol. 1, Vol. 2.
SKT.1, SKT.2   *Sources of Korean Tradition*, Vol. 1, Vol. 2.

References

Anthony, R. 1993. "Brotherhoods, Secret Societies and the Law in Qing Dynasty China," in Ownby and Heidhues, Eds., *"Secret Societies" Reconsidered*. Armonk, NY: M.E. Sharpe.

Beasley, W. and Pulleyblank, E., eds. 1961. *Historians of China and Japan*. London, Oxford University Press.

Boulais, A. 1924. *Manuel du Code Chinois*. Chang-hai: Imp. de la Mission Catholique.

Chan, H. 1984. *Legitimation in Imperial China*. Seattle: Washington University Press.

Cumings, B. 1997. *Korea's Place in The Sun*. New York and London: W. W. Norton and Company.

De Bary, W.T. and Chaffee, J., eds. 1989. *Neo-Confucian Education: The Formative Stage*. Taipei: SMC Publishing Inc.

Deuchler, M. 1995. *The Confucian Transformation of Korea*. Cambridge, MA, and London: Harvard University Press.

Dikötter, F. 1992. *The Discourse of Race in Modern China*. London: Hurst and Company.

Dikötter, F. 1997. *The Construction of Racial Identities in China and Japan*. Honolulu: University of Hawaii Press.

Dore, R. P. 1965. *Education in Tokugawa Japan*. Berkeley: University of California Press.

Duara, P. 1995. *Rescuing History from the Nation: Questioning Narratives of Modern China*. Chicago: University of Chicago Press.

Duncan, J. 2002. "Examinations and Orthodoxy in Chosôn Dynasty Korea," in Elman, ed., *Rethinking Confucianism*, 65–94.

Elman, B. ed. (2002). *Rethinking Confucianism*. UCLA Asian Pacific Monograph Series.

Fincher, J. 1972. "China as a Race, Culture and Nation," in Buxbaum and Mote, eds., *Transition and Permanence*. Hong Kong: Cathay Press, 59–69.

Jenner, W. J. F. 1992. *The Tyranny of History*. London: Penguin.

Keenan, B. 1977. *The Dewey Experiment in China*. Cambridge, MA: Harvard University Press.

Lee, C. 1963. *The Politics of Korean Nationalism*. Berkeley: University of California Press.

Lincicome, M. 1995. *Principle, Praxis and the Politics of Educational Reform in Meiji Japan*. Honolulu: University of Hawaii Press.

Mehl, M. 1998. *History and the State in Nineteenth Century Japan*. New York: St. Martin's Press.

Morris-Suzuki, T. 1998. "Becoming Japanese: Imperial Expansion and Identity Crises in the Early Twentieth Century," in Minichiello, ed., *Japan's Competing Modernities*. Honolulu: University of Hawaii Press, 157–180.

Palais, J. 1996. *Confucian Statecraft and Korean Institutions*. Seattle: University of Washington Press.

Purcell, V. 1965. *The Chinese in Southeast Asia*. London: Oxford University Press.

Robinson, G. 1961. "Early Japanese Chronicles: The Six National Histories," in W. Beasley and E. Pulleyblank, eds., *Historians of China and Japan*. London: Oxford University Press, 213–228.

Robinson, G. and Beasley, W. 1961. "Japanese Historical Writing in the 11th–14th Centuries" in W. Beasley and E. Pulleyblank eds., *Historians of China and Japan*. London: Oxford University Press, 229–244.

Shin, Y. 2000. *Modern Korean History and Nationalism*. Seoul: Jimoondang Publishing Co.

Su, S. 1998. "Woguo gudai de lishi jiaoyu he jiaocai [History Education and Teaching Materials in Ancient China]," in Kecheng jiaocai yanjiusuo, eds, *Kecheng jiaocai yanjiu 15 nian*. Beijing: PEP, 436–454.

Tsurumi, E. P. 1977. *Japanese Colonial Education in Taiwan, 1895–1945*. Cambridge, MA: Harvard University Press.

Tu, W., ed. 1997. *Confucian Traditions in East Asian Modernity*. Cambridge, MA: Harvard University Press.

Vickers, E. 2000. *History as a School Subject in Hong Kong: 1960's–2000*. [Ph.D. Dissertation]. University of Hong Kong.

Xiong, M. 1999. *Zhongguo jinxiandai jiaoxue gaige shi (A History of Education Reform in Modern and Contemporary China)*. Chongqing: Chongqing chubanshe.

Yamashita, S. H. 1996. "Confucianism and the Japanese State," in W. Tu, ed., *Confucian Traditions in East Asian Modernity*, Cambridge, MA: Harvard University Press, 132–154.

Yang, L. 1961. "The Origins of Chinese Official Historiography: Principles and Methods of Cheng-shih, T'ang–Ming," in W. Beasley and E. Pulleyblank, eds. *Historians of China and Japan*. London: Oxford University Press.

2
Changing the Past to Serve the Present: History Education in Mainland China

ALISA JONES

Note on citations: Many of the texts cited here are government documents such as education laws or national curricula. Teaching outlines excepted, the full title of the document and the date published are given in each instance, followed by the author's name or title of a reference volume in which the relevant document has been published.

"Who controls the past controls the future; who controls the present controls the past" is the party mantra intoned in Orwell's *Nineteen Eighty-Four* and echoed in many other fictional dystopias, where manipulating the past is standard practice for brutal totalitarian regimes, and self-censorship and memory repression a necessary precaution for their citizens. It is not, of course, only in fictional societies that the state carefully edits or even completely rewrites the past to justify present political and social circumstances, limn an idyllic future, inculcate desirable values and legitimating ideologies, or foster loyalty to the state and support for its causes. Presentist uses and abuses of history, and of the school history subject in particular, have been common the world over in both liberal democracies and totalitarian societies. They have, however, been particularly blatant in the latter, especially under regimes that derive their symbolic legitimacy from religious or utopian political ideologies. Indeed, it is widely believed that in China "the Orwellian nightmare has already visited" (Avery 1986, xi), with a malevolent scheming Communist Party controlling the past and present (if not necessarily the future) and blithely indoctrinating docile masses, opposed only sporadically by a handful of brave and selfless dissident intellectuals.

As discussed in the previous chapter, however, history and education in China became intertwined with regime legitimation, culture and value transmission, and the making of dutiful citizens more than two millennia ago, when the imperial government first began to provide official narratives of the past and edit the present for posterity and to implement a national curriculum that enshrined the values and *Weltanschauung* of the state. History was also invoked to explain and justify the Chinese world order, in which Our Country (*woguo*, a standard way of referring to China) had culture (*wenhua*) and was therefore immeasurably superior to neighboring "barbarian" states. While it would be erroneous to suggest that essential or immutable concepts or narratives of history and its didactic functions have been transmitted in toto across the centuries, it is evident that "using the past to serve the present" (*gu wei jin yong*) and promoting ideological conformity and state-sanctioned identities through education are far from novel brainwashing strategies devised by a big bad Communist Party. In fact, as shown below, the Chinese Communist Party (CPC) has been extremely unoriginal in its use of both historiography and public education for moral-ideological purposes, drawing heavily on the experience, policies, administrative structures and even the narratives produced under previous regimes, especially those of its immediate predecessor, the Nationalist Party (Kuomintang[KMT]). Furthermore, the KMT and CPC have shared many similar conceptions of Chineseness and a vision of modernity that would free China from encroachment by foreign economic and military power and restore the nation to its rightful place at the center of Asia and the forefront of the world stage, objectives that have been clearly reflected in the history curricula produced by both regimes. The CPC victory over the KMT in the civil war and the establishment of the People's Republic of China (PRC) in October 1949 may thus be seen as rather less of a watershed in history education, as in many other policy areas, than is often supposed, and certainly far less than has been claimed by PRC policymakers. Similarly, post–Cultural Revolution reforms in history education have neither broken as completely from the so-called incorrect lines of the early PRC years nor continued the correct ones as smoothly as contemporary commentators maintain.

This chapter seeks to bridge the 1949 and Cultural Revolution divides, examining the development of the history curriculum as an ongoing process from the period of KMT rule to the present "reform and opening" (*gaige kaifang*) era. Although the post–World War II period with which this volume is principally concerned marked the tail end of KMT rule in China, as it was weakened, defeated, and finally forced to flee to Taiwan in 1949, the goals and content of the history curricula that it implemented in regions under its control between 1945 and 1949 remained much the same as those of the early years; indeed, the history curricula subsequently imposed on the Taiwanese from the 1950s to 1980s (see Chapter 3) were in many respects barely modified from the KMT's first 1929 drafts. This chapter accordingly begins by examining the content of the earliest KMT history curricula, focusing on those issues most pertinent to questions of political legitimation, moral education, and national identity formation, and outlines the ways in which these curricula were modified up to 1949. It then analyses how and why the CPC revised or retained KMT curriculum development processes and history goals and content up to the end of the Cultural Revolution. Finally, it explores the influence of the post–Cultural Revolution reform and opening policies on the history curriculum and evaluates the latest claims to innovation of the so-called quality education (*suzhi jiaoyu*) drive and its actual effects on the history subject. Since primary school history has never been comprehensive and for parts of the period discussed here has been subsumed by social studies, and since senior secondary education has been neither compulsory nor universally accessible, the discussion focuses chiefly on the teaching and learning objectives and the content of the junior secondary history curriculum. While Chinese history has been heavily emphasised to promote identification with particular visions of the nation, it should be remembered that world history has been far from value-free, even if it has typically enjoyed a far smaller proportion of class hours. As countless scholars since Said (1978) have emphasised, we define ourselves, both past and present, in relation to our Others, and the very purpose of world history, therefore, may be to locate or create suitable Others against which one's own nation may be usefully (and usually favorably) compared. Indeed, how world history is narrated may reveal as much about national self-image as it does about those societies, peoples, and cultures it purports to portray. Thus, while this chapter focuses chiefly on the dominant Chinese history component of the curriculum, world history content is also considered. Local history, however, is not discussed, both for reasons of space and because it has been only a minor and, until very recently, optional element of the curricula, inconsistently implemented at the provincial or municipal/county level.

History in the Republic of China, 1927–1949

In the aftermath of the 1911 Revolution, China rapidly divided into de facto autonomous states governed by warlords. It was not until 1927 that the KMT reunified the country, albeit with the cooperation of the warlords they had been unable to defeat outright in the Northern Expedition. As shown in Chapter 1, although national curricula had been devised between 1911 and 1927, they had barely been implemented. They had, however, represented an attempt to move toward a liberal, child-centered form of education. Under the KMT, the liberal experiment came to an end. Education was centralised under the Ministry of Education (MOE), and the KMT even planned to produce unified textbooks. However, this idea was soon abandoned as impractical (Peake, 1970), and they merely updated the textbook inspection and approval system established in the early Republic. A rigorous process of national curriculum development was also established under the auspices of the MOE Primary and Secondary School Curriculum Standards Committee, involving many academics and educationalists in the initial drafting and subsequent discussion processes, although final approval rested with the MOE. As in the 1923 curriculum discussed in the previous chapter, separation was maintained between an overarching curriculum (*kecheng biaozhun zonggang*), which outlined general principles and allocated class hours, and individual subject curricula (also known as *kecheng biaozhun*) tailored to specific disciplinary goals and content, although the new curricula added lengthy instructions to guide teaching, study, and homework. Teaching and learning goals were also far more clearly specified and content was substantially altered, particularly in arts and social sciences, for although both the 1922 Education Decree and 1925 draft constitution explicitly stated that education must be independent of politics, the KMT instated Sun Yat-sen's Three Principles of the People (*sanminzhuyi*) as the guiding ideology of the state and its education system. Thus, it was directed that "everything which violates the Three Principles should be excised from curriculum materials," although, perhaps somewhat contradictorily, it was also stated that scientific methods and evidence were to be "the basis, so as to reduce the errors of subjectivity" (*Xiaoxue kecheng zanxing biaozhun zong shuoming* [1929], COCP, 117). It was clear, however, that politics was to have priority over science, and in addition to permeating the curriculum with the Three Principles of *minzu* (nationalism), *minquan* (People's Rights), and *minsheng* (People's Livelihood) and directly promoting the Nationalist agenda in citizenship, significant class time (2 to 6 percent) was allocated to the subject of Party Principles, and students were to learn military drills in Party Cadet classes. The curriculum for these subjects, moreover, was not issued by the MOE but by the Party Central Office (*Chuji zhongxue zanxing kecheng biaozhun shuoming* [1929], COCP, 119).

Although in primary schools history was integrated with geography and citizenship into a new social studies course, it retained an important place in the curriculum and was taught throughout junior and senior secondary school. In line with the nationalist ethos, Chinese and world history, which had been merged in the 1923 curriculum to provide a global perspective and promote internationalism, were separated, and approximately two-thirds of class hours focused on China alone. Meanwhile, moral didacticism, deemphasised in the 1923 curriculum in favor of a more critical-analytical approach, was regarded as crucial to saving the nation (*jiuguo*) and was accordingly restored as a central objective of the history subject, which was now expected to "nurture [students'] noble sentiments and the tireless spirit of serving the people (*renqun*)" (*Chuji zhongxue lishi zanxing kecheng biaozhun* [1929], COH, 21). Chinese history was to follow the Three Principles, narrating the development of the nation, People's Rights, and Livelihood, which had culminated (inevitably) in the Nationalist Revolution. This required a combination of political, economic, social, and cultural history, with an emphasis on recent history to demonstrate "how the Chinese national people [*Zhonghua minzu*] have suffered foreign invasions … [in order to] stimulate students' national [*minzu*] spirit and arouse consciousness of their responsibility to China's National Movement [*minzu yundong*]" (ibid.,). Indeed, the importance of this period to *minzu* consciousness-raising was such that in all curricula during the Nationalist period, teachers were explicitly warned to plan ahead to ensure sufficient class time for full coverage of China's humiliations. *Minzu*, however, was poorly defined. Despite this, the three principal themes highlighted as the core of Chinese history suggest efforts to create flexible boundaries that could be and, as shown below, were in fact moved as necessary. These overlapping themes were "the past glories of the Chinese *minzu*," "the relationship between history and present-day life," and "the extension of China's borders (*kuojiang*)" (ibid., 22). History thus narrated how past cultural and/or military superiority had allowed the "Han race" to assimilate (*tonghua*) or Sinicize (*Hanhua*) both its neighbors and barbarian invaders, thus expanding the national territory (*guotu*); how together as the Chinese national people (*Zhonghua minzu*) they had resisted recent invaders; and how evolving political and civic consciousness had led to the establishment of the Nanjing government and its correct social and economic policies. Racial, cultural, and political communities were thereby conflated in the rubric of both nation and state, KMT legitimate succession was successfully demonstrated, and the present territorial claims of the Republic were justified.

World history, meanwhile, traced the origins of the present international balance of power and required students to develop international knowledge and a broad outlook (ibid., 21). As in the 1923 curriculum, international sympathy and a spirit of fraternal cooperation, justice, and tolerance were to be cultivated but were now to be moderated to appropriate levels to prevent students from developing excessively lofty ideals that might lead them to "neglect the necessity of revitalizing and protecting the Chinese *minzu*" (*Gaoji zhongxue putongke waiguoshi zanxing kecheng biaozhun* [1929], COH, 37). Through examining the histories of other societies (predominantly European), students were to understand that

> capitalist imperialism in recent history has led to the oppression of workers and weak *minzu*. Since the First World War, these weak *minzu* have risen up to oppose imperialism and demand independence ... China is an important member of this group. Thus when teaching foreign history in China, special attention must be paid to the development of imperialism and independence movements so as to inspire citizens with the courage and diligence to cast off the bonds of imperialism and achieve liberation (ibid.).

The example of the imperialist powers, however, was to motivate the Chinese *minzu* to strive for similar greatness, although China would "not, of course, imitate imperialist policies ... The postwar world is, nonetheless, one in which might prevails, and thus [China] must not be seduced by ideals of Universal Harmony [*datong shijie*]." Despite the emphasis on self-strengthening and resisting imperialism, students were not to become unequivocally antiforeign; indeed history was to "correct narrow, antiforeign, *minzu* prejudice." It was also to provide practical precedents, and in a similar spirit to that of the "Chinese-learning-as-the-essence, Western-learning-as-practical-application" (*zhong-ti, xi-yong*) approach advocated by nineteenth-century Chinese reformers (see Chapter 1), students were to recognize the cultural (primarily recent scientific and technological) achievements of Europe and the United States and use them to supplement China's deficiencies (ibid., 37).

That Nationalist curricula and textbooks could take such an anti-imperialist stance vis-à-vis Europe, while lauding Han military conquests of foreign peoples/races (*waizu, yizu*) does not seem to have been regarded as a contradiction. A possible reason was the influence of Bolshevik ideas on the KMT and of historical materialism, then making rapid inroads among historians. This posited imperialism as an advanced stage of capitalism (the "highest stage," according to Lenin). Since China had been at the feudal or proto capitalist stage during its expansions, by definition it could not be imperialistic (an argument which continues to be used today). This, however, merely removed the opprobrious label of "imperialism"; it did not account for the national glory derived from Han subjugation of "weak *minzu*" or conquest of *their* national territory. It is probable, therefore, that the resemblance to imperialism was unseen because China's culture and her political system had long been regarded as benefiting barbaric peoples, bringing the light of civilisation where hitherto there had only been ignorance. Indeed, most history textbooks clearly "proved" that when uncivilied *waizu* invaded Han territories, they did so not simply to plunder, but because they craved civilisation. This Han Chinese expansion could not be compared with the European colonial project, not simply because the latter had no ideological justification, but because the European civilising mission was, in China's case, being brought to a society that regarded itself not merely as already civilised, but as "civilisation itself."[1] As the twelfth-century historian, Zheng Qiao, had written, "The myriad states have each their different ways, but all must join in the greater community which is China; only then may the outlying areas escape the ills of stagnation" (cited in Fincher, 1972, 64).

As Japanese encroachment intensified and the KMT felt increasingly threatened by the Communists, efforts were made to intensify moral-ideological education, most notably through the New Life Movement launched in 1934, which advocated adherence to the Confucian virtues of decorum (*li*), righteousness (*yi*), integrity (*lian*), and a sense of shame (*chi*). This, it was hoped, would raise the cultural level of the people so that they could better resist enemies both without and within. Somewhat surprisingly, neither New Life nor the subsequent outbreak of war significantly affected the history curriculum, although curriculum goals became increasingly presentist and more dogmatically nationalist, placing even greater weight on defending the *minzu* and the state, supporting the leadership, and opposing imperialism. A slight redefinition of the formation of the *Zhonghua minzu* was also displayed, with the terms *assimilation* (*tonghua*) and *Sinicization* (*Hanhua*), which implied Han superiority and, frequently, military conquest of other ethnic groups, abandoned in favor of the more egalitarian and peaceful process of ethnic integration (*minzu ronghe*). In addition, class hours were adjusted to increase emphasis on Chinese history (see chapter appendix tables 2.1 and 2.2); in fact, by 1948, world history no longer warranted a separate course of study but was to be inserted into the Chinese history course at appropriate junctures. As is evident from the 1948 revised syllabus, this scheme was not informed by the internationalist spirit of the 1923 curriculum but was adopted because world history was considered inessential to the paramount objective of propagating patriotism and loyalty to the KMT (*Xiuding chuji zhongxue lishi kecheng biaozhun* [1948], COH, 97–99). Other than the changes noted above, however, most syllabi and textbooks were barely altered during the turbulent 1937 to 1949 period, except to bring content up to the wartime present. What is astounding under these circumstances is that the KMT government found time and resources to revise the school curriculum at all. According to Li, this may be attributed to the "study to save the nation" (*dushu jiuguo*) theory popular among many educationalists and the associated KMT policy of "viewing wartime as peacetime," maintaining a semblance of normality and stability amidst the surrounding chaos. The war, it was thought, was going to be a lengthy affair, and skilled personnel as well as soldiers would be needed both for the resistance and postwar reconstruction. Education was thus to continue as usual (Li, 1995, 2–6; *Zhongxue kecheng biaozhun bianding zhi jingguo* [1940], COCP, 145).

History in Communist China, 1949–1976

New Regime, New System

The Nationalists were indeed correct that the war would be long and that skilled personnel would be needed for national reconstruction. By 1949, however, they were no longer on hand to supervise the reconstruction project, having been resoundingly defeated by the Communists before retreating to Taiwan to reestablish themselves as the government of Mainland China in absentia and plan the overthrow of the People's Republic. As the actual government of China, the Communists finally had the opportunity to implement in the national arena the policies they had tested in the liberated areas (*jiefangqu*) under their control during the war years. Once in power, however, the many policy experiments of the resistance years were abandoned in favor of a more traditional, centralised model, much along KMT lines but also heavily influenced by the USSR. Education was considered central to socialist transformation and modernisation and, with a new cause and ideology, it was thought that the education system and curriculum and textbook content would need to be substantially reformed as well as more closely controlled by the state. In "value-free" sciences and foreign languages, reform was not thought urgent, but in ideology-laden history and other humanities subjects, it was deemed essential immediately to adopt "Marxist-Leninist viewpoints and methods, and new democratic, scientific, mass, anti-imperialist, antifeudal culture to replace the reactionary idealist, mechanical materialist, feudal, comprador, fascist ideology and curriculum produced under reactionary Kuomintang rule."[2] To this end, it was decided that not only would the state continue to issue detailed national curricula, but it would also provide a public school system with a party-supervised education administration at all levels of government from central to local and would take charge of textbook publication. Clearly, this could not be achieved overnight, but after a brief transitional phase, during which policy would be locally set and textbooks selected from Yan'an editions, abridged versions of professional (preferably Marxist) scholars' work, or those books from the Nationalist era judged politically acceptable, China would finally adopt the USSR model, and all children would follow the same course, with the same textbook, at the same time.

The new education system was not, in fact, to be very different from that established by the KMT. Over the next few years, general Teaching Plans (*jiaoxue jihua*) and individual subject Teaching Outlines (*jiaoxue dagang*) replaced the Nationalists' Curriculum Standards, but the development process as well as the format and even much of the content of the new curricula were remarkably similar to the allegedly "feudal" and "fascist" incarnations produced by the Nationalists. The first Teaching Plans and Outlines were initially drafted by the MOE, while the task of producing unified textbooks was assigned to the People's Education Press (PEP), established in December 1950 as a subsidiary agency of the MOE. By the mid to late 1950s, however, PEP had acquired a virtual monopoly over primary and secondary school curricula. Not only did PEP produce all school textbooks and accompanying sets of teacher handbooks, but they also assumed responsibility for outline production, although comments and advice continued, in principle at least, to be sought from academic and pedagogical experts before curricula and textbooks were promulgated.[3] Meanwhile, under state and party supervision, an increasing number of education journals were published (several of them by PEP), various academic and professional associations were created, and individual subject research groups (*yanjiuzu*) were established in secondary schools to find ways to improve and standardise both the ideological and academic quality of teaching (*Xiaoxue zanxing guicheng, Zhongxue zanxing guicheng* [1952], COCP, 200–212).

The Purpose of History

Education in the New China was to unite Marxist-Leninist theory and China's revolutionary practice, as exemplified by Mao thought, and develop children's intellectual, moral, physical, and aesthetic abilities, preparing them to progress to the next level of schooling or to take up employment. Students were to learn to "love the motherland, the people (*renmin*), labor, and science, and develop civic morality and resolute courage to protect public property." They were also to be healthy and disciplined and to develop their creative abilities (ibid., 200, 206). Secondary education promoted similar objectives, and emphasis was placed on cultivating self-awareness or self-consciousness (*zijue*), so that students would internalise ideology, ethics, and discipline rather than simply obey instructions. They were thus to be taught "good study habits and the skills of analysis, criticism and independent thinking to enable them to understand and use the knowledge learnt in each subject, and to verify and develop it through practical application" (ibid., 209).

In addition to developing science and technology for China's economic modernisation, moral-ideological education was strongly emphasised as a means of creating model socialist citizens who would put the well-being of the nation and its people ahead of personal desires. With a clear politics curriculum yet to be determined,[4] history was selected early on as the principal conduit for inculcating new ideological precepts and socialist morality and transmitting and universalising the official narrative of legitimate succession, now scientifically proven by historical materialist laws. Although no individual subject curriculum was issued for secondary history until 1956, its basic goals were clear from the outset in both the Plans and the primary school History Outline. Its chief purpose was to provide children with "an elementary understanding of the laws of historical development: that the laboring people (*laodong renmin*) create history, and that class struggle drives history forward." This would gradually foster a "historical materialist viewpoint, the willpower for revolutionary struggle" and an awareness of China's "place and responsibilities in the endeavor to achieve world peace." At the same time, children would learn that the Chinese people (*Zhonghua minzu*) are "hardworking, brave and wise," that they have "made many great discoveries," and "occupy an important position in Asian and world history." This would nurture patriotism (*Xiaoxue zanxing guicheng* [1952], COCP, 204). Indeed, so important was history to moral-ideological training that in all Plans until 1957, it was consistently allocated approximately 10 percent of total class hours, behind only Chinese and mathematics.

During the New Democracy phase of the early People's Republic, as through most of the Nationalist era, Chinese history was allocated two-thirds of class hours. Both Chinese and world history were taught from ancient times to the present, and junior secondary content was simply repeated at senior secondary level in more depth. By 1953, however, China was "leaning to one side" and adopting USSR models, resulting in an equalised distribution of class hours between Chinese and world history. Moreover, world history was to precede Chinese, so as to situate the latter in a global context, while repetition at junior and senior secondary levels was avoided by arranging the curriculum in a continuous chronological narrative. Only ancient history was thus taught at junior secondary level and only modern history at senior secondary. Although this must have allowed for greater depth of study, Chinese educators thoroughly disliked it, feeling that it devalued the importance and uniqueness of China's past, as well as depriving the many students who did not progress to senior secondary level of the historical knowledge necessary to understand the modern world and provide motivation to build China anew. It may have been an acceptable structuring of the syllabus in the USSR, one Chinese textbook editor recalled, but the Soviets had a 10-year compulsory system, ensuring that all students would complete the entire course. Furthermore, "the USSR is a European country and has from ancient times on always had a relatively close relationship with the world … China's national situation is different … Ancient China's links with the world were not close, but the Teaching Plans (1953–1955) blindly copied [the USSR]" (Zhao 1989, 3).

History Content: The Materialist Conception of History

By the time the first History Teaching Outline and an accompanying set of PEP textbooks were issued in 1956,[5] a fairly coherent national and global historical narrative had been established, and despite some minor changes in the 1963 Outline and later textbook editions, and the rupture of the Cultural Revolution, this narrative has remained fundamentally intact into the post-Mao era. The new narratives (which were far less of a radical departure from Nationalist texts than Chinese writers have been wont to claim) sought principally to define the nation-state, its national people, and their unique characteristics and to compare China favorably against its Others, while incorporating traditional Chinese moral didacticism and incontrovertibly proving legitimate succession.

The theory of legitimate succession had, as already noted, been revised to prove the inevitability of CPC rule through historical materialist laws, although Mao's oft-quoted dictum, "Political power comes from the barrel of a gun," explicitly acknowledged the pivotal role of might. Synthesising China's actual historical development with an evolutionary model derived from European history and balancing ideological orthodoxy with patriotic and cultural-historical pride, however, was complex, as China's historians would attest, for they had labored long and hard to correlate theory (*lun*) with historical data (*shi*) (Dirlik 1978; Feuerwerker 1968). This had largely resulted in Sinification of the imported theory, particularly in school history classes where ongoing debates of the academic world were ignored or simplified to accommodate younger (and more impressionable) minds. Inexorable social evolution from primitive communist to slave, feudal, capitalist, and socialist society was thus modified to deemphasise the capitalist stage, since China had only developed the "sprouts of capitalism" (*ziben zhuyi mengya*) before repeated foreign invasions and reactionary, feudal, and fascist thinking on the part of China's corrupt rulers' obstructed progress, reducing the once great empire to a semi-feudal, semicolonial state.

Regime changes, meanwhile, were attributed primarily to class contradictions and struggle, and much attention focused on landholding patterns, taxation systems, and corresponding tensions between landlords and the peasantry that had culminated eventually in righteous peasant uprisings (*nongmin qiyi*). Although class relations and peasant uprisings were highlighted as history's motive force, Chinese history actually traced the rise and fall of dynasties (see table 2.1) and tempered economic determinism with voluntarism, assigning to individual figures prominent, and frequently decisive, roles in historical events. Consequently, efforts to emphasise the peasantry's gradual transition from spontaneous (*zifa*) resistance against oppression and exploitation toward class consciousness and self-aware (*zijue*) revolutionary action were mostly superseded by tales of Great Men, which focused on praising heroic rebel leaders and blaming their reactionary ruling class opponents, despite the fact that innate class morality had supposedly replaced acquired Confucian morality.

Table 2.1 Periodization of Chinese History

Historical Materialist Stage of Development	Era/Dynasty	Historical Period
Primitive Communism, 1.7m–2100 B.C.	Primitive, tribal (matriarchal, patriarchal) society	Ancient history 1.7m B.C.–1840
Slave Society, 2100–476 B.C.	Xia, Shang, Zhou	
Feudal Society, 475 B.C.–1840 A.D. (Since this accounts for most of China's recorded history, the curriculum normally divides feudal society into the five stages shown at right).	1. Warring States, Qin, Western Han, Eastern Han 2. Three Kingdoms, Western Jin, Eastern Jin, Northern and Southern Dynasties 3. Sui, Tang 4. Five Dynasties, Liao, Song, Xi Xia, Jin, Yuan 5. Ming, Qing (to 1840)	
Semifeudal, semicolonial, Bureaucratic capitalist, 1840–1949	Qing (post-1840)	Modern History 1840–1919
	Republic of China 1911–1927 (Warlordism)	Contemporary History 1919–
	Nanjing Government 1927–1949 (Nationalist Party)	
Socialist 1949–	People's Republic of China	

Whether it was because historical materialism (Sinified or otherwise) was at root a foreign theory, or simply that the cultural legacy retained a powerful grip on modern thinking, the CPC also sought to demonstrate legitimate succession in more strictly traditional terms of moral superiority over predecessors and the defense, restoration, and preservation of national unity. Accordingly, history Outlines and textbooks portrayed the CPC as the spearhead of the national restoration movement: organizing strikes and boycotts to protest against foreign imperialist exigencies and single-handedly leading the people in fighting the War of Resistance against Japan, while also improving rural conditions through land reform and education in CPC-held liberated areas. Conversely, the Nationalists were shown to have been profoundly corrupt, to have brutally exploited the people, and to have capitulated to or collaborated with the enemy, while simultaneously attempting to exterminate the Communists. Chiang Kai-shek and his (bourgeois self-seeking) Nationalists thereby forfeited the ruling mandate to the morally superior and more patriotic CPC and the (virtuous, disciplined, and working class) People's Liberation Army (PLA). This allowed the CPC to establish the People's Republic, ending the period of disunity and the "hundred years of humiliation" caused by foreign invasion, Qing conservatism, warlord rapacity, and KMT perfidy (*Chuji zhongxue Zhongguo lishi jiaoxue dagang* [1956], COH, 146–152; PEP [CZL] 1956, vol. 4; Ding 1953).

As previously shown, history not only legitimised regimes but also defined the parameters of the nation-state over which the regime presided and to which entity citizens were expected to show loyalty. For symbolic reasons of national continuity and other strategic and pragmatic concerns, the PRC, like the Republic, claimed most territories formerly controlled by the Qing empire. History thus charted the evolution of the nation-state in such a way as to demonstrate incontestable sovereignty over ethnic minority regions, Taiwan, and assorted oil- and mineral-rich atolls in the surrounding seas. A cornerstone of CPC ideology, however, was the promotion of egalitarianism and, like the Nationalists, opposition to imperialism. Unlike the Nationalists, however, the Communists did see problems with simultaneously opposing European imperialism and lauding Chinese expansionism. They therefore sought to prove that minority territories were not simply Chinese imperial conquests or that ethnic minorities were the culturally and technologically inferior objects of a Han civilizing mission; instead, non-Han or internationally contested territories were portrayed as "indivisible parts of China from ancient times onward" (*zigu yilai buke fenlie de lingtu*), and a primordial conception of the *Zhonghua minzu* was promoted, entwining both the majority Han and diverse minority nationalities in a common ancestry from Peking Man to a common destiny in a Communist utopia. Thus, what were once considered invasions by barbarians (the Xiongnu, Mongols, Manchus), bringing disaster for the legitimate (ethnic Han) rulers (Han, Song, Ming), were recast as internal clashes erupting within eternal national borders or were lauded as national unification movements. Such interethnic confrontations were mainly classified as class contradictions to emphasise the dominant theme of integration, unity, and friendship between nationalities. Meanwhile, uprisings against the dynasty that were not led by the peasantry, or which asserted independence from the center, were simply labeled as treasonous rebellions (*fanpan, panluan*). Despite efforts to portray ethnic relations as harmonious and egalitarian, however, traditional prejudices persisted in historical materialist guise, with most minority cultures categorised as feudal (backward), thus requiring the socialist (advanced) Han to modernize them.[6]

Integrating non-Chinese history and political ideology was relatively straightforward, mainly because there was far less at stake politically, but also because the deeply ingrained Sinocentric worldview meant that there was no longstanding tradition of studying the histories of other states or societies, a deficiency Soviet influence had failed to redress (Croizier 1990). Furthermore, world history was primarily Eurocentric, sitting more easily, therefore, with a historical materialist interpretation. Proving the objective laws of historical materialism appears to have been the principal purpose of world history, although it was also charged with inculcating internationalism and further inspiring patriotism and commitment to the Chinese revolution. Major ancient slave civilisations (Egypt, Greece, Rome) and the cultures of feudal empires in Europe, Asia, and the Arab world were thus surveyed both to demonstrate the relevant historical materialist stage and to prove China's greater antiquity and longevity; as one text on patriotic education explained

> Of the ancient civilisations which emerged on the stage of history at approximately the same time as China, some had long terminated their historical development, such as Ancient Greece and Babylon, while others had for long periods of time lagged far behind China in historical development, such as Egypt and India. Only when China had completed the great developmental phases of the Ch'un-ch-iu, the Warring States and the two Han periods, did the [ancestors of the] English of today begin to establish a number of small unintegrated states. As for the United States of America, it is hardly comparable to us, with its less than two hundred years of nation-making. (cited in Hu 1964, 8–9)

Most world history content, however, focused on the origins of capitalism, the evils of imperialism-colonialism, and their inevitable demise and displacement by communism. This involved great emphasis on changing modes of production and modern and contemporary European revolutions, especially the founding of the USSR. It also highlighted anticolonial or independence movements in the oppressed, proletarian nations of Asia, Africa, and Latin America.

Political Change and the Place of History

From 1952 to 1956, history was heavily influenced by Soviet models, and China sent teachers to the USSR to learn from Soviet experience and invited many Soviet education and history experts to recommend ways to improve Chinese practice (Xiong 1999, 330). History did not, however, blindly copy USSR curricula; indeed, the CPC established a committee to oversee issues in history and Chinese language education and ensure that these subjects were tailored to local conditions and fully reflected China's special characteristics. Later, as relations with the USSR deteriorated following Khrushchev's denunciation of Stalin and China reverted to a more Sinocentric and isolationist stance, the old two-to-one Chinese to world history ratio and the practice of repetition at junior and senior secondary levels were restored (*Chuji zhongxue Zhongguo lishi jiaoxue dagang* [1956], *Chuji zhongxue shijie lishi jiaoxue dagang* [1956], COH, 135–181). By the late 1950s, China had vowed no longer to borrow from its revisionist European neighbor — now viewed as just another European imperialist power masquerading as an international socialist one — but would find its own way to Communism and walk there on "two legs," blazing a revolutionary path for other oppressed peoples to follow.

In an increasingly revolutionary climate, the elite status, common sense, and work ethic of the red agricultural and urban proletarian classes were championed over effete, bourgeois, and potentially counterrevolutionary academic learning that alienated the expert few from the red many. The three cores of revisionism — textbook knowledge, classroom teaching, and the role of the teacher — were criticised, and teachers and students were instructed to leave the classroom and engage in situational education (*xianchang jiaoxue*) (Xiong 1999, 332). Total class hours were cut, labor education was increased, and politics supplanted history as the cornerstone of moral-ideological education. World history was first to be excised from junior history, as it was deemed unnecessary for basic moral-ideological training; ancient history was next, for the revolutionary ethos focused on the present and the utopian future. Although after experiments in devolution and local production of teaching materials during the Great Leap Forward, education was recentralised and academic learning reinstated as part of the gradualist path to socialism; this proved but temporary. By 1965, only 1 year of history was taught and content was oriented primarily to the Chinese revolutionary tradition, with peasant rebellions and vitriolic attacks on historical class enemies increasingly prominent. (See chapter appendix tables 2.3 and 2.4 for class hour distribution 1950–1965.)

When the Cultural Revolution was launched following the suspected allegorical criticism of Mao in historian Wu Han's play, *Hai Rui Dismissed from Office*, proletarian politics were put in command, and education through productive labor further increased. Schools and colleges, accused of being "breeding grounds for bourgeois intellectuals," run by "traitors, spies, and capitalist roaders," were closed down or transformed into sites of political slogan-mongering, while many education professionals were persecuted and dismissed from their posts. The entire education system was fragmented, and where classes were available, they were mainly staffed by underqualified personnel teaching a piecemeal curriculum that prioritized Maoist thought and a correct political viewpoint above all else. Perhaps aggravated by the "subversive" *Hai Rui*, many academic historians were viciously attacked, and school history was singled out as "a stew of feudalism, capitalism and revisionism" (*feng, zi, xiu da zahui*). The MOE Party Committee thus ordered printing, distribution, and use of existing history textbooks to cease, politics and Chinese to be integrated, and history classes abolished altogether (*Guanyu 1966–1967 niandu zhongxue zhengzhi, yuwen, lishi jiaocai chuli yijian de qingshi baogao* [June 13, 1966] cited in Xiong 1999, 332). As one veteran PEP textbook editor recalled, "the status and role of History were completely negated" (Su 1995, 243).

Farewell to Revolution

By the early 1970s, it was decided that "stopping classes to make revolution" (*tingke nao geming*) was obstructing China's modernisation goals, and efforts were made to regularise education and reestablish a broad curriculum under the slogan "restore classes to make revolution" (*fuke nao geming*).[7] Indeed, Zhou Enlai even questioned the wisdom of sending educated youth to the countryside and recruiting for tertiary education based on class background when he told a visiting foreign academic that he believed university students should be recruited directly from secondary school based on academic qualifications ("Setting things right in education" [Sept. 19, 1977], SWD). Although the April 1971 National Education Conference delivered the Two Appraisals, which asserted that during the entire 1949 to 1966 period the bourgeoisie had exercised dictatorship over the proletariat in education and that the political outlook of all intellectuals remained fundamentally bourgeois, education restoration was tentatively begun. Central control was not, however, immediately reasserted and administrative responsibility remained at the provincial or local level, albeit under the supervision of the State Council Science and Education Committee, which had replaced the defunct MOE (and the National Science Commission) in 1970.[8] History was reintroduced into the curriculum, and seven provincial-municipal education authorities were instructed to produce new curricula and textbooks, as the Two Appraisals rendered a return to pre–Cultural Revolution Outlines and textbooks unacceptable.

Both Chinese and world history textbooks were drafted, apparently modeled on those produced by the Beijing Municipal Education Committee (Wang 2000), but it is difficult to know exactly what was taught, since Cultural Revolution–era textbooks, regarded as worthless, full of lies, and Gang of Four propaganda, have not been preserved.[9] Reform-era writings have simply asserted that "during this period, there was no educational quality" for "politics replaced history" and "the masses of youth became 'historically illiterate.'" They thus dismiss the history courses reintroduced during the early 1970s as "a disaster" and "a travesty," in which history was "a small boat in a vast ocean, tossed violently by the unremitting waves of politics," with "the previous outline and textbooks repudiated and the ratio of ancient to modern, Chinese to world history thrown into chaos" (Su 1995, 240; Xiong 1999, 332). It is interesting, however, that a number of these writers, although clearly fearful of the erratic Cultural Revolution regime, were far from languishing on the Mongolian steppes or in labor reform camps; rather, they were employed in textbook production at regional education institutions. Yet, these history textbook writer-editors (many of whom remained in the profession in the reform era) have offered no insight into curricula and textbooks during the latter Cultural Revolution period, remarking only on the extreme leftist orientation. It seems that, like many of their contemporaries, their collaboration — however unwilling — in curriculum development during the Cultural Revolution is a part of history they prefer to forget.

The restoration of education begun in 1970 was temporarily interrupted by a last wave of revolutionary zeal, culminating in "the campaign to criticize Lin Biao and Confucius," but it was clear that the majority of CPC leaders favored recentralisation and standardisation of education over the Gang of Four's revolutionary model. PEP was reestablished in 1972 and many former editors were reinstated, charged with drafting new textbooks for all primary and secondary school subjects, and in January 1975, the MOE was reestablished. With Mao's death in 1976, Chi Qun and his colleagues, whom the Gang of Four had entrusted with overseeing the MOE and ensuring its adherence to the revolutionary path, were arrested along with their masters, and the Cultural Revolution officially came to an end.

History in the Post-Mao Era, 1976–

1976–1979: Bringing Order out of Chaos

After the Cultural Revolution, there was a brief period of hesitancy, during which Hua Guofeng, Mao's successor, followed the Two Whatevers policy of rigid adherence to all things Maoist.[10] It was soon acknowledged, however, that the ideological zealotry of the Cultural Revolution, which had exalted manual labor and derogated much intellectual endeavor as bourgeois and counterrevolutionary, had not only failed to deliver the long-promised modernist utopia but had also severely discredited the CPC and its legitimating ideology, left a legacy of systemic chaos and a chronic shortage of skilled personnel, and excluded many individuals and groups from full membership in the ranks of the people (*renmin*). Recentralising education and restoring academic standards were regarded as crucial to the rehabilitation and modernisation process, and personnel were reinstated and standard examinations reintroduced.

The primary, junior, and senior secondary school system was initially maintained at 10 years (divided 5-3-2), and although there was much debate over whether or when to restore the 12-year system, it was decided that reunifying and updating curricula and textbooks were more pressing concerns. In September 1977, therefore, the MOE convened a conference of more than two hundred reinstated PEP writer-editors and university academics and commissioned them to draft new outlines and accompanying textbooks.

The 1978 History Teaching Outline and textbooks were tentative, departing minimally from the basic historical narrative previously described, and closely following the prevalent political line. This lack of innovation was partly because time was limited; a central directive instructed the editors to complete both the outlines and textbooks in time for the 1978 autumn term (Su 1995, 240). Hua's Two Whatevers policy also prevented formal revocation of the Two Appraisals, and although Deng Xiaoping had denounced the Appraisals as absurd ("Setting Things Right in Education," [Aug. 1977], SWD), MOE leaders remained loath to initiate reform. It was unthinkable, therefore, that their subordinates would do so. Additionally, new or reformed interpretations of the past had not yet been agreed on, and "the most urgent priority was to erase the Gang of Four's pernicious influence on historiography" (Wang 2000, 389).

Besides transmitting "basic knowledge" of the past, therefore, teaching and learning objectives in the 1978 Outline closely followed those of its 1963 predecessor, emphasising using the past to explain the present and anticipate the future, but advising teachers to avoid historical allegories and metaphors in an oblique warning against using the past to critique the present (COH, 330). History was to continue teaching historical materialist laws and to provide education in the revolutionary tradition, patriotism, and internationalism, and teaching students to love the CPC, revolutionary proletarian exemplars, the masses, and the motherland (COH, 327–328). This entailed a continued focus on the changing forces and relations of production, on peasant uprisings, and on the "one hundred years of humiliation" (*bainian guochi*) China had suffered (beginning with the first Opium War of 1839 to 1842 and ending with the establishment of the PRC) at the hands of European capitalist imperialists and the Japanese. It also involved derogating the Qing dynasty and the KMT for weakness, corruption, and collaboration with the enemy and exalting Mao as the founding father and revered leader under whose revolutionary guidance "all our victories have been achieved" (COH, 352). Ethnic relations and national unity, meanwhile, featured more prominently than in previous outlines and textbooks, presumably to counteract secessionist and anti-Chinese sentiment in minority and border areas, which had been exacerbated by Cultural Revolution excesses. This entailed not only reiterating the one-nation message described above and warning against ethnic chauvinism and localism (i.e., separatism) but also reimagining periods of disunity (negative) as characterized principally by ethnic integration (positive) through trade and cultural exchange between rival centers of political power (COH, 331; PEP [CZL 1–4], 1978, 1979).

In scope, detailed syllabus coverage that had formerly ended in 1949 was extended to 1957, to include the period of CPC rule that was almost unanimously regarded as successful. The period from 1958 and the Great Leap Forward on was also covered in the outline, including the Cultural Revolution victory of the proletariat (over revisionism and rightist deviations), but broadbrush treatment was recommended, commensurate with the many issues awaiting formal address and resolution. The textbook, however, ended in 1957. Clearly, the history outline and textbook editorial committee were following Deng's advice that "it is best to say little about the living" (Su 1995, 240).

Deng Xiaoping assumed supreme leadership in December 1978, and although the Four Modernizations (in agriculture, industry, science and technology, and national defense) were vigorously promoted, it was some time before his authority was consolidated and the reform path secure. When revising the 1978 Outline and textbooks in 1980, therefore, curriculum and textbook developers prudently avoided sensitive issues and omitted post-1949 history altogether. The more revolutionary language and goals of the 1978 Outline and textbooks, such as "line struggle" and "ongoing revolution under the dictatorship of the proletariat" were, however, eliminated and discussion of class struggle was muted (PEP [CZL 1–4], 1980/1981; COH, 386). The exhortation to "love the revolutionary proletarian exemplars" was also deleted, since the Cultural Revolution overemphasis on red class background had been officially condemned and intellectuals were now deemed to be serving the nation with their expertise. As the roles of class struggle, revolution, and the masses were downplayed, so coverage of cultural history was increased, and several Great Men formerly derogated as feudal oppressors were reinstated. The most significant of these was Confucius. Object of a vicious "anti" campaign during the Cultural Revolution, in 1978 Confucius was still portrayed as a reactionary ideologue whose negative influence had obstructed social and economic development. In 1980, however, he was partially rehabilitated as "a thinker" and "educator" (COH, 392). Similarly, some "bourgeois" leaders of the late-nineteenth-century modernisation and reform movements were no longer dismissed as "collaborators" and "capitalist running dogs" but were credited with desiring "independence, strength, and prosperity for China" (COH, 403), an acknowledgment that all Chinese, regardless of class background, could be patriots. In a similar effort to embrace opening and dispel isolationist xenophobia, the Boxer movement, formerly depicted simply as a heroic "anti-imperialist struggle," was criticised for its "narrow and backward nature and generally antiforeign methods" (COH, 403).

Reflecting leadership changes and the anti-personality cult ethos, flattering references to "sagacious (former) Chairman Hua," were removed and, more importantly, the sycophantic ascription of all China's revolutionary successes to Mao's genius was replaced by a relatively subdued emphasis on collective Party leadership (COH, 411). Nowhere was Mao's "correct line" mentioned. As with other sensitive and unresolved issues, caution was paramount and curriculum developers clearly chose both to credit other revolutionary leaders, many of whom were in senior government positions in 1980, and to dissociate themselves from the awkward task of dispensing praise and blame where Mao and his correct (and incorrect) lines were concerned. As Su later noted, "In the past, the influence of leftist ideology meant that many historical issues were regarded as political issues ... History curriculum developers and textbook writers did not dare to question matters in this regard" (1995, 256).

1981–1986: Construction and Consolidation

Once Deng's authority was assured, a new era of "socialism with Chinese characteristics" was announced, in which pragmatism would take precedence over ideology and expertise over redness, famously summarised in Deng's dictum, "it doesn't matter whether the cat is black or white, as long as it catches the mouse." Although the Four Cardinal Principles (Marxism, dictatorship of the proletariat, leadership by the CPC, the socialist road) were enshrined in the constitution as official ideology, a reform and opening policy was adopted to accelerate construction of socialist material civilisation and deliver strength, prosperity, and international prestige. Whateverism and the Two Appraisals were formally revoked, and education was enjoined to "face modernization, the world and the future."[11] Education reform was begun in earnest and, in 1985, the administration was restructured, with the MOE upgraded to the status of State Education Commission (SEdC, the title MOE was restored in a 1998 reshuffle), with increased policymaking powers, and micro-management devolved to regional education bureaus and their subsidiary agencies (*Zhongyang guanyu jiaoyu tizhi gaige de jueding* [May 27, 1985], JYFQS, 66–72). Nine-year compulsory education (primary and junior secondary, split 6-3 or 5-4) was then legislated with implementation timelines staggered according to local conditions (*Yiwu jiaoyu fa* [passed April 12, 1986, effective July 1, 1986], JYFQS, 72–73). Additionally, it was decided to extend participation in curriculum development to include more expert advice from academics, teacher-training personnel, and senior teachers and to introduce limited textbook pluralism, under the "one Outline, many textbooks" (*yigang duoben*) system. New Outlines and textbooks would henceforth be ratified by Teaching Materials Inspection Committees (TMIC), which aimed at independent adjudication and objectivity, although since committee members were to be MOE-appointed and supervised it is difficult to imagine how such goals could be attained. At the same time, the economically advanced regions of Shanghai and Zhejiang were granted permission to design their own curricula as well as teaching materials as a pilot project in curricular devolution.

Education was not only charged with training a skilled workforce but was also intended to create a generation of new people (*yidai xinren*) with a high level of culture who were committed to building socialist modernity with Chinese characteristics and resistant to the pernicious influences of the West, already beginning to slip in through the open door. As a key source of moral-ideological education, history was restored to a more prominent place in the curriculum. The 1981 Teaching Plan increased history class hours by 25 percent and also moved it from junior secondary Years 2 and 3 to Years 1 and 2, presumably to ensure that students actually completed the course as classes were frequently abandoned in the third year to allow additional revision time for the core subjects tested in all-important senior secondary entrance examinations (history was not normally examined).[12] History received a further status boost in 1983 with a Propaganda Ministry Opinion on strengthening patriotism through formal and informal history education. Similar MOE guidelines on strengthening history and geography education and implementing the Propaganda Ministry directive were then issued, declaring that history (and geography) had hitherto been neglected. Schools, these documents stated, had reduced time-tabled class hours or cut the subjects altogether, and many trained history and geography teachers were being transferred to teach other subjects while those actually teaching were the "teachers who are unable to teach anything at all." Research institutes responsible for in-service teacher training and support did not have people or departments assigned to history and geography, and teacher quality could not therefore be improved. Moreover, the narrow focus on senior secondary and university entrance examinations that were weighted toward sciences (*like*) had a devastating impact on humanities (*wenke*), and not only did students lack knowledge of these important subjects and develop one-sidedly, but this deficiency was impeding the development of their political-ideological consciousness (*sixiang zhengzhi juewu*). Education departments and schools were accordingly instructed to follow Teaching Plan timetables, develop a corps of qualified teachers, and add more variety to teaching methods, including, where possible, combining classroom learning with visits to museums and important historical sites and using assorted audio-visual materials to stimulate students' interest (*Jiaoyubu guanyu gaijin jiaqiang zhongxue lishi he dili jiaoxue de tongzhi* [Aug. 8, 1983], JYFQS, 666–667). Study groups were to be organized to discuss patriotic education and, from the earliest possible age, the concept of the motherland was to be "engraved on children's minds," and the motherland, the CPC, and socialism were to be integrated as a single object of devotion (*Jiaoyubu guanyu xuexi guanche "guanyu jiaqiang aiguozhuyi xuanchuan jiaoyu de yijian" de tongzhi* [Aug. 24, 1983], JYFQS, 607–608).

History's improved status and the delivery of the official verdict on the pre–Cultural Revolution period in 1981[13] partially freed curriculum and textbook developers from their earlier caution, although increased official attention reminded them not to overstep certain boundaries. Nonetheless, continued efforts to minimize leftism and "the salience of struggle philosophy" (Wang 2000, 396) and to promote reform and modernisation as well as patriotism led to significant changes when the Outline and textbooks were revised once again in 1986. Historical materialist laws were downplayed and Communism was pushed into the background, while patriotism was highlighted as a timeless, class- and ethnicity-transcending, unifying force and the motherland was placed top of the "to love" list (COH, 448). Many peasant rebellions were deemphasised or excised, and although the socialist people remained the main actors of history, the masses were omitted from the syllabus' "to love" list. Clearly, agricultural and urban proletarian laborers were no longer to be exalted as role models; instead, inspiration was to be sought in the "achievements and noble spirit of outstanding persons" in Chinese history. Great Men who had contributed to (or detracted from) China's former preeminence were accordingly emphasised. Unequivocal distribution of praise and blame, however, was repudiated, and historical figures were to be evaluated in the spirit of "seeking truth from facts," rather than denigrated according to class background (Wang 2000, 392–393). This exhortation may have been a simple repetition of the oft-quoted reform mantra, but it also reflected the trend among professional historians toward integrating data and theory, (shilun jiehe) rather than using theory to lead data (yi lun dai shi).

The general portrayal of ethnic relations was unchanged, but "eradicating ethnic chauvinism and localism" was no longer listed as a curricular objective. Wang asserts that this was because "ethnic contradictions" had steadily diminished since 1949, disappearing completely by 1986, obviating the need for further mention (2000, 393–394). Ethnic problems, however, had clearly not been eradicated and were tacitly acknowledged in the highlighted historical role and the epithet "hero of the national people" (minzu yingxiong) awarded to Great Men from minority nationalities who had contributed to the glory of China (including that famous Chinese hero, Genghis Khan). Prominence was also given to "the peaceful liberation of Tibet." The former was presumably intended prophylactically, to demonstrate to wary minorities the inclusive nature of the Chinese nation, but the latter, which had not been mentioned in the 1978 Outline, was clearly a response to the growing pro-independence movement within Tibet.

Other significant changes included acknowledgement of KMT participation in the 1926 to 1927 Northern Expedition and 1937 to 1945 War of Resistance against Japan (COH, 474–477), reflecting, in part, curriculum developers' professional pursuit of accuracy but also gradual détente between the PRC and Taiwan that began in the early 1980s. Additionally, coverage of contemporary history was extended to the 1980s, although some sensitive issues, such as the 1957 Anti-Rightist Movement and factional struggles within the party were barely discussed (COH, 481). Perhaps the most important changes in 1986, however, were the expansion of pedagogical objectives to include training in analytical skills (although correct conclusions were still to be reached) and the restoration of world history to the junior secondary curriculum. The world history syllabus was a sweeping one-semester survey from primitive times to the 1980s and was a direct abridgment of the senior secondary course. Unlike Chinese history, it was heavily biased toward modern-contemporary history and emphasised historical materialist laws, revolutions, imperialism, and anti-colonialism. The addition of world history, however, was not unequivocally welcomed, for total history class hours had not increased, necessitating the reduction of Chinese history from four to three semesters to accommodate the world history component. Furthermore, despite the implementation of 12-year schooling, Chinese history had not been added to the senior secondary curric-ulum, and the combined class hour total was divided equally between Chinese and world history, which "given that China has such a long history, is not really appropriate" (Yu and Zhao 1999, 113). (That world history is also "long" does not seem to have had any bearing on the matter, nor does the fact that in primary schools, a 1-year history course, weighted three to one in favor of Chinese history, was also taught.)

1987–1995: History in Flux

The mid to late 1980s were a tumultuous period for China as reform and opening accelerated, bringing a potent mixture of economic growth, social problems, and criticism of corruption, cronyism, and the progress and scope of reform from both liberals and conservatives. Serious theoretical challenges to orthodox Marxism-Leninism-Mao Zedong thought were mounted, China's political future was hotly debated in the salons that sprang up in more developed areas and, in 1986, student demonstrations calling for democracy, human rights, and freedom erupted across a number of Chinese cities. Cam-paigns against spiritual pollution and bourgeois liberalisation, thought to be the products of over-Westernization, failed to stifle these complaints and, as in the past, history was harnessed as a vehicle for obliquely expressing popular dissatisfaction, most famously in the quasi-historical documentary *Heshang* (*River Elegy*). *Heshang* lambasted traditional Chinese culture, ridiculed its symbols of greatness as evidence of backwardness and ignorant isolationism, and implied that the CPC had wrought no improvements. Instead, it advo-cated a reorientation toward the blue (maritime) culture, an outlook per-ceived as characteristic of Western civilization (Su 1991). The CPC responded by banning *Heshang* and sponsoring a historical documentary, *On the Road: A Century of Marxism*. Each episode was based on one of the Four Cardinal Principles and demonstrated how China's travails since the mid-nineteenth century had finally ended with the establishment of the PRC (Barmé 1990). The counterattack was weak, however, and the party quickly resorted to more traditional methods of silencing its critics, expelling advocates of democratization from the CPC and imprisoning political activists.

If historical narratives were a vehicle for popular and academic criticism of the regime, history education was the regime's vehicle for promoting moral-ideological conformity. In this political climate, therefore, the 1988 Teaching Plan further boosted history's status, extending the course from 2 to 3 years. (This restored it to parity with politics, the first time history had been in such a position of strength since the mid-1950s.) With extra class hours, the 1988 draft Outline expanded the world history course to a full year, although it remained a simplified version of the senior secondary syllabus. Approximately five percent of total class hours were also allocated to ethnic minority or local history, the teaching of which had hitherto been sporadic, since previous outlines had designated it as supplementary and there was no organized publication of teaching materials. It is unclear whether this was a politically correct effort to celebrate, or at least display tolerance for ethnic and regional diversity, or a more cynical attempt to dictate the content of non-national histories and prevent any assertion of separate identities and secessionist dreams. What is certain, however, is that it aimed to promote understanding of local conditions and love for one's hometown, and thereby inspire the young to strive for local development. By extension, it was thought, this would nurture patriotism and contribute to national modernisation goals (Song 1990, 38–39).

Although political uncertainty led history curriculum and textbook developers to continue their cautious approach, the emphasis on historical materialist theory, class struggle, and peasant uprisings was further reduced in the 1988 draft Outline and textbooks. Space devoted to cultural history and Great Men was again expanded, reflecting continued repudiation of revolution and the promotion of patriotism and national self-confidence through nurturing pride in China's past glories. The demotion of theory was also a response to professional historical research, which — influenced by various foreign discourses on historiography now being translated into Chinese[14] — increasingly attempted not only to integrate theory and data but to release Chinese history from its historical materialist straitjacket altogether and derive (new) theories from data (*lun cong shi chu*). Such an approach was not evident in world history, which remained mainly concerned with providing illustrative examples of historical materialist theory and demonstrating past imperialist transgressions to alert the young to continued imperialist threats. Nonetheless, some cultural topics were added and, in a nod to internationalism, students were required not only to strive for socialist modernisation in China but also to develop a sense of responsibility and to strive for the peace and progressive undertakings of humanity (COH, 510). International relations were thus portrayed as having been typified by peaceful trade and cultural exchange, albeit punctuated by occasional wars. This internationalist spirit was, however, somewhat undermined by Sinocentric arrogance, which asserted that China had made great contributions (*gongxian*, purely positive) to humanity, while other cultures had influenced (*yingxiang*) China in both positive and negative senses (COH, 511).

Following academic trends, considerably more attention was directed toward pedagogy in the 1988 curriculum, in part because opening had permitted the study of new (mostly foreign) ideas and theories, and it was felt that traditional pedagogies were inadequate for the modernisation task, but also because matters such as teaching methods were perceived as apolitical and value-free. The History Inspection Committee approved the draft Outline and textbooks in 1988, permitting implementation on a trial basis, with nationwide promulgation slated for 1992 and 1993.

By the end of the 1980s, however, rampant nepotism and corruption had combined with spiraling inflation, wage stagnation, and abolition of subsidies to cause increasingly widespread dissatisfaction with the party. Therefore, when students took to Tiananmen Square in April 1989 to lament the death of the reformist leader Hu Yaobang, protest against corruption and call for further reforms, they were soon joined by thousands of disgruntled workers. The subsequent repression is well documented and need not be discussed here, but the complete failure of official campaigns to curb bourgeois liberalism and strengthen public morality, which had been adopted to avert such a crisis, led the party to reassert its "patriotic" credentials as China's past, present, and future savior. It thus asserted that having saved the nation from feudalism, imperialism, Japan, the KMT, the USSR, and the United States, it now had to protect it from China's own youth, who had, it was believed, tasted only the sweet fruits of modernisation and not the hard years of bitter struggle and were thus too easily led astray by the pernicious influences of decadent Western culture. Clearly what was being taught in schools was failing to eradicate the poisonous foreign weeds (*ducao*) that were taking root in young minds. Tiananmen thus prompted an intensified focus on ideological education, and especially on history, as a source of moral and ideological renewal and consolidation.

Over the next 2 years, the SEdC issued several directives on strengthening patriotism and education in national conditions (*guoqing jiaoyu*) through history. These were far more aggressive than previous directives and underlined the nation's commitment to socialism and the party. A 1989 Opinion, for example, emphasised that China would never "capitulate to foreign forces, nor completely Westernize (*quanpan xihua*), nor take the capitalist road" and that the party is "great, glorious ... and the correct long-term choice of the Chinese people. Only under Party leadership will the Chinese *minzu* be able to stand up in the world of nations" (*Guojia jiaowei guanyu zai zhongxiaoxue yuwen*, *lishi, dili deng xueke jiaoxuezhong jiaqiang sixiang zhengzhi he guoqing jiaoyu de yijian* [Nov. 8, 1989], JYFQS, 619–621). To convey this message, history (and other humanities subjects) was to reemphasize patriotism and socialist morality. In an unprecedented move, the provisions of the Teaching Plan and Outline were overridden in the middle of the academic year and, from the spring semester of the 1989–1990 school year, modern-contemporary Chinese history was added to the first-year senior secondary curriculum, which since 1978 had taught only world history (see chapter appendix tables 2.5 and 2.6). The new course and class hours were confirmed in the 1990 History Outline for senior secondary schools. At the same time, the 1986 junior secondary History Outline was revised as an interim measure until the 1988 draft Outline could be fully tested. The 1990 revised Outline made few changes other than to designate some topics — chiefly the few remaining peasant wars and economic history — as optional. World history content, however, was reduced, allegedly because current content was too taxing for students, but probably necessitated by the greater emphasis to be placed on Chinese history as the vehicle for patriotic education (ibid., 621; COH, 539–606).

While several other directives on moral education were issued both by the SEdC and other government bureaus from 1989 to 1990, the most comprehensive guidelines to emerge in response to the late 1980s crises were not promulgated until August 1991. In March 1991, the then Party General Secretary Jiang Zemin had written a letter to SEdC leaders, Li Tieying and He Dongchang, calling for greater attention to be paid to modern-contemporary Chinese history and to education in China's national conditions as a means of inculcating right attitudes to socialist modernisation and due caution with regard to foreign ideas and culture (*Jiang Zemin zongshuji zhi Li Tieying, He Dongchang qiangdiao jinxing Zhongguo jindaishi, xiandishi ji guoqing jiaoyu*, COH, 607–608). Unsurprisingly, this letter was subsequently published in the *People's Daily* and, widely circulated, became the basis for the August SEdC directives.

The "General Guideline on Strengthening Modern and Contemporary Chinese History and Education in China's National Conditions" used much more extremist language and was clearer in its targets of attack than earlier documents. The Guideline's stated objectives that dwelled primarily on strengthening patriotism, faith in the party, and cultural pride; on teaching the young that foreign ideas of democracy, human rights, and peaceful evolution were the sugar-coated bullets of reactionary enemy forces (capitalist and imperialist) conspiring to return China to a weak and easily exploited, semi-feudal, semicolonial state; and on teaching the young to understand China's national conditions, which would give them patience and determination to strive for socialist modernisation, so that China would never again be humiliated. Western capitalism was singled out for special attack, not only for its past imperialist transgressions against China, but as *innately* evil. This evil, exploitative nature was to be exposed through history and, in language reminiscent of the anti-Rightist and Cultural Revolution campaigns, "a clear line" was to be drawn between socialism (China, good) and capitalism (the West, bad). Although the working people of Western countries were to be recognized as fellow sufferers exploited by the ruling classes, the distinction between political-economic systems and national character (*guomin jingshen*) does not appear to have been made very clear, and the general tone certainly conveyed more than a whiff of antiforeignism. History was the core of this educational endeavor, and the guideline listed three key components: "five-thousand years of glorious culture," "more than one hundred years of struggle to save the nation from humiliation and annihilation by invading enemy forces," and 40 years of "world-beating transformation" and the establishment of "glorious future prospects" under the leadership of the CPC. CPC errors, meanwhile, were to be examined from a positive standpoint and narrating them was to result in positive conclusions (*Guojia jiaowei guanyu lingfa "zhongxiaoxue jiaqiang jindai, xiandaishi ji guoqing jiaoyu de zongti gangyao (chugao)" de tongzhi*, [1991], COH, 609–610; *Zhongxiaoxue jiaqiang jindai, xiandaishi ji guoqing jiaoyu de zongti gangyao (chugao)* [1991], 610–636). An appropriate syllabus was accordingly drawn up, although it did not differ significantly from the existing outline and was merely a list of topics deemed relevant to conveying the guidelines' core message. Education authorities, however, were to draw up more specific plans and "within two-three years should have integrated all the provisions of the guidelines into the curriculum of every school," although how this was to be done other than "by paying special attention to those subjects most important for this kind of education" was not specified (*Zhongxiaoxue lishi xueke sixiang zhengzhi jiaoyu gangya* [1991], COH, 637–655).

Personal attention from Jiang Zemin and the 1991 directives thrust history further into the spotlight, and the new Teaching Plan for compulsory education raised its official status even further by adding an extra weekly class hour in the second year of junior secondary school to be devoted to modern-contemporary history. When the 1988 draft History Outline and textbooks were finally promulgated in 1992, however, there were few changes from the 1988 drafts. Some of the vitriol of the 1991 directives was incorporated, and history was ordered to "expose the invasive nature and extortionist crimes of capitalism and imperialism" (COH, 658). It was acknowledged, however, that socialist China was not yet perfect. History was thus to teach students that

> In the history of the world, creating and consolidating any new [political] system has always involved a long period of struggle, during which there have been many twists, turns and setbacks; feudalism was like that, capitalism is like that, and socialism is even more so ... [S]ocialism will

inevitably triumph the world over, but the road to victory will be tortuous. (COH, 658)

Understanding national conditions (*guoqing*), upholding the Four Cardinal Principles, opposing "peaceful evolution plots," and so forth were accordingly emphasised and "socialist" preceded almost every mention of motherland. At the same time, however, as had been emphasised by Deng on his 1992 Southern Tour, China was not to revert to isolationism but was to continue the reform and opening process. The Outline thus stated that the closed door policies of late imperial times were to be criticised for having retarded China's development (COH, 667).

1996–: Quality Education

Since the mid-1990s, of the Four Cardinal Principles, only leadership by the CPC has been truly retained; socialism is little in evidence and reform and opening have accelerated dramatically. Increasingly it is believed that "creative consciousness and creative ability … [are] important factors in overall national power" and that "the capital with which to engage in international competition is the quality of the national people (*minzu suzhi*) and science and technology; that is, education and talented persons" (Ouyang 1999, 18). The drive for national greatness, increased exposure to foreign pedagogies and practices, and expanded participation in policymaking by often foreign-trained, non-party professionals have thus led to calls for more thorough reforms, a deemphasis on the examination-centered curriculum, and the cultivation of creative and independent thinking skills. At the same time, the "little emperor" syndrome and juvenile delinquency have impelled the authorities to reiterate the centrality of moral education and have spurred research by educationalists into child psychological development. This has underpinned the emergence of quality education (*suzhi jiaoyu*) as the guiding principle of current reforms. While the nature-nurture conundrum that underpins the concept of *suzhi* has obstructed formulation of a precise definition of quality education (Huang 1996; Sun and Cheng 1997), some general principles regarding its practical functions and goals have been agreed on, and quality education was adopted as the official education policy mantra in 1999 (*Beijing jiaoyu kexue yanjiuyuan*, 45–65, 66–78).

The overarching goal is to "raise the quality of the national people" (*tigao minzu suzhi*), a concept that has much in common with earlier calls under both the KMT and CPC to improve the cultural level of the masses through education, and with much older Confucian notions about transforming the backward mindset and habits of the lowly. In order to accomplish this, education must center on holistic (*quanmian*) development, nurturing the individual's moral, intellectual, physical, and aesthetic strengths (*de, zhi, ti, mei*);

improving areas of weakness; and ensuring psychological and social well being. It must also cater to the needs of all students, so that no child is left behind. Additionally it must provide a balanced curriculum that integrates teaching and learning, preactive and active curricula, and abstract knowledge and concrete practice. Although this has clearly not yet been achieved, new curriculum standards (*kecheng biaozhun*), which depart considerably from the traditional Outline format, and new textbooks that at least aspire to these goals, have been drafted. Additionally, many experimental courses have been devised and textbook pluralism extended.

While history remains fundamental to moral-ideological education, efforts to make the subject more holistic, skills-oriented, and relevant to contemporary life have persuaded education policymakers not only to reform the history subject but also to create new integrative courses such as social studies and history and society. In the case of the conventional history subject, PEP, for the first time in more than 40 years, has had little involvement in the outline drafting process, although it has produced a set of textbooks to accompany the new History Curriculum Standards (HCS). Perhaps partly because of the involvement of new personnel, including many educationalists as well as historians (under the guidance of Beijing Normal University, one of China's premier teacher training institutions), the HCS attempt to move away from overly prescriptive syllabus content and to increase concrete pedagogical guidance. HCS have thus been praised by some for their innovation, liveliness, and creativity, while being maligned by others (in private at least) for lack of structure, sketchiness, and blind trend-following. Some textbook editors have also complained that they are insufficiently detailed to enable them to produce textbooks that fully "comply with all the requirements stipulated by the Teaching Plans and Outlines," a prerequisite for passing MOE inspection (*Guojia jiaoyu weiyuanhui zhongxiaoxue jiaocai shending biaozhun* [Oct. 10, 1987], JYFQS, 1090–1091). However, the final, official verdict on the new curriculum has not yet been delivered, as the HCS and the new integrated history subjects have only been implemented on a trial basis in selected schools and regions since autumn 2001. As in the past, this experiment will continue for several years, gradually expanding its scope until it is implemented nationwide. In the interim, since no curricular changes other than class hour adjustments (see chapter appendix table 2.5) and minor editorial revisions of textbooks had been made since the 1992 Outline and textbooks were produced, comprehensive revisions were commissioned in 2000 and promulgated in autumn 2001.

The 2000 Outline has made few changes to the 1992 format and syllabus, but goals and teaching methods have been revised to reflect the new priorities outlined above. History is no longer forced to pursue abstract ideological goals of constructing socialist material or spiritual civilisation, and pedagogical goals have instead been highlighted. "Teaching students to learn" is the fundamental objective, to be accomplished through a variety of activities and methods that must be appropriate for students' "level of cognitive development." History must nurture skills and abilities, such as historical thinking, creative consciousness, independent study, and cooperation with others, as well as the more specific skills of note-taking, using maps, and so forth elaborated in the 1988 draft and 1992 Outline (COH, 715). Although skills and abilities remain rather poorly defined, guidance on methods of fostering them has become more detailed in response to criticisms of vagueness and a lack of concrete examples and explanations (Nie 1999; Zhang 2000).

This heightened focus on pedagogy has by no means entailed the demise of ideology. Nurturing love of the motherland (no longer prefixed by socialist) and developing national self-respect and confidence remain central goals. "Patriotism, socialism, the revolutionary tradition, national conditions, and ethnic unity" are also emphasised, but references to the Four Cardinal Principles and following the party's basic line have been expunged. Dialectical and historical materialism have also been retained, but integrating theory and data and, more importantly, deriving theories from data are explicitly stated to be the guiding theoretical principles that must be upheld (COH, 715). Moreover, the analysis and evaluation of historical events and people are is no longer explicitly required to be correct, and students are to use imagination, association, comparison, and generalisation to develop their own opinions based on data from both the textbook and other sources.

In an apparently more genuine internationalist spirit, history is also seen as a means of "enhancing understanding of the world ... leading students to respect the fruits of other countries' and peoples' civilizations," although this has not entailed substantial reform of world history coverage. Finally, the importance of personal development and public morality are highlighted, with history described as assisting students to develop a rounded personality, "healthy aesthetic consciousness and interests," and the "determination to strive for ideals, honesty, and goodness." Despite much talk of individuality and independent thinking, however, the morality and viewpoints that even quality history education is expected to inculcate remain fundamentally prescriptive, with the adjective "correct" recurrently used to define desirable types of consciousness and values. Curriculum developers may thus increasingly reject the tenets of historical materialism and old historical narratives, and they may scorn direct imposition of ideas and values. However, in practice, they seem neither ready nor willing to challenge absolutist concepts of true and false or right and wrong when discussing the past or the present.

Conclusion

"To destroy a nation, its history must first be erased," wrote Chinese statesman and scholar Gong Zizhen (1792–1841), succinctly expressing the idea that shared memories of a real or imagined past are an essential component of communal identities and social cohesion. As argued in the introduction and throughout the present volume, this notion has underpinned nation-building projects worldwide, rendering history, and especially the school subject of history, with its large, young, impressionable and, above all, captive audience, a site of frequently bitter contest over who "We" are, and where "We" should be heading. In both Nationalist and Communist China, history has been crucial to the transmission of state-authorized memories on which state-authorized identities may be constructed and to the suppression or control of histories that may support alternative ethnic, regional, or political identities. However, although history production has been restricted directly by government control mechanisms and indirectly by self-censorship, and the standardised, examination-centered national curriculum has often ensured considerable homogeneity across syllabi, textbooks, and classroom teaching, this does not necessarily mean that the Chinese regime has persuaded its citizens to subscribe lock, stock, and barrel to the state-sanctioned vision of Chineseness. It is one thing to produce official histories, but dictating how they are consumed and suppressing all competing sources of historical memory are impossible tasks. No matter how often an official history is reiterated (and more or less the same history is recapitulated at all stages of the Chinese education system), people can only be forced to know, not to believe; official histories and may even actively resist them (as happened in the Soviet bloc) precisely because they are state-sponsored (Wertsch 2000).

In the PRC today, some resistance to official discourses of historical and national identity obviously exists, erupting at times into open dissent in independence-seeking minority regions, such as Tibet and Xinjiang, where the majority regard themselves as conquered and colonized by the (Han) Chinese state and dismiss the one-nation message as propaganda; indeed, Hansen (1999) suggests that emphasising a unified Chinese identity rooted chiefly in Han culture and history, while downplaying minority cultural and historical difference, often strengthens separate ethnic identities. By contrast, among the Han population (including many democracy activists and dissidents), it appears that official histories have been largely accepted, although economic determinism and the inevitability of CPC rule are increasingly questioned. As many people are wont to claim, "I love the country, but not the party" (*ai guo bu ai dang*), indicating that it is considered perfectly possible to be patriotic without supporting the current regime or political system. This attitude has tallied with the recent rise among China's youth of a militant popular nationalism (exemplified by the best-seller *China Can Say "No"*), which sees China as a peace-loving state that has never fought an unjust war or invaded another country and has been cruelly victimized by foreign imperialists past and present. The public outcries following the North Atlantic Treaty Organisation's 1999 bombing of the Chinese Embassy in Belgrade and the collision in

2001 between a U.S. reconnaissance jet and a Chinese F-8 fighter, for example, were couched in the language of historical grievance, with international gunboat diplomacy deplored as a throwback to China's nineteenth-century victimisation. Similarly, Japanese wartime atrocities and their lack of coverage in many Japanese school textbooks are frequently invoked in popular discussion and in depictions of Japan by the Chinese media as well as in formal Sino-Japanese exchanges. Most Han Chinese also appear to genuinely believe that Tibet, Taiwan, Mongolia, and other recent territorial acquisitions are not Chinese conquests, but eternal and indivisible parts of the motherland, although they do not always regard the indigenous inhabitants as fully Chinese even if they are recognized as fellow citizens.

How far the history curriculum shapes or is shaped by popular sentiment is difficult to ascertain; there is certainly much apparent congruence between official narratives and popular opinion, although this may be because the omnipresence of official narratives in education, the media, and other state-supervised arenas forms a dominant discourse that permeates the language and structure of all histories, even heterodox ones (Wertsch 2000). Furthermore, curriculum developers are not necessarily party stalwarts; some are not even party members, and obviously they are not immune from bottom-up influences, just as they are not simply instruments of top-down policymaking. Regardless of who or what is influencing who, it is clear that curriculum and textbook developers have discarded the legitimating ideology of Marxism-Leninism-Mao Zedong thought as inappropriate for children and irrelevant to Chinese (if not to world) history, and perhaps also because they view it as increasingly obsolete. They have also encouraged the development of historical thinking skills that may be an attempt to defend history's territory and status in the school curriculum, or reflect genuine concern to make history more useful to students, but could also perhaps involve a subversive promotion of critical thinking as the basis of informed citizenship. In addition, curriculum developers have focused on Chinese dynastic and cultural heritage rather than on historical materialism, and on the national people rather than on the socialist people, indicating a decisive reorientation away from class to ethnicity and from socialism to nationalism. The regime has, of course, permitted and even encouraged this reorientation, seeking to distance itself from the Cultural Revolution debacle of revolutionary socialism and to accentuate its traditional Chinese characteristics, even publicly endorsing the virtues of Confucianism. But this is a dangerous game, for the nation-centered narrative of history posits a primordial people and eternal motherland that transcend the transient historical category of the (Communist) state (Tang 1999, 79). It is this nation descended from the Yellow Emperor, its culture and ancestral lands — not the historically contingent regime and its political maneuvering — with which history exhorts the Chinese people to identify and for the betterment of which they should strive; "the state," as Tang wryly observes "will sooner or later become obsolete and end up in the museum, whereas the motherland will have as long a life as humankind itself" (ibid.,).

Endnotes

1. This paraphrases Harrison (2001, 7). The original quote reads, "In the eyes of the emperor's subjects, the [Chinese] empire was not a country, but the country, not a culture, but culture itself."

2. RMRB, "*Renzhen shishi wenfa xueyuan de xin kecheng*" Oct. 14, 1949. This exhortation is frequently cited or adapted by writers on the history of education. The RMRB exhortation is an elaboration of the Chinese People's Political Consultative Conference (CPPCC) Common Program, which declared, "The cultural education work of the People's Government should raise the cultural level of the People, nurture talented persons for national construction, eradicate feudal, comprador and fascist thinking, and develop ideology which serves the People" (quoted by Su 1995, 119).

3. PEP was to assume Outline drafting duties by 1959, but the reins were actually handed over by 1957 (*Guanyu zhongxue lishi, dili, wuli, shengwu dengke jiaokeshu de jingjian banfa* [1957], COH, 236).

4. The first Politics Outline was issued in 1959. In the meantime, assorted courses in various aspects of socialist thought were taught.

5. This was the second complete set of textbooks drafted and published by PEP, but the first attached to the national curriculum.

6. For a full discussion of the civilising project and PRC historiography of minority nationalities, see Harrell (1995).

7. This slogan had originally been used in 1967 for the same purpose, but had met with little success.

8. From 1973, this committee was only responsible for education, as responsibility for scientific work was transferred to the Academy of Sciences.

9. From personal communications with staff at PEP and various universities in Beijing and Shanghai.

10. The Two Whatevers refers to the statement "We will resolutely uphold whatever policy decisions Chairman Mao made, and unswervingly follow whatever instructions Chairman Mao gave."

11. Deng formulated this dictum in an address to the Jingshan School in Beijing on 1/10/1983. It was later included in the 1985 Decision on Reforming the Education System and is almost universally incorporated in most official directives and academic articles on education reform.

12. Senior secondary entrance examination requirements are determined by provincial-level education departments. Most regions examine Chinese, mathematics, English, physics, chemistry, and politics.

13. "Resolution on Certain Questions in the History of Our Party."

14. Foreign theorists translated during the 1980s include E. H. Carr (*What Is History?*), Croce (*The Theory and Practice of History*), Collingwood (*The Idea of History*), and Popper (*The Poverty of Historicism*) (Qu 1988).

References
Abbreviations

CES   *Chinese Education and Society.*

COCP   *Ershi shiji Zhongguo zhongxiaoxue kecheng biaozhun, jiaoxue dagang huibian: kecheng (jiaoxue) jihua juan* (Collected twentieth century standard curricula and teaching outlines for Chinese primary and secondary schools: Curriculum (Teaching) Plans).

COH   *Ershi shiji Zhongguo zhongxiaoxue kecheng biaozhun, jiaoxue dagang huibian: lishi juan* (Collected twentieth century standard curricula and teaching outlines for Chinese primary and secondary schools: History).

CSL   *Chuji zhongxue shijie lishi*, 1–2 (Junior secondary World History textbook, Vols. 1–2).

CZL   *Chuji zhongxue Zhongguo lishi*, 1–4 (Junior secondary Chinese History textbook, Vols. 1–4).

HCS   *Quanrizhi yiwu jiaoyu lishi kecheng biazhun (shiyangao)* (Full-time compulsory education: History Curriculum Standards [trial ed.]).

JDC   *Jiaoyu da cidian* (The Dictionary of Education).

JYFQS   *Zhonghua renmin gongheguo jiaoyufa quanshu* (An Encyclopaedia of PRC Education Law).

JYSD   *Zhongguo jiaoyu shidian* (A Compendium of Events in Chinese Education).

LSJX   *Lishi jiaoxue* (History Education).

RMRB   *Renmin ribao* (*People's Daily*).

SWD   Selected Works of Deng Xiaoping (online edition).

ZXLS   *Zhongxue lishi* (History Teaching in Middle Schools).

References

Avery, M. 1986. Translator's Introduction in Zhang Xianliang, *Half of Man Is Woman*. London: Penguin.

Barmé, G. 1990. "Small Screen, Small Minds." *Far Eastern Economic Review* (Oct. 25, 1990):32.

COCP: Kecheng jiaocai yanjiusuo, eds. 2001. *Ershi shiji Zhongguo zhongxiaoxue kecheng biaozhun, jiaoxue dagang huibian: kecheng (jiaoxue) jihuajuan.* Beijing: PEP.

COH: Kecheng jiaocai yanjiusuo, eds. 2001. *Ershi shiji Zhongguo zhongxiaoxue kecheng biaozhun, jiaoxue dagang huibian: lishi juan.* Beijing: PEP.

Croizier, R. 1990. "World History in the People's Republic of China." *The Journal of World History* 1, 2 (Fall 1990):151–170.

Deng, Xiaoping. *Selected Works of Deng Xiaoping, Vols. 1–3* (online ed.,). http://english.peopledaily.com.cn.dengxp.

Dirlik, A. 1978. *Revolution and History.* Berkeley: University of California Press.

Feuerwerker, Albert. 1968. *History in Communist China.* Boston: MIT Press.

Fincher, J. 1972. "China as a Race, Culture and Nation," in Buxbaum and Mote, eds., *Transition and Permanence.* Hong Kong: Cathay Press, 59–69.

Gries, P. 1999. Face Nationalism: Power and Passion in China's Foreign Relations. [Ph.D. dissertation]. University of California, Berkeley.

Hansen, M. 1999. *Lessons in Being Chinese.* Seattle: University of Washington Press.

Harrell, S., ed. 1995. *Cultural Encounters on China's Ethnic Frontiers.* Seattle: University of Washington Press.

Harrison, H. 2000. *The Making of the Republican Citizen.* Oxford: Oxford University Press.

HCS. 2001. Beijing: Beijing shifan daxue chubanshe, 2001.

Hu, C. T. 1964. "The Teaching of History in Communist China," proceedings of *China Quarterly* conference. Oxford.

Huang, F. 1996. "Suzhi jiaoyu beilun." *Beijing shifan daxue xuebao (shehui kexue ban)* 5:81–84.

JYFQS. 1995. Beijing: Beijing guangbo xueyuan chubanshe.

Keenan, B. 1977. *The Dewey Experiment in China.* Cambridge, MA: Harvard University Press.

Li, D. 1995. *Kangzhan shiqi Chongqing de jiaoyu.* Chongqing: Chongqing chubanshe.

Nie, Y. 1999. *Zhongxue lishi jiaoyu lun.* Shanghai: Xuelin chubanshe.

Ouyang, B. 1999. "Lishi ketang jiaoxue yu chuangzaoxing siwei." *ZXLS* 4:18–20.
Peake, C. 1970. *Nationalism and Education in Modern China*. New York, Columbia University Press, orig. pub. 1932.
Qu, Q. 1988. "Tashan zhi shi, he yi wei cuo." *GMRB* (Oct. 19, 1988).
Said, E. 1978. *Orientalism*. New York: Pantheon Books.
Song, E. 1990. "Dui jiaqiang xiangtu shi jiaoxue de sandian renshi." *LSJX* 2:38–40.
Su, S. 1995. *Shibian shiyi*. Beijing: PEP.
Su, X. 1991. *Deathsong of a River*. Ithaca, NY: East Asia Program, Cornell University.
Sun, X. and Cheng, Y. 1997. "Quality, Development and Education" *CES* 30, 6 (Nov./Dec.):12–14.
Tang, Z. 1999. "Rethinking the Problem of Patriotic Education in the Subject of History in High Schools." *CES* 30, 6 (Nov./Dec.):78–81.
Wang, H. 2000. *Lishi jiaocai de gaige yu shijian*. Beijing: PEP.
Wertsch, J. 2000. "Is It Possible to Teach Beliefs, as Well as Knowledge about History?" in Stearns, Seixas, and Wineburg, eds., *Knowing, Teaching and Learning History: National and International Perspectives*. New York and London: New York University Press.
Xiong, M. 1999. *Zhongguo jinxiandai jiaoxue gaige shi*. Chongqing: Chongqing chubanshe.
Yu, Y., Ye, X. and Zhao, Y. 1999. *Lishi xueke jiaoyuxue*. Beijing: Shoudu shifan daxue chubanshe.
Zhang, J. 1999a. "Dui lishi kecheng xianzhuang de fenxi," in Wen, ed., *Xianshi yu chaoyue*, vol. 2. Beijing: Beijing chubanshe, 423–430.
Zhang, J. 1999b. "Kecheng gaige xuesheng wenjuan de diaocha yu fenxi," in Wen, ed., *Xianshi yu chaoyue*, vol. 1. Beijing: Beijing chubanshe, 57–72.
Zhao, H. 1989. "Zhongxue lishi jiaoxue shijian sishinian." *LSJX* 9 (1989)2–7.
Zhao, Y. 1997. *Zhongxue lishi jiaoyuxue*. Beijing: Zhongguo jiancai gongye chubanshe.

APPENDIX: CLASS-HOUR DISTRIBUTION FOR SECONDARY SCHOOL HISTORY, 1929–2001

Abbreviations

I, II, III	First, second, third year of school	A	Ancient history	Ch	Chinese history
i, ii	First, second semester	M	Modern history	W	World history
x	Class hours per week	C	Contemporary history		

Dates in bold indicate History Curriculum Standards or History Teaching Outlines; other dates refer to Teaching Plans or other government directives affecting class hours.

1929–1949

Appendix Table 2.1 Junior Secondary

	I.i	I.ii	II.i	II.ii	III.i	III.ii
1929*	Ch/2x	Ch/2x	Ch/2x	Ch/2x	W/2x	W/2x
1932	Ch/2x	Ch/2x	Ch/2x	Ch/2x	W/2x	W/2x
1936	Ch/2x	Ch/2x	Ch/2x	Ch/2x	W/2x	W/2x
1940	Ch/2x	Ch/2x	Ch/2x	Ch/2x	Ch/2x	W/2x
1948#	Ch(+W)/2x	Ch(+W)/2x	Ch(+W)/2x	Ch(+W)/2x	Ch(+W)/2x	Ch(+W)/2x

Appendix Table 2.2 Senior Secondary

	I.i	I.ii	II.i	II.ii	III.i	III.ii
1929*	Ch/2x	Ch/2x	Ch/2x	W/2x	W/2x	W/2x
1932	Ch/4x	Ch/2x	Ch/2x	W/2x	W/2x	W/2x
1936	Ch/2x	Ch/2x	Ch/2x	W/2x	W/2x	W/2x
1940	Ch/2x	Ch/2x	Ch/2x	Ch/2x	W/2x	W/2x
1948##			Ch/2x	Ch/2x	Ch., W/2x	W/2x

* Suggested class hour distribution. Class hour allocation in the 1929 draft curriculum was not given; rather, a credit system was employed, 1 credit = 1 term of 1 class hour p/w. History for both junior and senior secondary was to consist of twelve credits over 3 years — 8 Chinese: 4 world for junior secondary, 6:6 in senior secondary.

\# Class hour distribution unspecified. Suggested only that world history be integrated with Chinese history.

\## Precise class hour allocation unspecified; distribution specified as 60 percent Chinese, 40 percent world.

1950–1965

Appendix Table 2.3 Junior Secondary

	I.i	I.ii	II.i	II.ii	III.i	III.ii
1950	Ch/3x	Ch/3x	Ch/3x	Ch/3x	W/3x	W/3x
1953	W/A/3x	W/A/3x	W/A/3x	Ch/A/3x	Ch/A/3x	Ch/A/3x
1954	Ch/A/3x	Ch/A/3x	Ch/A/3x	W/A/3x	W/A/3x	W/A/3x
1955	Ch/A/3x	Ch/A/3x	Ch/A/3x	Ch/M-C/3x	W/A/3x	W/A/3x
1956	Ch/A/3x	Ch/A/3x	Ch/M-C/3x	Ch/M-C/3x	W/3x	W/3x
1958	Ch/3x	Ch/3x	Ch/2x	Ch/2x	W/2x	W/2x
1959	Ch/2x	Ch/2x	Ch/2x	Ch/2x	W/2x	W/2x
1963			Ch/3x	Ch/3x	Ch/3x	Ch/3x
1964			Ch/4x	Ch/4x		

Appendix Table 2.4 Senior Secondary

	I.i	I.ii	II.i	II.ii	III.i	III.ii
1950	Ch/3x	Ch/3x	Ch/3x	Ch/3x	W/3x	W/3x
1953	W/M-C/3x	W/M-C/3x	W/M-C/3x	Ch/M-C/3x	Ch/M-C/3x	Ch/M-C/3x
1954	W/M-C/3x	W/M-C/3x	W/M-C/3x	Ch/M-C/3x	Ch/M-C/3x	Ch/M-C/3x
1955	W/M-C/3x	W/M-C/3x	W/M-C/3x	Ch/M-C/3x	Ch/M-C/3x	Ch/M-C/3x
1956	W/M-C/3x	W/M-C/3x	Ch/A/3x	Ch/A/3x	Ch/M-C/3x	Ch/M-C/3x
1958	W/M-C/2x	W/M-C/2x	Ch/A/2x	Ch/A/2x	Ch/M-C/2x	Ch/M-C/2x
1959	W/M-C/2x	W/M-C/2x	Ch/A/2x	Ch/A/2x	Ch/M-C/2x	Ch/M-C/2x
1963					W/3x	W/3x
1964					W/3x	W/3x

1978–2001

Appendix Table 2.5 Junior Secondary

	I.i	I.ii	II.i	II.ii	III.i	III.ii
1978			Ch/A/2x	Ch/A-M/2x	Ch/M-C/2x	Ch/C/2x
1980			Ch/A/2x	Ch/A/2x	Ch/M/2x	Ch/C/2x
1981	Ch/A/3x	Ch/A-M/3x	Ch/M-C/2x	Ch/C/2x		
1986	Ch/A/3x	Ch/A-M/3x	Ch/C/2x	W/A-C/2x		
1988*#	Ch/A/2x	Ch/A/2x	Ch/M/2x	Ch/C/2x	W/A-M/2x	W/M-C/2x
1990	Ch/A/3x	Ch/A-M/3x	Ch/C/2x	W/A/2x		
1992	Ch/A/2x	Ch/A/2x	Ch/M/3x	Ch/C/3x	W/A-M/2x	W/M-C/2x
1994	Ch/A/2x	Ch/A/2x	Ch/M/2x	Ch/C/2x	W/A-M/2x	W/M-C/2x
2000	Ch/A/2x	Ch/A/2x	Ch/M/2x	Ch/C/2x	W/A-M/2x	W/M-C/2x
2001#	Ch/A/2x	Ch/A/2x	Ch/M/2x	Ch/C/2x	W/A-M/2x	W/M-C/2x

* Class hours listed here are for the more common 6-3 (6-year primary, 3-year junior secondary) system. Where the trial Outline was tested in 5-4 system schools, however, history was taught in junior years I, II and IV, with 3 hours per week in the second year. When the 1988 draft was promulgated nationwide as the 1992 Outline, it allotted equal hours to both systems and moved history from year IV to year III in the 5-4 system.

Trial version of Outline.

Appendix Table 2.6 Senior secondary compulsory (*bixiu*) classes

	I.i	I.ii	II.i	II.ii
1978	W/A-M/2x	W/M-C/2x		
1980	W/A-M/2x	W/M-C/2x		
1986	W/A-M/3x	W/M-C/3x		
1990	Ch/M-C/2x	W/A/2x	W/M/2x	W/M-C/2x
1996	Ch/M/3x	Ch/C/3x	W/M/2x	W/M-C/2x
2000	Ch/M/3x	Ch/C/3x		

3
Identity Issues in Taiwan's History Curriculum

MEI-HUI LIU, LI-CHING HUNG, AND EDWARD VICKERS

As was noted in the introduction to this volume, the school curriculum is commonly seen as a tool whereby dominant social groups transmit their own sets of values and effectively impose these values on the rest of society. Many scholars have argued that the ways societies choose, classify, deliver, and evaluate knowledge reflect patterns of power allocation and social control (Althusser 1972; Bernstein 1977; Giroux 1981). However, neo-Marxist or postmodernist views of the state often overlook the possibility that in certain circumstances school curriculum may function as an instrument of liberation rather than of simply as on control or domination. In Taiwan, in the period since the late 1980s, the state has shifted from an authoritarian model to a far more democratic are, and this has been reflected in changes to the school curriculum. These have involved attempts to move away from the overt indoctrination that characterized the curriculum under the Kuomintang (KMT) toward an increasing emphasis on fostering critical thinking skills and active citizenship. However, underlying this change has been the shift from official promotion of a monolithic vision of Chineseness to an increasing recognition of a distinct Taiwanese identity; a recognition that in turn has both reflected and facilitated the transformation of Taiwanese society and culture during this period.

The principle feature of this transformation has been the emergence of an increasingly assertive Taiwanese consciousness — a celebration of Taiwan as a cultural, social, and political entity distinct from China. This has not necessarily involved a denial of Taiwan's cultural Chineseness, but it has witnessed an increasing dissociation on the part of many Taiwanese between their cultural identity as *huaren* and their more immediate political identification with the Taiwanese (or Republic of China [ROC]) state. In other words, many Taiwanese today do not identify with the Chinese state in the political sphere, but they identify with their ancestors' homeland in the cultural sphere. The evolution of Taiwanese and Chinese identities on Taiwan over the past century has been a complex and fraught process, as the island has undergone first invasion and colonization by the Japanese, then forcible reunification under the KMT (Nationalist Party), and finally over 50 years of isolation from the Chinese mainland (Huang 2000). During the period of Japanese colonial rule, the sense of distinctive Taiwaneseness was relatively weak, since resistance to attempts to promote Japanese language and culture on the island tended to manifest itself in expressions of Chinese identity (Ching 2001). The formative period for the emergence of Taiwanese consciousness was the period of KMT military rule, from Taiwan's retrocession to the Republic of China in 1945 to the end of martial law in 1987. It was the experience of political and cultural repression under the KMT regime, dominated by mainlanders (*waishengren*) who fled to the island after the losing the Civil War with the Communists, that prompted many native Taiwanese (*benshengren*) to reject the chauvinist, homogenizing vision of Chineseness propounded by the KMT and develop instead their own more pluralist vision embodying a strong sense of Taiwan's cultural, historical, and political separateness from the rest of China. In the years since the lifting of martial law in 1987, *benshengren* have played an increasingly prominent role in the political and cultural life of the island as Taiwan has shifted from authoritarian uniformity toward greater democracy, openness, and pluralism. This process has been viewed with outrage and trepidation both by die-hard traditionalists within the KMT and by the Communist regime on the main-land, whose repeated threats directed at Taiwan separatists have arguably only strengthened the alienation of many Taiwanese from their "one China" vision (Huang 2000).

The strengthening of Taiwanese consciousness has been reflected in school curricula, especially in the curriculum for history. Before the 1980s, the cur-riculum was overwhelmingly China-centered, and Taiwan hardly figured in teaching materials for schools. During the 1980s, however, the six southern counties governed by the (proindependence) Democratic Progressive Party (DPP) began to support efforts to use the Taiwanese dialect in schools (the KMT had banned this, requiring the use of Mandarin in all public contexts). This largely grassroots educational movement later influenced the moves made during the 1990s by the central government, under the *benshengren* president Lee Teng-hui, to develop Taiwanese history and culture as independent sub-jects for primary and junior high schools. The most notable initiative of this period was the development of the *Renshi Taiwan* (Knowing Taiwan) course. This course is discussed in detail in Chapter 4, which focuses on the mecha-nisms of the reform, its political and symbolic significance, and the nature of the Taiwanese nationalism it expressed.

The purpose of this chapter is to explore how Taiwan's official school history curriculum has dealt with the issue of political and cultural identity during the postwar period, with a particular focus on developments since about 1980 (curricular changes before the 1980s were generally minimal). The authors have analyzed curriculum standards and the textbooks for elementary and junior high schools, focusing primarily on the levels at which history is a compulsory subject. At the elementary level, it is integrated into social studies (*shehui xue*), and the analysis thus focuses on the history units in the social studies textbooks based on the 1975 and 1993 curriculum standards. At the junior high school level, history is a separate subject, and the analysis of the curriculum at this level is based on the 1983 and 1994 editions of the history curriculum standards and the relevant textbooks. Under the Nine-Year Integrated Curriculum implemented in 2001, history is combined with social studies for grades 1 through 9. Since the textbooks for this latest curriculum are still being drafted at the time of writing, only the curriculum guidelines for social studies could be analyzed. However, the author include some discussion of the most recent (2002–2004) controversy over history education in Taiwan, which relates to plans to revise the curriculum for senior high schools.

Tension and Transition: The Historical and Political Context of Taiwanese Identities

From Japanese Colony to Anticommunist Base

Taiwan did not become a full province of China until 1887, by which time three major ethnic groups inhabited the island. The island's indigenous inhabitants were not Han Chinese, but Malayo-Polynesian tribes whose languages belonged to the Austronesian family. These aborigines had had Taiwan more or less to themselves until Han settlers, consisting of two distinct groups from Fujian and Guangdong provinces, migrated there from the seventeenth century onwards, initially with the active encouragement of the Dutch East India Company, which governed much of southern Taiwan between the 1620s and the 1660s. The settlers from Fujian (variously referred to as "*Minnanren*" or "*Hoklo*") were speakers of local variants of the *Minnan* or *Hokkien* dialect, whereas the immigrants from Guangdong generally belonged to a distinct Chinese ethnic group known as the *Hakka*. The forces of the Ming loyalist Zheng Cheng-gong (Koxinga) displaced the Dutch in the mid-seventeenth century, and it was not until 1683 that the authority of the Manchu imperial government was established on the island. From then until 1887, this island frontier of the Qing Empire was governed as a dependency of Fujian Province.

In 1895, China lost control of Taiwan after the Japanese victory in the Sino-Japanese War. The island remained a Japanese colony for 50 years and was subjected to a thoroughgoing process of Japanification; Japanese became the sole language of instruction in schools, and education aimed to socialize Taiwanese as Japanese subjects. Following Japan's defeat in 1945, China's KMT government under Chiang Kai-shek took over Taiwan and sent administrators to govern the island. The Chinese soldiers and officials were initially welcomed enthusiastically by the island's inhabitants, many of whom had harbored a sentimental attachment to the motherland from which they had been forcibly estranged during the decades of Japanese rule. However, due to a combination of poor economic policies, cultural differences, and a series of incidents involving maltreatment of local Taiwanese by KMT soldiers or officials, tensions between the authorities and the local population mounted, culminating in demonstrations on February 28, 1947, that were bloodily suppressed. In the ensuing period of repression, thousands of Taiwanese were killed, sowing the seeds of an enduring resentment on the part of many *benshengren* against their *waishengren* overlords. (For an overview of Taiwan's modern and contemporary history, see Rubinstein [1999] or Roy [2003].)

By late 1949, the Communists had won China's Civil War and gained control of most of the Chinese mainland, so the KMT regime withdrew to Taiwan, bringing with it nearly 2 million refugees, including government officials and military personnel. In order to bolster its authority and legitimacy, the KMT constructed a political system designed to reinforce Taiwan's status as simply a province of the ROC and to foster Chinese consciousness among the local population (Huang 1987; Hughes, 1997). The KMT emphasised that the ROC was the only legitimate government representing the whole of China. It claimed that moving to Taiwan was a temporary expedient and that the recovery of the lost territory on the Chinese mainland was the mission of all patriotic citizens — thus Taiwan was officially referred to as the *fuxing jidi*, or the "base for recovery [of the mainland]." Martial law was maintained for four decades, contact with the Chinese mainland was forbidden, and a system of military conscription was instituted that served the dual function of socialising Taiwanese youths as loyal defenders of the ROC regime and strengthening the island's defenses against the forces of the Communist People's Republic of China (PRC), which aspired to liberate Taiwan. Meanwhile, until the early 1970s, many of the world's most powerful nations recognized Taipei, rather than Beijing, as the legitimate government of China. The ROC maintained control of the Chinese seat on the United Nations Security Council, and this global recognition helped the KMT consolidate its authority in Taiwan and foster a sense of Chinese national identity among Taiwanese.

The KMT shared with their Communist rivals across the Taiwan Strait a homogenous and totalising vision of One China, embodying the very simple premises that: (1) Taiwanese are Chinese (2) Taiwan is a part of China (3) the government of the ROC on Taiwan has to maintain a political system that can represent the whole of China. This official discourse reflected a highly conservative interpretation of China's 5,000-year-old history and culture, which was seen as constituting the defining inheritance for Chinese on Taiwan just as for their compatriots on the mainland. The KMT withdrawal from the mainland was regarded as a national crisis, and the Chinese Communists were portrayed as traitorous rebels who were destroying Chinese tradition and culture. Therefore, the revival of culture and the maintenance of the nation's life were portrayed as the special mission of Taiwan's Chinese population. Mainland Chinese culture (or mainstream culture as defined by the KMT) was officially promoted and the cultures of Taiwan's different ethnic groups, whether Han or aboriginal, were either suppressed or officially ignored. Nothing better symbolized the KMT's vision of Chinese culture, and Taiwan's role in its preservation, than the collection of imperial treasures housed in the massive National Palace Museum just outside Taipei — treasures rescued by the Nationalists from the barbarian philistinism of the Communists on the mainland and stored and displayed in a templelike edifice for the edification of Chinese generations to come.[1]

Democratization and the Rise of "Taiwanese" Consciousness

As a result of the Sino-Soviet split and the subsequent rapprochement between the Americans and the Communist regime in China, the ROC was forced to withdraw from the United Nations in 1971, and its claim to constitute the legitimate government of China was thus considerably weakened. The United States formalized its diplomatic relations with the PRC in 1979. The deterioration of the ROC's diplomatic situation threatened to undermine the KMT's unequivocal stance on the Chineseness of Taiwan and was one factor in persuading the regime, still dominated by aging mainlanders, to look for ways of broadening its political base on the island.

The 1970s have been seen as the turning point for the rise in Taiwanese consciousness (Wang 1989), although Friedman (2004) argues that the key episode in this respect was the Meilidao incident and the subsequent KMT repression in 1980 and 1981. This, he claims, marked the definitive break between an earlier pattern of largely loyalist opposition and the emergence of an increasingly independence-oriented search for a Taiwanese consciousness. Between the death of Chiang Kai-shek in 1975 and the lifting of martial law in 1987, Taiwan moved fitfully from repressive authoritarianism toward growing democratization. Chiang Ching-kuo (Chiang Kai-shek's son and successor) initiated the process of Taiwanizing the KMT by sharing power with the Taiwanese because he recognized that Taiwan "could be torn apart by long suppressed ethnic tension" (Rubinstein 1999). In addition to sharing power with local Taiwanese, the government modified its political system by institutionalizing and legalizing opposition parties and introduced popular elections at the local and national levels. The DPP, which was mainly (though not exclusively) composed of *bensheng* Taiwanese activists, was established in 1986. Its political platform consisted essentially of two planks: democratization and Taiwanese independence. On Chiang Ching-kuo's death in 1988, Lee Teng-hui succeeded him, becoming Taiwan's first native-born president. With Lee's accession, the mainlanders gradually lost their dominance of the KMT.

The rapid rise of Taiwanese consciousness throughout the 1980s and 1990s was a cultural as much as a political pheomenon. In literature, writers such as Zhang Xi-guo had begun as early as the 1970s to write novels depicting the increasingly affluent and Westernized lifestyle of young Taipei urbanites; however, from the mid-1980s onwards, a new generation of novelists published works that, through historical fiction or allegory, sought more explicitly to address themes related to Taiwanese identity. One of these was *The Tale of Mt. Taimu* by Li Qiao, published in 1984, which depicts a writer (modeled on the writer Lu Heruo) on the run in the aftermath of the February 28, 1947, massacres, also called the "228 Incident." (though the historical references are discreet and unobtrusive; Yee 2001). Although ultimately the hero perishes from a snakebite, aborigines from the Atayal tribe save him from capture by the KMT — a storyline that, as Margaret Hillebrand has noted,[2] presages more recent discourses that have emphasized the unity of Taiwan's ethnic groups. The story also draws parallels between the KMT takeover and the Japanese invasion 50 years earlier. Several years later, the filmmaker Hou Hsiao-Hsien famously took the 228 Incident as the subject matter for his prize-winning 1989 film *City of Sadness* (*Beiqing Chengshi*).

The events of the 228 Incident have been central to the mythology of the emerging proindependence Green camp since the 1980s,[3] when many figures associated with the DPP campaigned to force the KMT regime to publicly acknowledge the events of 1947 and to apologize to the victims (an apology was eventually made by President Lee Teng-hui in the mid-1990s). This incident can perhaps be seen as playing a role in the formation of a distinctive Taiwanese consciousness similar to that played by the local post-Tiananmen protests in the emergence of a distinctive and politicized sense of Hongkongese identity, although Hong Kong's protests were at the same time very self-consciously an expression of (outraged) *Chinese* patriotism. In both cases, concerns over the public representation (or lack of it) of these events in school textbooks, museums, and official discourse more broadly have come to symbolize for local democrats the illiberalism of the existing regime. Moreover, the success of Taiwan's Greens in securing recognition of the 228 Incident in official historiography contrasts tellingly with the Hong Kong (and Beijing) authorities' continuing refusal to countenance comprehensive and balanced coverage of the events of 1989 in school textbooks or museums. In 1996, Chen Shui-bian, then the DPP mayor of Taipei, opened a new museum in the center of the city devoted entirely to the 228 Incident. At the time, the museum project was the target of vituperative protests from die-hard conservatives within the KMT. However, Ma Ying-jeou, Chen's KMT successor as Taipei Mayor, tacitly endorsed the museum — an indication, perhaps, that at least for younger Taiwanese (*waishengren* as well as *benshengren*) the 228 Incident is beginning to be perceived as part of a common narrative of the national past, rather than simply as a source of rancor and division between Greens and Blues.

Nevertheless, attempts to give greater prominence to Taiwan's own history, let alone controversial episodes like the 228 Incident, continue to be greeted with outrage by a number of KMT traditionalists. For some of the dwindling but still influential band of mainlanders and conservatives that dominate both the KMT leadership and certain quarters of the academic establishment, the sudden rise of Taiwanese consciousness since the 1980s, the moves toward nativization under Li Teng-hui in the 1990s, and the attempts by the Green camp to further promote this process since capturing the presidency in 2000 have appeared "absurd and threatening" (Friedman 2004). The more die-hard traditionalists tend to subscribe to the kind of neoreligious, didactomoralistic, state-centered approach to Chinese historiography championed by Qian Mu, the founder of New Asia College in Hong Kong, and the Confucianist "ultras" associated with him (some of whom were responsible for the initial development of the Chinese history curriculum for Hong Kong's schools [see Chapter 5]). For such figures, Taiwan, like Hong Kong, has been seen as an uncultured frontier, an irrelevant backwater, important or useful only because it has served as a temporary refuge for the exiled bearers of the sacred flame of Chinese civilization. The dominance such conservatives have enjoyed over the Academia Sinica, Taiwan's premier center for research in the humanities, partly explains why the Centre for Taiwan History has for years remained only at a preparatory stage.

One instance of the kind of near-hysterical reaction that challenges to the One China orthodoxy arouse among conservatives was the response in the late 1990s to the *Renshi Taiwan* course for junior secondary schools, discussed in Chapter 4. More recently, the cultural policy pursued by the administration of Chen Shui-bian has provoked similar outrage. For example, ministers such as Wu Mi-cha (Deputy Minister for Culture) and Tu Cheng-sheng (earlier one of the leading lights of the *Renshi Taiwan* project) have sought to promote a vision of Taiwan's history that emphasizes its Asian and multicultural heritage, rather than focusing simply on its Chineseness. As head of the National Palace Museum from 2000 to 2004 (when he was made Education Minister), Tu developed a strategy for repositioning this quintessentially Chinese institution, involving plans to construct a new branch museum in southern Taiwan that would showcase the Asian treasures in the museum's collection. Meanwhile, the Education and Culture Ministries, as well as a number of county governments, have lavishly funded the construction of new museums devoted to aspects of Taiwan's history and prehistory.[4]

The celebration of the cultures and heritage of Taiwan's aboriginal peoples has been a prominent theme in discourses of Taiwaneseness; however, in museums (as in school textbooks), discussion of aborigines has noticeably tended to be confined to prehistory, archaeology, anthropology, culture, and customs. The history of the aborigines in the period following Han settlement, and the story of their conflicts with Chinese immigrants, is generally given little, if any, attention, even in a museum such as that at Shi San Hang (near Tanshui, northwest of Taipei) that is devoted entirely to remains left by plains aborigines who were subsequently wiped out or assimilated by the Chinese. The implicit aim of such displays seems to be to emphasize the aspects of Taiwan's heritage that distinguish it most starkly from the Chinese mainland, while at the same time leaving the impression that the history of relations between the island's different ethnic groups has been one of peaceful and harmonious coexistence. Nevertheless, the increased attention devoted to aboriginal history and culture, however much it has been manipulated for political purposes, does reflect a sense in Taiwanese society at large of a need to right past wrongs — perhaps comparable to the sense evident in recent North American or Australian attitudes toward indigenous populations. President Chen's much-derided decision to rename the street outside the presidential palace in Taipei after an aboriginal tribe matches similar symbolic gestures made in Australia and Canada and contrasts favorably with what Friedman has called the "contemptuous museumification" of minorities in the PRC (Friedman 2004).

Harmony was famously little in evidence during the demonstrations that followed President Chen's narrow election victory in 2004, but the ferocity of the KMT reaction disguised the actual closeness of the policy platforms on the basis of which the KMT and DPP had fought. Voters were divided principally over their perceptions of Chen's administrative competence and the wisdom of his more provocative stance vis-à-vis the mainland. Following the election, the hysteria of the core group of protestors, who were predominantly middle-aged *waishengren*, appears to have alienated most voters and alarmed younger KMT moderates such as Ma Ying-jeou (who studiously distanced himself from the protests). Many in the Blue camp have perceived phenomena such as the trend toward Taiwanese nativism and the promotion of *Taiyu* (the language spoken by most *benshengren*) as racist, with some KMT figures during and after the election campaign even comparing President Chen to Hitler or Ben Ladin. However, such intemperate accusations do not seem to resonate with the majority of Taiwanese, whether from mainland or native backgrounds. (For further analysis of the mentality of Taiwan's Blues, see Corcuff 2004.)

According to a recent investigation, most people in Taiwan have a sense of dual identity or mixed identity, describing themselves as "both Chinese and Taiwanese." The dual identity is expressed in two different ways. Some people perceive themselves as Chinese in the cultural domain and as Taiwanese in the political domain. Some accept that Taiwan is geographically part of China but nonetheless possess a strong sense of a distinctive Taiwaneseness (Chiang 1998). For many, (perhaps most) Taiwanese, identity is still primarily defined in ethno-cultural terms, as witnessed by the fashion among many families in recent years to trace their often highly tenuous or dubious aboriginal roots. Some of those who take a Taiwanese nativist position seek to establish it on a monolithic ethno-cultural basis that to some extent mirrors (just as it rejects) the "Great Han Chauvinism" characteristic of mainstream Chinese nationalism.

However, some scholars have also detected a growing sense of civic nationalism in some quarters, whereby Taiwaneseness is defined not primarily in essentialist, ethno-cultural, or even linguistic terms, but more broadly and inclusively as a sense of belonging to Taiwan.

Official Historiography, Schooling, and Taiwan's Political Transition

The Republic of China on Taiwan maintained a highly centralized system of curriculum development and textbook production from the 1940s until the late 1990s, when central control was loosened somewhat. The Ministry of Education (MOE) has controlled the national curriculum for elementary and secondary schools through its appointed Curriculum Reference Revision Committee, which is composed of university professors, school teachers, and educational administrators. The official curriculum prescribes the goals, time allocation, scope, sequence, and implementation guidelines for each subject. Until the late 1990s, the National Institute for Compilation and Translation (NICT; *Guoli Bianyi Guan*) had the job of preparing textbooks and teaching materials based on these curriculum references. Since 1998, however, the MOE has opened up the textbook market to competition among private publishing companies, and the NICT has lost its role as a textbook compiler and publisher. Under the new law, all competing textbooks are field tested and scrutinized before they are adopted.

Corresponding to the phases of political transition, three periods in social studies education in Taiwan can be distinguished: those of "traditional social studies education" (1950–1980), "new social studies education" (1980–2000), and "nine-year integrated social studies" (2001–present). In the first period, education was part of the overall KMT strategy of fierce opposition to the PRC and promotion of a vehemently anticommunist outlook. The school curriculum, and especially that for social studies, indoctrinated students into a belief that the adherence of Chinese leaders to communist ideas had led to desperate living conditions for people in mainland China. Sun Yat-sen's Three Principles of the People were used to provide the ideological underpinning for opposition to Communism and were a required subject at high school and university level. The question of how to develop a strong sense of national identity was seen as another crucial issue at this time. The KMT aimed to reinforce its authority and legitimacy in Taiwan and, through the school curriculum, taught students that loyalty and devotion to the ROC as a nation was the primary duty of all citizens.

One of the strategies for building national identity was to cultivate students' appreciation of Chinese culture and their understanding of the antecedents of the ROC. The medium through which the curriculum was delivered was itself part of the nationalist message, since schools were required to operate exclusively in the official lingua franca, Mandarin Chinese — a language spoken at home only by the *waishengren* immigrants, and not by *benshengren* Taiwanese.

In school textbooks, Taiwan was treated merely as one of the provinces of China, and china was the principal focus of history and geography, with coverage of Taiwan taking up only a very small proportion of the social studies curriculum. The traditional social studies curriculum focused on the inculcation of an uncritical, state-centered patriotism and a specific set of values associated with the official version of traditional Chinese culture.

The nature of the history taught in schools was fairly uniform across the different levels, so that students studied more or less the same chronological narrative at both junior and senior levels, only in greater detail the second time around. In this respect, the approach was identical to that adopted on the Communist mainland and for the Chinese history subject in Hong Kong. Just as there was no space for coverage of Hong Kong's own history in the state-centered narrative that formed the core of the Chinese history course there, so in Taiwan local history was ignored — but not entirely. The only period during which Taiwan figured in the historical narrative was in the very last section of the books on Chinese history (after the completion of which, students went on to study the books on world history). This section was entitled "The Achievements and Development of the Base for Recovery" (*fuxing jidi de chengjiu yu zhanwang*). Until the 1990s, this was also the only section of the history textbooks that underwent significant revision from one edition to the next, since it had to be updated to cover the most recent achievements of the ROC state. This section focused on the triumphs of the ROC regime in constructing Taiwan's infrastructure; building schools, universities, and hospitals; promoting economic development; and generally improving the quality of life for Chinese citizens on Taiwan. Awkward episodes such as the 228 Incident were not mentioned.

The second period of curricular development in postwar Taiwan can be said to have begun after the 1987 lifting of martial law, though change was at first very slow and incremental. The Three Principles of the People became an optional course and the emphasis on anticommunist ideology diminished. The purpose of social studies education was gradually adjusted, bringing it more into line with what has been termed the "social sciences tradition" (Barr, Barth, and Shermis 1977). The purpose of social studies defined as social science was that young people should acquire the knowledge and skills associated with particular social science disciplines so that they became informed and effective as citizens. This approach was intended to help students learn how social scientists gather and analyze knowledge, so that they would acquire skills that would enable them to participate more fully and actively in the community. However, as was the case with social studies in Hong Kong, the degree to which the various disciplines were actually integrated within the textbooks, let alone in classroom practice, was limited. The approach to history remained highly didactic, conventional, and chronological.

Two major changes were made to the social studies curriculum during the 1990s. First, a new subject, *Renshi Taiwan* (Knowing Taiwan), was created for grade 7. This move marked a highly significant break with the unremittingly China-centered perspective that had pervaded the entire school curriculum throughout the postwar era. The themes of Knowing Taiwan include: people and language, family and relatives, festivals and customs, historical sites and cultural crafts, education, economics, politics, leisure, religions, and social issues. The emphasis here is clearly more on relatively harmless social and cultural themes than on more contentious political issues, but the new subject was nonetheless fiercely criticized by conservatives for supporting Taiwan independence. The case of Knowing Taiwan illustrates how curriculum developers in the Lee Teng-hui era attempted to navigate a middle course between proponents of outright independence, on the one hand, and die-hard KMT supporters of reunification on the other. (See chapter 4 for a full discussion of this subject.)

Second, a new subject called Native Place Teaching Activities (NPTA; *xiangtu jiaoxue*), focusing on the study of students' local living environments, was created for grades 3 to 6. Each county was encouraged to edit and publish its own textbooks for NPTA. Although Knowing Taiwan and NPTA were symbols of Taiwanese consciousness raising, the textbooks were still ambivalent regarding the question of national identity. They avoided using the term "Taiwanese people" (*Taiwanren*), instead preferring the form "the people of Taiwan" (*Taiwan renmin*). Similar ambivalence surrounds the issue of how Taiwan should be described — as the Republic of China, the Republic of China on Taiwan, or Taiwan? Should it be considered an independent country or a province of China? Should the people term themselves Taiwanese or Chinese? Discussion of national identity in curricula and textbooks remains ambiguous because these basic questions cannot be directly addressed. Meanwhile, NPTA and related government initiatives, such as the program to establish local museums in each county, aim to reinforce a sense of local belonging and pride in Taiwanese culture and heritage while avoiding outright or explicit denial of Taiwan's Chineseness.

Since the late 1980s and early 1990s, the increasing openness and vibrancy of Taiwan's civil society has been reflected by growing public interest in education. This is evident in the number of education-related pressure groups that have sprung up during this period. Most of these groups want Taiwan's education system to become more "decentralized, flexible, diversified, autonomous, and depoliticized" (Murphy and Liu 1998); depoliticization in this context generally refers to ridding the curriculum of the political indoctrination and the monolithic and totalizing vision of Chineseness, that pervaded schooling during the martial law era. The effectiveness of such lobbying can be seen in the wide range of reform policies issued by the MOE since the mid-1990s (Ministry of Education 1995) and the Council on Education Reform established by the Executive Yuan (Council on Education Reform 1996).

One of the most significant large-scale educational reforms has been the Nine-Year Integrated Curriculum Plan for Elementary and Junior High Schools,[5] which began to be implemented in the 2001 school year. This curriculum plan is widely regarded as a turning point for curriculum decentralization because it involves the replacement of the previous curriculum standards by nonprescriptive curriculum guidelines, while the centralized and prescriptive national curriculum will be replaced by school-based curricula. Other major changes include:

- Designing the curriculum framework from grades 1 through 9, rather than separating the elementary level from the junior high school level.
- Replacing the separate subjects approach with an interdisciplinary approach, targeting seven major subject areas (languages, math, social studies, nature and technology, arts and humanities, health and physical education, and general activities).
- Concentrating on ten basic learning capabilities or skills (such as critical thinking and, information processing) rather than knowledge content.
- Shortening the school year from 260 to 200 days and from 6 to 5 days a week.

The new curriculum guidelines attempt to reduce the number of school subjects by integrating subjects of a similar nature. For example, geography, history, and civics are to be integrated as social studies at junior high school level in order to ensure more continuity with social studies at the elementary level. In addition, the guidelines state that the organization of the history curriculum will be more issues-centered and that history will be more connected with other social science disciplines. "Authentic instruction,"[6] aiming to develop students' higher-order thinking and research abilities, is also advocated.

This shake-up appears to raise the prospect of radical reform to the curriculum for history and other humanities subjects, and one clearly aimed at bringing teaching more into line with the changes in Taiwanese society and politics over recent years. In general, the capacity of sweeping, centrally imposed reforms to effect real change at classroom level needs to be viewed with skepticism, given that new curricula will inevitably be implemented, by and large, by the same teachers who implemented their predecessors; but, in the case of Taiwan, it must be borne in mind that many teachers taught to the old KMT textbooks not out of any great belief in the narrative these books related, but because they had no choice. More to the point, the curriculum for senior secondary level remains highly prescriptive and examination-driven, and this looks unlikely to change unless the *liankao* examinations for university entrance are radically reformed. Meanwhile, as elsewhere in East Asia, the washback effect of high-stakes examinations at more senior levels may create pressures on teachers and textbooks at junior levels to adopt the content focus, and the more conventional style of pedagogy, that is seen as likely to maximize examination results later on. Analysis of implementation must be left to future studies, but the likely persistence of many old attitudes and values "at the chalkface" should be borne in mind when considering the discussion below of changes to official curricula.

History in the School Curriculum before and since the 1990s

The following analysis of the portrayal of history in Taiwan's school curriculum focuses on curriculum goals, curriculum organization, and the coverage of particular topics in textbooks. Since space does not allow for a comprehensive analysis here of all history-related subjects, we focus first on the syllabi for social studies (which give a broad overview of the range and nature of historical coverage at the compulsory stage), before looking in more detail at the treatment in various textbooks of specific topics related to the issue of identity. Since curriculum development and textbook production were both, until very recently, functions of the central government in Taiwan, the correspondence between official curricular guidelines and textbook content during most of the period discussed was much closer than is often the case in more decentralized systems.

Curriculum Goals

The syllabi for elementary and junior high level before 1990 are summarized in table 3.1. The 1975 social studies syllabus for elementary schools evinced a strong ideology of social control. Each goal began with the term "to guide," implying an authority leading students toward a rigid and predetermined set of values, and ended with a nationalistic term, such as "national spirit," "loving the nation," or "constructing the nation." These goals reflected the KMT ideology of patriarchal authoritarianism, patriotism, and nationalism.

These syllabi were imbued with a strong sense of a monolithic and homogenizing Chinese identity. For example, Goal 2, "cultivating the attitudes of loving the nation through understanding Chinese culture," stressed that the ROC was the political and cultural embodiment of the whole of China and that Taiwan was a part of China. The assumption here was that the best strategy for building national identity was to cultivate students' appreciation of Chinese culture (understood as a singular, timeless, and undifferentiated entity) and their understanding of the antecedents of the ROC. The history component of the syllabus stressed the importance of nurturing students' good conduct through the study of historical figures as moral exemplars, an approach shared by the Chinese history subject in Hong Kong (and reflecting the influence of Confucianist traditionalists such as Qian Mu on curriculum developers on both sides of the Taiwan Strait). One of the subgoals of the Taiwanese syllabus, "to guide students to respect Dr. Sun Yat-sen's and Chiang Kai-shek's contribution to the national revolution," aimed at fostering what was tantamount to leader-worship. This was a reflection of the official hagiography surrounding

Table 3.1 Goals of the Social Studies Curriculum

Version	Goals
1975 Elementary school	**Major Goals** To guide students to experience interpersonal relationships through their schools, families, and community life in order to develop the abilities and attitudes needed to adjust to and serve society, to practice national ethics, and to enhance the national spirit. To guide students to understand the relationship between Chinese culture and modern society through the process of historical evolution in order to cultivate love for the nation and a willingness to contribute to building the community and the nation. To guide students to understand the relationship between the environment and daily life, in the context of both the local and national environment, in order to develop a love for the locality, a consciousness of the need to improve the environment, and a willingness to construct the nation. To guide students to comprehend world trends and the development of modern culture, especially in its contributions to human dignity, social improvement, and revolution, through the progress of ethics, democracy, and science. **Subgoals for grades 3 and 4** To guide students to understand Taiwan's history and the great men who have made contributions to the development of Taiwan. To guide students to understand the development of political, material, social, ethical, and psychological construction and enhance their willingness to contribute to local construction. To guide students to understand the importance of Taiwan as a base for the recovery of mainland China. **Subgoals for grades 5 and 6** To guide students to understand the history of China's revolution and of ethnic immigration in order to enhance their sense of self-respect. To guide students to understand the superior national attributes of the Chinese, such as wisdom, competence, and morality in order to build national confidence. To guide students to understand and glorify Chinese tradition and. culture. To guide students to understand China's achievements in the fields of technology, invention, and institutional development during the dynastic period. To guide students to understand modern world trends and the relationship between China and the West.

Version	Goals
	To guide students to respect Dr. Sun Yat-sen's and Chiang Kai-shek's contributions to national revolution. To guide students to know the brutalities of the Communists and the opposition between liberalism and totalitarianism.
1983 Junior High School	To understand the evolution of China and the change of its territory in different dynasties. To understand the political, economic, social, and cultural development of our nation, and to enhance patriotism, love for the nation, and a spirit of cooperation. To understand our nation's traditions, people's status, and responsibility through the study of the history and culture of our nation.
1993	To develop a proper conception of the individual self, of the harmonious relationship between individuals and the group, and to cultivate good habits in order to develop a wholesome personality. To guide students to understand the living environment, and the nation's history, geography, and culture in order to nourish their affection and love of homeland, society, and nation. To guide students to understand the development of the world, and to broaden their horizons and their minds in order to promote the universal ideals of equality, reciprocity, and cooperation. To develop students' abilities in the spheres of critical thinking, value judgment, and problem-solving in order to prepare them for participation in a democratic society.
2000	To understand the environment, humanity, diversity, and the problems of the locality and other communities. To comprehend the interaction of people, society, culture, and ecology and the significance of environmental protection and resource exploitation. To impart a basic knowledge of the social sciences. To develop local and national identity and an attitude of concerned citizenship embracing a global perspective. To nurture democratic literacy, law-abiding concepts, and responsible attitudes. To nurture self-understanding and self-realization, along with positive, self-confident, and open attitudes. To develop abilities in the spheres of critical thinking, value judgment, and problem solving. To develop abilities and aptitudes related to social participation, decision-making, and the practical sphere. To develop the abilities of self-expression, communication, and cooperation. To develop an interest and ability to investigate, create, and process information.

Table 3.1 (Continued)

the figures of Sun and, to a lesser extent, Chiang more generally in Taiwan throughout the postwar period (and into the 1990s).

In the 1975 syllabus, Taiwan was marginalized and treated simply as a minor locality. One of the goals indicated how Taiwan's role was then still regarded by the KMT authorities: "To guide students to understand the importance of Taiwan as a base for the recovery of mainland China" (*fuxing jidi*). The curriculum standards stressed that it was every citizen's duty to obey the laws and the government and to serve society as a whole. Politics were a very sensitive matter in these years and, as also in Hong Kong during this period teachers were discouraged from discussing political matters or controversial issues with students. Discussion of Taiwanese independence was completely taboo during this period.

In the 1983 syllabus for junior high schools, the first goal called for the "cultivating of [Chinese] national consciousness." The goals relating to history stressed "understanding the development of the Chinese nation and the changes of its territory" and "understanding the national spirit through the study of our nation's long history and brilliant culture." The focus of political-cultural identity thus remained the Chinese motherland rather than Taiwan itself.

Compared to the 1975 syllabus, the 1993 social studies syllabus, a document of the Lee Teng-hui era, put far less emphasis on indoctrination and nationalism. Concepts or sentiments related to nationalism such as national spirit, loving the nation, constructing the nation, leader worship, anticommunism, and the recovery of China were omitted or downplayed. The focus of identity had shifted from a purely China-centered vision to a multidimensional one, encompassing the local community, society, and the nation. At the same time, the focus of the syllabus drafters appeared to have shifted from a nation-building agenda to a more student-centered approach concerned with fostering thinking skills and encouraging discussion and debate. In other words, the concern was now more with answering the question "What kinds of skills or capabilities do students need?" rather than simply "What kind of students does the nation need?" As Corcuff discusses in chapter 4, similar concerns and aspirations also animated many of those responsible for developing the *Renshi Taiwan* course for junior high schools in the mid to late 1990s — though at the same time nation-building aims remained high up the political agenda (albeit with an increasing drift toward Taiwanese nativism and away from One China orthodoxy).

The most recent Nine-Year Curriculum Guidelines (encompassing schooling at elementary and junior high levels) adopt a far more competence-oriented approach than comparable documents have done in the past. The backgrounds of those involved in the development of curriculum standards reveal considerable exposure to American influences, particularly the National Reference for social studies published by National Council for the Social Studies in 1994. The new 9-year curriculum guidelines for social studies refocus the subject away from Chinese nationalism toward local (*bentu* or "own territory") understanding. There is now less emphasis on general Chinese history and more attention to Taiwan's culture and history as well as global topics. Among the ten goals, only one is related to national identity. According to one analysis (Liu and Doong, forthcoming), seven out of thirteen performance targets in Theme 1, People and Time, relate to people, events, culture, and so on in the local community and Taiwan. Four performance targets call for the understanding of historical development and civilizations concerning all human beings. Only two performance targets involve the understanding of Chinese history and its interrelationship with other countries/cultures in Asia and the world. It would appear that the trend among curriculum developers is to view China less as the all-important national homeland and more as Taiwan's closest and most significant East Asian neighbor — a revered ancestor, perhaps, but no longer a brooding mother.

Curriculum Organization

The 1975 social studies syllabus adopted a local-national-global approach that expanded the scope from Taiwan to China and finally to the whole world. Table 3.2 lists the unit titles of the social studies syllabus. In Book 6, Taiwan was defined as the "native place" (*xiangtu*). Books 8 to 10, which focused on Chinese accomplishments, cultural exchange, and ethnic intermingling and assimilation, were used to foster Chinese identity. Books 9 and 10 dealt with national history, and Taiwan did not receive any attention. Thus, while according Taiwan more coverage than it received in the curriculum for history at more senior levels, the social studies textbooks nonetheless kept the island firmly in its place. Taiwan was discussed as "our living place" in the same ahistorical manner that Hong Kong during the same period was portrayed in school textbooks for the subject of economics and public affairs; in other words, it was depicted as a place without a significant identity or history of its own — a home for the Chinese people who happened to have ended up there, but one with little more cultural significance than an anonymous concrete tower block.

Elementary social studies was established as an interdisciplinary subject composed of history, geography, and civics. Originally, the proportion of the subject content taken up by history was approximately one-third. However, the 1993 social studies syllabus was structured differently, being composed of anthropology, sociology, psychology, political science, economics, geography, and history. Given that the amount of classroom time allocated to the new social studies subject was the same as for its predecessor, the time available for teaching history was effectively halved. The new social science approach was intended to enrich the content of the subject by incorporating elements of six disciplines as opposed to the previous three. However, it was felt by some edu-

Table 3.2 Unit Titles for Social Studies Textbooks

Book	1975	1993
6	Understanding our native place Loving our native place	Our native place I — town, city Our native place II — county
7	Taiwan's geography Taiwan's natural resources Taiwan's development	Taiwan, Kinmen, and Matsu Islands Taiwan's natural resources Taiwan's development
8	Chinese inventions and life Customs and life	Taiwan's economic development Taiwan's revolution Customs and life in Taiwan
9	Chinese living environment Chinese immigration The establishment of the ROC	Government and people
10	Economic construction Chinese accomplishments	The living environment in mainland China Chinese cultural migration Chinese culture
11	Our world Chinese-Western cultural exchange Traditional thought and the changing society	Our world Civilization and life Chinese-foreign cultural exchange

cators that trying to cram too much into the subject could easily to lead to content overload and confusion.

The new syllabus also saw a marked decrease in the amount of overtly ideological content in the curriculum. However, as already noted, the dilution of the nation-building content in the curriculum has been highly controversial, raising the hackles in particular of conservative Blues but also of some of the more ardent Green nativists, who have aspired to turn the curriculum into a vehicle for Taiwanese nation-building. Among these have been many academic historians, who have insisted that the history curriculum should promote national education because its central purpose is to foster political and cultural identification with the nation (whether China or Taiwan). Meanwhile, more and more professional educators have insisted that the curriculum should become more student-centered and less ideologically prescriptive, and these people — along with those academic historians who share a similar view — have tended to find themselves caught in the crossfire between the more entrenched partisans of the Blue and Green camps (Peng 2000).

In the 1993 social studies syllabus, the historical content was outlined in a concentric pattern: Taiwan-China-world (an approach that was also promoted by the advocates of *Renshi Taiwan* later in the 1990s). The scope of the native place (*xiangtu*) was confined to county, town, and city. Taiwan itself was no longer defined as a mere local community. The affiliated islands, Kinmen and Matsu, were also included in the textbooks. The coverage of Taiwanese history was expanded to a whole book. Chinese identity and Taiwanese identity coexisted in the history curriculum, and the distinction between the two was made clearer than it had previously been. For example, the title "The Chinese Living Environment" was replaced by "The Living Environment in Mainland China," thus distinguishing political China from geographical China — or mainland China from Taiwan.

In addition, as already mentioned, the rise of Taiwanese identity led to the establishment of two new subjects: NPTA for grade 3 and Knowing Taiwan (*Renshi Taiwan*) for junior high school level, both subjects focusing on the history, geography, and society of Taiwan. The goals of *Knowing Taiwan — Society* are defined as "reinforcing the understanding of the social environment of Taiwan, Penghu, Kinmen, and Matsu," "cultivating the sentiment of love for the community and the nation," and "developing a consciousness of the 'community of life'" (*sheng ming gong tong ti*).[7] The goals of *Knowing Taiwan — History* include "understanding the history of the ancestors of each of the ethnic groups in Taiwan, Penghu, Kinmen, and Matsu," although the teaching materials studiously avoid references to past conflicts between Han settlers and aboriginal tribes, instead painting a highly misleading picture of harmonious and peaceful coexistence. In the appendix to the syllabus, the significance of this new subject is emphasized: this is the first time that Taiwanese history has ever been taught as a formal subject at junior high school level.

As noted above, despite efforts to steer the content of the subject away from the most sensitive themes and issues, Knowing Taiwan nonetheless provoked heated controversy. Some scholars criticized it for "eulogising the era of Japanese colonial rule," "adopting the historical perspectives of Japanese imperialism," "promoting anti-Chinese [nationalist] ideology," and "portraying Chinese history as foreign history." One legislator went to the MOE to protest that the textbooks were propaganda for "Taiwanese independence" and demanded the suspension of the new subject (Wang 1999).

The *Renshi Taiwan* controversy is discussed more fully in the next chapter. However, very similar protests on the part of conservatives have greeted more recent proposals for the reform of the history curriculum for senior high schools. As in Hong Kong, local history was introduced at the junior level before being incorporated into the curriculum for senior high schools. The high school curriculum for particular subjects is usually reviewed every 10 years in Taiwan, and the history curriculum for high schools was up for review in 2002–2003. A committee consisting of academics, teachers, and civil servants was appointed to consider proposals for reform and, in part because of greater timetable constraints in the senior forms, the option of creating a separate subject along the *Renshi Taiwan* model for the junior years was not seriously discussed. Instead, a more radical overhaul of the history curriculum was contemplated, with some

DPP politicians originally hoping that the committee would devise a curriculum that made Taiwan's history the core of the narrative.

The committee was reluctant to go as far as some in the DPP were pressing it to go but was nonetheless in favor of giving Taiwan's own history a prominent place in the new syllabus. Like their Hong Kong counterparts, curriculum developers in Taiwan have been keen to stress the pedagogic and cognitive advantages of teaching local history: it ties in better with visits to museums and local historical sites, and leads to more opportunities for students to work with primary sources and engage in project work. The promotion of local history within the curriculum is thus linked to a vision of history education that emphasizes the role this can play in fostering critical and analytical skills and attitudes associated with active citizenship in a liberal democracy. The appeal of this vision is certainly genuine for many curriculum developers in both Hong Kong and Taiwan, coinciding as it does with the broadly liberal-democratic values and aspirations of the bulk of public opinion in both societies. However, the deployment of these kinds of arguments for teaching Hong Kong or Taiwanese history is also one way of attempting to deflect accusations from conservatives that an increasing emphasis on the local past is in any way linked to a plot to dilute the Chinese identity of students.

The committee appointed to revise the senior secondary curriculum produced a proposal that envisioned teaching the narrative of Chinese history up to 1500 but then incorporating coverage of China within the world history section thereafter, while the history of Taiwan from the seventeenth century to the present would be covered separately. This was fiercely attacked by both local Blues, who saw it as an attempt to promote a Two China vision and accused the committee of ignoring the Republic of China,[8] and by the mainland media, who sarcastically portrayed the proposals as a manifestation of "Cultural Taiwanese Independence" (*Wenhua Taidu*),[9] and as part of a "little game" (*xiao dongzuo*) on the part of the Taiwan authorities (*Taiwan Dangju*).[10]

The controversy over the senior high school curriculum was by no means the most serious or threatening of President Chen's first term, but during the close-run election campaign of early 2004, the whole issue was effectively kicked into touch by the announcement after the election that a new committee would be appointed to review the proposals of the first. Following the DPP's narrow victory, however, and especially given the subsequent appointment of Tu Cheng-sheng as the new minister of Education, it looks highly unlikely that the government will press for any decrease in the emphasis accorded to Taiwan's history in the original proposals.

The Coverage of Particular Topics in Textbooks

The Nature of the Chinese Nation. Coverage of history in Taiwanese textbooks has always begun at the beginning: with the prehistoric origins of the Chinese race-nation (*minzu*). The junior (*Guomin Zhongxue*) textbooks up to the 1990s opened with an unambiguous statement of Han chauvinism and Chinese cultural superiority. The summary of "the special characteristics of our country's history" (*woguo lishi de tese*) ran as follows:

1. Its length: from the establishment of our country by the Yellow Emperor (*Huang Ti*) to the present day, more than four thousand six hundred years have passed. ... The ancient civilizations of Mesopotamia and Egypt have long disappeared, and the present-day countries in those regions are unrelated to them — in contrast to our country, where traditions have been passed down in an unbroken line from generation to generation.

2. The assimilation of ethnic groups (*minzu ronghe*): the Chinese race is an amalgamation of all the ethnic groups within the national borders. After a long process of contact, intermingling and cultural exchange, they have gradually formed the great Chinese race-nation (*weidade Zhonghua minzu*). The basins of the Yellow River and the Yangtse were the main regions where this process of assimilation took place.

3. The emphasis on propriety: our country's traditional culture is based on Confucianism, so the emphasis placed by Confucianism on concepts of ritual propriety and morality has very naturally become the basis on which individuals govern their behaviour in their daily lives. ... Propriety and morality are the essence (*jinghua*) of our national culture, and constitute the unique characteristics (*dute de xingge*) of the Chinese race-nation.

4. The love of peace: the Chinese are a peace-loving, warm-hearted people, whose relations with their neighbors have been governed by their sense of morality, and who have very seldom mounted armed invasions [of neighboring countries]. Despite possessing a cultural heritage that has been admired and coveted by her neighbors, China has never taken a selfish or small-minded approach to interaction with other states, but has freely shared her cultural inheritance. Japan, Korea and Vietnam are the three countries that have been most profoundly influenced by Chinese culture. (Junior Middle School [*Guomin Zhongxue*] history textbook, 1987–1997 edition: Book 1, 2–4.)

These statements, and the brief discussion of Chinese prehistory that preceded them, were accompanied by two maps: one depicted the major sites of the prehistoric world, with China shown shaded (within the official borders of the ROC — including Outer Mongolia); the other map showed China alone, highlighting the valleys of the Yellow and Yangtse Rivers and the names of the major minority *minzu* (Manchus, Mongols, Tibetans, Uighurs, and the rest) with arrows pointing inwards toward the area between the rivers, where the characters "*Zhonghua Minzu*" (Chinese Race-Nation) were printed in bold.

The 1998 edition of the history textbooks for junior secondary level adopt, the same chronological narrative, and more or less the same structure and coverage of historical events (Chinese history in the first two volumes, concluding with a section on the history of the Republic of China on Taiwan; then two volumes on world history). However, although the text is clearly adapted from that of the earlier edition, a significant difference in tone is evident from the first pages of Book 1. The first chapter begins with a discussion of the questions "What is history?" and "Why do we study history?" that includes the declaration that "history can not only help us to 'foresee the future by reviewing the past,' but can also foster our investigative and analytical abilities, and our critical judgment." It then moves on to a discussion of "the formation of the Chinese nation," which — like the previous edition — emphasizes China's immense antiquity, and the fact that of all the civilizations of the ancient world, it alone has survived. However, the other defining features of Chineseness enumerated in the previous edition are omitted, as are the maps that implicitly portray the boundaries of the Republic of China as primordial features of the geographical and cultural landscape. The Great Han chauvinism that characterized the earlier narrative is diluted here to the statement that China's political system and philosophical tradition "have become not merely the heritage of the Chinese nation alone, but a great contribution to the culture of the whole world." This is perhaps in part a reflection of the influence in Taiwan in recent years of Tu Wei-ming and the Harvard Confucianists, who similarly argue that Chinese culture should not be regarded as an incommensurable essence belonging exclusively to those who are racially Chinese. Moreover, this more open, flexible, and inclusive definition of Chineseness, separating the cultural realm from those of nation or race, clearly chimes with the views of those on Taiwan who insist that the island should remain politically separate from the PRC. (Junior High School textbook, 1998 edition, Book 1, 2–3.)

Descriptions of National Territory. In the 1975 edition of the official social studies textbooks, Taiwan was regarded merely as a province and China was the major focus. Taiwan's outlying islands were ignored altogether. Book 9 used the title "Our Territory" (*woguo de jiang yu*) to introduce the Chinese mainland. It stated, "Taiwan is located in the southeast of *our country*" (*woguo*). The definition of Our Territory encompassed mainland China, Taiwan, Penghu, Kinmen, and Matsu islands, together with the entire territory of the Qing Empire as of 1911 (including Outer Mongolia). Maps of the Republic of China showing these borders hung until the late 1990s on the walls of every classroom throughout Taiwan. However, the 1993 edition of the social studies textbooks revised its description of the national territory, with the statement that "Taiwan is located to the southeast of *mainland China*" (*Zhongguo dalu*). This description implies an equal status for Taiwan and mainland China —

without explicitly defining Taiwan as a separate nation. Penghu, Kinmen, and Matsu islands, which were previously neglected, were included in the textbooks. The realistic term "the ROC on Taiwan" was used in the textbook to reflect the current situation of Taiwan. The term "the territory of Taiwan" (*Taiwan zhekuai tudi*) also appeared several times. Overall, the textbook effectively promoted a form of pseudonational identity through encouraging identification with the territory of Taiwan, rather than an overtly political identification with the state.

The 1980s editions of history textbooks for junior high level included a section entitled "The Achievement and Prospects of the Base for [National] Recovery" (*Fuxing Jidi de Chengjiu yu Zhanwang*). In the 1998 edition, a similar section was retained but was retitled "The Development of the ROC on Taiwan" (*Zhonghua Minguo zai Taiwan de Fazhan*). This change in title reflected the ROC's de facto status and implied that recovery of the lost territory on mainland China was no longer the overriding mission of Taiwan's government or people.

Japanese Colonial Rule. In the 1975 social studies textbooks, Dr. Sun Yat-Sen's establishment of the ROC in China was emphasized in order to foster a sense of identification with the motherland.

> During the fifty years of Japanese colonial rule, Dr. Sun Yat-Sen led the National Revolution in mainland China and built the ROC … In 1945, we won the War of Resistance. Japan surrendered and returned Taiwan to our country. Taiwanese people excitedly greeted their reunification [with the rest of China]. On October 25, Taiwan returned to the arms of the motherland. (Book 7, 79–81)

By contrast, the 1993 social studies textbook stated that "Japan surrendered and returned Taiwan to 'the ROC'" instead of "our country." This served simply to remind students that Taiwan belonged to the ROC rather than the PRC, but emotive or overtly nationalistic terms such as the motherland were no longer used to refer to China.

The traditional KMT textbooks described only the negative impact of colonialism to contrast this with the constructive measures introduced by the Nationalist government after 1945. However, the new history textbooks, in stressing the contrast between democratic Taiwan and authoritarian China, adopt a less jaundiced view of Taiwan's colonial legacy. The positive as well as the negative effects of Japanese colonialism in Taiwan are discussed, and Taiwan's situation is described as being governed rather than simply occupied by Japan. The new books emphasize the achievements of the colonial Japanese authorities, such as "the increase of population," "the fostering of the rule of law," and "the spread of modern knowledge concerning health and hygiene." The treatment of Japan in contemporary Taiwanese textbooks is thus in marked contrast to the way Japan is dealt with in the history books used in mainland Chinese schools, where the emphasis is still very much on the portrayal of the Japanese as hated invaders. For the Taiwanese, drawing attention to the closeness of their island's historical relationship with Japan has become yet another way of stressing their distinctiveness vis-à-vis mainland China.

The KMT in Taiwan. The 1983 edition of the history textbook for junior high school level eulogized the KMT's contributions to Taiwan and never mentioned any negative effects of KMT actions or policies. The textbook described the Chinese Communists' reign of terror and the distress of their people in graphic terms, comparing the experience of life on the mainland to living in "deep water and hot fire." The aim was to highlight the benevolence of the KMT's administration and to reinforce students' sense of political identity.

By contrast, the 1994 edition conveyed a far more neutral perspective on the KMT's administrative record. While acknowledging the KMT's contribution to economic development, the textbooks also criticized its "great China policy" and its monopoly on political power.

> After the government moved to Taiwan, the KMT controlled all political power for the first thirty years. Its power permeated both the civilian and military spheres. It was very difficult for opposition parties to develop or establish themselves. In order to maintain strong central control and prevent any challenge to the government's legitimacy, the National Assembly was never reelected. As a result, it was criticized as "the thousand years National Assembly." Chiang Kai-Shek used "the recovery of mainland China" and "anti-Communism" as his principal political slogans, so the administration was dominated by "great China" considerations and the KMT's determination to cling on to political power. (Book 2, 177)
>
> Since the ROC on Taiwan broke with the traditional historical patterns, cross-Strait relations and the unification-independence battle have become people's major concerns. (Book 2, 180)

"Breaking with the traditional historical patterns" can perhaps be taken as an oblique reference to the shift in people's sense of identity, whereby Chinese identity is no longer seen as the only form of identity for Taiwanese due to the emergence of a strong and distinctive sense of Taiwanese identity.

Ethnicity, Culture, and the Aborigines. As already noted, the coverage of history in most textbooks tends to be organized chronologically, with an emphasis on political and military history — fields in which minorities (not to mention women) are largely excluded from the narrative or tend to be portrayed purely from the perspective of the dominant (male) majority. The newer textbooks devote more attention to different ethnic groups than their predecessors, but the proportion of content devoted to these groups is still very limited.

In terms of cultural identity, both the old and new textbooks focus on Chineseness.

> Chinese is the general name for the ethnic groups that constitute the Chinese nation, including Han, Manchus, Mongolians, Moslems (*Hui*), Tibetans, Miao, Yao, ... and Taiwanese aborigines. (Book 9, 10)
>
> Our ancestors moved to Taiwan at different periods. The original inhabitants were aborigines who composed a small group. (Book 7, 51)

In terms of their ethnic origins, Taiwan's aborigines are completely unrelated to the Han Chinese. However, the 1975 editions of the textbooks stressed that the aborigines, along with all other Chinese ethnic groups, have acquired a common ethnicity after 5,000 years of assimilation (*ronghe*). The textbooks indoctrinated students into the belief that the people of Taiwan all belong to the same Chinese ethnic group. Until the 1990s, Taiwanese textbooks, like their mainland counterparts, thus remained wedded to an ethnocentric Han Chinese discourse, neglecting the fact that the Taiwanese aborigines are a Malayo-Polynesian people whose languages belong to the Austronesian family.

One folk story that used to be told to Taiwanese schoolchildren, and was included in official textbooks until the late 1980s, reflects the sort of attitude that then prevailed toward the aborigines (or the mountain people — *shandiren* — as they were more commonly known). This was the story of Wu Feng, a virtuous official of the old school, whose family was said to have migrated to Taiwan from Fujian Province during the reign of the Kangxi Emperor in the early eighteenth century. Shocked by the custom of headhunting then prevalent among the aborigines in his region, Wu resolved to educate them out of this unfortunate habit. He won the trust and friendship of the local tribe, who desisted from headhunting for 40 years. Eventually, however, a famine occurred, which the tribe attributed to a lack of heads to present to their gods, and they told Wu that it was essential for them to obtain a fresh head. Seeing it was impossible to dissuade them, Wu told them that at noon the next day a man wearing a red hat would pass near his office, and that they could kill him. This they duly did, only to find that their red-hatted victim was none other than Wu himself. Moved by this noble gesture, the tribe then abandoned headhunting once and for all. This story, now generally considered to be fictitious, was finally excised from official school texts during the late 1980s, after numerous protests by aboriginal groups.[11]

Textbooks published from the mid-1990s onwards have eschewed such a condescending approach toward the indigenous population in favor of a self-consciously multicultural vision. The most recent history textbook describes Taiwan's four ethnic groups and their origins as follows:

> Some ancestors of the current inhabitants of Taiwan migrated from mainland China, while others have been settled here for a long time.

> Approximately 400 years ago, large numbers of people from Fujian and Guangdong provinces migrated to Taiwan. From then on, more and more residents of other provinces also migrated to Taiwan. (Book 7, 91)

The status of the aboriginal people has been raised in current textbooks by including more references to their contributions to Taiwan's culture and history in the text. Some editions of the history textbooks describe the culture of specific tribes, such as the Amis or Atayal.[12] However, other books continue to refer to them simply by the general term "aboriginal people," implying a uniform (and uniformly primitive) cultural and ethnic background.

The Distinctiveness of Taiwan. The old curriculum or textbooks for history or social studies did not emphasize Taiwan's distinctiveness and accorded it marginal status as a province of China. By contrast, in the recent *Renshi Taiwan* textbook, Taiwanese status and consciousness are constantly underlined and reinforced. The textbook uses the term mainland China rather than simply the mainland (which was often used in the old history textbooks), with the effect of downplaying or minimizing the significance of the connection between China and Taiwan. The first direct presidential election in 1996 is taken to mark a turning point whereby the people became the masters of Taiwan. The book never uses the descriptor "the Chinese" *(Zhongguoren)* to refer to Taiwan's inhabitants and simply uses the terms "*Hanren*" (referring to those of Chinese ethnicity) and Taiwanese ("*Taiwanren*") (encompassing the four ethnic groups—aborigines, *Minnan*, *Hakka*, and *waishengren*) to describe the people living in Taiwan. Only one paragraph touches explicitly on the issue of unification with mainland China:

> In 1991, our government passed "the Guidelines for National Unification" and ended the "Temporary Provisions Effective During the Period of Communist Rebellion." It hopes the two sides of the Strait will achieve the ultimate aim of unification through three stages: "exchanges and reciprocity", "mutual trust and cooperation" and "consultation and communication." However, cross-straits relations have not made a breakthrough because the PRC overlooks the fact of separation and insists on its "one country two systems" policy. (*Knowing Taiwan — History*, 100)

Far more emphasis is given to the issue of how to build a prosperous new Taiwan. The last chapter of *Understanding Taiwan — Society* is entitled "Building New Taiwan," implying that the future of Taiwan should be decided by the whole body of the residents of Taiwan.

The textbook thus treats the ROC and PRC as two distinct political entities, describing Taiwan's status as follows:

President Lee Teng-hui applied a 'pragmatic diplomatic policy' (*shizhi waijiao*) [i.e., fostering connections with some nations through economic cooperation notwithstanding the absence of official diplomatic relations]. The policy no longer insists that the ROC is the only legitimate government of China. It emphasizes that China has separated into two equal regimes. The ROC is an independent sovereign entity that has broken through the PRC's diplomatic blockade by virtue of its economic strength, and has thus maintained its international status. (*Knowing Taiwan — History*, 97)

Nevertheless, although Taiwanese consciousness is raised in the new history textbook, advocacy of outright independence for Taiwan is still taboo.

The foregoing analysis of the content of the history curriculum shows that treatment of the identity issue has changed dramatically over the past 20 years. In the 1980s, the official curriculum for history reflected and promoted a sense of Chinese identity in the territorial, cultural, ethnic, and political domains. The textbooks stressed the relationship between Taiwan and China and the superiority of Chinese culture. However, by the mid-1990s, a sense of a distinctive Taiwanese identity began to be recognized in the history curriculum, and the proportion of syllabus and textbook content devoted to Taiwan markedly increased. The textbooks attempted to draw a distinction between cultural identity and political identity. Chinese culture continued to be portrayed as a common, shared cultural heritage, but the existence and distinctiveness of Taiwanese culture began to be emphasized as never before. Issues of identity nonetheless remain the source of considerable confusion, in particular regarding the problem of how to reconcile conceptions of ethno-cultural and civic nationalisms in order to construct a truly coherent vision of Taiwaneseness. The new textbooks, for example, describe the ethnic origins of the Hakka and Fukienese inhabitants of Taiwan in order to underline that "we are [culturally] all Chinese," but at the same time acknowledge that the aboriginal people are not Han and possess an entirely different ethno-cultural heritage. Meanwhile, in the political sphere, as a result of the unification-independence controversy and Chinese communists' threats, the textbooks continue to use the vague and nowadays increasingly incongruous term "the ROC on Taiwan" to define the political community.

Conclusion

Taiwan has peculiar problems with defining its sense of historical identity. Over the past century, it has been subject to the influence of two external governing forces: Japan, from 1895 to 1945, and the KMT, from 1945 to 2000, both of which have used education in their attempts to shape the identity consciousness of the local population. Acute contradictions persist between the way national identity is portrayed at an official level, and how it is perceived by many ordinary Taiwanese, reflecting an enduring ambivalence in Taiwan's identity as seen both domestically and abroad.

From 1945 until the 1990s, the KMT regime ensured that the history curriculum encouraged identification with a homogenous and totalizing vision of Chinese culture, with little or no allusion to Taiwan's historical distinctiveness. However, the lifting of martial law in 1987 was followed by a relatively rapid process of democratization, lifting the taboo on discussion of Taiwanese independence. This has raised the possibility that Chinese identity will gradually be replaced by a sense of Taiwanese identity, and recent developments do indeed point to a marked shift in the portrayal of Chinese/Taiwanese identity in the school curriculum. However, does this involve the replacement one monolithic (Chinese) vision of identity with another (Taiwanese) vision? Or are changes to the history curriculum leading to an open acknowledgement of Taiwan's history of multiple and conflicting identities?

Concerns have certainly been voiced in some quarters — and not only among the ultraconservative KMT old guard — that the DPP administration in power since 2000 has been attempting to use cultural policy in general, and schooling in particular, for a program of indoctrination similar in style, if not in substance, to that pursued for 50 years by the KMT. However, given the repression to which native Taiwanese were subjected during the martial law era, including the denigration of their language and culture, it is perhaps surprising that the backlash under the DPP has been so restrained. The divisions within Taiwanese society, dramatically exhibited by the demonstrations of April 2004, are unsurprising given the island's recent history and, as Friedman (2004) has pointed out, are less severe than the divisions affecting many other societies emerging from long periods of authoritarian rule (South Africa, for example); after all, for all the sound and fury generated by the KMT protests in early 2004, violence was minimal. What makes the situation in Taiwan so potentially dangerous, and the divisions potentially suicidal, is the very real threat posed to Taiwan's liberal-democratic society by mainland China. This threat raises the stakes in Taiwan's search for a new basis for social cohesion — a vision of Taiwanese identity and values that can accommodate both Greens and Blues.

The recent emphasis on Taiwanese consciousness in the school curriculum may help Taiwanese to reconnect with their own history and acquire a stronger and more secure sense of their own identity. In an ideal world, history education would perhaps also challenge students to critically engage with multiple and conflicting perspectives on the past, in such a way as to encourage skepticism regarding some of the more extreme claims of both the One China conservatives and the more extreme Taiwanese nativists. However, even in many more established democracies, history education falls short in this respect, and sensitive and controversial topics are sidelined or ignored (see Chapter 10). The international environment in which Taiwan finds itself is far from ideal, a fact highlighted by the image on the back cover of the latest edition of the junior high history textbook (Book 4), which shows the United Nations Building in New York lit up in celebration of the organization's fiftieth anniversary. Neither students nor teachers need reminding that Taiwan was not invited to that party. Until the question of the island's international status is resolved, it is hard to see how the school curriculum can address the issue of Taiwanese identity through the history curriculum in a more balanced and critical, or less ideologically charged, fashion.

Endnotes

1. A classic exposition of the KMT view of modern Chinese history — and the place of Taiwan in it — is *Zhongguo Xiandai Shi*, edited by Guo Ting-yu and published by the Zhong Zheng Shu Ju in 1980. This adopts the same interpretation as school textbooks of the period and was widely used by schoolteachers as a reference work.

2. In a lecture on the 228 Incident in Taiwanese literature, presented at School of Oriental and African Studies in the Autumn term, 2003.

3. "Green" is the term commonly used to refer to the proindependence camp and has no environmentalist connotations. The KMT's color is Blue.

4. Edward Vickers interviewed Wu Mi-cha and Tu Cheng-sheng on Friday, January 9, 2004, and Monday, January, 12, 2004 respectively.

5. "Nine-Year" because Taiwan has 9 years of compulsory education.

6. Authentic instruction is significant and meaningful instruction, which is distinct from trivial and meaningless instruction. There are three criteria of authentic instruction: (1) instruction involves students in higher-order thinking, (2) instruction is the process of knowledge construction and substantive conversation, (3) instruction makes the connection to the world beyond the classroom (Newmann 1996).

7. "Community of life" is a new term developed by the former President Lee Teng-hui. He indicated that the people in Taiwan should live on this island peacefully and cooperatively, no matter which ethnic group came to Taiwan first or last. All residents of Taiwan are new Taiwanese and should relate to each other as a single community regardless of their different ethnic backgrounds.

8. Edward Vickers interviewed Professor Chen Guo-dong of the Academia Sinica (one of the members of the Curriculum Committee) on Tuesday, January 13, 2004.

9. For example, the *People's Daily*, September 29, 2003: *Ping Taiwan Dangju Huangmiu Juelun de Lishi Guan* ("A Criticism of the Taiwan Authorities' Preposterous and Nonsensical View of History").

10. *People's Daily*, September 29, 2003: *Taiwan Dangju de "Wenhua Taidu" Xiao Dongzuo* ("The Taiwan Authorities Little 'Cultural Independence' Ploy").

11. We have been unable to locate a textbook version of the story, but it has been posted on the Xinsheng website (http://xinsheng.net/xs/articles/big5/2003/7/3/22134.htm). We are grateful to Dr. Patricia Huang for bringing this story to our attention.

12. Amis and Atayal are the biggest tribes of Taiwanese aboriginal people in terms of population.

References

All references to textbooks in this chapter are, unless otherwise stated, to books published by the National Institute for Compilation and Translation (*Guoli Bianyi Guan*).

Althusser, L. 1972. "Ideology and ideological state apparatuses," in B. Cosin, ed., *Education: Structure and Society.* England: Penguin Books, 243–280.

Barr, R. D., Barth, J. L., and Shermis, S. S. 1977. *Defining the Social Studies.* Arlington, VA: National Council for the Social Studies.

Bernstein, B. 1977. *Class, Codes and Control*, 2nd ed. Boston: Routledge.

Chiang, Y. H. 1998. *Liberalism, Nationalism and National Identity.* Taipei: Young-Chi. (Chinese).

Ching, Leo T. S. 2001. *Becoming "Japanese": Colonial Taiwan and the Politics of Identity Formation*

Corcuff, S., ed. 2002. *Memories of the Future.* New York: M. E. Sharpe.

———. 2004. "The Supporters of Unification and the Taiwanization Movement. Feelings of Emergency and a Crisis Mentality in the Blue camp during the Presidential Election Campaign." *China Perspectives* 52 (May–June), 49–66.

Friedman, E. 2004. Paranoia, Polarisation and Suicide: Unexpected Consequences of Taiwan's 2004 Presidential Election, Annual SOAS Taiwan Lecture, presented at SOAS, London, June 24, 2004.

Giroux, H. A. 1981. *Ideology, Culture and the Process of Schooling.* Philadelphia: Temple University Press.

Guo, T. Y. 1980. *Zhongguo Xiandai Shi (Contemporary Chinese History).* Taipei: Zheng Zhong Shu Ju.

Huang, C. C. 2000. *Taiwanese Consciousness and Culture.* Taipei: Zheng Zhong Shu Ju.

Huang, K. K. 1987. "Taiwanese Complex and Chinese Complex." *Chinese Forum* 289:1–19 (Chinese).

Hughes, C. 1997. *Taiwan and Chinese Nationalism: National Identity and Status in International Society.* New York: Routledge.

Kuo, J. 2000. "Building a Taiwanese national identity." *Taipei Times*, Jan. 6.

Liu. M. and Doong, S. Forthcoming. "Civic Education Reform in Taiwan: Directions, Controversies, and Challenges." *Education Pacific Asia.*

Ministry of Education. 1983. *Curriculum Reference for Junior High Schools.* Taipei: MOE. (Chinese)

———. 1994. *Curriculum Reference for Junior High Schools.* Taipei: MOE. (Chinese)

———. 2000. *Curriculum Guidelines for Nine-Year Integrated Curriculum—Social Studies.* Taipei: MOE. (Chinese)

Murphy, C., and Liu, M. 1998. "Choices Must be Made: The Case of Education in Taiwan." *Education 3 to 13* 26, 2:9–16.

Newmann, F. M. 1996. *Authentic Achievement: Restructuring Schools for Intellectual Quality.* San Francisco: Jossey-Bass Publishers.

Roy, D. 2003. *Taiwan: A Political History.* Ithaca: Cornell University Press.

Rubinstein, M. A. 1999. "Political Taiwanization and Pragmatic Diplomacy: The Eras of Chiang Ching-kuo and Lee Teng-hui, 1971–1994," in M. A. Rubinstein, ed., *Taiwan: A New History.* Armonk, NY: M. E. Sharpe, 436–483.

Shih, G. S. 1993. *Ideologies and Taiwan's Textbooks.* Taipei: Chien-Way. (Chinese).

Wang, C. H. 1989. The Political Transition and Opposition Movement. *Taiwan Social Research Quarterly* 2, 1:71–116 (Chinese).

Wang, C. L. 1999. *National Identity and the Controversies Regarding the New Subject: Knowing Taiwan in the ROC.* ERIC Document Reproduction Service No. ED 432–530.

Wu, M. C., and Chiang, W. W. 1994. *Screening Elementary Textbooks*. Taipei: Chien-Way. (Chinese).

Yee, A. C. 2001. "Constructing a Native Consciousness: Taiwan Literature in the 20th Century." *Special Issue: Taiwan in the 20th Century, China Quarterly* 165 (March 2001):83–101.

Young, Y. R. 1994. *Education and National Development: Taiwan Experiences*. Taipei: Keui-Kuan. (Chinese)

4

History Textbooks, Identity Politics, and Ethnic Introspection in Taiwan: The June 1997 Knowing Taiwan Textbooks Controversy and the Questions It Raised on the Various Approaches to "Han" Identity

STÉPHANE CORCUFF

Textbooks are one of the mediums extremely susceptible to centralized political control and to uniformity of message, particularly when they are published by government printing houses and circulated through many if not all of the nation's schools, as they are in both Taiwan and China.

— Roberta Martin

The present chapter aims to bring to the reader's attention a process crucial to an understanding of the Taiwanese laboratory of identities in the 1990s: the reform of the history and geography junior high textbooks in June 1997. It provoked a heated debate that both reflected and further stimulated introspection among intellectuals regarding Taiwan's cultural heritage and provided a revealing indication of the state of Taiwanese *mentalités* in relation to the debate over national identity in the tenth year of Mr. Lee Teng-hui's presidency.[1]

As the Kuomintang's (KMT's) Chinese Nationalists retreated to Taiwan in 1949, they feared that the Chinese consciousness (*Zhongguo yishi*) of the islanders might have been seriously weakened by the insularity of Taiwan, the influence of Japanese colonization (1895–1945), and the bloody repression of the 1947 uprising against the corruption and inefficiency of the new Chinese administration sent to Taiwan after the departure of the Japanese colonial government. For five decades — from 1945 to the mid-1990s — the KMT used national education and military conscription as tools of political socialization with the aim of nurturing in Taiwanese minds a desire for unification with the Chinese motherland (see Chapter 3). School textbooks were conceived as one of the most fundamental tools to disseminate in Taiwanese society a new "Chinese consciousness": a feeling of belonging to a cultural and historical China.[2] That China only survived in memories and ideas and was distinct from the politico-administrative notion of the Communists' People's Republic of China (PRC). However, Chinese consciousness was supposed to facilitate Taiwanese allegiance to the Nationalists' Republic of China, despite the way in which postwar developments created a serious legitimacy problem for the Nationalist government, not least by reducing the scope of the its authority to the single province of Taiwan.[3] Indeed, a sense of the fragility of its legitimacy no doubt helped to reinforce the urgency with which the regime sought to raise nationalist consciousness through education.

As democratization set in from the late 1980s, the way Taiwan's national identity was perceived, debated, and expressed underwent a transformation: Taiwan's constitutional status as an insular province of Republican China began to be openly challenged by the political project of an emerging Taiwanese nation. The instrumentalization of a national education serving the pan-Chinese ideology became logically increasingly problematic. Eventually, in 1994, a grand project of educational reform was launched by a Taiwanized KMT presided over by Lee Teng-hui, with Lien Chan as premier. A consensus was quickly reached among reformers: the most urgent task was to revise the school textbooks.

This reform was a major step in the ongoing policy of deepening what is distinct in Taiwan's identity and of rendering its distinctiveness more widely known and acknowledged by Taiwanese themselves, by China, and by the world at large.

In this chapter, I first present the context of the reform and the position of the major political parties on educational restructuring prior to the event. I then try to shed light on the main objectives of the authors of the new manuals. Next, I analyze the reactions of the opponents to the reform and the counterarguments offered by the supporters of the reform. Lastly, I discuss what I term here the "phenomenon of introspection/distantiation of Taiwanese intellectuals from the island's Chinese cultural heritage," a phenomenon to which this event gave a new impetus.

Apart from being a study of the historical and political importance of what is a milestone in Taiwan's contemporary history, this chapter is a study of what becoming aware of the inherently pluralistic and fluid character of identities means for a country's elite in their perception of political socialization and national historiography.[4]

The New Textbooks: From the Initial Version to the Official Version

The three manuals of the Knowing Taiwan (*Renshi Taiwan*) textbook series were adopted in 1997 after a short but intense ideological challenge launched by conservative politicians opposed to the Taiwanization movement and astonished by the boldness of the sudden changes. Designed for the first year of junior high (or students between 12 and 13), the program consisted of three manuals addressing historical, geographical, and societal questions. Each of the three was accompanied by a teacher's manual; in addition, a workbook supplemented the geography book.[5]

The manuals went through several revisions even before they actually reached the schools. The first version was a working one, used internally by the National Institute of Compilations and Translations (*guoli bianyi guan*; hereafter, the Institute), the official body in charge of writing school textbooks. This version, finished and printed in May 1997, was called the "model version," or *moben*, on its cover, and the "first edition" (*chuban*) at the end of the books. For purposes of clarity, I call it the "initial" version.

This initial version was modified at the end of June 1997 and formally printed the following month. The date originally chosen for the official publication was August 1997, and this anticipated date was printed on these two versions. The second version, with only minor changes to the content, at first retained the designation "first edition" on the copyright page at the end of each manual and then went on sale during autumn under the denomination "trial version" (*shiyong ben*). This third version was used during the 1997–1998 school year, until an "official version, first edition" (*zhengshi ben chuban*) was published in August 1998, for use during the following year. In this fourth version, there were noticeable changes in the content of the society manual. Finally, a "new edition of the official version" (*zhengshi ben zaiban*) was published in August 1999, to be used thereafter. It is this fifth version that is currently in use in Taiwan's schools.[6]

The initial version, a copy of which I obtained in May 1997 at the Institute, was never published or distributed to the public. It is this version that sparked the intense controversy of June 1997. In order to gauge their opinions regarding the new program, the Institute sent copies of this version to teachers, one of whom provided copy to Lee Ching-hua, a conservative prounification legislator, and started the controversy. Since the initial version is the version to which he reacted by initiating and leading the controversy that forms the subject of this chapter, it is on this initial version that the content analysis of the reform in this paper is based.[7]

The Context of the Reform: Criticisms Formulated Against Traditional Textbooks

Four major criticisms had long been leveled at the Nationalists' educational system in Taiwan: the definition of the programs and the textbook editing process were too centralized; a systematic ideology of Chinese consciousness was disseminated in the manuals, with a quasi absence of courses on Taiwan in consequence; emphasis was placed more on memorization than on reflection or critical thinking; and the content of the manuals was largely, and increasingly, outdated. In general, progressive intellectuals argued that the Nationalists had used education largely for ideological and political purposes. In fact, the 1947 Constitution itself stipulated that nationalist consciousness-raising was to be one of the core functions of the education system.[8]

The government centralized the preparation and publication of school textbooks in a 1968 reform that gave the Institute a monopoly. Textbooks of history and *guowen* (national language and literature) were to teach Taiwanese that they were "Chinese," with no possibility to question the exact meaning of this word. Very few classes were taught on the island's own history and geography. Relatively little was said about political and economic developments on the island since the 1945 takeover, despite the usual propensity of dictatorships worldwide to highlight their own achievements. The explanation probably lies in the perception of the Nationalists under Chiang Kai-shek that their stay in Taiwan would only be temporary and that focusing on Taiwan's recent development would undermine the "correct" historical perspective of *emphasizing the Mainland over the Island*. Lastly, the content of the manuals was outdated. The Ministry of Education's (hereafter: the Ministry) last *Curriculum Reference* (*kecheng biaozhun*) for junior high schools had been published in 1985, and subsequent events had already dramatically altered the state of the world.[9] According to a history professor, Cheng Jui-ming of the National Taiwan Normal University, changes to the history books had been minor between 1948 and the death of Chiang Kai-shek in 1975, and the textbooks used were those already used by the regime during its continental era.[10] This was hardly surprising, since no one would have expected the KMT regime to suddenly change its historical perspective, just because it had lost the civil war.[11]

In consequence, following the liberalization of the island's politics and media from the late 1980s, those Taiwanese intellectuals disagreeing with an instrumentalization of knowledge by the political power — or at least with its instrumentalization by a *Chinese* government on Taiwan — soon started to consider Taiwan's national education as one of the main propaganda tools of the government, often referring to it as a "strategy of keeping the people in ignorance" (*yumin zhengce*) or, adopting a Western term as, obscurantism.[12]

Soon after martial law was lifted in 1987, the first pressures on the government were felt in the Legislative Yuan. The Executive Yuan (the executive branch, headed by the premier) responded slowly, establishing a small reform group to study the question. In 1994, under renewed pressure and after Lien Chan became premier, an official commission was established: the Executive Yuan commission on the study of educational reform (*xingzhengyuan jiaoyu gaige shenyi weiyuanhui*). This second commission set about its task discretely, but quickly, setting the tone for the rest of its work until 1997. The following year, the Ministry published a brand new *Curriculum Reference* for the junior high programs, which precisely laid down the outline of the future Knowing

Taiwan textbook series. In March 1996, ignorant of the reform process and of the existence of the new *Curriculum Reference*, several National Taiwan University students organized an auto-da-fé, attacking the Ministry for being on the side of the pro-China camp.[13] Just a few months later, a new reform commission, which had in the meantime succeeded to the previous one, placed the goal of changing the school textbooks at the top of the reform agenda in its final report published on December 2.

The Position of the Major Political Parties on Educational Reform

What was the position of the three major political parties on the island before the controversy erupted in June 1997? In 1986, a Taiwanese journal, *Education Studies* (*jiaoxue yanjiu*), published a short study on the position of the KMT, after two staff writers visited the party's general headquarters. They did not get any precise information other than a vague mention of the objective of developing a "worldwide view" or a "vision open to the world" (*shijie guan*), on which no details were apparently provided to the reporters. Nothing was said about developing nativist (or local) education (*xiangtu jiaoxue*) or about teaching Taiwanese and aboriginal languages, even though the debate over these issues had already begun.[14]

The position of the Democratic Progressive Party (DPP, or *Minjindang*) had been laid out 2 years earlier, in 1995, in the electoral manifesto entitled "Give Taiwan a Chance" (*gei Taiwan yige jihui*). The DPP expressed an unequivocal commitment to a desinicization of national education on the island and its adaptation to the contemporary reality of Taiwan, a reality that the word *plurality* perhaps describes best. The DPP's demands were numerous: a bilingual education system (with the main local language, *Hoklo*, being granted equal status to Mandarin); competition in the editing and publication of school textbooks (ending the Institute's monopoly); general pluralization (*duoyuan hua*) of the educational system; the promotion of a consciousness of Taiwanese citizenship (*Taiwan guomin yishi*); the development of curricula for history and literature that take Taiwan as the central subject (*yi Taiwan wei zhuti*);[15] respect for the distinct identity and cultural integrity (*zhuti xing*) of each ethnic group; and the protection of aboriginal cultures.

The position of the New Party (*Xindang*) should also be noted, since this was the party most strongly opposed to the nativization policy pursued by President Lee Teng-hui. The New Party interprets the Taiwanization movement as an ideological menace to the ultimate goal of unification with China. On the one hand, one might suggest that no political party can survive for long without adapting to the actual conditions of the society in which it is competing for electoral mandates. And indeed, before the 1997 political tempest over the new manuals, the New Party had announced that it was in favor of a curriculum that would encourage the islanders to love their Taiwanese homeland, but without forgetting their Chinese motherland. In 1995, the New Party published a white paper pleading for a strategy of "cultural pluralism" and supporting the idea of a "nativist education" to help Taiwanese nurture "a feeling" toward their land, but it added that this should not be done "at the expense of the unifying national language."

Until a concrete question was raised and before a strong disagreement actually emerged, it seems that there was a relative consensus among political parties regarding the necessity of reforming the national education system and devising a more nativist curriculum.

Launching the Reform

In 1995, the Ministry, its reform commission, and the Institute jointly established a new Commission for Editing New Junior High School Textbooks (*guomin zhongxue xin kecheng jiaoliao yongshu bianshen weiyuanhui*; hereafter, the Commission), which was put in charge of writing the three manuals of the Knowing Taiwan course. The composition of this commission clearly demonstrates an ambition to give back to educators the responsibility of designing curricular content, while correspondingly reducing the degree of supervision exercised by the Ministry's bureaucrats.[16] Its presidency was given to Lee Yuan-tse, the 1986 recipient of the Nobel Prize for Chemistry, president of the prestigious Academia Sinica, and a proreform intellectual widely respected in Taiwan. The meetings started in June 1995 and finished in February 1997.

The content of any one of the three manuals of the program was enough to arouse anxiety among the conservatives: the history book (*lishi pian*) because it focused only on Taiwanese history; the society book (*shehui pian*), perceived as presenting Taiwan as an emerging nation; and the geography volume (*dili pian*), which clearly confined the limits of such a nation to the island of Taiwan and its neighboring islets. The history and society books provoked the biggest controversy, and thus are the main focus of this chapter. The scholars who chaired the teams working on those two books were respectively Huang Hsiu-cheng (professor of history at Chung-Hsin University, history) and Tu Cheng-sheng (then director of the Center for History and Language Studies of the Academia Sinica, society).

Huang and Tu, along with other scholars and teachers who contributed the content of the textbooks, gave several interviews to Taiwanese journalists in June 1997. These interviews were of great help to an understanding of their aims, for those who were able to decipher their declarations, the scholars were frank, in general, but still expressed themselves with some self-restraint — a strategy probably designed to defend the program from conservative attacks by toning down its revolutionary character. Conducting a cross-analysis of the context of the reform, of the actual content of the new manuals, and of the declarations of their authors to the press, is indeed necessary to understand the understated and to grasp the true significance of this dramatic event in the political history of Taiwan during the 1990s.

The Objectives of the Authors of the Program

The first obvious aim of the authors was to separate, as much as possible, the political ideology from the educational content. For them, it meant above all removing from the manuals the ideology of Chinese consciousness and its nationalistic corollary, commonly referred to by Taiwan's reformist intellectuals and proindependence militants as the "Greater China ideology" (*da Zhongguo yishi xingtai, da Zhongguo zhuyi*, or *da Zhonghua zhuyi*) or the "Great Han ideology" (*da han zhuyi*). Five decades of an intense curricular focus on the Chinese continent had led to general ignorance among Taiwanese pupils regarding Taiwan's history and geography. History books at the junior high school level, before the reform, devoted only three short chapters to Taiwanese history since the 1945 takeover (in the last volume; on this point, see Chapter 3). In 1999, in his book *Taiwan's Point of View* (*Taiwan di zhuzhang*), former President Lee Teng-hui indicated that he had become interested in educational reform as early as the period of his vice-presidency (1984–1988). In the spring of 1996, he expressed his support for the ongoing reform by calling upon Taiwan to look at its educational system with a "new thinking" in order to nurture the feeling of a "common destiny."[17] At the peak of the June 1997 controversy, he declared to the press: "Everyone is learning history and geography, but we just learn about the length of the Great Wall. The Great Wall is not longer than five thousand kilometers, but the irrigation system built in Taiwan by our ancestors totaled twenty thousand kilometers; and yet no one knows about it."[18]

The second major goal was to evaluate again Taiwan's colonial period under Japanese rule. It is not rare to find hatred against Japanese among Taiwan's "New inhabitants," the Taiwanese of recent continental origin,[19] at least among those who experienced China's war against Japan (1937–1945). In the past, the positive aspects of the Japanese colonial experience in Taiwan were systematically erased from history books, whereas its negative aspects were often highlighted. The manuals also not very astutely overemphasized the "patriotic resistance" of the Taiwanese in the years after the Japanese took control of Taiwan, between June and November 1895. The following is an example of the tone used in the junior high school history textbook before the reform:

> Once the separation of Taiwan[20] was formalized, the Taiwanese compatriots decided to resist to the death … On the initiative of Chiu Feng-chia[21] and others, on the fifth month of the twenty-first year of Kuang-hsü's reign,[22] the Democratic Republic of Taiwan was established, and T'ang Ching-sung[23] was designated the President. At the beginning of May, the Japanese military approached a bay on the Taiwanese coast, and then landed. In mid-May, as Keelung was occupied, T'ang Ching-sung fled, and Taipei fell into the enemy's hands. Under the supervision of General Liu Yung-fu, an army of volunteers continued the combat. With the Black

flag army,[24] the force did not consist of more than a few thousand men, who bloodily resisted the elite of the Japanese marine corps for several months, leaving historical footprints which illustrate our determination not to yield, which comes from the spirit of our race.

In addition to the concluding allusion to the Han "racial spirit," the reader will probably have noticed how a history book written and printed in Taiwan for Taiwanese students speaks of "Taiwanese compatriots," just as if the author was situating himself on the other side of the Taiwan Strait. The text also omitted to mention the willingness of the Taipei gentry, led by the business-man Koo Hsien-jung,[25] to open Taipei's doors to the Japanese in order to stop looting and killings by Chinese troops and their desire to move forward to the new era, given that Taiwan had been ceded to Japan anyway.[26]

It is this kind of viewpoint and partial presentation that the authors of the new manuals had decided to avoid, even though writing a history book without any ideological preconceptions is certainly almost impossible. The new version of the history book chose to speak of a "war of courageous resis-tance" (*yingyong kangzhan*), which was a strong term, but from which any strong ideological connotations had disappeared. Regarding the ensuing colonial period, which was pushed into the background in the former manuals, the Commission chose a more balanced historical analysis, mentioning the cru-elty of Japanese repression of the resistance after taking over Taiwan as well as the positive consequences for Taiwanese of five decades of development of the economy, industry, urban infrastructure, and transport.[27]

The new manuals also provided an occasion to present, for the first time, a constitutive dimension of Taiwan's identity and an issue at the core of the national identity debate: the plurality (*duoyuan hua*) of the island's ethnic structure and historical experience. The Nationalists' curricula had systemati-cally understated the effect of Taiwan's exposure to various experiences with rulers arrived from overseas: the Dutch and the Spanish before the Chinese and the Japanese after them. They deemed Taiwan's past worthy of consider-ation only after Chinese settlers arrived on its shore, or when Chinese missions were occasionally sent to the island. Everything prior to this was regarded with the ancestral contempt the Han have long had for any "raw" (sheng) inhabit-ants of remote lands. Regarding this historical diversity, the leader of the his-tory team, Huang Hsiu-cheng, wrote in the *China Times* (Taipei) during the June 1997 controversy:

The development of Taiwan's history shows complex international rela-tions with the Netherlands, Spain and Japan, which all once occupied Taiwan, giving Taiwan's culture, to a certain extent, the colors of a for-eign country.[28]

Here, in one of Taiwan's largest daily newspapers, is an explicit reference to an issue the New inhabitants had been forced by the government's policies to ignore, if not deny, and to what the pre-1990s school books had tried to erase from the Taiwanese collective memory: the plurality of historical experience and what this meant in terms of Taiwanese identity.

The reform was thus an excellent opportunity for the authors of the new program to foster a debate over the emergence of a naturally pluralistic configuration of national identification. Whether out of conviction or a sense of prudence, the advocates of reform and their supporters have not been willing, at least publicly in the manuals or in their declarations to the press, to draw a conclusion regarding the necessity of terminating ties with China. Instead, they envisioned an identification with both Taiwan and China, in concentric circles (*tongxin yuan*): a concept that in Chinese may also carry a more poetic shade of meaning, as "circles of shared feelings." Paraphrasing Lee Yuan-tse and the Commission, Kuo Wei-fan, then Minister of Education, presented the idea in an April 8, 1996 internal speech to the KMT, during a Dr. Sun Yat-sen Memorial Talk.[29] His speech criticized openly the ideological content of the manuals and their "grand-Han" historiographical perspective and explained the new concept of *tongxin yuan*:

> If we look at things from the point of view of the structure of school textbooks, a student book must start by presenting knowledge from the immediate environment, before extending step by step the domain studied: first to the local culture and to the ethnic group that influences [most] the society, then to a knowledge of the cultures of the various ethnic groups and of the territory of the nation; last, to the world's culture ... In consequence, the *Curriculum References* for primary and junior high schools have recently been modified following a strategy of "Standing on Taiwan, having consideration for continental China, opening our eyes on the world" (*lizu Taiwan, xionghuai Dalu, fangyan shijie*).

The allusion to Taiwan's specificity was clear, and other parts of his speech were also clearly directed against the influence of nationalist of ideology on education.

However, Minister Kuo Wei-fan was no proponent of Taiwan's independence from China. If we take away (insofar as it is possible) ideology from the debate on education, everyone could easily agree, I suggest, on the interest and soundness of a principle of identification by concentric circles. In a way, the major political parties in Taiwan had even shown, before the controversy, a clear disposition to accept such an idea. Kuo was later sent to Paris as Taiwan's representative, where I met him on several occasions. During one of our interviews, which followed his reading of a long discussion of the 1997 textbook reform in my Ph.D. dissertation, he denied having been bold over this reform. This surprising comment may help us interpret his 1996 move and the significance of the role he played between 1994 and 1996. He was in favor of a reform that common sense seemed to dictate and had the courage to defend a new vision within KMT circles. But he gave an indication that the task, in fact, might not have been so hard within administrative circles: as long as it was not politicized, the necessity of such a reform was so clear by this stage that reluctant KMT stalwarts could not easily voice opposition. In other words, the trend toward reform was already becoming unstoppable. His declaration was also a confirmation that the principle of a curriculum beginning with textbooks focused on Taiwan, followed by textbooks dealing with China, and finally by books on the wider world, did not necessarily constitute a proindependence policy, at least in the eyes of the Ministry. This may help to explain why the pro-independent militants, as we shall see, had ambivalent feelings about the reform.

However it may be, the notion of identification in concentric circles was still a revolutionary departure in the official discourse of a KMT Minister of Education. It is this notion of identification in concentric circles that was to serve as the basis for the history, geography, and society textbooks during the 3 years of middle-school in a Taiwanese pupil's life: in the first year, knowing Taiwan; in the second year, knowing China; in the third, knowing the world.

Removing from the textbooks an ideology inherited from a period that was drawing to a close; overturning the tradition of Great Han historiography; adapting manuals to the geography of Taiwan; establishing a new point of view that acknowledged the contributions of various ethnic groups to Taiwan's history; incorporating a new evaluation of the Dutch, Spanish, and Japanese colonial experiences; letting different figurations of national identification express themselves in a pluralistic society — all this would appear, in a stable liberal-democratic country, as natural elements of a democratic national education. However, in the Taiwan of 1997, they still constituted the ingredients of bitter political and ideological controversy, launched immediately by the conservative camp in the face of a progressive coalition determined to hold firm and to grasp what they saw as an opportunity to advance a crucial step.

The reform had been prepared during several months and years. It involved non-KMT intellectuals outside the state-party apparatus along with civil servants from within. For both proreformists and antireformists, the stakes were unprecedented. For these reasons, understanding the significance of the June 1997 Knowing Taiwan textbook controversy is crucial to a comprehension of the national identity transition under Lee Teng-hui's presidency. As we shall see, the outcome was a comprehensive defeat for the prounification, antireform camp; not only was the reform passed but also the intense reaction of a few opponents helped mobilize a large number of supporters, initiating an islandwide debate in the printed press. This outcome appears in fact as nothing else than the logical consequence of the steady ideological marginalization of the conservative camp. In 1997, 10 years after the lifting of the martial law, this marginalization was already obvious, in spite of the conservative camp's apparent dominance of positions within the administration, the army, and academia, as well as its close association with several of the island's main media networks.

The Reaction of the Prounification Camp

Commentators, scholars, and politicians adopted at least three interpretations of the reform during the month of June 1997. The first was the conservative portrayal of the program as the result of an ideologically motivated plot hatched by the proindependence camp, with the aim of severing future generations' psychological ties with China. They clearly viewed the new manuals as a propagandist opus, and several contrasted the traditional historiographical approach, regarded as neutral, to the new one, which they branded ideological.

The second type of interpretation was adopted by people who considered reform to be necessary and who opined that it was only the exaggerations of the previous manuals that made the new textbooks look like an ideological manipulation. They viewed the new manuals as the result of a more realistic attempt to render the complexity of Taiwan's historical experiences. However, as we will see below, this second view was espoused by supporters of the reform, and some tended to overlook or downplay those elements of the new program that did indeed introduce considerable changes in the overall curricula. Did they know they themselves could hardly escape from having a particular ideology, as most progressive intellectuals are no less aware of the importance of education in modeling society?

The third type of interpretation was that of the openly proindependence militants, who accepted the reform because they considered it a step forward but who nevertheless considered it a disappointing compromise with traditional historiography, and thus an unsatisfactory and incomplete measure.

On the part of the conservative and prounification camp, the attack was led by a legislator, Lee Ching-hua, who rapidly printed and distributed through the Taipei headquarters of the New Party a short pamphlet entitled "Knowing Taiwan? Or Misunderstanding Taiwan? About Doubts Concerning the Quality of the Content of the Knowing Taiwan Textbooks."[30] In his eyes, Knowing Taiwan was no less than a plot devised by a proindependence camp determined to cut ties with China by removing Chinese history and culture from school textbooks and by enhancing the colonial period's image, all this engineered for Lee Teng-hui's glory. These three ideas were illustrated in the aphorism "*qinRi, fan-Hua, pengLi*" (pro-Japanese, anti-Chinese, flattering Lee Teng-hui).

The Japanese colonial period was undoubtedly the most sensitive issue of all.[31] One of the very few scholars to take sides with the antireform movement,

Wang Hsiao-po, was for instance quoted by a major newspaper as saying: "The program Knowing Taiwan is a school book that views positively the Japanese colonial period."[32]

The conservatives' dissatisfaction started with terminology. Since Japan formally relinquished control over Taiwan on October 25 and the subsequent arrival of a Chinese government, the Japanese colonial period had been called "*Riju shidai*" or "*Riju shiqi*," meaning the period of the Japanese occupation, an expression that denied legality to the Japanese presence between 1895 and 1945, in spite of its legal basis — a bilateral treaty[33] — and Taipei's postwar peace treaty with Japan — an interesting position, since the legality of the ROC's sovereignty on Taiwan is itself a disputed legal matter.[34] The authors of the new manuals preferred the more neutral expression "the period of Japanese colonial rule" (*Riben zhimin tongzhi shiqi*). Given the sensitivity of the conservative mainlanders on the question of Japan, in large part due to their experience of Japan's wartime atrocities, it was felt to be all the more unacceptable that the expression, when abbreviated, was read "*Rizhi shiqi*," or the period of Japanese rule, which they saw as an attempt to imprint in the students' minds a political message: "the period when Taiwan was Japanese." This is a good example of how interpretation matters: de facto and de jure, Taiwan was indeed Japanese. The conservatives believed that it was not true in terms of identity — but what is identity? This is the central issue here. And for them, the failure of the authors to use the usual pejorative expression meant that they had adopted a positive perspective toward Japanese colonization. For them, this was equivalent to adopting an anti-Chinese point of view.

Conservative vigilance on the Japanese question encompassed the smallest details. For instance, on page 21 of the initial version of the history textbook, it was stated that some Japanese priests had been present among the Spanish missions in the seventeenth century, which is indeed surprising. The inclusion of this detail may not have been innocuous and was interpreted as an effort by the authors to trace back to as early as possible a Japanese interest in and presence on the island (the detail did not appear in the later trial version). Another example noticed by the conservatives was the use, in the society manual, of the words "Taiwanese soul" (*Taiwan hun*), an expression drawn directly from the Japanese language and from the Japanese colonial period and clearly meant to evoke a Taiwanese specificity. This was criticized repeatedly by the conservatives, but the expression was nonetheless retained in the following versions of the text.

Regarding the question of Taiwan's relations with China, Lee Ching-hua bitterly reproached the authors of the History manual for not having used any Chinese archives, for failing to cite any of the ancient Chinese expeditions to Taiwan, and for not having once used the words "Chinese" or "Chinese race" to qualify Taiwan and the Taiwanese. He also reproached the authors of the society manual for not having tackled or even mentioned unification when dealing with Taiwan's future in the last chapter and for having preferred the use of "*Zhongguo Dalu*" (mainland China) to "*Dalu*" (Mainland). On this last point, a proindependence militant would say "it is the same anyway" and that only the replacement of "Mainland China" by "China" would signify a real change. The fact that Lee Ching-hua still had something to say about such a tiny difference in words, which are basically expressing the same idea, showed the extreme sensitivity of the conservatives and, at the same time, the precautions taken by the reformers, who were careful not to call China simply "China." To a certain extent, it also shows a prounification camp partially out of touch with reality, since most in Taiwan now recognize China and Taiwan as two different countries.[35] Last, it illustrated the situation of a camp increasingly unable to reverse the Taiwanization trend: Lee Ching-hua was leading a pointless fight over an invisible issue, while the whole society manual was a revolution. And in spite of his critique, the volume was adopted and the reform passed.

On the question of the island's national identity — whether it should be seen as a nation of its own or as part of a bigger nation — the reform's detractors immediately perceived the particular tone employed by the authors in the society manual to describe the existence of a Taiwanese people sharing a community of destiny on their island. They interpreted the last paragraphs of the manual as a declaration of Taiwan's national character. According to Lee Ching-hua:

> We can read in the manual that "All the citizens of Taiwan have an identity card." Is "Taiwan" a country?[36] … We can read in the manual that "the new Taiwan" … wants to transform itself into a civilized country. Has "Taiwan" a national character?[37]

Yet, it would be natural for many islanders — including the so-called Mainlanders — to simply answer yes to his two questions. Many people do indeed consider Taiwan as a country (*guo*), even though some of them still favor unification. This shows the discrepancy between the reality of Taiwan's society and the discourse from which this legislator could not depart, and several other pro-unification politicians with him.

The conservatives also vehemently criticized the way the books depicted Lee Teng-hui's presidency. In the early 1990s, the KMT was divided between conservative and progressive factions, split into two, with a breakaway faction soon constituting the New Party, radically opposed to Lee Teng-hui and his Taiwanization policy. Unsurprisingly, the inclusion in the history books of Lee's presidency, which had not yet come to an end, was difficult for the conservatives to accept, even though political developments since he assumed power had been numerous and far-reaching. The conservatives were caught between the impossibility of denying that history continued and the difficulty of accepting the changes that history's continuation involved. In order to escape this contradiction, and to try to prevent any mention or discussion of this period in schoolbooks, some privately used the argument that the interpretation of this part of recent history was "not yet consensual" and thus should not be evoked. Similar arguments were used by the conservatives in Hong Kong during the 1990s to justify the reluctance to include in textbooks any mention of the student movement of 1989. In the case of Taiwan's conservatives, this not only reflects their unease with the current ideology, which is not theirs, but perhaps also the influence of a longstanding tradition in orthodox, state-centered Chinese historiography that holds that officially sanctioned verdicts (*dinglun*) ought to be delivered on particular historical events — verdicts that scholars and students alike should subsequently respect as the truth.

Moreover, the conservatives found in the book a mistake that was too big to be ignored. The accusation that followed is of great significance and thus deserves detailed consideration. An error attributed to Lee Teng-hui the decision to lift martial law in 1987, a decision that had in fact been taken by his predecessor, Chiang Ching-kuo, son of Chiang Kai-shek's first wife and president from 1978 to 1988. The opponents of the reform, and Lee Ching-hua in particular, drew the conclusion that this was a politically inspired distortion of the truth and proof that the book was in fact the product of a proindependence conspiracy prepared in connivance with President Lee Teng-hui.

The thesis of an intentional mistake does not stand up to careful analysis. Most people in Taiwan know who lifted martial law: some pupils might not know, but their parents and their teachers could hardly be ignorant on this score. It is difficult to imagine that a conscious attempt was being made to deceive people regarding such an established and well-known historical fact. What is more probable is that this was an unintentional mistake, perhaps made by a subordinate writer rushing to meet a deadline, who confused the lifting of martial law by Chiang Ching-kuo in 1987 with the lifting of the Temporary Provisions in 1991 by Lee Teng-hui. In fact, the 1991 decision had, in several respects, a much greater impact on Taiwan's political system.[38] If anything, it was Lee Ching-hua who may have been guilty of a disingenuous manipulation of the truth. The legislator loudly denounced the error made in the teachers' manual but kept silent regarding the fact that in the students' book responsibility for lifting martial law was clearly accorded to Chiang Ching-kuo and not to Lee Teng-hui.

The attempt to blow up this rather trivial typographical error into a full-blown political scandal appears, in fact, to have been part of a premeditated political strategy on the part of the conservatives. It has in fact become a traditional tactic of the anti–Lee Teng-hui camp throughout the 1990s: denouncing a plot fomented by proindependence forces while taking every opportunity to demonize Lee Teng-hui in order to discredit his attempts to change the system erected by the Mainlander elite over the previous for decades. When Lee Ching-hua paid a visit to the new Minister, Wu Ching, during the June 1997 controversy, he branded Knowing Taiwan as a *heixiang zuoye*, or a conspiracy conceived in the dark. Two days earlier, he had described the program as having been "written jointly by Lee Teng-hui and Shiba Ryotaro," the Japanese historian in the presence of whom, in 1994, Lee Teng-hui had made a declaration that infuriated the conservatives for several years.[39] In his opinion, as well as in the eyes of other opponents of reform, the president of the Republic of China was colluding with Japan to brainwash Taiwanese students out of their sense of identification with the Chinese motherland.

Yet the conservatives themselves knew very well that neither Lee nor Shiba had written the manuals. The accusation was yet another example of the prounification camp's interpretation of political events and of their discursive treatment of political reality, a mixture of rhetorical exaggeration and of deliberate manipulation that shows an interesting side of the conservative camp's psychology.[40] On this point, as on others, Lee Ching-hua received full support from other conservative prounificationists, though his active supporters remained very few in number. In general, opponents of the reform kept silent, probably out of a consciousness of their inability to reverse the new course of Taiwanese politics or overturn the new dominant ideology.

The Reaction of the Proreform Camp

Since the outbreak of the controversy, Lee Yuan-tse, the president of the Commission, had been attempting to inject a note of calm and sanity into the debate. He declared to the newspaper most widely read by the conservatives, the *United Daily News* (*Lianhe bao*), "History is a very difficult thing to write. Let history return to history. If we look at history with different ideologies, we will have endless disputes."[41] Whether this statement could really appease the conservatives can be questioned, but Lee at least appeared to have this goal in mind.

The defense of the new history book in Taiwan's newspapers mobilized three prominent contributors to the manual: Huang Hsiu-cheng, mentioned above, the leader of the history team; Huang Fu-san, researcher and director of the Institute of Taiwan History at the Academia Sinica; and Chang Sheng-yen, professor of history and director of the history department of Taiwan's National Central University. Huang Hsiu-cheng focused on the main point of contention: the Japanese issue, citing the text to illustrate what had been said about the harshness of the Japanese repression of resistance by aborigines and other Taiwanese.[42] But he also chose to defend the idea that there existed "a Chinese perception of Taiwan" and a "Taiwanese perception of Taiwan," the latter taking into consideration the diversity of Taiwan's history and its long experience of direct relations with countries other than China.[43] Huang Fu-san organized his arguments around two ideas. The first was that Japan's colonial policy in Taiwan was indeed an imperialist one but that it would be "hard to find another example [as positive as this one] elsewhere in the world." First, he said, the

Japanese soon considered Taiwan as part of their territory and had designed a "project of development of the island over one hundred years." Second, he insisted, the effort to spread literacy among the population was "without equivalent," and he cited the figure of 70 percent of the population having received primary education by the end of the colonial period. The second idea developed by Huang was that the defense of Knowing Taiwan should not be undertaken at the expense of the stability of Taiwan's interethnic relations. He claimed that those who had experienced the war crimes of the Japanese on the Mainland — a severe form of oppression that most Taiwanese did not experience — should be understood, and thus called for a reformulation of certain passages, in order to respect their sensitivitles.[44] Chang Sheng-yen, for his part, straightforwardly territorialized a Taiwanese nation: "Our national territory," he said, has precise territorial limits, which are Taiwan, Penghu, Kinmen and Matsu."[45]

As far as the society manual was concerned, its defense was mainly the responsibility of the head of the working team, Tu Cheng-sheng, who intervened frequently, as his manual was the focal point of the attacks. He regularly defended himself against the charge of attempting to cut psychological ties with China, once concluding, "If we look at Taiwan through the eyes of the Chinese communists, then even eating and sleeping can be suspected of being pro-independence [activities]."[46]

Let us now see what arguments were used by the scholars who defended the reform without actually having taken part in the reform. Analyzing their arguments, presenting their statements and assessing their moderation or their passion will also help us to understand the precise state reached by the gradual maturation of the national identity debate in 1997 and the profound changes in terms of national identity symbols with which the conservatives were confronted during Lee Teng-hui's presidency.

Some supporters of curricular Taiwanization chose to insist on the aboriginal component of Taiwan's identity. Academia Sinica's Chang Sheng-yen, for instance, argued that the new history books should give Aborigines the place they deserved. He also insisted on "Taiwan's independent character and Taiwanese specificity."[47] Others chose to reflect on the nature of the history discipline itself.[48] For instance, the above-mentioned history professor Cheng Jui-ming insisted that historiography cannot compromise with ideology and argued that historians should not produce political statements; at the same time, he stated that it was also natural for the content of history books to evolve with time, because the way history is understood also changes with time.

Several self-appointed defenders of the reform chose to minimize its significance, apparently hoping to pass it off as a politically innocuous move. For instance, an editorial in the *Taiwan Daily News*, a proindependence southern newspaper, declared that criticisms leveled at the program by the two sides (i.e., the prounification camp and the proindependence camp) showed that "there [was] no ideology in this text." It nevertheless acknowledged that "History is a sacred text written by the hand of the winner,"[49] apparently recognizing the naivety of claims that history writers can take ideology (in its broadest sense) out of schoolbooks.

The history professor Lee Yung-chi, of National Taiwan University, declared: "The railroad network and the [infrastructures of] public hygiene during the Japanese era were built by the Japanese. It is history that says this, and it has nothing to do with the debate over Taiwan's independence."[50] This may be true as far as it goes, but coming from a man who was to become, 3 months later, the spokesman of the Taiwan Independence Party (Jianguodang, or TAIP), what is significant is his failure to acknowledge the formidable might that history has, as a unique provider of identification markers: knowing is starting to identify with; and in Chinese, "knowing" (*renshi*) starts with the same character as "identifying with" (*rentong*), and this is no coincidence. "Knowing Taiwan" is thus, semantically as well as conceptually, very close to identifying with Taiwan. The Japanese infrastructure achievements in Taiwan are historical facts, but they are transl(oc)ated into the present of Taiwanese *mentalités* by the transmission of knowledge; they became a part of collective memory, and they now influence the islanders' scheme of national identification — not to mention that any historical fact is partially constructed by the history writers of every period, who place them in narratives particular to their period or personal systems of belief.

The strategy of trying to tone down the revolutionary aspect of the new textbooks explains that the heart of the question — is Taiwan a nation? — has not been discussed directly by many on the reformist side, with most intellectuals trying to moderate their words. The words "*Taiwan guo*" (the country of Taiwan) and "*Taiwan minzu zhuyi*" (Taiwanese nationalism) have in general been carefully avoided. In the transitional phase Taiwan is experiencing, intellectuals who want to explore further political possibilities are conscious of the risks involved in going too fast; political militants are not always conscious of these risks, and this is one of the points that distinguishes them from their more intellectual sympathizers. For that reason, intellectuals mainly called upon schoolbooks to "take Taiwan as the central subject,"[51] at that time an already controversial political stance, but not a recklessly provocative one.

The more militant advocates of a change to the regime's name (*gai guohao*, one of the technical issues behind the so-called declaration of independence, along with constitutional change and redefinition of national boundaries)[52] also conducted their own analysis of the textbooks, which was voiced at the peak of the June 1997 controversy by four groups: the TAIP, the Taiwanese Association of University Professors (*Taiwan jiaoshou xiehui*), a Front for a New Country (*Xin guojia zhenxian*) in the Legislative Yuan, and an Alliance for Justice (*Zhengyi lianxian*) in the National Assembly (the upper house).

The views adopted by the first two groups can be summarized thus: though the manuals do not mention the history of the Taiwan independence movement and still "go on referring to the Republic of China,"[53] which is not acceptable, the new manuals are nevertheless greatly preferable to their predecessors. They should thus be accepted, but pressure on the government to proceed with a more thoroughgoing reform should not be relaxed. On July 4, 1997, the two movements organized a joint conference and issued a communiqué that concluded, "At least it is a good start to let the Taiwanese people understand better their own nation, Taiwan."

The Front for a New Country adopted a harsher evaluation of the reform. Much more reluctant to accept the reform, its members regarded the new program as a mere adaptation for student consumption of the pragmatic ideology of Lee Teng-hui's Taiwanized KMT. The Front legislators asked the reformers to go much further in the reform, while their colleagues of the National Assembly organized a protest on June 24 in front of the Institute. On their banderoles, one could read: "If you love Taiwan, please know Taiwan; if you love China, please go back to China!" (*ai Taiwan, qing renshi Taiwan; ai Zhongguo, qing huigui Zhongguo*).

The Spirit of the Reform: The Influence of the Movement of Indigenization

The reform of 1994 through 1997 reflects quite well the evolution and the complexity of the national debate in Taiwan 11 years after the start of liberalization, and in the tenth year of Lee Teng-hui's presidency. On the one hand, we find in the new manuals clear marks of the influence of years of indigenization of political thought, symbols, and institutions; of a more neutral and balanced historiography, particularly as regards the period of Japanese colonization; and of the ideas of Lee Teng-hui, who as president defended a cautious and moderate version of Taiwanese nationalism. All this suggests a pragmatic move in the direction of curricular localization, rather than a conspiracy on the part of proindependence militants.

However, it is also undeniable that we find in the new books, especially in the society volume, several sentences and paragraphs that could not fail to alarm the conservatives. It appeared to most that the authors of the society book had not maintained the same level of detachment toward their topic as the authors of the history book. The topic itself may partly explain this: not that history writing is not subject to passion, but in the sense that it is even more difficult to remain neutral when writing on a society like Taiwan's, which is characterized by a severe ideological divide. In addition, a sentiment of exasperation on the part of scholars who had spent years working in an atmosphere dominated by an almighty ideology of Chinese consciousness doubtless prompted them to reveal their identification to Taiwan now that such an opportunity presented itself.

This strong influence of years of indigenization of the polity is clearly illustrated by the geographical scope of the curricular content: the Tai-Peng-Jin-Ma area, in other words, Taiwan, Penghu, Kinmen, and Matsu, the four main insular groups over which the Republic of China (Taipei) exerts effective jurisdiction. Giving the new manuals that spatial scope was not a deliberate choice made by the authors on their own authority; it was the decision taken by the Ministry at the outset of the reform.[54] This confirms the interpretation of this reform that was made above: the Ministry clearly decided to increase Taiwanese students' knowledge of and identification with Taiwan, but no decision was ever taken to focus all textbooks for each grade exclusively on Taiwan — as stated above, Knowing Taiwan was conceived as a program only for the first year of junior high school, and was to be followed in Year 2 by classes on China and in Year 3 by courses on the rest of the world. But the actual application of the Ministry's directive could hardly produce anything other than what in fact resulted: a history book focusing exclusively on Taiwan's own history; a geography manual dealing with the Tai-Peng-Jin-Ma area; and a society textbook that could hardly avoid, if it wanted to justify its existence, a focus on the feeling of common destiny in Taiwan that is palpably felt by most inhabitants of Taiwan and that was not simply invented by proindependence scholars intent on instituting a scheme of anti-China brainwashing.

In consequence, it could be said that the conservatives might have better directed their reproaches at the Ministry's new 1995 curriculum — and especially the decision to include a new discipline, with the introduction of a society book — than at the authors' 1997 work. We have here an illustration of the historical contradiction in which the Taiwanization movement places the prounification camp: the latter cannot and, as shown, did not deny the necessity to localize the school curriculum, but when the concrete consequences of such a policy materialized, it was harder for them to accept them, and this contradiction — constant since the beginning of 1990s — shows how delicate their position is in the context of the current trends of Taiwanese politics.[55] This raises the following question: if the conservatives were in principle prepared to accept a localization of the school curriculum, what form could this localization have taken that they might have found acceptable? The example of contemporary Hong Kong, where curricular localization has religiously abided by the dictates of China's "one country" ideology, perhaps suggests the answer (see Chapter 5).

For its part, however, the society manual appears much more strongly committed than the history manual to the defense of the idea of a Taiwanese community of destiny. In the first chapter of the initial version, a subchapter is entitled "We are all Taiwanese" (11), an expression that even the prounification camp uses — in its case, to reject any accusation of being unfaithful to Taiwan — but that is nevertheless an explicit reference to the community of fate of a politically isolated island. This community is based on "ethnic pluralism" (8, 11, and 92) that, "with the discreet influence of culture and an objective political environment, has produced the so-called Taiwanese consciousness" (11). But speaking of a community where every islander can be called "Taiwanese" can only be possible "if every ethnic group respects each other" (14). Today's population inherited from preceding generations "a certain number of life habits" that, according to the manuals, would justify the use of the terms "Taiwanese soul" and "Taiwanese spirit" (50). A romanticized presentation of Taiwanese history follows, which deploys language reminiscent of revolutionary mythology accompanying the birth of a new nation; in a subchapter entitled "Equality, Liberty, Dignity," it is stated that the Taiwanese historical experience

> has caused interpersonal relations to be based on a greater equality and, thanks to the profound esteem in which Liberty is held [in Taiwan], has caused people to reject governments that oppress society and to bravely defy authority. (52)

What is clearly implied here is a tradition of opposition to the successive foreign rulers, the Manchus (1683–1895), the Japanese (1895–1945), and the Chinese (1945–1988). Further on, the theme of the island's tragic history is invoked to legitimize the assertion of a separatist claim. In a subchapter entitled "We Can Be Our Own Masters and Decide by Ourselves," it is stated that: "During most of the last four hundred years, the people have not been masters at home, and have not been able to decide their own fate," an expression very close in content and tone to the statements made by intellectuals and politicians of openly proindependence sympathies.[56] The authors of the society manual consider that "Taiwanese political history is the sad history of a [form of] political control which dispensed with [the need for] people's approval and participation" (63). A few lines further on, we read this expression, the literal meaning of which corresponds to reality, but whose political significance goes much further: "In the thirty-fourth year of the Republic [i.e., 1945], at the end of the second Sino-Japanese war, the Nationalist government received (*jieshou*) Taiwan [from the Japanese]; Taiwan then started to be ruled by the government of the Republic of China" (*Taiwan shi you Zhongghua mingguo zhengfu tongzhi*; 64). This formulation clearly indicated that a parallel was being drawn between KMT rule and other previous periods of foreign rule. The conservatives might have derived some comfort from the fact that the authors counted years in Republican years (with 1912 as Year 1), whereas it is not at all rare in Taiwan today to count years the Western way. It would also be hard for them to deny that this presentation is factually accurate. But the choice of certain terms over alternative equivalents was enough to expose substantial differences in opinion and to provoke the outrage of a camp rendered oversensitive by its growing sense of helplessness in the face of gradual, but relentless and systematic, symbolic changes under Lee Teng-hui's presidency.

It would be possible to give several more examples of phrases and concepts drawn from or reflecting the rhetoric of Taiwanese nationalism. The very last chapter of the society volume is entitled "Building a New Taiwan," and this deals with the island's future. These very words seem directly borrowed from the political lexicon and phraseology of former President Lee, who in late 1994 coined the expression "Managing Greater Taiwan" for one of his speeches, later popularized by a book with the same title he published in January 1995. The two expressions are very close: *ying zao xin Taiwan* (society manual) and *jing ying da Taiwan* (Lee's book). Noticeably, Lee Teng-hui's thought inspired even more obviously the designers of the new middle-school *Curriculum Reference* published in 1995 by the Ministry, which insisted that the society textbook be able to "nurture a capacity for self-control, directed toward tolerance, generosity and humanism, and to help concentrate on the consensus about a community of life" (*shengming gongtongti*). The expression *shengming gongtongti* was coined in Chinese by or for Lee Teng-hui and has been one of his favorite slogans for years. The final chapter calls upon Taiwanese to now use "our point of view," adding that "even before the end of the 20th century, the word 'Taiwanese' ha[d] already become the name of all of us within the international community" (88). A few lines after, it concluded: "No deity, and no hero, has the power to decide Taiwan's fate" (*renhe yi zun shenming huo renhe yi wei yingxiong dou wu fa jueding Taiwan de mingyun*; 89).

The Intellectuals' Introspection-Distantiation

The Knowing Taiwan controversy of June 1997 had a side effect that the conservatives would certainly have desired even less than the adoption of the manuals: it helped to reinforce a trend towards of introspection regarding the Han Chinese origins of the Taiwanese.

The discourse of many militant advocates of Taiwanese identity can be as primordialist (based on a perception of identity as mainly a matter of primordial attachments) as that of the conservatives themselves; they tend to deny plurality and evolution as fundamental features of identity processes. Instead, they essentialize identity, reifying it and elevating it to the status of an inalienable heritage, an attribute rather than an process. In consequence, proindependence militants often pass over in silence, and even occasionally deny, the ethno-cultural foundation of Taiwanese culture, which is in large part "Chinese." But the use of quotation marks here underlines the risk that by using the label "Chinese" we may in turn fall into the trap of an essentialized vision of Chineseness. What does "Chinese" mean? What concretely does it mean to have "Chinese cultural origins"? In a politicized debate between China and the world, between China and Taiwan, and between prounificationists and proindependence militants on Taiwan, the word "Chinese" is unfortunately never defined, since a constructionist interpretation of the term risks undermining a set of categories often brandished as an apolitical tool legitimizing everything that need to be legitimized, from China's special terms for entering the World Trade Oraganization to the denial by Taiwan's mainlanders that the Taiwanese might have the right to envision a separate future for themselves.

Meanwhile, however, a few intellectuals in Taiwan have defended a more sophisticated — and courageous — approach, tackling head-on the issue of the origins of Taiwan's society and culture and deducing from the history of their development the pluralistic and fluid character of identities. Nation-builders do not need to deny the plurality of the culture they inherit and that they try to change; once it is accepted that identity evolves over time, there is no reason to see as incompatible an origin situated within a culture increasingly considered as foreign and a future envisioned as distinct. In other words, a common cultural matrix does not impose a shared future. Identity is by definition pluralistic and evolving, and it is possible to acknowledge this widely accepted theoretical argument while pursuing a nation-building movement. However, it is practically risky to attempt to incorporate such an approach into a political rhetoric that is, by nature, an attempt to mobilize and, as a consequence, has a tendency to simplify. Accepting plurality while attempting to define a nation reflects the maturity of a political movement, and that was one of the intellectual issues at stake during the 1997 reform, as it is more generally in the ongoing process of defining Taiwanese nationhood. This process or debate continues to involve tensions between ethnic and civic, and between moderation and inclusiveness on the one side and extremism and exclusiveness on the other.

Since the mid-1990s, there has been an effort in university circles to conceptualize Taiwanese identity in more complex and potentially more inclusive terms. Here, as an example, is what professor Hsü Chün-hsiung, who teaches Chinese literature at National Taiwan Normal University, wrote in June 1995:

> Taiwanese historians have already initiated a deep introspection, they have understood better and better mutations in Taiwanese society, and are finally able to make judgements in a different manner than previously, when their analysis was informed by a Han perspective; the history of Taiwan's society was forged jointly by each of the ethnic groups on the island ... Let us adopt a new type of point of view to combat and eliminate the wide-ranging Han hegemony; the very large scope of Taiwanese literature has been created together by the Aborigines, the Minnan, the Hakkas, and the Waishengren,[57] and, in fact, we should state this plainly. There has never been an equal emphasis placed in Han culture on agriculture, plains, mountains and oceans as has been the case in our local culture and the literature of the past ... What literature reveals in terms of pluralism, directions of thought, in material of creation ... can also produce an interaction between ethnic groups, a stimulant of creativity, of development, and of radiance ... With an island that is attracting little by little the attention of international society, at a moment when scholars from the Mainland, from Japan, from the United States elsewhere are deepening their study of Taiwanese literature, at a time when

they are establishing university departments in this field, we have no reason to shy away; being conscious proponents of a better knowledge of Taiwan will help us keep our own eyes open, and appreciate this central question: the existence of a pluralistic people, of which each part is bound to share the fate of the other parts, in what is happy and what is sad.[58]

The plurality of Taiwanese identity is presented here through an emphasis on the ethnic variety of Taiwanese society. It is interesting to note the logical character of the author's argumentation: he criticizes the hegemony of the traditional Han point of view and, as a logical consequence of his vision of Taiwanese society as pluralistic, he calls upon Taiwanese to accept the idea that every component of their society, including the last wave of immigrants from China, has contributed to the richness of Taiwanese society and history. In this plurality, the mainlanders, or New inhabitants, have their place, and just that — they no longer dominate, but they nonetheless still belong.

Such a discourse was still uncommon in the Taiwan of 1995; it was certainly unheard of on the prounification side but also very rare on the part of proindependence activists who, out of perhaps understandable acrimony arising from years of persecution, were prone to forget (or deny) that the New inhabitants also belonged to this land. Two years later, during the June 1997 ideological tempest, the arguments used by the intellectuals defending the reform were elaborate variations on the fundamental themes expressed by Hsü Chün-hsiung and a few others, an indication that such arguments represent the national thought of a growing number of Taiwanese intellectuals.

What is also remarkable in this text is the consciousness that the author has of being Han himself — if this vague ethnic label has any real sense — and the ease with which he copes with what many would see as a contradiction: being Han (or potentially regarded as Han) and criticizing the so-called Great Han ideology. Trying to keep under wraps a Chinese ancestry that would be considered embarrassing is not an option; he prefers to develop a vision of plurality, which involves a degree of introspection and distantiation from an ethnic marker considered by some to be at the heart of Taiwanese identity. That is why I try to characterize, through the example of the Knowing Taiwan textbook controversy, this deep change at play in Taiwan as an introspection-distantiation on the part of the island's progressive intellectual elite regarding Taiwan's ethno-cultural matrix. I hope thereby to illuminate this reflection on plurality (and the claim of the right to enounce it publicly), which upsets the ideological, historiographical, and cultural prejudices that gave psychological comfort to the mainlander minority during the 40 years of their rule over Taiwan.

It is also important to note that this text was written in elegant Chinese, which is perhaps to be expected of a professor of Chinese literature but also has a political significance: a deliberate choice to show that loving Taiwan does not mean being ignorant, that seeing Taiwan as a nation does not mean rejecting Chinese culture, that one can be at the same time well-versed in Chinese classical literature, while also understanding the modern aspiration to let an insular identity evolve and express itself naturally. Such an attitude, which is undoubtedly shared by this author as it is by several literati in Taiwan, helps the comprehension of two constitutive characters of identity: plurality and fluidity. It renders possible the formulation in the realm of ideas and concepts what is already a concrete political reality: the legitimacy of the separation between race or ethnicity and governance. This could be expressed in the following manner: The claim that I would belong to the same race as you does not imply that I have to live under the same roof, the existence and the consciousness that I have of the common roots I share with you do not prevent my identity from evolving in a different way from yours, and this claim of a specificity in my character and of an independence in my movements is in no way a disownment of my origins. And who has the right to say I belong to you anyway?[59]

This reasoning involves several steps: looking back on oneself, becoming conscious of one's origins rather than passively internalizing a received narrative, measuring the distance of an evolution, admitting the emergence of differences with others who also evolving themselves; and asserting the legitimacy of such evolutions. This process of introspection and distantiation did not begin suddenly in June 1997. It is the result of a long process of maturation in Taiwan's identity. The June 1997 controversy has highlighted and confirmed the extent of the changes that had taken place in the mentality of Taiwan's progressive intellectual elite, but the lack of interest exhibited by the broader public in this issue (as I felt during the controversy by asking questions to numerous friends, contacts, and casual acquaintances) shows that the controversy was nevertheless largely confined within the circles of the printed media, intellectuals, and politicians. However intense the controversy may have been, and no matter how extensive these circles are, the debate was carried on mainly among the elite.

Nevertheless, this does not mean that the changes were superficial or contingent and unrelated to any more profound historical trends. The New Party and the conservative circles, had they possessed the power to do so would certainly have stopped or tried to stop the reform. But they no longer had this power, and even if they had still had it, they could probably not have simply forced the progressive intellectual elite to return to the positions they held on Taiwan's identity before the start of the nativization movement. Mentalities do not easily return to a status quo ante, and potent governments can only freeze political evolutions temporarily. The genie of Taiwanese consciousness, once released, would not be squeezed back inside its bottle.

It is no surprise that this phenomenon of introspection and distantiation resurfaced immediately during the intense debates provoked by the presentation of the new textbooks in June 1997. The above-mentioned researcher Chang Sheng-yen expressed the idea that "Han people" would not know how to "read history" and to draw conclusions from it. In the past, he said, the tradition was to learn from history only the material useful for imperial exams — a tradition imported to Taiwan for other types of exams. He thus exhorted Taiwanese to distance themselves from this tradition and to learn how to draw from their history lessons of wisdom.[60] On his side, Yü Kuo-chi, then deputy executive director of the editorial office of the *Liberty Times*, argued that it was time to reexamine Han culture to see whether it had not also had a negative influence (*fumian yingxiang*) in Taiwan, and whether the values of the Taiwanese people had not, by their specific evolution, distanced themselves little by little from the traditional values of the "Han people":

> Old manuals seriously lacked any criticism of the negative influence of Han culture. We must study the question of whether or not Han culture has had a negative impact on our life-style, and whether or not our system of values has distanced itself from this Han culture.[61]

Lin Shih-ji, assistant to a member of the National Assembly, insisted on the same idea:

> There are two axes in the historical development of Taiwan since the Qing took control of it [in 1683]. One is China's influence, and Taiwan's incorporation into China. The other is Taiwan's separation from China and its insertion into the international community. The foundations of Taiwan's relations with China are a geographic link and a blood link. The Han people of Taiwan arrived from Fujian and Guangdong. When coming to the island, they brought with them the customs and folkways of the Han, their beliefs and their traditions. Several generations have passed. The ancient Han immigrants have all put down roots in Taiwan and become Taiwanized. Not only they have identified with Taiwan, but in addition their difference with the Han of contemporary China is great.[62]

The affirmation that an original ethnic community existed (whether a myth or not, considering the debates on the notion of ethnicity) is not detrimental to a proindependence discourse, and this text exemplifies it. Its author, probably without being well versed in theories of identity and ethnicity, nevertheless treats identity in the same way a growing number of social scientists do: as a social construct in permanent evolution. As this text shows, the author is conscious that it is useless to deny that a certain community between China and Taiwan used to exist and, for those who believe in the disputable concept of Han ethnicity, that immigrants and mainlanders shared a common ethnicity, because a common origin, says this author, does not preclude the possibility of a divergent evolution, which is a natural process. Of course, there is a risk that such an analysis, after legitimizing a new identity born from these evolutions, stops short and gives way once again to a more traditional, primordialist-like reading of this new identity, the new discourse replacing the old one and, another essentialist approach toward identity replacing the other. Not all Taiwanese proreform intellectuals escape this danger.

The Knowing Taiwan textbooks controversy constituted an excellent occasion for the expression of ideas revealing what is called here introspection and distantiation, a movement that seems a necessary preliminary step to envisioning the Taiwanese nation. It is not surprising that these discussions alarm those of the New inhabitants who remain wedded to a primordialist conception of identity — and they are numerous: How, they wonder, can Taiwanese forget that they are Han? This is the central point of their incomprehension. But to ask that question, one should first ask this one: What does the word "Han" really mean? Is it a valid concept? Does this ethnic label have a real capacity to explain a complex reality? Has it ever been carefully defined and critiqued?

Taiwan's de facto, if not de jure, independence from an irredentist China is the background context of an identity search that has transformed Taiwan, during the 1990s, into a "laboratory of identities."[63] It is often said that Taiwan is inventing Taiwaneseness in the course of its nation-building process. But generally unnoticed is the fact that Taiwan, by the very same process, might also be contributing to the reinvention of Chineseness, by simply trying to verbalize its content beyond its ideological meaning. The different texts presented above all bring us back to the same question: What does it mean to be a Han? If one can say that Taiwan's Han and China's Han are now different (Lin Shih-chi), is it still relevant and meaningful to describe them all as Hans? If so, what is this Han character? If the scholars who debate these questions are considered to be Han, while detaching themselves so much from a Han heritage, is it legitimate to decide for them who they are and to call them Han, a label they might dispute? If the idea that identity evolves is accepted, can a common origin supply an exclusive and eternal identity marker? If not, then we must ask ourselves if we can accept the word "Han" without questioning it first, as it is a term that belongs above all to the realm of political argumentation and is usually imposed in a narrow, unreflective manner as an identity marker that is not supposed to be questioned. "You are a Han, how can you forget it?" is a common question asked in Chinese communities around the globe to people of Chinese descent who try to imagine an identity other than the ethnicist definition of what they are supposed to be.

By progressively conceptualizing a distinction between ethnicity and governance, some Taiwanese intellectuals are inevitably raising questions about the construction of ethnic labels that were previously accepted without question. It is my belief that the notion of Han is, concretely, of poor scientific value;

however, precisely because of its extensive political use, it has a social meaning deserving examination.

In other words, if Taiwan's identity search contributes to an understanding that Chineseness might be found elsewhere than in an ill-defined and overpoliticized concept, this laboratory of identities can help to explore what it means to be Chinese today, at a moment when the question is of pressing importance in China proper. It is through the confrontation of two mutually incomprehensible discourses (a conservative one, based on the strength of primordial attachments, and a progressive one, based on a constructionist perception of identities) that a fertile reflection has emerged in Taiwan on what it means to be what one is supposed to be. The degree of the incomprehension can be expressed in this sentence from Wang Chien-hsüen, one of the founders of the New Party, in an interview a few weeks after the June controversy: "But how can Taiwanese forget that their fathers all came from continental China?"[64]

What if this question is not at all relevant any more?

Of course, not all declarations that were made during the month of June 1997 were moderate. Some clearly reflected an exasperation with what was felt to be a fundamental contempt for Taiwan on the part of a former elite who ruled the island as colonizers and who, after they finally lost power, have continued to try to halt the efforts of the local elite to enhance Taiwan people's comprehension of and love for their own land. For instance, in an opinion column entitled "Are You Afraid of 'Knowing Taiwan'? Or Are You Afraid that Historical Facts Annihilate the Dream of a Unified Greater China?"[65] Chen Chieh-chüan, also an assistant to a member of the National Assembly, declared:

> The idea of knowing (*renshi*) Taiwan had become, in fact, a taboo in our national curriculum; it has now become a source of considerable anxiety in the hearts of the supporters of unification ... If Taiwanese understand (*liaojie*) their own land, this will surely create a concrete feeling of love for it, and the dream of the love for a Greater China will go up in smoke ... Lee Ching-hua grew up by eating Taiwanese rice, and he is the son of a dignitary; he has been a legislator for many years, and has never thought about the question of education; how can he suddenly feel a passion for "Knowing Taiwan"?[66]

Later in the text, he asked: "Eight years of war against Japan, what is the link with Taiwan?" showing how wide the difference can be between the New inhabitants and the proindependence militants on such a sensitive point. He continued in a strongly worded conclusion:

> In order to construct perfect national institutions, we must teach the sons and daughters of Taiwan how to know Taiwan, understand its past and envision the future of its people. If the supporters of unification do not identify with this, then they can just go back to China immediately.[67]

Conclusion

The movement of educational reform between 1994 and 1997 has reversed Taiwan's postwar historiographic tradition. The reason behind the quasi-ignorance of Taiwanese history in previous textbooks was that Taiwan was considered a peripheral territory; a marginal land; an appendage to a central, ancestral, and splendid China; an island worthy of historicity only from the time Chinese people started to colonize it. Knowing Taiwan has thus given an impulse to the notion of pluralistic national identity and national identification.[68] It has provided some intellectuals with a golden opportunity to defend a constructionist definition of identity, claiming the legitimacy of a separate fate in spite of a common origin, even if, at times, it was later to justify an identity that risks being viewed in an essentialist (primordialist) way.

It is always hard for scholars, and among them, historians, to escape ideology totally; the conservatives were of course not wrong in describing the reform as an ideological move. In this respect, however, the difference between the old textbooks and the new ones is clear: the new ones have to a real extent managed to remain much more neutral in presenting points of contention, such as Taiwan's Chinese cultural matrix, the Japanese era, the February 28 uprising and the following massacre, and the authoritarian period of the regime. It would be naïve to pretend that no ideology informs the writing of the new books — since history and ideology (in its broad sense) are intertwined — even though the authors were probably sincere in their wish to make a break with the style of the old nationalistic, politicized history books. Their own ideology is manifest when they talk, for instance, of a "Taiwanese soul"; but again, this is the society book and not the history book. All in all, they were successful in depoliticizing history, and the reaction of the conservatives was not simply a product of the inevitability of ideology's presence in any historical text, but was marked above all by their own unwillingness to accept that another ideology should replace theirs.

But the major difference in the reading we can make of the conservatives' ideology versus the new one is perhaps the moral legitimacy of the world view that the second proposes: democracy, pluralism, and a civic nationalism that transcends ethnic diversity and replaces a chauvinist ethnic nationalism that used to militarize the spirit of school education. It simply appeals more to us today than the conservative, passé, prounification ideology of the KMT. This latter was based on a postulated necessity to make the ethnic community coincide with the polity, justifying on purely emotional grounds the necessity of reunifying Taiwan and China. Justifying Taiwan's unification with China by invoking an invented Han community cannot be an intellectually satisfactory explanation, especially at a time when the disastrous state of the contemporary world gives countless examples of the dangers of such an ideology.

Endnotes

1. I would like to thank three persons who kindly reviewed this chapter and gave me very useful comments: Sylvie Pasquet, a researcher at the National Centre for Scientific Research in Paris; Patricia van der Eeckhout, who teaches social history at the Vrije Universiteit Brussels; and Edward Vickers, the editor of this volume. I remain, of course, the only person responsible for any mistake this chapter may contain.

2. I proposed in French to describe this as "*une Chine* idéelle," meaning "existing in ideas," distinct from the notion of "*une Chine idéale*," an ideal China.

3. On the question of the logical links between the necessity to find political legitimization, the suppression of Taiwanese identity, and the dictatorial shape of the Nationalist government, the French-literate reader may want to have a look at my M.A. dissertation, *Legitimization at the Test of Time: The Political Equilibrium in the Republic of China, 1949–1972*, Paris, Institute of Political Studies, 1993, 128 p.

4. In the present text, "historiography" is not used in the sense of the body of literature published on historical matters. It will be used exclusively (1) in the sense of "the way history is written"; (2) to designate the reflection conducted on how history is written: an introspective research on the technical and ethical rules of the discipline aimed at showing how a historian works, how different schools of history have evolved, alerting historians to their social power and responsibility and to what dangers they must avoid, such as confusing historical analysis and ideological statements.

5. Precise references on the manuals will be found in the references section on page 167.

6. The "new edition of the official version" mentions on the last page of each manual only one "trial version," the one that was distributed to the public in September 1997. However readers of this volume now know that two internal versions preceded this.

7. This document will presumably be hard to find in the future. As time has now passed since I wrote this paper in 1999, I realize that most analyses of the *Knowing Taiwan* textbooks done subsequently have been based on the public versions and not on the internal version, the one that started the crisis, a priceless version that very few, I believe, possess. My opinion is that this initial version is the one most worth analyzing if the object is to investigate the political meaning of the reform at the moment of Lee's presidency.

8. Article 158, the first of the ten articles devoted to national education in the constitution, states that "Education culture is to develop the nationalist spirit of the citizen, a spirit of autonomy, physical health, science and intelligence."

9. By the beginning of the 1990s, the United States of Soviet Republic did not exist any more, the Cold War was over, and the two sides of the Taiwan Straits had engaged in a dialogue.

10. *Ziyou shibao*, June 16, 1997.

11. As Hai Ren notes, "[the] Kuomintang was obsessed by its continental past … and lived in a displaced history, which was nevertheless the present of Taiwan." In "Taiwan and the Impossibility of the Chinese," in Melissa J. Brown, ed. *Negotiating Ethnicities in China and Taiwan.* Berkeley: Berkeley University Press, 1996, 93–94.

12. In June 1997, the Kaohsiung legislator Chen Chi-mai of the Democratic Progressive Party wrote for instance in an opinion column: "For more than forty years of martial law in our country … national education has constantly fallen into the state of a brainwashing tool serving our governing institutions." *Zili zaobao*, June 8, 1997.

13. In the traumatic atmosphere of the 1996 presidential election, marked by the missile crisis (when China test-fired ballistic missiles in the Taiwan Strait), a proindependence student organization of National Taiwan University organized a sit-in in the February 28 Peace Park in Taipei, calling on the Ministry and its employees to "stop being history's criminals" (*bu yao zuo lishi de zuiren*) and finally burning manuals published by the Institute. Their leaflets asked for textbooks that took "Taiwanese ethnic consciousness as a central topic" (*yi Taiwan minzu yishi wei zhuti*; leaflet distributed on March 20, 1996, third demand).

14. This absence of precision can be explained in several ways. One will immediately think of the party's reluctance to change the school programs. However, as we have seen in the previous section, the reform had already started to be implemented by that time. An explanation of the lack of information given by the KMT can perhaps be found in the fact that, the party having been in power for five decades already, its heavy and slow bureaucracy was not inclined to produce programs and explain its policies as a normal party would do if placed in a situation of open electoral competition. More simply, the KMT cadre interviewed might also have known little about the reform that was being conducted at the same moment.

15. This idea of replacing a "China-centered point of view" by a "Taiwan-centered point of view" is central to the proindependence activists' protest against the KMT schoolbooks.

16. For each discipline (history, geography, and societal questions), the Commission was composed of working teams made up of specialists in the relevant disciplines (40 percent of the membership), active teachers (35 percent), specialists in educational psychology and other fields of educational science (10 percent), specialists in "media production" (5 percent) (since the production of textbooks was now opened to the

private sector) and, lastly, officials from the Ministry and the Institute (only 10 percent).

17. Speech in *Tamsui*, May 26, 1996.

18. *Lianhe wanbao*, June 9, 1997.

19. Usually and inaccurately called "Mainlanders." On this question, see Stéphane Corcuff, "Taiwan's Mainlanders, New Taiwanese?" in Stéphane Corcuff, *Memories of the Future, op. cit.*, 163–165.

20. Separation with China, by the April 17, 1895 treaty of Shimonoseki, which ceded Taiwan to Japan.

21. A Taiwanese Hakka, who in 1894 founded a militia that later reach the number of eighty battalions and that became one of the most important forces to fight the Japanese.

22. May 23, 1895.

23. He was first the treasurer of the governor Shao You-lien, then became governor himself in October 1894, and was designated President of the brief Democratic Republic of Taiwan (*Taiwan minzhuguo*) in April 1895.

24. A contingent of three thousand men of the Yue (Guangdong and Guangxi) army sent by the Emperor to Taiwan in July 1894, after the Fall of Seoul and the growing Japanese menace toward China.

25. The father of Koo Cheng-fu, Taiwan's chief negotiator with China today.

26. See Andrew Morris, "The Taiwan Republic of 1895 and the Failure of the Qing Modernizing Project," in Stéphane Corcuff, *Memories of the Future, op. cit.*, 3–24.

27. Part 8 of the new history textbook.

28. Here *Huang* probably means "Foreign to China," trying to cautiously depart from a Han-centered historiography. *Zhongguo shibao*, June 6, 1997.

29. Chen Chih-chia (2000, 21) mentions in her bibliography a speech the same year on the same topic at the presidential palace, entitled *Jiaoyu gaige de gongshi yu qiyi* (Consensus and differences in the interpretation of educational reform; no pagination given).

30. This text is the main source for my analysis of the arguments employed in June 1997 by the reform opponents, at times completed by a few declarations they made to the press.

31. Interestingly, this indicated that, by the end of the 1990s, the question of Japan was still very divisive in ideological debates in Taiwan, especially between those believing in Chinese consciousness and those believing in a Taiwanese consciousness.

32. *Zhongguo shibao*, June 5, 1997.

33. The Shimonoseki treaty of April 17, 1895.

34. Japan handed Taiwan over to the Allies, represented by Chiang Kai-shek, by the will of MacArthur, and not to the ROC proper—this is indeed the way it is officially stated in the Japanese surrender document.

35. And among them, an increasing number of New inhabitants. I suggest readers who read Chinese refer to my essay on this question, "*Feng he ri nuan: Taiwan Waishengren yu guojia rentong di zhuanbian.*" Taipei, Yunchen wenhua, 2004.
36. Lee Ching-hua, *Knowing Taiwan?* (1997), 8.
37. Ibid., 9.
38. The provisions were the legal dispositions that had frozen the normal constitutional life of the Republic from April 18, 1948, to May 1, 1991.
39. The interview was published by the weekly magazine of the *Asahi Shinbun*, Tokyo, May 5–13, 1994. In this interview, Lee Teng-hui talked about the "sorrow of having been born Taiwanese" (*sheng wei Taiwanren de beiai*) and described the party of which he was president, the KMT, as "a political force which came from outside" (*wailai zhengquan*). In his 1999 Taiwan di zhuzhang, Lee Teng-hui made a sort of inventory of the cultural influences he had received, the first one cited being the Japanese. Lee, who declared until 1945, he was Japanese, has fully recognized his Japanese heritage, which has provoked outrage in the prounification camp.
40. I recently published an analysis of the use of the theory of conspiracy by the same anti-Taiwanization, conservative, mainly Mainlander political camp during the 2004 presidential election. The reader can refer to it to see what appears as an extraordinary consistency of arguments, techniques and, ultimately, psychology, on the part of a camp that is conscious of both its progressive marginalization and its inability to stop it. In its effort to survive it has resorted to a political strategy of denouncing, exaggerating, manipulating, which is equivalent, as Edward Friedman puts it, to "political suicide." See Stéphane Corcuff's "The supporters of unification and the Taiwanization movement: Feelings of emergency and crisis mentality in the Blues' camp during the 2004 presidential election campaign," in *China Perspectives* 53 (May–June 2004):49–66. The text by Professor Friedman is the text of a June 24, 2004 lecture he gave at the School of Oriental and African Studies (London) entitled "Paranoia, Polarization and Suicide: How Taiwan's 2004 Presidential Election Revealed Deep Societal Fissures."
41. *Lianhebao*, June 8, 1997.
42. *Zhongguo shibao*, June 6, and *Lianhebao*, June 10, 1997.
43. *Zhongguo shibao*, June 6, 1997.
44. *Lianhebao*, June 10, 1997.
45. *Ziyou shibao*, June 16, 1997.
46. Ibid., June 6, 1997.
47. Ibid., June 16, 1997.
48. See note 3.
49. *Taiwan ribao*, June 7, 1997.
50. *Minzhong ribao*, June 15, 1997.

51. See note 11.
52. The reader can see a box entitled "What independence?" on Taiwan's status de facto and de jure about the technical question of independence, in my paper "The Supporters of Unification," *China Perspectives*, op. cit.
53. We should nevertheless mention that the teachers' society manual contained several documents to serve as a base for students' work that present the February–March 1947 massacre, the "White terror" of the 1950s, the "Formosa Incident" of 1979, and the numerous social movements that put pressure on the KMT after the lifting of the martial law to liberalize the society. See *Renshi Taiwan lishi pian, jiaoshou ce*, 163 et seq. (trial version).
54. The first two objectives of the program devised for the society manual were: (1) to increase the knowledge of the societies of Taiwan, Penghu, Kinmen, and Matsu (2) to develop a perception of them that corresponds to a pluralistic culture, nurture love for one's local land that enables an even stronger love for the nation (Curriculum *Reference*, 133). The same wording can be found in the history book (ibid., 147) and the geography one (ibid., 155).
55. The passage between these two notes was added to my initial French version. On this interpretation of the prounification camp's delicate position, I advise again my reader to have a look at the paper I published on this topic after the 2004 Presidential election, "The Supporters of Unification and the Taiwanization Movement," op. cit.
56. The second sentence of Lee Teng-hui's *Taiwan di zhuzhang* reads: "For a very long period, Taiwanese have not been able to be masters in their own home" (Lee, op. cit., 34.)
57. The common word in Chinese for those called in English "Taiwan's Mainlanders" and that I propose, in my work, to call the New inhabitants. See above, note 15.
58. *Zhongguo shibao*, June 26, 1997.
59. I use here the disputed notion of race to express in a few words only what would take much longer to explain
60. *Ziyou shibao*, June 16, 1997.
61. Ibid.
62. *Zili zaobao*, June 18, 1997.
63. See Corcuff, op. cit., 2002, "Intro: Taiwan, A Laboratory of Identities," xi–xxiv.
64. Interview with Wang Chien-hsüen, Taipei, July 15, 1997.
65. *Zili zaobao*, June 25, 1997.
66. An argument by Lee Ching-hua in the opening of his pamphlet. In a diplomatic, but not very convincing way, Lee says that in principle, he thinks the manuals are "good manuals" and really interesting. Then follows with a long list of criticisms.

67. Contrary to what the printed press said after a few changes were made to the manuals at the end of June 1997, these were in fact not made under pressure from the conservatives. Had the press carefully compared the versions, they would have realized that the Institute even took the opportunity of being asked to look again at its text to add a few changes going against the conservatives' wishes: for instance, replacing "the activities (*huodong*) of the Dutch and the Spanish" by "the era when Taiwan was ruled (*tongzhi*) by the Dutch and the Spanish." As mentioned above, the controversial point regarding the Japanese priests was suppressed, and the society manual was indeed slightly remastered. But changes from the *mo ben* to the *shiyong ben* were only nominal. For instance, the contentious subchapter entitled "We are all Taiwanese" was renamed, only for this expression to be used instead as the title for a paragraph elsewhere in the same chapter. The defeat of the conservative camp in 1997 was thus total. But in 1998, an official version (*zhengshi ben*) was published, after the trial version (*shiyong ben*) had been officially circulated and used during the first school year following the adoption of the reform. This official version showed that pressures from the conservatives probably continued after the public phase of the controversy. Substantial changes were made to the two most sensitive chapters of the society manual, illustrating the difficulty of bedding down new reforms, during the transition experienced by Taiwan since 1987. The fact that the reform might at times not be linear is another illustration of the state reached by the ethnic and ideological power transition in the tenth year of Lee Teng-hui's presidency: the power of the conservative mainlanders remained strong, both ideologically and numerically in political and administrative circles. Nevertheless, the reform was adopted in spite of a huge protest. And this protest was led by what was already a very limited number of persons, whose final failure to prevent Taiwan from changing indicated clearly the progressive extinction of their influence in the final years of Lee's presidency.

68. For a larger analysis of the notion, those who can read French may want to refer to my Ph.D. dissertation, *Une identification nationale plurielle: Les Waishengren à Taiwan et la transition identitaire à Taiwan, 1988–1997* (A Pluralistic National Identification. Waishengren and the National Identity Transition in Taiwan, 1988–1997), Lille: Presses du Septentrion, 2000, 821.

References

The Curriculum Reference Book

Guomin zhongxue kecheng biaozhun (Junior high Curriculum Reference). Taipei: Ministry of Education, 1995, 926.

Textbooks of the "Knowing Taiwan" Series

Renshi Taiwan dili pian (Knowing Taiwan — Geography). 1997. Student book. (Internal) working version (*mo ben*). Taipei: Guoli bianyi guan, May, postdated August, 109.

Renshi Taiwan dili pian (Knowing Taiwan — Geography). 1997. Student book. (Published) trial version (*shiyong ben*). Taipei: Guoli bianyi guan, August.

Renshi Taiwan dili pian (Knowing Taiwan — Geography). 1997. Student book. (Published) official version, 2nd ed. (*zhengshi ben zaiban*). Taipei: Guoli bianyi guan, August, 109.

Renshi Taiwan dili pian, jiaoshi shouce (Knowing Taiwan — Geography). 1998. Teacher book. (Published) official version, first edition (zhengshi ben chuban). Taipei: Guoli bianyi guan, August 1998, 122.

Renshi Taiwan dili pian, xuesheng xizuo (Knowing Taiwan — Geography). 1999. Student exercise book. (Published) official version, 2nd ed. (*zhengshi ben zaiban*). Taipei: Guoli bianyi guan, August, 64.

Renshi Taiwan lishi pian (Knowing Taiwan — History). 1997. Student book. (Internal) working version (*mo ben*). Taipei: Guoli bianyi guan, May, postdated August, 114.

Renshi Taiwan lishi pian (Knowing Taiwan — History). 1997. Student book. (Published) trial version (*shiyong ben*). Taipei: Guoli bianyi guan, August, 114.

Renshi Taiwan lishi pian, jiaoshi shouce (Knowing Taiwan — History). 1998. Teacher book. (Published) official version, 1st ed. (zhengshi ben chuban). Taipei: Guoli bianyi guan, August 1998, 234.

Renshi Taiwan lishi pian (Knowing Taiwan — History). 1999. Student book. (Published) official version, 2nd ed. (*zhengshi ben zaiban*). Taipei: Guoli bianyi guan, August, 116.

Renshi Taiwan shehui pian (Knowing Taiwan — Society). 1997. Student book. (Internal) working version (*mo ben*). Taipei: Guoli bianyi guan, May, postdated August, 107.

Renshi Taiwan shehui pian (Knowing Taiwan — Society). 1997. Student book. (Published) trial version (*shiyong ben*). Taipei: Guoli bianyi guan, August 1997, 107.

Renshi Taiwan shehui pian (Knowing Taiwan — Society). 1999. Student book. (Published) official version, 2nd ed. (*zhengshi ben zaiban*). Taipei: Guoli bianyi guan, August, 94.

Renshi Taiwan shehui pian, jiaoshi shouce (Knowing Taiwan — Society). 1998. Teacher book. (Published) official version, 1st ed. (*zhengshi ben chuban*). Taipei: Guoli bianyi guan, August, 207.

Reports, Books, Pamphlets, and Newspaper Articles
(Not including newspaper articles quoted in bibliographic endnotes.)

"Faxian Taiwan" (Special issue "Discovering Taiwan"). 1991. *Commonwealth Magazine (Tianxia zazhi)*, Taipei, November 18.

"Gei Taiwan yi ge jihui" ("Give Taiwan a chance"). 1995. Taipei, Democratic Progressive Party.

"Jiaoyu yu tiyu" ("National education and physical education"), Central News Agency (*Zhongyang tongxun she*), 1997 World Almanac (1997 *shijie nianjian*). Taipei, 291–295.

Kuo Wei-fan (Guo Weifan). 1996. "Dangqian jiaoyu gaige de keti" ("The question of the current educational reform"). Unpublished speech for the April 8, "Dr Sun Yat-sen Memorial Talk" within the Kuomintang, Taipei, 28.

Lee, Chen-wen (Li Zhenwen) 1996. "Zhengdang zhengzhi yu jiaoyu zhengce (Party politics and education policy)." *Educational Studies (Jiaoxue yanjiu)* 47, 2 (1996):4–22.

Lee, Ching-hua (Li Qinghua). 1997. "Renshi Taiwan ? huo wujie Taiwan ? —Dui guozhong Renshi Taiwan jiaokeshu neirong di zhiyi" ("Knowing Taiwan? Or misunderstanding Taiwan? About doubts concerning the quality of the content of the Knowing Taiwan textbooks"). Taipei, New Party, June 16, 12.

Lee, Teng-hui (Li, Denghui). 1999. "Taiwan de zhuzhang" ("Taiwan's Point of view"). Taipei, Yuanliu.

"Qinxiu neizheng ai Taiwan: Xindang gonggong zhengce baibishu" ("Reforming national policy, loving Taiwan: The New Party's White Paper on public policy"). 1995. Taipei, New Party, 133.

"Taiwan Jiaoyu" (Special Issue on "Taiwan's national education"). 1996. *Commonwealth Magazine (Tianxia zazhi)*, Taipei, November 15.

"Xingzhengyuan jiaoyu gaige shenyi weiyuan hui" ("Executive Yuan commission on the study of educational reform"). 1996. *Jiaoyu gaige zong ziyi baogao shu* (General discussion report on the reform of education), Taipei.

Interviews (With Interviewee's Occupation at the Time of the Textbook Reform)

Ms. Fang Chih-fang, head, edition department for the junior and junior high schools of the National Institute of Compilation and Translations (Taipei, NICT, July 24, 1997).

Mr. Wang Chien-hsüen, secretary general, New Party, 1997–1998 (Taipei, New Party, July 15, 1997).

Mr. Lee Yuan-tse, president, Academia Sinica, 1994– (Taipei, Academia Sinica, December 22, 1997).

Mr. Kuo Wei-fan, Minister of Education, 1993–1996. (Paris, Taipei Representative Office, November 26, 1999).

Mr. Tu Cheng-sheng, head, society textbook writing team, 1995, and Head, Junior High history programs edition department, National Institute of Compilation and Translations, 1997 (Taipei, National Palace Museum, April 24, 2001).

General references

Martin, Roberta. 1975. "The socialization of Children in China and on Taiwan: An Analysis of Elementary School Textbooks." *China Quarterly* 62.

Meyer, Jeffrey E. 1988. "Teaching Morality in Taiwan's schools: the message of textbooks." *China Quarterly* 144:267–284

Tai Shih-tsun (Dai Shicun). 1994. "Lishi jiaoyu yu guojia rentong. Guomin zhong/xiaoxue Taiwan shi jiaoyu zhi jiantao" ("Historical education and national identity. A criticism of education in Taiwanese history in Junior High"), in *Xiandai yanjiu xueshu jijinhui (Foundation for modern academic research),* ed., *Guojia rentong xueshu yantaohui lunwenji (Proceedings of an academic conference on national identity).* Taipei: Foundation for modern academic research, 115–138.

Shi Chi-sheng (Shi Jisheng) et al. 1995. *Yishi xingtai yu Taiwan jiaokeshu (Ideology and the school textbooks),* 2nd ed. Taipei: Qianwei (1993), 102.

Chen, Ya-ling. 1995. "Da Zhongguo yishi de fushen" ("Rise and fall of the Greater China Ideology"), Guanghua (Sinorama, domestic edition), Taipei, May, 18–26.

Hsüeh Hsiao-hua (Xue Xiaohua). 1996. *Taiwan minjian jiaoyu gaige yundong: guojia yu shehui de fenxi (The civic movement for educational reform in Taiwan: An analysis of the state and of the society).* Taipei: Qianwei.

Hsieh Chia-hsiang (Xie Jiaxiang). 1997. "Guomin jiaoyu yu renshi Taiwan" ("National education and Knowing Taiwan"). *Guojia zhengci shuangzhou kan (National policy bimonthly)* 168 (Aug. 8):15–16.

Hughes, C. and Stone, R. "Nation building and curriculum reform in Hong Kong and Taiwan." *China Quarterly* 160:977–991.

Chen, Jyh-Jia. 2000. Hegemony, Official Knowledge and Textbooks: A Preliminary Approach to the Politics of Deregulating National Standardized Textbooks in Taiwan. Paper presented to the Sixth Annual Conference of the North American Taiwan Studies Association, Harvard, June 16-19, 22.

Law, Wing-wah. "Educational Reform in Taiwan: A Search for a 'National' Identity through Democratization and Taiwanization." *Compare* (32-1):61–81.

Wang, Ching-kuei (Wang Qinggui). 2002. *Taiwan shixue wushinian (1950–2000): chuancheng, fangfa, quxiang (Fifty Years of Teaching of History in Taiwan (1950–2000): Tradition, Methods and Directions).* Taipei, Maitian.

Works by the Promoters of the Reform

Tu, Cheng-sheng (Du Zhengsheng). "Yige xin shiguan di dansheng" ("The Birth of a New Historical Reading/Perspective). *Dangdai* 120 (August):20–31.

Tu, Cheng-sheng (Du Zhengsheng). 1998. "Lishi jiaoyu yu guojia rentong. Taiwan lishi jiaokeshu fengbo de fenxi" (History education and national identity. An analysis of the controversy over Taiwan's history books), in *Taiwan xin, Taiwan hun (Taiwanese heart, Taiwanese soul).* Kaohsiung: Hepan, 153–154.

Works by the Detractors of the Reform

Lee, Ching-hua (Li Qinghua). 1997. Renshi Taiwan? Huo wujie Taiwan ? —Dui guozhong Renshi Taiwan jiaokeshu neirong di zhiyi ("Knowing Taiwan? Or Misunderstanding Taiwan? About Doubts Concerning the Quality of the Content of the Knowing Taiwan Textbooks"). Taipei, New party, June 16, 12.

Hsü Nan-tsun (Xu Nancun). 1999. sous la dir. de. "Renshi Taiwan" jiaokeshu pingxi (Criticism and Analysis of the School Textbooks "Knowing Taiwan"). Taipei, Renjian, 191.
Wang Chung-fu (Wang Zhongfu), ed. 2001. *Wei lishi liuxia jianzheng. "'Renshi Taiwan' jiaokeshu cankao wenjian" xin bian (Leaving a Testimony for History: A New Edition of the "Reference documents on 'Knowing Taiwan'"*). Taipei: Haixia xueshu, 2001.

Journalistic Analyses of the Knowing Taiwan Textbook Reform

Chen, Shu-mei. 1997. "Shei jueding zhishi? Jiaokeshu xinshidai lailing" ("Who Takes Discussion over Knowledge? A New Era for the School Textbooks Arrives). *Guanghua* (Sinorama, domestic edition) Taipei, Sept., 6–14.

Academic Analyses of Knowing Taiwan

Kang, Peter. 1998. "Knowing Whose Taiwan? Construction of the Chinese Identity in the High School History Education of Taiwan." *Journal of Hua-lien Teachers College* 6 (June):217–237.
Lu Chien-jung (Lu Jianrong). 1999. "Jiuqi nian lishi jiaokeshu zhengyi shijian" ("The 1997 Controversy over the History Textbooks), in *Fenlie de guozu rentong 1975–1997 (An Ambivalent National Identity, 1975–1997)*. Taipei: Maitian, Feb., 273–283.
Corcuff, Stéphane. 1999. La réforme des manuels scolaires à Taiwan de 1989 à 1997. Unpublished manuscript (available upon request), May, 97.
———. 2001. "L'introspection han à Formose. L'affaire des manuels scolaires "Connaître Taiwan" (1994–1997)". *Études chinoises* 20, 1–2 (Spring-Fall):41–84.
———. 2002. "The Symbolic Dimension of Democratization and the Transition of National Identity under Lee Teng-hui," in Stéphane Corcuff, ed., *Memories of the Future: National Identity Issues and the Search for a New Taiwan*. Armonk, M. E. Sharpe, March, 83–92.
——— (Gao Gefu). 2004. "Bentuhua: Waishengren guojia rentong zuobiaodian di dafu gaibian" ("Localization: Profound Changes in the National Identification Reference Points of the Mainlanders"), in *Fenghe rinuan: Taiwan Waishengren yu guojia rentong de zhuanbian (Light Wind, Warm Sun: Taiwan's Mainlanders and the transition of national identification)*. Taipei: Yunchen Wenhua, January, 72–92.
Wang Fu-chang. 2001. "Minzu xiangxiang, zuqun yishi yu lishi — "renshi Taiwan" jiaokeshu zhengyi fengbo de neirong yu mailuo fenxi" (Nationalist Imagination, Ethnic Consciousness and History — An Analysis of the Context and Content of the Controversy on the 'Knowing Taiwan' Textbooks). *Taiwanshi yanjiu* 8, 2 (Dec.):145–207.

Recent European Dissertations on Educational Reform

Corcuff, Stéphane. 2000. "La réforme des manuels scolaires de 1989 à 1997" (The reform of school textbooks in *Une identification nationale plurielle. Les Waishengren à Taiwan et la transition identitaire à Taiwan, 1988–1997* — A Pluralistic National Identification. Waishengren and the National Identity Transition in Taiwan, 1988–1997), Ph.D. thesis in political science, Paris Institute of Political studies, Sept. Lille: Presses du Septentrion, 181–204.
Huang, Min-yuan. 2002. *La représentation et la réinterprétation de l'histoire. Une étude comparative des deux systèmes d'éducation identitaire à Taiwan de 1895 à 1988*. M.A. dissertation (sociology), Paris, Ecole des Hautes Études en Sciences Sociales, Sept., 182.
Tchao, Aurélie. 2003. *Quête de l'identité taiwanaise et aspiration à un changement du système éducatif*. B.A. dissertation (Chinese language and civilization), Paris, University of Paris VII, Sept., 119.
Song, Xiaokun. 2004. "Conceptualisation of the Taiwanese Nation in the Cultural Arena," in *Between Civic and Ethnic: The transformation of Taiwanese Nationalist Ideologies* (1895–2000). Ph.D. thesis (political science), Brussels, Vrije Universiteit Brussel, March, 232–247.

5

The Re-education of Hong Kong: Identity, Politics, and History Education in Colonial and Postcolonial Hong Kong

EDWARD VICKERS AND FLORA KAN

There is a wide chasm between the CE [Chief Executive] and the people. His linking of national security with being Chinese *continues to make people uncomfortable. His belief that once Article 23 [the controversial "national security" legislation] is dealt with, he can get on with the economy also misses the point that Hong Kong people's real issue with the CE is how he sees and handles things.*

— Christine Loh [our emphasis]

The massive demonstrations that rocked Hong Kong in early July 2003 appeared to take many people by surprise, not least Chief Executive Tung Chee Hwa himself. As Christine Loh observed at the time, a key element of Tung's governing strategy had been to attempt to bolster the legitimacy of his regime by invoking the blood-bond between local Chinese and their "motherland." Indeed, phrases such as "We are all Chinese" had become something of a mantra for Tung in the years since he took office in 1997. The vision of Hong Kong as a harmonious, apolitical, capitalist utopia, bound together by Chinese values and presided over by a benevolent neo-Confucian patriarch in the person of its Chief Executive, was evidently not shared by the half a million citizens who took to the streets on July 1. Nevertheless, the central rhetorical role played by this concept of Chineseness during the post-1997 period begs several questions. Firstly, to what extent is the chasm that has undoubtedly opened up between Hong Kong's new leadership and the bulk of local people a reflection of widely differing visions of what it means to be Chinese in the Hong Kong context? Secondly, if widely differing visions do exist, what are their origins? And thirdly, how have these varying visions been reflected in the school curriculum, and what role has been assigned to the curriculum itself in shaping local people's sense of their Hongkongeseness and Chineseness?

171

In this chapter we propose to focus on the third question (or pair of questions). However, before analysing the role of education — and of the history curriculum in particular — in official attempts to mold identity consciousness in Hong Kong, we provide a brief survey of the political, social, and cultural changes that the territory (or region) has undergone since the 1940s. We examine the different dimensions of Hong Kong's political and cultural identity — local, pan-Chinese, and international or global — as these have developed over the years, and consider the tensions between them. The neoconservative political, cultural, and educational agenda pursued by the Tung regime since 1997 is then analysed, both as it relates to the local context and to the rise of neoconservatism across the border in mainland China. Noting the curious affinities between Tung's post-1997 Confucian patriarchy and Britain's pre-Patten colonialist paternalism, we discuss why and how both British- and Chinese-sponsored local regimes have in general chosen to downplay the significance of any distinctive sense of local identity.

Turning to the school curriculum, we then examine how these issues relating to culture and identity have been reflected in or influenced by the content of school subjects. While our principal focus is on the two distinct subjects of history and Chinese history, of most direct relevance to any consideration of the role of education in identity formation, we also take into account the nature of the broader school curriculum. In particular, we note peculiarities in how language and literature have been taught in local schools and argue that these have also had an important bearing on the way a sense of local or Chinese identity is presented through the school curriculum. We do not attempt to measure or quantify the importance of the curriculum as compared with other factors (such as popular culture) in shaping identity consciousness among local students, nor do we assume that the political messages that syllabi and textbooks convey are transmitted in any simple, direct, and unmediated fashion. The actual impact of the curriculum on students' learning is a matter for further investigation; here we confine ourselves to examining the relationship between the political and cultural context and the process of curriculum development. Our analysis of the curricula for the two history subjects demonstrates that local political realities and the centralized, official nature of the curriculum development process have effectively prevented curriculum developers and textbook authors from promoting any strong and distinctive sense of local identity. This conclusion leads us finally to consider the relationship between education, historical consciousness, and Hong Kong's democratic development.

Identity Politics in Hong Kong — A Three-Dimensional Survey

The Local Dimension

Hong Kong in the three decades following the Second World War was essentially a refugee society, with a population consisting overwhelmingly of migrants from the Chinese mainland who had fled to the colony during the Chinese Civil War of the late 1940s or during subsequent upheavals such as the Great Leap Forward and the Cultural Revolution. At first, these refugees tended to maintain strong affective loyalties to their native places in China and evinced a relatively weak attachment to Hong Kong itself. Even in the realm of popular culture, Mandarin-medium output produced by artists exiled to Hong Kong from various parts of the mainland predominated in the local film and popular music industries into the 1960s. Lack of interest in local history was one symptom of a generally weak sense of identification with Hong Kong among the local Chinese population. In the early 1970s, a trainer of history teachers recently arrived from Britain to take up a post at the University of Hong Kong expressed surprise to a local colleague that no Hong Kong history was taught in local schools. "Well, I can understand why you should be interested in Hong Kong history," came the reply. "But why should I be? I'm Chinese. Hong Kong's history is an irrelevance."[1]

By the 1970s, however, this state of affairs had begun to change as the result of a number of factors, including the rise to maturity of a second generation, born and bred in Hong Kong; the ending of the Cultural Revolution and the discrediting of the extreme brand of anti-imperialist Maoism associated with it; and a steady growth in local economic prosperity. The large riots of 1966 and 1967, partly inspired by the Cultural Revolution, but also partly the product of local grievances against the colonial regime, are generally seen as a watershed, marking the end of the era of classic colonialism in Hong Kong and the start of a period during which the British administration, local elites, and the wider community sought to establish a social and political order that was less obviously, and less humiliatingly, colonial. An additional motive from the British point of view was related to the restoration of diplomatic ties with the Beijing government and the latter's accession to China's seat at the United Nations (UN) in 1971. This process involved the removal of Hong Kong, at the joint request of the British and Chinese governments, from the UN's register of colonies in 1972; henceforth, official British documents referred to Hong Kong as a "territory," rather than a colony.

The late-1960s and early 1970s witnessed the emergence of a number of pressure groups that lobbied the colonial administration on issues such as the status in Hong Kong of the Chinese language (which was not made an official language until 1974) and rampant corruption in the local police force. The Students' movement of the time, which played a part in pushing for the Chinese language to be granted official status, was inspired by anticolonialist, pan-Chinese ideals, and many students (in Hong Kong as in the West) were attracted to the idealism of the Great Proletarian Cultural Revolution. These were, of course, the years in which the bulk of Britain's remaining colonies obtained their freedom and in which protests against the imperialism perceived as animating American intervention in Vietnam rocked university campuses around the world. (The Vietnam conflict had a considerable economic and demographic impact on Hong Kong, which was an important port of call for the U.S. Navy and which, from the 1970s onwards, became a major destination for Vietnamese boat people.) Anti-imperialist sentiment certainly existed in Hong Kong, but almost uniquely for a colonial society, it never manifested itself in an organized struggle for independence. This was mainly because, as many refugee parents of 1970s students were no doubt at pains to remind their offspring, the only realistic alternative to British rule was control by the as yet unreconstructed Communist regime across the border.

As the truth emerged concerning what had really happened in China during the Cultural Revolution, and as the People's Republic opened its borders to Hong Kong visitors from the late 1970s onwards, the ideological and material gulf that separated local people from their mainland cousins became starkly apparent. Many locally raised businessmen and tourists visiting China for the first time in the late 1970s were shocked by what they found there. The much-vaunted motherland turned out to be an ill-kempt, uncultured, scrounging delinquent — the sort of relative you would be tempted to lock away in the attic sooner than introduce to your friends. During the 1980s and early 1990s, *daaihluhkyahn* or mainlanders tended to be portrayed in local films and television soap operas as idiotic country bumpkins, sinister gangsters, corrupt Party cadres, or indigent migrants scrabbling to enter Hong Kong's Promised Land (Leung 1996). A "Great Hong Kong Mentality" took root, reflecting a widespread desire on the part of local Chinese to assert their distinctiveness from the *daaihluhkyahn*. We are *Heunggongyahn* — Hongkongers — said the new generation: more sophisticated, more cosmopolitan and, above all, richer than the yokels across the border in the benighted mainland.

Then there was the language issue — not Chinese versus English this time, but Mandarin versus Cantonese. While schools in the rest of China (including those in Kuomintang-ruled Taiwan) were swept up in the drive to promote *Putonghua* (the common speech), as Mandarin is known on the mainland, at the expense of local dialects, in Hong Kong alone a nonstandard variant of Chinese held the field. Well over 90 percent of the local population were, and remain, Cantonese speakers, and when a Hong Kong person asks whether you can speak *Jungmahn*, or Chinese, what they mean by Chinese is Cantonese. In the same way, when Chinese was finally made an official language in 1974, the particular form of Chinese on which this status was bestowed was never specified; it was taken as given that the spoken language of Hong Kong's Chinese population was Cantonese. The official written language was Modern Standard Chinese (more or less the same as *Putonghua*), but it was Chinese written in the traditional, full-form characters — not the simplified characters used in the People's Republic and in Singapore. In the popular press, moreover, a considerable number of nonstandard characters and expressions were and are used to represent Cantonese terms excluded from the standard lexicon, with the result that a mainlander would very likely find the headlines of a popular Hong Kong newspaper such as the *Pihngguo Yahtbou* (*Apple Daily*) all but incomprehensible. In this way, perhaps more than any other, Hong Kong still feels foreign to visitors from the rest of China — and vice versa. In short, as far as most Hongkongese are concerned, for someone to be considered a true *Heunggongyahn*, the most basic criteria are Chinese ethnicity *and* Cantonese language. Thus, one of Tung Chee Hwa's many failings in local eyes is the fact that he speaks Cantonese with a distinct Shanghainese accent.

Such prejudices do, it must be said, reflect a dark side to the assertion of local distinctiveness vis-à-vis outsiders of various descriptions. This is evident especially in antimainlander prejudice — a widespread sentiment that was shamelessly exploited during the 1999 Right of Abode crisis by the then-Secretary for Security, Regina Ip.[2] In addition, blatantly racist attitudes pervade local society, directed particularly (but not exclusively) against the substantial Filipino community, the smaller but long-established communities of Indians and Pakistanis, and refugees or economic migrants from Vietnam. Hong Kong until very recently lacked any law outlawing racial discrimination — a state of affairs that the government attempted to justify on the grounds that "there [was] no popular demand" for such a law on the part of the majority of the local (overwhelmingly Chinese) community.[3]

Analyses of the Hong Kong identity have tended to focus on issues of life-style and, to some extent, also of language, neglecting the political component integral to the sense of local distinctiveness. The Hong Kong ethos has famously been characterized as one of strongly procapitalist "utilitarianistic familism," involving a focus on personal and family enrichment, in which political concerns have no place. However, the vision of Hong Kong as simply a depoliticized place to do business — a vision jointly cherished by local business leaders and mainland cadres — fails to account for the high levels of political engagement demonstrated by Hong Kong people at moments of crisis. Often these have been related to political events or movements on the mainland, as was the case with the riots of the late 1960s, the street-fights during the 1950s between gangs supporting the Kuomintang and the Communists and, earlier, the engagement of Hong Kong Chinese in the anti-Japanese struggle of the 1930s and 1940s, in anti-British or anti-Japanese strikes and boycotts and, in the early years of the twentieth century, in reformist or revolutionary activism.[4] Indeed, the current Beijing regime and Hong Kong's post-handover administration have been keen to remind Hongkongers of such past examples of patriotic activism, while simultaneously ignoring campaigns directed at local issues or local ends, implying that Hong Kong itself possesses no legitimacy as a site for political engagement. Hong Kong, the mantra runs, is not and has never been a political city.

Perhaps the most striking instance of political activism in Hong Kong's history (and certainly one that continues to haunt pro-Beijing policymakers) was the massive demonstrations that followed the June 4, 1989 massacres in Beijing, in which about a sixth of the entire local population are estimated to have participated. Election results since the early 1990s have consistently shown substantial majorities supporting prodemocracy, anti-Beijing parties, on turnouts comparable to those seen for recent elections in established democracies such as the United Kingdom or the United States. Some public opinion surveys have shown that many local people evince a somewhat idiosyncratic understanding of the concept of democracy, though this should perhaps not surprise us, given the highly peculiar structure and history of Hong Kong's representative institutions and government. Hong Kong's substantial middle classes appear firmly wedded to a set of distinctly liberal-democratic values, including the rule of law and civil liberties such as freedom of expression. These values, as well as an explicit rejection of Communism, constitute an important component of the sense of Hongkongeseness that distinguishes local Chinese from their mainland "compatriots."

Nevertheless, as the affluence of the 1990s gave way to economic uncertainty in the period following 1997, so the brash self-confidence that used to typify Hong Kong suffered a severe dent. In the 1980s or 1990s, it was possible to imagine local newspaper headlines declaring "Fog in Harbor — Mainland Cut off!", but by the early years of the new century it was Hong Kong that was more likely to feel isolated and becalmed by the shifting trade winds. Amid the fanfare surrounding the announcement in early 2003 of a new Closer Economic Partnership Arrangement (CEPA) between the mainland and Hong Kong, it was made perfectly clear that this was a case of the former assisting the latter. It was no longer possible for Hongkongers to regard their cousins across the border with the same arrogant assurance of economic superiority. The more prosperous coastal regions of the mainland were fast catching up, and a new generation of highly educated mainland yuppies were aspiring to the sort of ultramaterialistic consumer culture that had previously been more exclusively associated with the Hong Kong lifestyle. With jobs and people migrating at an escalating rate in both directions across an increasingly porous border, the fate of Hong Kong's cultural distinctiveness began to seem as uncertain as its economic future.

The Pan-Chinese Dimension

To say that Hongkongers since the 1960s have developed a strongly distinct identity should not be taken as implying that local society has necessarily become any less Chinese. While surveys of public opinion from the 1980s onwards have consistently shown that, when given the choice between defining themselves primarily as Chinese or as Hongkongese, the majority of local people choose the latter, few if any would regard the two categories as mutually exclusive. The sense of Hong Kong's distinctiveness vis-à-vis the mainland coexists, as it always has, with a profound consciousness of cultural and even racial Chineseness.

If the popular demonstrations of summer 2003 against the Tung administration can be interpreted as defiant assertions of Hong Kong's autonomy and
way of life, then other recent manifestations of public opinion display a rather
different facet of local identity. In 1999, when North Atlantic Treaty Organization planes bombed the Chinese embassy in Belgrade, apparently by accident,
Hong Kong's Chinese-language media were virtually unanimous in voicing the
patriotic outrage of local Chinese and in refusing to entertain the possibility
that the bombing could have been anything other than intentional. Famously
(or notoriously) anti-Beijing figures belonging to organizations such as the
Democratic Party were among the most strident and vociferous patriots.
Three years earlier, many of the same individuals had been involved in noisy
protests against the Japanese occupation of the Diaoyutai/Senkakuji islands —
an archipelago of uninhabitable rocks northeast of Taiwan that are disputed by
China, Taiwan, and Japan. This dispute has played a significant symbolic role
in local politics since the 1970s, with local activists periodically mounting loud
protests in response to perceived Japanese provocation. In 1999, after a group
of extreme Japanese nationalists had visited the islands, ostensibly to rebuild a
lighthouse, small but vociferous demonstrations ensued in Hong Kong. These
culminated with a trip to the islands by a band of outraged patriots, in which
one protester died attempting to swim ashore in heavy seas. Other protestors
were rescued by the Japanese navy, but this did not prevent the local media from
hailing the dead man as a martyr to the cause of patriotic resistance against
Japanese imperialism.

Episodes such as these demonstrated an acute local sensitivity to any actual
or imagined foreign challenges to China's territorial sovereignty or national
dignity. Implicitly or explicitly, protests by Hongkongers over such issues also
pointed up the failure of the Chinese government itself to defend the honor of
the motherland. As Ian Buruma has written with regard to early twentieth-
century Japan: "When governments rule without popular representation or
even consent, one form of rebellion is to be more nationalistic than the rulers.
If the rulers are traitors to the nation, they should be overthrown" (Buruma
2003, 53).[5] In late twentieth and early twenty-first century Hong Kong (and in
mainland China itself), ultranationalist protest serves as a politically telling
and emotionally satisfying means of impugning the virility of the national
leadership.

However, there is more to expressions of outraged patriotism than simply
implied criticism of the Beijing authorities. Chinese patriotism is for many
Hongkongers a heartfelt, almost visceral sentiment — all the more so, it has
been suggested, because of Hong Kong's historical detachment from the Chinese mainland (Luk 1998). In fact, the China with which local people tend to
identify most strongly is long gone, if, that is, it ever existed at all. The fascina-
tion with a semimythical Chinese past manifests itself in the popularity of
martial arts comics and novels such as the *Gam Yung* (*Jin Yong*) epics, in the

vogue for television dramatizations of old folk tales such as the Judge Pao series, in costume dramas and irreverent slapstick comedies of court life in ancient China, and in the adherence to folk customs and celebration of traditional festivals (Leung 1996). This folk Chineseness, divorced from (and transcending) the realities of contemporary life in mainland China itself,[6] is a cultural attribute that Hong Kong shares with Taiwan, where even campaigners for Taiwanese independence will describe themselves as *Huaren*, a term that Hongkongers also use to designate all Chinese — including overseas Chinese (Roy 2003, 1). In English, the closest approximation to this concept would be the term *Anglo-Saxon*, which was once freely used by British, Americans, Canadians, Australians, and others to assert and celebrate the ethno-cultural unity of the English-speaking peoples, but which has now generally fallen out of favor (except with the French, who tend to use it as a term of abuse). As the term *Anglo-Saxon* did for a nineteenth-century Englishman or American, *Huaren* (or *Wahyahn*) for a twenty-first-century Taiwanese or Hongkonger carries distinctly racial as well as cultural overtones.

Despite this shared acknowledgment of an essential Chineseness, important differences exist in how citizens of Taiwan and Hong Kong typically conceptualize their identity vis-à-vis China. This is perhaps most strikingly evident in the terminology used to describe the local languages. In Taiwan, the local variant of the *Minnanhua* language spoken by most ethnic Chinese residents of the island is commonly referred to as *Taiyu*, or Taiwanese. In Hong Kong, by contrast, there is no concept of a Hongkongese language — no *Gongyu* or *Gongmahn*; as noted above, Hongkongers typically describe their language simply as *Jungmahn*, or Chinese. Moreover, there exists, at least among many more educated Hongkongers, a pronounced inferiority complex regarding the status of their version of Chinese as compared with Mandarin. Cantonese may be the badge of a true *Heunggongyahn*, but at the same time it is generally seen, in defiance of international linguistic categories, as an inferior dialect and not a true language at all. Even while they may share the common prejudices against Mandarin-speaking mainlanders, educated Hongkongers frequently confess to feelings of embarrassment or shame at their own inability to speak good *Gwokyu* (national language, as Mandarin is commonly called both in Hong Kong and Taiwan), as if this somehow diminishes their claim to true Chineseness. To explore the reasons for this would involve too large a digression from our theme; suffice it to note that history, politics, economics, geography, and genealogy mean that Hong Kong's bonds with its mainland hinterland remain far more intimate than Taiwan's.

The International Dimension

We are here concerned primarily with the more political aspects of Hong Kong people's identities, and the way in which these identities both influence and are influenced by the school curriculum. However, in their everyday lives, local residents arguably identify far less readily with politico-historical abstractions such as Hong Kong or China than they do with their company, workplace or, above all, their families. Indeed, as noted above, the Hong Kong ethos has been characterized as one of "utilitarianistic familism" (Lau 1981), a set of attitudes which, in layman's terms, could be summed up by Margaret Thatcher's notorious dictum, "There is no such thing as society; there are only individuals and families." Other commentators have disputed this vision of the typical Hongkonger as an apolitical economic animal as something of a caricature, but there can be little doubt that in Hong Kong, as in any society, relationships developed through work and family constitute central components of any individual's sense of his or her identity (Degolyer and Scott 1996).

It might be expected that workplace and family ties would tend, if anything, to pull inwards and promote a more parochial outlook, and there is indeed a strong element of parochialism in the typical Hong Kong worldview. There is also, however, a widespread sense of pride in Hong Kong's status as an international city. What is meant by the phrase "international city" is seldom explored in any depth and, in terms of cultural and ethnic diversity, Hong Kong is not remotely in the same league as, say, London, New York, or Singapore for that matter. Nevertheless, in economic and familial terms, the extent of Hong Kong's global ties is impressive. Even if the workforce is overwhelmingly Chinese, a considerable proportion of it is employed by multinational companies involved in financial services or entrepôt trade, in locally based companies with a global reach, or in the sizeable tourism and hospitality industries catering to a largely international clientele. Moreover, a history of large-scale overseas emigration means that many Hongkongers have close relatives or friends resident in Canada, Australia, the United States, the United Kingdom, or elsewhere, and many more have themselves worked or studied abroad for extended periods before returning to the territory. In the case of Hong Kong, therefore, the most intimate networks of relationships centered around family and workplace have in many cases tended to pull the individual outwards, from a parochial toward a more international outlook.

The international facet to Hong Kong's identity was strengthened in the 1980s and 1990s as a direct consequence of fears surrounding the territory's impending retrocession to China. During this period, thousands of people, often relatively affluent professionals, migrated overseas — in particular to Australia, Canada, and New Zealand — primarily to secure foreign nationality for themselves and their families, and thus a bolt-hole abroad in the event of political or economic repression on the part of the post-1997 regime. Thousands more applied for passports under the British government's controversial scheme that granted full British nationality to middle-ranking professionals in certain key positions. Meanwhile, a large proportion of Hongkongers who were unable to secure full right of abode overseas took out British National Overseas passports. Although exact figures are unavailable, a very high proportion of Hong Kong's educated Chinese middle class thus holds foreign citizenship in one form or another.

As far as legal citizenship rights are concerned, Hongkongers do seem, to borrow Lau's term, to take a utilitarianistic attitude, seeing no contradiction, for instance, in using an Australian passport for overseas trips, but a Home-going Certificate (*Wuihheungjing*) for visa-free travel to mainland China (ignoring the PRC's strictures against dual nationality). The extent to which possession of, for example, an Australian passport impinges on a Hong Kong person's fundamental sense of identity is a moot point; someone who has grown up with a sense of themselves as *Heunggongyahn* and *Wahyahn* is unlikely to feel that identity erased or supplanted the moment they are issued a foreign travel document. For many children of such passport holders, educated overseas for all or part of their school career, it may be a different matter altogether (and many children of returned emigrants in fact continue to follow foreign school curricula within Hong Kong, in the territory's large international schools sector). What is certain is that, though Hong Kong's population may seem relatively homogenous in terms of ethnicity (well over 90 percent Cantonese-Chinese), in terms of legal nationality, educational experience, family ties, and career history, the picture is far more complex and diverse.

Politics and Identity Post-1997: The Tung Administration's *Kulturkampf*

Immediately after the 1997 handover, the troops of China's People's Liberation Army (PLA) installed themselves in the various barracks and bases that had previously been occupied by the British Army's Hong Kong Garrison. The most prominent of these was the Prince of Wales Barracks in Admiralty, a prime location on the island shore of Victoria Harbor. The occupation of the Admiralty site was symbolic rather than strategic. The PLA was clearly not in Hong Kong to guard against any external security threat; its purpose was above all to symbolize, by its very presence, the restoration of Chinese sovereignty over the territory. The message was spelled out in large characters on huge banners draped across the sides of the Prince of Wales Barracks: *Ai Zuguo; Ai Xianggang* (Love the Motherland; Love Hong Kong) — strictly in that order.

Beijing's policy regarding the role of the PLA in Hong Kong was a reflection of the regime's overall attitude toward the territory and its people. Hong-kongers, it was felt, had been led astray politically and culturally as a result of British colonial influence, most flagrantly so under the last Governor, Chris Patten. Their love for the motherland had been deliberately undermined by the colonial authorities, in large part, it was alleged, through manipulation of the education system, and their consequent political unreliability had been brought home to the central government by their fervent support for the student demonstrators during the 1989 Tiananmen protests. A top priority for the posthandover regime was therefore to coax or cajole these wayward compatriots back into the Chinese fold, primarily by means of exhortation and education (Tung 1997).[7]

As discussed in Chapter 2, it has long been a prevalent belief among the Chinese that effective government and education go hand in hand; in other words, that the state (traditionally in the person of the emperor) can and should attempt to educate the populace in morally correct behavior, just as a father lectures and admonishes his children (Spence 2002). This view of the state's educative, paternalistic role is still widely adhered to by Hong Kong people, even though it might seem to sit uneasily alongside the democratic aspirations that many of them also harbor. The colonial government consciously adopted such a role through various exhortative public campaigns, from appeals to "Keep Hong Kong Clean" to advertisements reminding citizens of the dangers of throwing old television sets out of the windows of high-rise apartments. However, in stark contrast to the mainland regime, the Hong Kong authorities were emphatically not interested in the political socialization of the local population, except in a negative sense. Thus, in defiance of widespread assumptions concerning the nature of colonialism, the British did not, at least during the latter decades of their stewardship, make any effort to instill in Hong Kong people a sense of Britishness — quite the opposite. The government in London was anxious to minimize any potential costs or pressures for immigration from its remaining colonies, and it therefore took steps to deny right of abode in Britain to the majority of Hong Kong's British subjects. It suited London's purposes, as well as the avowedly liberal-democratic principles of postcolonial Britain, to position the Hong Kong Government as, to all intents and purposes, the government of a culturally Chinese but politically autonomous international city state. During the 1970s, the colonial government effectively underwent a makeover with the granting of official status to the Chinese language, public campaigns to promote a depoliticized civic consciousness (as for example in the "Hong Kong Is Our Home" campaign), and a belated but determined effort to stamp out police corruption. The British were anxious to discourage identification on the part of local Chinese with the Communist regime across the border, but they were also, at least prior to the Patten governorship, distinctly ambivalent about the emergence of any strong, politicized sense of local belonging. To have encouraged the development of any movement bent on asserting Hong Kong's political distinctiveness not only from Britain but also from China would have been to invite an open challenge to the legitimacy of the colonial regime, while simultaneously incurring the wrath of Beijing (Turner 1995).

The Tung administration has in many respects evinced a hankering after the era of the 1960s and 1970s, when the colony was run by a coterie of senior government officials and city fathers drawn from the local business community and when the bulk of the general population had hardly begun to think of itself as Hongkongese (Vickers S., 2000). Like pre-Patten British governors, Tung has sought to emphasize the Chinese and, to some extent, the international dimensions of Hong Kong's civic identity, while downplaying or ignoring the significance of the local dimensions. Unlike his British predecessors, however, he has tried to give local Chineseness a distinct political flavor — one that carries the unmistakable whiff of the Beijing kitchen — and has done so in a context in which local political palates have become accustomed to a far more democratic recipe. The new government's slogan for Hong Kong is "Asia's World City, and a Major City in China," thus defining Hong Kong primarily in terms of its relationships with China, Asia, and the world. In 2001, a consultation document produced by the government-appointed Culture and Heritage Commission reported that commission members had reached a consensus to the effect that

> Hong Kong's culture is a component of Chinese culture. The long tradition of Chinese culture offers a great treasure house for the sustained development of Hong Kong culture. It is our long-term goal to expand our global cultural vision on the foundation of Chinese culture, drawing on the essence of other cultures to develop Hong Kong into an international cultural metropolis known for its openness and pluralism.
>
> Our mission is to encourage Hong Kong people, in particular the young generation, to appreciate and participate in the arts; to enrich their lives with a greater emphasis on culture; to strengthen social cohesion and shared values; and to build up the confidence and pride of Hong Kong people in their country and society. (Culture and Heritage Commission 2001, 8)

In common with other official statements on Hong Kong's culture and identity (such as the curricular documents discussed below), this declaration implicitly adopts a vision of Chinese culture as a homogenous and totalizing essence and sees Hong Kong's culture as a mere subset of this greater whole. Hong Kong's cultural distinctiveness is seen as deriving from its function as a sort of international entrepôt for trade in cultural essences, but in such a manner that the essential Chineseness of local culture is never compromised. The idea that Hong Kong culture might itself offer a distinctive vision — or even several competing visions — of what it means to be Chinese in the modern world is nowhere entertained, since pluralism is here defined not as something internal to Chinese culture but as an outcome of the interaction between Chinese and international cultures. There is, in short, no official vision of Hong Kong primarily as *Hong Kong*, since the Tung administration clearly feels this to be incompatible with a correct interpretation of Beijing's One China orthodoxy.

The meaning and significance of One China — or the one country element in Deng Xiaoping's "one country; two systems" formula for the reunification project — is an issue that has formed the subtext to many of the key political, legal, and educational debates in posthandover Hong Kong, with the government consistently choosing interpretations that emphasize the One Country over the two systems element. At least in the cultural and educational fields, however, care has been taken to avoid the appearance of overt interference in day-to-day policymaking, reliance instead being placed largely on unofficial channels — such as the pro-Beijing press — or on platitudinous official or semiofficial statements (such as Tung's own policy addresses and the above-quoted report of the Culture and Heritage Commission) to remind middle-ranking bureaucrats, academics, publishers, and others of the ideological parameters within which they should work. Conformity with the One China principle is thus achieved more through self-censorship or guided self-censorship than as the result of any draconian system of central controls (Vines 1998).

One example of the outcome of such an approach is the permanent exhibition at the new Hong Kong Museum of History, opened in 2002. Replacing an older museum that was closed down soon after retrocession, this vast and lavish display takes the visitor on a journey through 6,000 years of Hong Kong history. It does so, moreover, in a way that ignores or sidelines all the most controversial issues in local history: the ethnicity of Hong Kong's early inhabitants (who were not Han Chinese) is not discussed, and the conflicts between these inhabitants and early settlers from the north is not mentioned; the Opium War receives fairly orthodox coverage from a nationalist perspective; the nature of the British colonial administration, and the collaborative relationships with local Chinese elites upon which it depended, is hardly discussed; the contribution of Hong Kong to revolution and in particular to the anti-Japanese war effort on the Chinese mainland is emphasized, but there is no recognition of the contribution made by non-Chinese groups (particularly Indians) to Hong Kong's early development; and the coverage of post-1945 Hong Kong renders the British presence in the territory almost totally invisible. While the exhibition was being prepared, there was some debate in the local press over the sensitive issue of whether or not to include coverage of the 1989 demonstrations, which are widely recognized as a defining event in Hong Kong's recent history. The demonstrations do in fact feature in the final audio-visual presentation of the exhibition, but they do so in the form of a brief clip in a narrative of the events leading up to the 1997 handover. Under the caption "Blood Is Thicker than Water," the local reaction to the Tiananmen tragedy is bizarrely subsumed into a celebratory account of the territory's glorious progress toward reunification. The museum thus focuses exclusively on the significance of this event as a manifestation of Hong Kong people's Chinese patriotism, implicitly referring to their blood union (*huet tong*) with their racial brethren on the mainland. In this way, the role of the 1989 events in accentuating both local people's alienation from the mainland regime and their sense of Hong Kong's distinctiveness is deftly sidestepped (Vickers 2003, ch. 3).

The central thrust of the post-1997 regime's cultural policy thus appears to be the assertion of Hong Kong's eternal and indissoluble ties with the Chinese motherland and the denial of any elements in local history or culture that might qualify or weaken this vision of the Special Administrative Region's unequivocal Chineseness. Such a vision does not preclude a nod in the direction of the international facet of local identity, but Chineseness and foreignness, notwithstanding official acknowledgments of the virtues of pluralism, are still implicitly regarded as distinct essences rather than fluid or porous categories. This appeal to the pan-Chinese aspect of the Hong Kong mentality as a means of encouraging closer identification with the Chinese mainland is made more possible by the tectonic ideological shifts that have taken place across the border since the 1970s. As Beijing has, to all intents and purposes, abandoned communism as its ideological mainstay in favor of free-wheeling capitalism and One China patriotism (Barmé 1999), it has become better able to appeal to the Han chauvinism and latent xenophobia that remain important components of the ethno-cultural consciousness of many Hong Kong Chinese.

Nevertheless, as was demonstrated in 1989, and in subsequent elections to the local legislative council, Chinese patriotism for most Hongkongers by no means entails unquestioning support for the Beijing-appointed Tung regime. As far as most adult residents are concerned, attempts by a figure such as Tung to quell local dissent through appeals to patriotic duty are liable, if anything, to further fuel resentment, as is suggested by the quotation from Christine Loh at the start of this chapter. With schoolchildren, however, it is a different matter, and the Tung administration has made no secret of its ambition to socialize the younger generation as Chinese patriots first and foremost, uncritically supportive of Beijing's One China agenda.[8] The remainder of this article examines the role that has been assigned to the local school curriculum, in particular to the history subject, in winning young hearts and minds for the motherland. It discusses the ways the curriculum has or has not served as a vehicle for the distinctively local, pan-Chinese, and international facets of Hong Kong's cultural identity and how and why syllabi and textbooks have shifted their treatment of sensitive issues related to local history and culture both prior and subsequent to the territory's return to Chinese rule.

History and Identity in the Hong Kong School Curriculum up to 1997

In the media frenzy that preceded Hong Kong's retrocession, both Chinese and overseas journalists tended to take it for granted that, since Hong Kong was a colony, the local school curriculum must present students with a stereotypically colonial vision of the territory's past and present. The fact that most secondary schools used (or claimed to use) English as their medium of instruction was taken by some as confirmation of an ingrained colonialism pervading the education system as a whole (Pennycook 1998). In particular, however, it was alleged that the curriculum for history — always the most politically sensitive of school subjects — had been manipulated by the colonial government in order to put across a pro-British vision of the local past. It was inevitable — indeed, some implied, only natural — that the history curriculum should become the site for a struggle over the political socialization of Hong Kong's youth. As the British journalist Steve Vines put it in 1998, "The British were shameless in offering an imperial version of history. The post-British regime has been busy with the scissors and wants to ensure that the new generation learns its version of the past" (258).

Statements such as this seemed superficially plausible but were in fact totally unsupported by the evidence. What was most striking about the pre-1997 school curriculum was not the prevalence of imperialist propaganda, but its absence. It is necessary to go back as far as the 1960s to find a time when local students were presented with a triumphalist account of Hong Kong history as one component of a larger narrative of British imperial progress. For example, *Fragrant Harbour*, by the British historians G. B. Endacott and Arthur Hinton, and published in 1962, ends its first chapter with a quotation from Sun Yat-sen's address to the students of Hong Kong University in 1923:

> My fellow students; you and I have studied in this English Colony and in an English University and we must learn by English examples. We must carry this English example of good government to every part of China. (5)

However, this textbook does not appear to have been widely used, since even in the 1960s little time was generally devoted to the study of Hong Kong's own past, most teachers choosing to concentrate on topics related to modern European history (Vickers E. 2000, ch. 6).[9]

By the 1970s, British history had virtually disappeared from the school curriculum, and local history along with it, leaving students to subsist on a curricular diet of Chinese history (mostly ancient) and world history (mostly East Asian and European, with very little British content). Oddly, given the nationalist passions it continues to arouse among many Chinese, the only episode in local history that was still included in the junior and senior secondary curricula was the Opium War. Otherwise, students were presented, through the junior secondary subject of Economics and Public Affairs (EPA), with an ahistorical vision of Hong Kong as a cosmopolitan capitalist utopia (Vickers 2003, ch. 4; Morris, McClelland, and Wong 1997).

Meanwhile, within the predominantly English-medium school curriculum, there persisted throughout the period of British rule an unassailable redoubt of Chineseness in the form of the Chinese language subjects: Chinese language and literature and Chinese history. As Bernard Luk has argued, and as we have discussed in previous publications, these subjects purveyed a depoliticized, culturalist vision of Chinese identity rooted in the ancient glories of that civilization and entirely divorced both from contemporary mainland politics and from the local context (Luk 1998; Vickers, Kan, and Morris 2003; Kan and Vickers 2002). Following the Communist victory in China in 1949, the curriculum development process in Hong Kong primarily involved the bureaucratic control of school subjects and curriculum materials via model syllabi, approved textbooks, and exhortation regarding appropriate or effective teaching methods. The rationale for this approach arose from the government's desire to combat the spread of Communist influence in schools. Therefore, the literary output of post-1949 China was excluded from the curriculum, as were works by any Hong Kong authors. In the case of Chinese history, the effective end-date of the curriculum was set even earlier, and the chronological scope of the Certificate of Education Examination (CEE) syllabus was only extended to 1911, 1945, and 1949, in 1965, 1972, and 1979 respectively. In the 1995 CEE revision, the scope was extended only to 1976, thus excluding the 1989 June Fourth Incident.[10] Hong Kong history was not covered at all. For the émigré scholars who shaped the curriculum in the 1950s and 1960s, Hong Kong had no status whatsoever in the grand narrative of the Chinese past; it was a peripheral backwater, a traditional haven for pirates (Chinese or foreign), a colonial stain on the national character, and an occasional refuge for reluctant exiles from the motherland. For these scholars and their students, who continued to influence the development of the Chinese history curriculum right into the twenty-first century, the essence of Chinese history was the traditional dynastic narrative, and the moral lessons thence to be derived through the correct apportionment of praise and blame (Vickers, Kan, and Morris 2003).

It was one of the curious anomalies of Hong Kong's school curriculum that it boasted not just one but two history subjects, since in addition to Chinese history there was a completely separate subject called history. This situation had its roots in the curriculum for the Anglo-Chinese schools in the 1950s and 1960s. History's content originally consisted primarily of British and world history but, since it made little sense to teach Chinese history to Chinese students in English, the practice had arisen of using Chinese-medium history textbooks produced on the mainland to teach the history of China. However, as the political tensions associated with the Chinese Civil War and the subsequent Communist-Kuomintang stand-off spilled over into Hong Kong from the late 1940s onwards, the colonial authorities became increasingly anxious to prevent inflammatory antiforeign teaching materials being used in local schools. Steps were therefore taken to secure the collaboration of highly conservative émigré scholars in the development of a Chinese history curriculum especially for Hong Kong schools, a curriculum that would ignore the recent Chinese past, whose memory was so distasteful to them and so dangerous to their colonial masters. Instead it would concentrate on celebrating the ancient dynasties as a source both of ethno-cultural pride and of exemplars of the

Confucian virtues, not least that of obedience to established authority. Many of these individuals were associated with the group of exiled conservatives centered around the eminent historian Qian Mu, who in the 1950s established New Asia College (later to form the core of the Chinese University of Hong Kong) as a base for the preservation and transmission of traditional Chinese learning, a task the exiles felt had been betrayed by both the Communist and Kuomintang regimes. So successful was the project of establishing an autochthonous and distinct curriculum for Chinese history in Hong Kong that, by the 1970s, the subject had become entrenched as a potent symbol of and vehicle for the ethnic pride of a Chinese population uncomfortably wedged between the barbarous excesses of communism, on the one hand, and the humiliating anachronism of colonial subjecthood on the other (Kan and Vickers 2002; Luk 1998; Vickers, Kan, and Morris 2003).

The by then patent anachronism of Hong Kong's political arrangements was, it seems likely, one reason why topics related to both imperial and local history were quietly dropped from history syllabi around 1970, with the exception of an unpopular optional module in the A level syllabus that was retained until 1984. From the 1970s onwards, curriculum developers responsible for the history subject (mostly locally raised Chinese along with a handful of British academics) embraced a broadly liberal-internationalist perspective. They shifted the focus of syllabi onto progressively more contemporary periods and issues, while tending to devote about half of the subject content to topics in Western (mainly European) history and half to the history of modern Asia, and in particular of China. A number of local educationalists associated with history and other humanities subjects were also aware of new international trends in history and social studies pedagogy, such as the New History movement, that from the 1970s enjoyed growing popularity amongst teachers in the United Kingdom, North America, and elsewhere. Curriculum developers in many Western countries were attempting to make history education less stuffily academic and more skills-based and relevant to students in terms of both teaching methods and subject matter, in an era of universal compulsory secondary education. Hong Kong's schools were likewise moving rapidly from secondary provision for a privileged elite toward universal provision, and local curriculum developers were thus starting to face some of the same problems that had earlier confronted their Western counterparts. In addition, with competition intensifying among rival subjects for space in a crowded school curriculum, the rationale for maintaining two entirely distinct history subjects began to look decidedly shaky to a number of education policymakers (Vickers 2003, ch. 4).

In 1974, a self-consciously progressive group of expatriate educators returned from an international conference on social studies education in Japan with a proposal to launch a new social studies subject that would bridge the divide between history and Chinese history by offering a new course incorporating elements of both Chinese and foreign history, geography, and civics, to be taught through the medium of Chinese (i.e., Cantonese). Despite what were felt to be its impeccably liberal credentials, this proposal was met with howls of protest from supporters of the Chinese history subject — teachers, academics, and elements in the Chinese-language media — who portrayed it as an insidious colonial plot to erase the Chinese identity of local students. To reduce the amount of time available for teaching the entire narrative of dynastic history, while attempting to teach the history of China in the context of a broad global narrative, was seen as a wholly unacceptable denationalization of the curriculum. The government, acutely conscious of its fragile legitimacy, and highly sensitive to accusations of colonialist behavior, quietly backed away from its intention of reforming the Chinese history curriculum (Morris, McClelland, and Wong 1997). From 1975 until 1997, education policymakers tiptoed round this sacred grove of Chineseness. While attempts were made to reform other school subjects, Chinese history alone remained inviolable.

The history subject, by contrast, underwent major reforms between the mid-1980s and 1997. Looking for ways to enhance their subject's relevance and popularity, curriculum developers for history introduced data-based questions aimed at fostering critical and analytical skills, trimmed the content of syllabi, and adopted a more contemporary focus. They also, from the late 1980s, took steps to reintroduce coverage of local history, a topic clearly of maximum relevance to local students. The reintroduction of local history, first at sixth-form and junior level, and later at senior secondary level, came at a time when consciousness of Hong Kong's distinctive identity had become an incontrovertible sociological fact. A 1989 document explaining the decision over local history stated that the initiative aimed to "enhance pupils' understanding of the local setting [and] enforce their sense of identity to the local community" through "appropriate elaboration and discussion on the development of Hong Kong in the context of global issues" (Cheng 1989, 17–18). No mention was made here of the importance of the national or the Chinese context.

Unsurprisingly, given their overriding concern with ancient periods and the doings of emperors and their ministers, curriculum developers for Chinese history evinced no enthusiasm either in the early 1990s or subsequently for the teaching of Hong Kong history in schools. However, a number of commentators in the Chinese-language press were highly critical of the decision to include local history in what was commonly referred to as the world history subject rather than in Chinese history. Once again, it was implied that a colonialist plot was afoot to internationalize Hong Kong history, at a time when Chinese officials were accusing the British authorities of attempting to internationalize the territory politically as a means of countering or undermining Beijing's influence there.[11] The message emanating from Beijing was that Hong Kong was — and always had been — solely and essentially the legitimate concern of China. It is striking that all reference to the aim of encouraging, let alone enforcing, a sense of local identity through the teaching of local history was omitted from official documents from the mid-1990s onwards. The new ideological parameters within which curriculum development would have to take place were spelt out in a 1995 statement by the Education Department:

> Since the signing of the Sino-British Joint Declaration in 1984, local educators believe that students of Hong Kong should have a more comprehensive understanding of the history of Hong Kong and her development. On the one hand, through teaching the developmental process and factors of success of Hong Kong, teachers can help students appreciate the efforts of the predecessors and value their achievements, and thus cultivate a sense of sentiment and responsibility towards Hong Kong; on the other hand, when they realize the close linkage between Hong Kong and China in history, the students would strengthen their sense of identity with their mother country, nation and culture. These two aspects could facilitate the return of Hong Kong to China and the implementation of "one country, two systems".[12]

Far from strengthening any sense of local distinctiveness, the teaching of local history was thus now envisaged, in anticipation of the 1997 retrocession, primarily as a means of reinforcing awareness of Hong Kong's eternal and indissoluble ties with the Chinese motherland. The obligation to tow the party line on this issue clearly weighed heavily upon developers of the curriculum for history, as is evident from revisions made at the drafting stage to the local history sections of new syllabi for sixth form and, in particular, for junior secondary level. The local history component of the new junior syllabus of 1995 was adapted from the teaching package for a pilot project in local history teaching conducted during the early 1990s. Like the pilot project, the new syllabus focused largely on safe topics in social history and on local heritage, in the form of archaeological sites and prominent old buildings, and did not address many of the more controversial issues in Hong Kong's past. Nevertheless, the syllabus suffered even more than the preceding pilot project from controversy-avoidance syndrome. A section in the pilot package entitled "The Refugee Problem" was omitted from the syllabus altogether (description of Chinese fleeing mainland China for Hong Kong as "refugees" was impermissible); explicit references to the British or British rule were deleted; and an entire new section was devoted to relations with China (Vickers 2003, ch. 6). The original suggestion for the inclusion of the latter section appears to have come from a teacher responding to a consultation questionnaire, who proposed the following three themes:

> How China influenced Hong Kong and vice versa
> Hong Kong's role in the modernization of China
> Hong Kong's contribution to China

By contrast, the subthemes eventually listed in the syllabus were:

Hong Kong and the 1911 Revolution
China's contribution to the development of Hong Kong
Transition to a Special Administrative Region[13]

The emphasis of the original suggestion was thus effectively reversed, so that Hong Kong would in no sense appear as an equal partner in its relationship with the mainland, let alone as a modernizing influence or model for China's development, but rather as a subordinate client, the recipient of benefits bestowed by Beijing.

When textbooks for the new junior secondary history curriculum were published, they conformed to the typical Hong Kong pattern and followed the letter of the syllabus. Publishers had always been nervous lest the Education Department should find any reason to leave their books off the official lists of recommended textbooks, but in the run-up to the 1997 handover and in the years since, an additional element of self-censorship came into play. A reluctance to offend mainland sensibilities has been accentuated not only by the transition to Chinese rule but also by the fact that many of the major local publishers of school textbooks have become eager to gain a foothold in the potentially massive textbook market across the border. Shortly before Hong Kong's retrocession, publishers hastily revised their history and, in particular, their Chinese history textbooks to ensure that these conformed with the new political correctness. The results were sometimes too "correct" even for the Education Department, with an official recalling that one publisher submitted a revised edition in which all references to Hong Kong had been changed to Hong Kong SAR [Special Administrative Region] even in sections devoted to prehistoric life in the territory (Vickers 2003, 180). Partly in an attempt to forestall such overzealousness on the part of publishers, the Department produced its own list of necessary changes to textbooks, most of which related to terminology (such as the politically acceptable ways of referring to Taiwan and the Kuomintang). Nevertheless, in deciding which terms and definitions were acceptable, officials themselves were obliged to take on board the received verdicts handed down by mainland historians. For example, references to Hong Kong before 1997 as a colony were deemed problematic, since this description was seen as a tacit recognition of the legality of the Unequal Treaties under which the territory was ceded or leased by China to Britain (and whose legality was vehemently denied by Beijing). This stipulation in particular would require exceptional verbal dexterity on the part of authors and publishers. Rather than refer to Hong Kong itself as a colony, they avoided using any specific term to describe the territory's political status and instead used phrases such as "British administration," "British rule," or "British control" (Vickers 2003).[14]

The new junior secondary textbooks published by Hong Kong Commercial Press (HKCP) are typical in the way they tread, and occasionally traverse, the line between historical accuracy and nationalist orthodoxy in their narrative of the local past (Wong 2001). Indeed, the layout and even some of the illustrations found in the HKCP books are virtually identical to those in texts published by their main competitor, Aristo (Kan 2003). The account begins with the daily life of Hong Kong's prehistoric inhabitants, skips to a description of a famous find of a Han dynasty tomb, and then to the southward migrations that brought *Wahyan* (*Huaren*) to the region during the Tang and Sung Dynasties. However, while the author offers a relatively detailed description of the origins and customs of the various groups and clans of Han colonists, the question of what happened to the previous inhabitants of the area is nowhere addressed (Wong 2001, Book 1, ch. 2). Evidence in contemporary chronicles suggests that the aboriginal tribe occupying Lantau Island was ethnically cleansed by Han troops after a rebellion in the twelfth century (Ng and Baker 1983, 22–24), but no such conflicts are mentioned in school textbooks.

The account of Hong Kong's history under British rule focuses on the social and economic progress made by the local Chinese community during this period, while also acknowledging efforts made by the administration in the areas of law and order, education, public health, and housing. The main thrust of the narrative is a happy story of progress toward the prosperous capitalist utopia that is contemporary Hong Kong, briefly if rudely interrupted only by the 4 years of Japanese occupation during the Second World War. As in the new Hong Kong Museum of History, so in the HKCP textbooks the British steadily fade from the picture as we move into the postwar period, until we reach the section on "China's Contribution to the Development of Hong Kong." The contributions made by China during the postwar period are seen as including not only the provision of basic amenities for Hong Kong (in particular the supply of drinking water from across the border in Guangdong) but also, bizarrely, encompass the provision of investors and capital to jumpstart the local economy in the post–Civil War years and of a labor force consisting of those who fled to the colony from China during the same period. The fact is, of course, that these capitalists and workers, who were fleeing war, persecution, or starvation on the mainland, saw themselves as anything but part of some far-sighted Chinese project to boost the development of Hong Kong. However, the new history textbooks invite students to construe this mass influx of refugees during the postwar period as an instance of the motherland's benevolence. This account of China's contributions provides a fitting prelude to the uncritical, celebratory concluding section that describes the Sino-British negotiations over Hong Kong's future, the drafting of the Basic Law (Hong Kong's post-1997 mini-constitution), and the handover of sovereignty itself.

It is important to note that these textbooks, though published after 1997, follow the junior syllabus that was finalized in 1995, a good 2 years before Hong Kong's retrocession. This serves as a reminder that the formal transfer of sovereignty did not constitute the kind of neat cut-off between colonial and postcolonial politics that many at the time and since have assumed that it did. The central tenets of post-1997 political correctness were already becoming clear by the mid-1990s, and curriculum developers and publishers, anxious to conform to the standards that would be expected of them under the new dispensation, were already trimming their sails to the prevailing wind from Beijing. The drive on the part of history curriculum developers to ensure that their subject would become more relevant to generations of students for whom Hongkongeseness meant as much if not more than Chineseness was therefore already becoming subordinated to the nation-building priorities of the incoming administration, even before 1997.

Promoting Patriotism through the School Curriculum — Chinese History for the New Hong Kong

The importance attached by the Tung administration to the socialization of young Hongkongers as Chinese patriots has already been noted. The school curriculum, and the history subjects in particular, would naturally constitute the principal vehicle for such a program and, as the above discussion of the treatment of local history in some of the newer textbooks demonstrates, the curriculum for history has very palpably begun to serve a nation-building function. However, the continuing existence of two entirely separate history subjects with very distinctive subject cultures needs to be borne in mind.

Notwithstanding the way in which local history was eventually presented in junior-level syllabi and textbooks, the idea of using history education as a vehicle for the promotion of uncritical, state-centered patriotism has remained unpalatable for many of the curriculum developers responsible for the history subject. This is demonstrated by the struggles both before and since 1997 over the way local history should be dealt with in school curricula. In 2002, a minor furor erupted in the Chinese-language media when a consultative draft of a new curriculum for senior secondary history listed a topic on "administrative and constitutional reforms from Mark Young [a reformist postwar governor] to Christopher Patten" (Curriculum Development Institute [CDI] 2002, 1).[15] The subsequent draft not only omitted all reference to Young or Patten (famously designated a criminal by Beijing), but was rewritten so that in the local history section references to "Hong Kong society" or "Hong Kong culture" were replaced with phrases such as "the local Chinese community" or the "coexistence and interaction of Chinese and Western culture [in Hong Kong]" (CDI 2002, 2). The list of aims in the syllabus draft, meanwhile, included the importance of promoting national identity through history education, but it was the last item on the entire list.

Nothing better underlines the contrasting philosophies informing the development of the history and Chinese history subjects than the priority accorded to the promotion of national identity. For history curriculum developers, deeply influenced by overseas developments in pedagogy and assessment, the potential of their subject for training students in the skills of critical and analytical thinking has since the 1970s become of paramount importance, and an emphasis on promoting uncritical patriotism is clearly incompatible with such an approach (Vickers 2003, 205–216). Teachers and curriculum developers associated with Chinese history, on the other hand, have faced no such tension between conflicting values. The subject has always been firmly wedded to a state-centered, Han chauvinist account of the Chinese past, with an emphasis on cultural superiority reflected in such statements as this:

> Through learning about technological inventions, cultural exchanges with foreign countries, and intellectual and religious thought, pupils will come to understand that Chinese culture has the spirit of accommodating other cultures and making innovative creations. In the process of development, Chinese culture could assimilate other nations' cultures. (CDC 1997, cited in Kan 2002)[16]

This long-standing core belief in the existence of an eternal, immutable national essence — surviving and transcending China's historical encounters with the foreign world — sits easily with the post-handover emphasis on political unity, or the One Country element of the "one country, two systems" formula for Hong Kong's reunification. Thus the 1997 syllabus for junior secondary Chinese History stipulates that:

> One of the objectives of history teaching is, through understanding the nation's culture and history, to establish in pupils a sense of recognition and belonging to the nation. The ultimate aim is to unite the nation and build up the nation. (CDC, 1997, 7)

This readiness to embrace the political socialization agenda of the post-1997 regime reflects more than simply a pandering to political authority on the part of those responsible for Chinese history (though there may be an element of that as well). It is a reflection of deeply held convictions, regarding the virtue of patriotism, the ethno-cultural unity of China and, at a more general level, the belief that one of the principal functions of history is as a vehicle for didactic moralizing. These beliefs are evident in the guidelines provided in the 1997 syllabus concerning how Chinese history can be used to promote patriotism, linking specific learning objectives to particular episodes from the Chinese past and to named exemplars of the patriotic virtues, as shown in table 5.1.

The adoption in the run-up to 1997 of an explicitly state-centered approach to patriotism in place of the traditionally more culturalist approach

Table 5.1 Learning Objectives in 1997 Syllabus

Learning objective	Example in Chinese history
Show concern for the nation's development	The nation was partitioned into the South and North Dynasties. The Sui Dynasty unified the nation and developed national power
Wholeheartedly serve the nation	Officials' deeds in defending the nation against the Jin and the Mongols
Be selfless, and not gain personal benefits at the expense of the nation's interest	The deeds of Gao Zong and Yue Fei
Wholeheartedly serve the nation and protect the nation's interest	The deeds of Lin Zexu
Cultivate patriotic ideals	The late Qing revolutionary movement
	May Fourth Movement
Love peace. However, in the face of foreign invasion, one has to have a brave spirit and be willing to sacrifice oneself for the nation	War against the Japanese invasion
Strive for ethnic unity and national unification	The establishment of the People's Republic of China

Source: From CDC (1997), 20–35.

does not represent as much of a seismic shift for Chinese history as might at first be assumed. Although the Chinese history curriculum had originally been designed as a depoliticized, decontextualized treatment of the national past, its depoliticization had essentially consisted of an avoidance of twentieth-century history (and especially the Communist-Kuomintang conflict) and the adoption of a focus on more ancient periods. This had not prevented curriculum developers and textbook authors from embracing a far more antiforeign interpretation of, say, the Opium War, than their history subject counterparts (Kan and Vickers 2002). After 1997, this nationalist perspective was made more explicit in textbooks and was extended to the contemporary period with a celebration of the role of the People's Republic in unifying China (though no celebration of Communism as an ideology). References to "China" or "the Chinese" in textbooks were in many cases replaced by terms such as "the nation" or "compatriots," but the narrative otherwise remained largely unaltered (Kan 2002, ch. 8). Some terminological tinkering was required with respect to the status of The Republic of China (ROC) on Taiwan, ruled by the Kuomintang, but by the late 1990s, this issue was far less explosive than it had been in the 1950s. Research suggests that rhetorical appeals to nationalism in syllabi and terminological alterations to Chinese history textbooks have by and large not led to significant changes in how the subject is actually taught in classrooms. The Chinese history curriculum was in any case already infused with an intense sense of cultural nationalism and ethnic pride in China's ancient heritage. Hong Kong traditionalists, mainland Communists and, for that matter, Kuomintang right-wingers in Taiwan could all agree on their commitment to national unity above all else and on their die-hard opposition to separatism in any shape or form.

Indeed, in their treatment of China's so-called national minorities (*shaoshu minzu*), Hong Kong's Chinese history curriculum developers and, more especially, many ordinary teachers, had always tended to be far more openly chauvinist than would be acceptable in Beijing itself. For the mainland regime, which combines its dominion over the Han population of China proper with rule over the vast and (at least until recent large-scale Han immigration) non-Han territories of Tibet, Xinjiang, and Inner Mongolia, it has been a priority to emphasize the historical unity of these peripheral regions with the Han center. There are occasionally heated discussions in the mainland press over whether traditional Han folk heroes such as the Song Dynasty general Yue Fei, who fought Jurchen invaders in the twelfth century, can legitimately be designated national heroes (*minzu yingxiong*), since they displayed their heroics not in fighting bona fide foreign invaders, but in fighting the Jurchen — who as every Chinese schoolboy knows (or should know) are not foreigners but a brother nationality (*xiongdi minzu*) of the Han. Apocalyptic episodes such as the Mongol invasions of the thirteenth century are thus — in more orthodox mainland accounts — seen as strictly domestic conflicts, and Genghis Khan himself is posthumously honored in textbooks as "one of our country's great political and military leaders from the Mongol nationality" (People's Education Press 1993, see chapter 2). Not so in Hong Kong. Here, far away from Mongolia, Tibet, and Xinjiang, the legitimacy of Chinese rule over minority areas is not an issue, and the heroic status of figures such as Yue Fei is not a matter for debate. Chinese history teachers in Hong Kong as a matter of course have always set internal examination questions that explicitly define Mongols as non-Chinese, without any fear of attracting criticism from the authorities. Thus one typical question runs: "In the Yuan dynasty, the Mongols adopted oppressive policies against the Chinese. Give an account of the way in which the Han people and the Southerners were subject to political and legal discrimination" (Kan 2002, 292).

While this interpretation of the Mongol invasions is in fact probably fairer than one that portrays them as a minor domestic tiff when it comes to the history of Hong Kong itself, the position taken in official curriculum documents for Chinese history is rather more questionable. Prior to 1997, the Chinese history subject made no provision whatsoever for the teaching of local history, since from a Chinese nationalist perspective the topic was regarded as simply too peripheral and unimportant. However, following the retrocession and, perhaps more to the point, the implementation of a new junior secondary history subject curriculum that included local history, officials responsible for Chinese history felt it necessary to stake their own claim to this patch of curricular territory. Their claim took the form of a special teaching package issued by the Education Department's CDI in 1999. In contrast to the syllabi and textbooks for the history subject, which to some degree at least attempt to cover local history from a local perspective, in the Chinese history teaching package the focus is entirely on the role played by Hong Kong in the state-centered narrative of the national past. The first two paragraphs of the package encapsulate the general flavor:

> From many archaeological discoveries, we have learnt that Hong Kong's history can be traced back six thousand years to the New Stone Age. In the early period, it was inhabited by the people of the Hundred Yue Tribes, most of whom lived near the shore and fished and foraged for a living. Following the continuous progress of human civilisation, the culture of the northern central plains began to blend with the culture of the Southern Yue people, and Hong Kong gradually fell under the influence of the northern culture. By the time of the Qin and Han dynasties, Hong Kong had already come under the administration of China's central government, and had become part of the Great Chinese National Family.
>
> Hong Kong's long and close relationship with the inner regions of China has been proved by the teams of archaeologists who have been to Panyu County, photographed the Han Dynasty tombs there, and compared them with Hong Kong's Han Dynasty tomb at Lei Cheng Uk. This historical fact can enable students more deeply to appreciate that Hong Kong has been part of China from time immemorial. (CDI 1999, i)

Thus the Chinese history teaching package makes explicit the message that in the curriculum for the history subject is merely implicit; in other words-even the aboriginal inhabitants of Hong Kong were essentially Chinese, or were painlessly assimilated into the great Chinese *volksgemeinschaft*, though it is far from clear that this was the case. At the same time, in stark contrast to the approach adopted in the history subject, the local history teaching package for Chinese history contained a preface emphasizing that local history was merely an optional appendix to the main syllabus, to be taught only if time allowed.

The nationalist message is also the central theme of the new syllabus for senior secondary Chinese history, repeated again and again throughout the document in a way that marks a clear break with the depoliticized tone of official syllabi prior to 1997 (CDI 2002, 3). Interestingly, however, this was not the case with an earlier draft of the new syllabus, released for consultation in April 2001 (CDI 2001). Reflecting pressures brought to bear on curriculum developers by reformist elements within the CDI and the Hong Kong Examinations Authority (HKEA), this draft would have drastically reduced the proportion of the curriculum devoted to ancient history and correspondingly increased the proportion devoted to twentieth-century history. It also contained a list of eight optional special topics for in-depth study, from which students were required to choose three. The first two on the list related to the history of Taiwan and Hong Kong, although predictably the first teaching aim of the Taiwan option was defined as "recognising the fact that Taiwan has been part of Chinese territory from time immemorial" (CDI 2001, 5). Even this was insufficient to pacify the outraged fundamentalists of the Chinese history lobby, who fulminated in the local Chinese-language press against this attempt to water down the chronological coverage, dynasty by dynasty, of the full 5,000 years of China's glorious past (Vickers 2003, 219–220).

The would-be reformers were forced to give ground and to accept a new syllabus that retained more of the content of its predecessor, and which — for good measure — hammered home the importance of Chinese history's role in "strengthening national education and fostering students' sense of their national identity" (CDI 2002, 3). Moreover, when the textbooks for the new curriculum were published in early 2004, their increased coverage of modern Chinese history included accounts of the June 4th Incident of 1989 that in no case even mentioned that anyone had been killed in the military crackdown, an omission for which they were pilloried in the local press (Ling Kee 2004).[17] The narrative consisted, as before, almost exclusively of the doings of Great Men, and all else derived its significance only from its relationship to the political center. Thus, in the expanded account of the modern period, Tibet, Mongolia, and Taiwan appeared only as sites for the struggle to defend the sovereignty of the central Chinese state against the British, the Russians, the Japanese, or (in the case of contemporary Taiwan) other Chinese compatriots. The histories of these peripheral regions were otherwise entirely ignored, leaving students with no understanding of to what extent, or why, the authority of the central government had been recognized or rejected by the local inhabitants. What was true of Tibet and Taiwan was also true of Hong Kong itself. The syllabus called for a student-centered approach to the teaching of Chinese history; in the Hong Kong context, this might have been expected to involve attempts to relate events such as the Japanese invasion, the Civil War, the Great Leap Forward, and the Cultural Revolution to the impact that they had on local history. Textbooks might also have been expected to relate their coverage of the June 4th Incident to the massive local demonstrations that occurred in Hong Kong in reaction to that event. Instead, Hong Kong was only mentioned in connection with the Opium War, the return to Chinese rule in 1997, and its mediating role in relations between the mainland and Taiwan.

This was not the first time since 1997 that an attempt to reform history teaching in Hong Kong's schools had been scuppered by resistance from the Chinese history subject community. The first such occasion had been in 1999, when the CDI floated a proposal, strongly supported by the history subject officer at the time, to create a New History subject at junior secondary level that would combine world history and Chinese history in a common curriculum. A predictable uproar ensued, and the partisans of Chinese history were spurred to form a subject association, "The Chinese History Educators' Society," to lobby for the preservation of their curriculum in toto. As a result, New History went the way of Social Studies in the mid-1970s and was quietly shunted into a CDI siding, where responsibility for drafting the new curriculum was assumed by a former subject officer for Chinese history (Vickers 2003, 221–226; Kan and Vickers 2002).

The fate of these attempts since 1997 to reform the teaching of history, and the curriculum for Chinese history in particular, is symptomatic of the disarticulation that has characterized the policymaking process for education as for other areas under the Tung administration (Morris and Scott 2003). On the one hand, the government would like a modern school curriculum for a twenty-first century international metropolis, offering thorough training in information technology (IT) and in the critical and creative skills considered necessary for success in the knowledge economy. This requires the freeing-up of more space in the school curriculum for IT and for other subjects considered to be relevant to the achievement of these goals, and thus the trimming back of time allocated to other subjects. The retention of two entirely distinct history subjects appears in this light to be entirely indefensible, especially given that since 1997 most schools have switched to teaching history as well as Chinese history through the medium of Chinese/Cantonese. However, the administration has repeatedly failed to force any fundamental restructuring of history education, primarily because it finds itself the prisoner of its own nationalist rhetoric. Since Hong Kong's retrocession, supporters of the existing Chinese history curriculum have been tireless in stressing the nationalist credentials of their subject, not because they are mere tools or dupes of Beijing but because, given the political climate that both Tung and his Beijing masters have helped to create, they know that by doing so they strengthen their hand in an ongoing struggle with their local rivals — and in particular the history subject community — over curricular territory.

Conclusion

Hong Kong's schools therefore find themselves saddled for the foreseeable future with an anachronistic curricular division between two entirely distinct history subjects — a division that has its origins in the colonial politics of the 1950s, but which has derived new justification from the nation-building priorities espoused by the post-handover regime. In a sense, the two subjects of history and Chinese history reflect the conflicting identities and ideals that characterize Hong Kong society as a whole: on the one hand, a worthy but vague commitment to internationalism, on the other a profound conviction of ethno-cultural distinctiveness (or even superiority), and somewhere between these two poles a space in which local identity uneasily subsists. Local identity in Hong Kong is a powerful social and cultural reality, but one that possesses only shallow roots in any consciousness of local history and is therefore potentially vulnerable to attempts to smother local distinctiveness through appeals to an equally powerful belief in a transcendent, all-embracing Chineseness. Just such an attempt is integral to the overall project of Hong Kong's reunification with the motherland and has manifested itself in changes to the school curriculum, and in particular to the two history subjects, from the mid-1990s onwards. The original purpose of the reintroduction of local history, for example, has been partially subverted through a calculated distortion of significant aspects of the local past, and in particular of the key historical relationships that have shaped the Hong Kong of today, namely those with the Chinese mainland and with Britain.

In a political context in which allegations of colonialism (or neo-colonialism) and assertions of nationalism continue to color debate over the region's future, not least in the field of education, it is essential that Hongkongers should be able to look critically at their own past. A school curriculum that really sought to engage local students with the history that has made them who they are would invite them to critically analyze the historical interrelationships between Hong Kong, China, Britain, and the wider world. It would encourage them to reassess what it means to be at once Hongkongese, Chinese, and perhaps even British, Australian, Canadian, or American as well. It would acknowledge the contributions made to Hong Kong's development by ethnic groups other than the Chinese but at the same time would not shy away from confronting students with the uglier aspects of the local past, recognizing that "the attempt to portray Hong Kong history as the result of consensus politics [is] fundamentally dishonest and politically distracting" (Faure 2003, xiv).

Instead, however, recent changes to the history curriculum in Hong Kong have tended to stress the homogenous Chineseness of the region, at the expense of the many other elements that have shaped its past. Moreover, the prospects of this approach being superseded in the near future by a more critical, multifaceted, locally oriented perspective appear to be slim indeed, since for this to happen the current political regime would need to be replaced by one that did not feel obliged to base its claims to legitimacy upon assertions of nationalist political correctness. In other words, as a minimum (but not necessarily sufficient) requirement for meaningful reform to the history curriculum, Hong Kong's political system would need to be democratized, since only an elected administration would have the will or the authority necessary to take on a vested interest such as the Chinese history lobby. Meanwhile, in the absence of such democratization, it is perhaps not inconceivable that the One Country orthodoxy that now pervades the school curriculum might gradually succeed in indoctrinating Hong Kong's youth, and thus begin to turn historical fiction into political fact.

Endnotes

1. Professor Anthony Sweeting recalled this exchange in an interview with Edward Vickers in 1999.

2. The government raised the spectre of 1.6 million impoverished mainlanders flooding into Hong Kong in order to mobilize public opinion against a ruling by the Court of Final Appeal upholding the right of children of Hong Kong permanent residents to come to Hong Kong from the mainland. This ruling was subsequently overturned by a committee of the National People's Congress in Beijing, in an intervention widely seen as seriously undermining Hong Kong's judicial autonomy.

3. See the official website of the Hong Kong Human Rights Monitor (www.hkhrm.org.hk), for example, their "Shadow Report to the United Nations Committee on the Elimination of Racial Discrimination Regarding the Report of the Hong Kong Special Administrative Region of the People's Republic of China" (July 2, 2001).

4. In early 2004, plans were approved for a new museum in Hong Kong dedicated to Sun Yat-sen (who studied in the colony and used it as a base for his revolutionary agitation on the mainland).

5. Buruma goes on to observe that this "is a pattern that has occurred over and over again in east Asia, and it is not very conducive to liberal democracy."

6. And for that matter divorced from the realities of the Chinese past as well. It is notable, for example, that few if any of the historical costume dramas on local (or mainland) television portray women in traditional China hobbling around on bound feet.

7. Unlike the statements of some mainland officials prior to 1997, Tung's policy addresses and public statements have tended to focus less on criticisms of colonialism (which would also imply criticism of local Chinese who collaborated with the British) and more on the importance of increasing knowledge of and affective loyalty to the Chinese motherland among local people.

8. For a discussion of changes to the civic education curriculum before and since the handover, see Morris, Kan, and Morris (2000). In the present article we do not discuss the civic education curriculum, since in most local schools, civic education as a distinct curricular area does not feature prominently. The official guidelines for civic education have reflected the same political influences that have affected the process of curriculum formation for subjects such as history and Chinese history, with an increasingly explicit emphasis on the importance of promoting patriotic sentiment among students.

9. This statement is based on interview testimony from a small sample of subjects who were either students or teachers of history in local schools in the 1960s.

10. Since the syllabus covered the entire 4,000 or 5,000 year history of China, and since most teachers tended to teach it chronologically, the more modern periods and topics tended to be neglected or crammed into the last few weeks of term. See Kan (2002).

11. See the review of press reaction to the move to reintroduce local history in Lee (1996), cited in Vickers (2003, ch. 6).

12. From *Wen Wei Pao*, translated and cited by Lee (1996, 59).

13. From "A Summary Report on the Evaluation of Local History Pilot Scheme, 1992–3," cited in Vickers (2003, 171).

14. A copy of the full list of terms that were required to be changed by publishers is reproduced as an appendix in Vickers (2000).

15. For a fuller discussion of the drafting process and the press reaction to the proposals, see Vickers (2003, 205–216).

16. Kan makes the point that this particular syllabus aim remained unchanged through the period of Hong Kong's transition to Chinese rule.

17. See also the textbooks published by the Hong Kong Educational Publishing Company and Everyman. Articles lambasting the new textbooks in the South China Morning Post alone included pieces by C. K. Lau ("Unsettling History of Omission," Saturday, June 5, 2004), Linda Yeung ("Textbooks Rewrite Tiananmen History," Saturday, June 5, 2004), and Edward Vickers ("Two-headed Mutant Freak of HK's Curricular Circus," Saturday, June 26, 2004).

References

Barmé, G. R. 1999. *In the Red: On Contemporary Chinese Culture*. New York: Columbia University Press.

Buruma, I. 2003. *Inventing Japan*. London: Weidenfield and Nicholson.

Cheng, J. 1989. "History, A New Perspective." *History Newsletter* 1 (Hong Kong: Advisory Inspectorate, Education Department).

Culture and Heritage Commission. 2001. *Consultation Paper*. Hong Kong: Culture and Heritage Commission Secretariat, March.

Curriculum Development Council (CDC). 1997. *Chinese History Syllabus (F. 1-3)*. Hong Kong: CDC, 1997, 5. Cited in Flora Kan, Chinese History in Hong Kong: The Secondary School Curriculum, 1946–2001, unpublished Ph.D. dissertation, University of Hong Kong, 281.

Curriculum Development Council (CDC). 1999. *Chinese History Subject, Special Package on Local History*. Hong Kong: CDI.

———. 2001. *Chinese History Subject (S4-5), Revised Curriculum, First Consultation*. Hong Kong: CDI, April.

———. 2002:1. *Revised S4-5 History Curriculum, First Consultation*. Hong Kong: CDI, March.

———. 2002:2. *S4-5 History Curriculum Framework (Draft for Second Consultation)*. Hong Kong: CDI, October.

———. 2002:3. *Chinese History Subject (S4-5), Revised Curriculum, Second Consultation*. Hong Kong: CDI, October.

Degolyer, M. and Scott, J. L. 1996. "The Myth of Political Apathy in Hong Kong." *The Annals of the American Academy of Political and Social Science — Special Edition on the Future of Hong Kong* (September).

Endacott, G. B. and Hinton, A. 1962. *Fragrant Harbour*. Hong Kong: Oxford University Press.

Faure, D. 2003. "Introduction," in D. Faure, ed. *Hong Kong: A Reader in Social History*. Hong Kong: Oxford University Press.

Kan, F. 2002. "Chinese History in Hong Kong: The Secondary School Curriculum, 1946–2001" (Ph.D dissertation, University of Hong Kong).

Kan, F. and Vickers, E. 2002. "One Hong Kong, Two Histories: History and Chinese History in the Hong Kong School Curriculum." *Comparative Education* 38, 1 (February):73–89.

Kan, Nelson 2003. *Journey through History: A Modern Course*, 2nd ed., books 1–3. Hong Kong: Aristo Educational Press.

Lau S. K. 1981. "Utilitarianistic Familism: the Basis of Political Stability," in Ambrose Y. C. King and Rance P. L. Lee, eds. *Social Life and Development in Hong Kong*. Hong Kong: Chinese University Press.

Lee C. H. 1996. "An Investigation into the Factors that Shape the Design and Formulation of a Curriculum Package: A Case Study of the Local History Package for Lower Secondary Schools of Hong Kong" (M. Ed. dissertation, University of Hong Kong).

Leung, Benjamin K. P. 1996. *Perspectives on Hong Kong Society*. Hong Kong: Oxford University Press.

Ling Kee (various authors). 2004. *Tansu Zhongguo Lishi (Exploring Chinese History)*, book 5. Hong Kong: Ling Kee Publishing Company.

Loh, C. 2003. *Christine Loh's Newsletter*. Hong Kong: Civic Exchange. July 7 e-mail newsletter.

Luk, B. 1998. "Chinese Culture in the Hong Kong Curriculum: Heritage and Colonialism," in Philip Stimpson and Paul Morris, ed., *Curriculum and Assessment for Hong Kong*. Hong Kong: Open University of Hong Kong Press, 51–74.

Morris, P., Kan F., and Morris E. 2000. "Education, Civic Participation and Identity: Continuity and Change in Hong Kong." *Cambridge Journal of Education* 30, 2 (2000):243–262.

Morris, P., McClelland, G., and Wong, P. M. 1997. "Explaining Curriculum Change: Social Studies in Hong Kong." *Comparative Education Review* (February):27–43.

Morris, P. and Scott, I. 2003. "Educational Reform and Policy Implementation in Hong Kong." *The Journal of Education Policy* 18, 1:71–84.

Ng, P. and Baker, H. 1983. *New Peace County*. Hong Kong: Hong Kong University Press.

Pennycook, A. 1998. *English and the Discourses of Colonialism*. New York, Routledge.

People's Education Press (PEP). 1993. *Zhongguo Lishi (Chinese History)*, book 2. Beijing: PEP.

Roy, D. 2003. *Taiwan: A Political History*. Ithaca: Cornell University Press.

Spence, J. 2002. *Treason by the Book*. Harmondsworth: Penguin.

Tung C. H. 1997. *Building Hong Kong for a New Era, Tung Chee-hwa's Policy Address to the Legislative Council*. Hong Kong: The Printing Department of the Hong Kong Special Administrative Region, October.

Turner, M. 1995. "60's / 90's: Dissolving the People," in *Hong Kong's Cultural Identity*. Hong Kong: Hong Kong Arts Centre.

Vickers, E. 2000. "History as a School Subject in Hong Kong" (Ph.D. dissertation, University of Hong Kong).

———. 2003. *In Search of an Identity: The Politics of History as a School Subject in Hong Kong*. New York: Routledge.

Vickers, E., Kan, F., and Morris, P. 2003. "Colonialism and the Politics of Chinese History in Hong Kong." *The Oxford Review of Education* (March).

Vickers, S. 2000. "'More Colonial Again'? — The Post-97 Culture of Hong Kong's Governing Elite." *The International Journal of Public Administration*, special edition on the effects of Hong Kong's handover.

Vines, S. 1998. *Hong Kong: China's New Colony*. Hong Kong: Aurum Press.

Wong S. K. 2001. *Chuansuo Shijie Lishi (World History)*, books 1–3. Hong Kong: Hong Kong Educational Publishing Company (a division of Hong Kong Commercial Press).

6

History Education and the Construction of National Identity in Singapore, 1945–2000

GOH CHOR BOON AND SARAVANAN GOPINATHAN

The half-century since the end of the Second World War has been witness to momentous historical events, namely, the end of colonial empires and the transition to statehood of colonial territories; the rise, first of internationalism, and later of globalization and transnationalism; technology-driven economic change; and the emergence of China and India as new centers of economic and military power. Events in the recent past, most notably the attack on the United States in September 2001 and the U.S.-led wars in Afghanistan and Iraq, the doctrine of unilateralism and preemptive military action, the decline of the influence of the United Nations, and the rise of an activist political Islam that transcends national borders, suggest a period of uncertainty in international relations and a strengthening of the role of individual states in guaranteeing the rights and security of the individual citizen within the nation-state. It is also the case that the promise of widespread development and democratization that shone so brightly in the 1960s has failed to materialize for many states in South Asia, Sub-Saharan Africa, Central Europe, and Central and South America. Some postcolonial states are fragmenting and the politics of identity are once more coming to the fore. East and Southeast Asia, by contrast, have shown more promise of sustainable socioeconomic development and the emergence of strong and credible states, yet the politics of national identity has not been subsumed by economic prosperity. Throughout East Asia, many states have sought to define the parameters of national identity and to promote among their citizens a profound sense of patriotism. History education has been one of the most important means by which these states have sought to achieve such goals, and Singapore has been no exception.

This chapter explores changes in the assumptions and practice of history education in Singapore's schools (secondary and junior colleges) between 1945 and 2000, examining the sociopolitical factors that influenced history curriculum development and the needs that drove the curriculum decision-making process. Changes to history curriculum content are analyzed from the perspective of identity formation, recognizing that identity is contested and changes over time. By stressing the politics of national identity and history teaching, this chapter explains why history is such a contentious subject in Singapore's school curriculum. We ask: What version of history should be taught in Singapore schools and why? Why did the subject become particularly problematic in the last quarter of the twentieth century? And what are the challenges and issues facing Singapore's history teachers at the start of the twenty-first century?

To answer such questions, however, it is first necessary to understand the nation's political history, the view of history advanced by its powerful elites and their efforts to legitimize their position and promote consensus, especially if the polity is plural and state formation has been a contested process. Historians and educators might wish for history education to be a vehicle for the "development of student's historical knowledge, understanding and a critical historical consciousness" (Crawford 2003, 115) but the reality is that in both developed and developing states, these aims are often subordinated to or undermined by the use of history education for purposes of political socialization.

It is also necessary to understand the role played by textbooks, and especially by history textbooks, in the schooling process. Hein and Selden (1998) argue that textbooks provide one of the most important ways nation, citizenship, the idealized past, and the promised future are articulated and disseminated in contemporary societies. It is now widely acknowledged that what is constitutive of official knowledge is presented selectively, and the stronger the state and more centrally run the education system is, the stronger and more hegemonic the representation will tend to be (Apple and Smith 1991). Textbooks are the key pedagogic vehicle for transmitting official knowledge, and all textbooks, perhaps especially those dealing with sensitive curricular areas such as history, social studies, civics and moral education, and economics are often vetted and have to be approved for use by ministries of education. An analysis of textbooks therefore provides a very useful way of detailing the intricate and often shifting relationships between the state, popular culture, and society. From a more pedagogic point of view, textbooks are also vehicles for imparting knowledge to students, and the instructional strategies embedded in these materials represent views of desirable teaching and learning styles. Typically, students read and remember the facts and explanations — and "by the very nature of the genre, (readers) are discouraged from contesting" the viewpoints expressed in textbooks (Ludmilla 2000, 19). Indeed, because most textbooks "seek to be fair and uncontentious, the sparkle, the sense of what the stakes are in divergent views of the past, sometimes gets lost" (ibid.). This must not however be taken to mean that reception of the intended messages by students, or even teachers, can always be treated as unproblematic.

Education and State Formation

The rise of the East Asian "developmental states" of first Japan, then South Korea, Taiwan, Hong Kong, and Singapore (and now Thailand and Malaysia) demonstrates the potential for state-building via economic growth, to which in turn education and training may make a significant contribution. State formation and national identity development had unpromising beginnings in the first group of countries. Japan, fueled by nationalistic pride, embarked on a disastrous war that ended with the first use of atomic weapons on a civilian population. It had to rebuild the state out of the rubble of military defeat, and its subsequent successful economic development did much to strengthen the state and set an example to others in the region. The division of the Korean Peninsula created a sense of insecurity for South Korea, which sought to distinguish itself from the North by its adoption of a different political and economic model, and by a strong alliance with the United States. Both Taiwan and Hong Kong have had troubled relationships with the Communist-ruled Chinese mainland, and this has played a key role in shaping their political identities and conceptions of statehood, while at the same time their regimes have derived some legitimacy and autonomy from rates of economic growth that until recently dramatically outstripped that of China. Even within secure states, however, conceptions of identity, state-citizen relations, and international relationships can continue to be problematic, and such problems as exist are typically reflected in the history curriculum, as Japan's continuing textbook controversies show (Crawford 2003; Hein and Selden 1998; Nozaki and Dierkes, this volume).

One major problem for the development of fair and balanced history syllabi, history textbooks, and history pedagogy is that they have to induct young minds into the discipline of history, to enable them to evaluate sources and come to defensible judgments, while often at the same time satisfying the demands of a political elite seeking to establish as truth a particular version of the past. In recent years, the approach to history education (and the school curriculum in general) in Singapore has shifted toward a thinking curriculum, which requires students to acquire both content knowledge and historical thinking skills. Official curricula now state that students should be taught to appreciate that there can be multiple and conflicting interpretations of historical events. As we detail later, however, there are several unsettled aspects of Singapore's historiography, for example with regard to the Japanese Occupation. This was by all accounts a period of brutal oppression, but at the same time, it demolished the myth of British invincibility and hastened the end of the empire. Also, the Japanese are now economically successful and a major source of investment for countries throughout East and Southeast Asia, including Singapore. How, then, is this history to be told? Will this investigative process and search for the truth create a more critical generation of Singaporeans who might not be so easily convinced by the official narrative of history?

Secondly, the heritage of colonial divide-and-rule policies in the interwar years left a legacy of bitterness among the non-English-educated population, especially the Chinese. Many Chinese-educated Singaporeans were inspired by postfeudal China's efforts to liberate itself and to modernize, and some became militantly anticolonial and leftist. They joined forces with moderate Chinese in the People's Action Party (PAP) in the 1950s to compete for power in a decolonizing Singapore, but split in the early 1960s over differences in politics, language, culture, and economic management. That in itself is not unusual, but the political labeling of the defeated group as Communist and chauvinistic continues to be controversial, with powerful stakeholders seeking to seal an official version (Lee Kuan Yew 1998; Drysdale 1986) while others attempt more critical evaluations of the past (Wee 1999; Lau 1992). With such issues unresolved, history teaching in a state-dominated education system is likely to be tilted toward official versions or victor's history. Harper (2001) calls these sorts of texts "authorised versions," some of which, while acknowledging the role of significant oppositional figures, characterizes them within the narrative as misguided. Singapore's first separate general history (following independence from Malaya/Malaysia in 1965), *The First 150 Years of Singapore*, was written by Donald and Joanna Moore (1969) — academics who were not historians. Three other significant books, Turnbull's *A History of Singapore, 1819–1975*, first published in 1977 and reissued in 1989 in an expanded version with the title *A History of Singapore 1819–1988*; Drysdale's *Singapore: Struggle for Success* (1984), and Bloodworth's *The Tiger and the Trojan Horse* (1986), were all written by Westerners who were generally sympathetic to the dominant perspective regarding "how it happened and why." Harper's comment that "the accounts by seemingly disinterested observers reflect Cold War imperatives and are dominated by stark political categories, [and] were written to edify and instruct" is an apt one. In 1998, Lee Kuan Yew published a two-volume account of the shaping of Singapore's modern history that, given his dominant role in Singapore's recent history, stands as a testament to how it should be viewed; this is particularly true of the first volume, *The Singapore Story*. There is now, however, an attempt to produce a fuller and more complex view of the contribution of other political figures to the making of Singapore's history. *Lee's Lieutenants* (1999) and *Comet in Our Sky: Lim Chin Siong in History* (2001) represent a welcome break from the official narrative, which could hopefully lead to the writing of multiple-perspective and nonlinear accounts of the story of Singapore.

Postwar School History: British Legacies and Western Dominance

Following the end of the war in 1945 and the reestablishment of British authority over Singapore, history education and history textbooks in English-medium schools were strongly influenced by British curricular models, and Chinese-medium schools likewise by those in China; this was due to the fact that during the colonial period, a large non-state-controlled sector of Chinese-medium schools had developed. This was a period when the British, in the face of rising nationalism among the people of Singapore (and their colonial subjects elsewhere in Southeast Asia) worked hard to restore lost prestige and control. Though the history syllabus then used in the schools was ostensibly based on the narrative of human progress, it essentially held up as an ideal the achievements of European civilization to "less-developed" countries like Malaya and Singapore. Filling the pages of primary and secondary textbooks of the period were European heroes, conquerors, explorers, saints, reformers, inventors, builder, and doctors — Alexander the Great, Julius Caesar, Christopher Columbus, Socrates, Joan of Arc, Francis Xavier, Archimedes, Florence Nightingale, Marconi, to name just a few. As an example, in the textbook *The Story of Malaya and Her Neighbours*, twenty-two out of thirty chapters were devoted to the achievements and dominance of the Europeans in Southeast Asia (Nazareth 1961). As late as the 1960s, the study of Commonwealth history was also strongly emphasized at the secondary level. Pupils read about the achievements of British India, "The Jewel of the British Empire," and the roles of various governor-generals in preserving the glory and benefits of British rule in India (and in other "backward" colonies). There was no mention of the negative impact of Britain's "civilizing mission" on the social and economic fabric of Indian villages and cottage industries.

Singapore's postwar political development owes much to events in the early twentieth century, when sociopolitical development and education were deeply intertwined. British colonial policy was content to leave the different ethnic groups largely to their own devices, while the growth of the port and trade allowed for sufficient employment opportunities. Without much central direction there evolved a four-language-stream model of schooling. The political turmoil in China in the early part of the century (and later, the civil war, the Communist takeover, the Japanese occupation of Manchuria, and conflict in the Korean Peninsula) all had a considerable impact on the local Chinese community. Singapore was both a haven and mobilization point for Chinese revolutionaries like Sun Yat Sen. The largely Chinese-educated population became progressively more anti-British, especially when the colonial administration sought to curtail their political activities. During this period, curricula in the clan- and community-supported Chinese-medium schools sought to project an overseas Chinese identity and affiliation with the Chinese mainland. The British responded by seeking more control over the administration and curricula of these Chinese schools and began to provide more aid to those schools that agreed to expand the teaching of English (Gopinathan 1974). During the 1950s, attempts were made both in Malaya-Singapore and in Hong Kong (see the previous chapter) to break the link between local Chinese schools and the education systems of Nationalist and, especially, Communist China — with the Communist insurgency in Malaya lending special urgency to efforts by the colonial administration there to exclude mainland Chinese teaching materials and propaganda.

In 1959, Singapore attained self-government under the PAP with Lee Kuan Yew as the prime minister. Attempts were made to develop an education policy based on equal respect for the four main ethnic groups — Chinese, Malays, Indians, and Eurasians — and all schools were required to use indigenized Malayan-centered syllabi and textbooks. Even then, local history in history textbooks of the 1950s had a largely British orientation (as the previous chapter noted was the case with local history in Hong Kong at this time) — British personalities such as Francis Light and Stamford Raffles, "founders" of Penang and Singapore respectively, figured prominently, and the narrative focused on issues such as the establishment of the Straits Settlements and the positive economic impact of the opening of the Suez Canal — in short, the bestowing of the peace and prosperity of the Pax Britannica on the indigenous peoples of the Malay Peninsula. This was a subtle and idealized representation of the core-periphery imperialism of the once-powerful British Empire. The loss of Singapore to Japan, regarded by Winston Churchill as the worst military disaster in British history, was not dwelt upon at any length. Indeed, this Eurocentric approach to the writing of history textbooks was reinforced by the prominent role of expatriate teachers, many of whom wrote the textbooks while living in England, Hong Kong, Madras, or Shanghai. As observed by Yong Nyuk Lin, then Education Minister, these writers could not play the role of nation-builders. He reiterated that the "Government's education policy should in time unite the different peoples and encourage loyalty for Singapore" (*Straits Times*, June 7, 1960).

Prewar colonial policy, the Japanese Occupation, contestation over political and civil rights, and the struggle first to merge with Malaya and then to come to terms with the aftermath of separation made the decade and a half from 1950 to 1965 a period of intense political debate about the nature of Singapore society and its political identity. Broadly speaking, the plural nature of Singapore society precluded the use of an ethno-cultural conception of national identity, although, as we shall see, later in the 1980s there were attempts to utilize an ancient civilization origins perspective to justify the desired socio-moral order. What then of the argument that East Asian state development was strongly nationalist and anticolonial? Here too it is necessary to avoid sweeping generalizations. It is clear that, in the Singapore case, there were struggles between English-educated and Chinese-educated groups and deep divisions over the nature of the state that was to be formed. In the Singapore case, the minority English-speaking elite, which advocated a strong capital-based economic modernization model, won the argument, and its capacity to deliver on its promise transformed postwar politics. In many ways, the acrimonious merger experience with Malaysia, a period of a mere 3 years, came to rankle more than one-and-a-half centuries of colonial rule! Thus, in comparison with the experience of violent anticolonial movements elsewhere, in the Singapore case, there was no serious rupture with the colonial period. Indeed, the convention has been to see Singapore's history as beginning in 1819, when Raffles established his trading post, and not to locate it in an earlier period, when Singapore was part of Malay empires.

Though Singapore attained self-government in 1959, the issue of independence was rendered problematic by a number of factors. The PAP argued that Singapore, with its Chinese-dominated population and with no hinterland, was not viable on its own; the Malaysians and the British concurred, fearing that an independent Singapore would quickly become pro-Communist and threaten Malaya and British interests there.

The solution to this dilemma of political identity was Singapore's merger with Malaysia, and to counterbalance the Chinese majority in Singapore the states of Sabah and Sarawak were included to form the Malaysian Federation in 1963. However, the merger solution was deeply divisive in Singapore and heightened political and ethnic divisions. Singapore's merger with Malaysia was in any event short-lived and ended with the island's ejection from the Federation in August 1965, but its legacy has been continual political differences over a number of issues with Malaysia.

History Education during the Survival Phase, 1965–1978

On August 9, 1965, Singapore became an independent republic. Lee Kuan Yew and his ministers immediately began tackling the three most pressing problems that would determine the survival of the small state — defending the nation, building social cohesion, and preparing its citizens for economic survival. With its expulsion from Malaysia, the island now had no direct access to its hinterland. It was seen as crucial for the government to educate the people to meet the challenges of a new era. Thus, curricular reform was essential, both to prepare school leavers for the industrial skills needed for economic growth and also to lay the foundations of a Singaporean identity. A few months earlier, in November 1964, Education Minister Ong Pang Boon had already called for the writing of a "common content syllabus for all schools" so that "national consciousness among our youth" could be strengthened (*Straits Times*, November 24, 1964).

Though history was a school subject, the content of textbooks suggested that it was not seen as a key tool for developing national consciousness and integrating the various communities. On the contrary, national history — the story of how immigrants from many countries came and settled down and how communal tension and suspicion led to mass riots and destruction — was not the core content. The fear was that an emphasis on the multiethnic and cultural identities of the people would further strengthen communal jealousies and rivalries. Rajaratnam, a leading ideologue in the PAP, asserted the need to be cautious about using the past: "Knowing where you are going to is more important than knowing where you came from" (cited in Lau 1992, 50). In line with this reasoning, the teaching of topics such as the Second World War and the Japanese Occupation of Singapore, which saw the dominance of one race over others and sometimes the use of extensive violence against some groups, were seen as potentially harmful to social stability and to the development of a multiethnic, multireligious Singapore. It must also be noted that the 1950s and 1960s were turbulent years in Singapore's short modern history, marked by islandwide racial riots initiated by left-wing radicals and racial chauvinists.

Education in Singapore during this survival-driven phase (1965–1978) was geared primarily toward raising literacy and numeracy levels and imparting technical skills to prepare the young to support the rapid industrialization programs initiated by the government. Singapore's first industrial park at Jurong at the western end of the island, once perceived by many as a white elephant when the forest and swamp were cleared at high cost in the late 1960s, was rapidly transformed into a haven for multinational corporations who were attracted to the Republic through a range of tax incentives and pioneer status benefits. Thousands of skilled and semiskilled blue-collar workers were needed to fill the factory floors. Schools were built rapidly to cater to the baby boomers of the 1950s and 1960s. Technical education was made compulsory for all secondary students. Polytechnic education was also expanded and more engineering courses were introduced at the University of Singapore. Under this national agenda to create a technically proficient workforce, arts subjects (such as history and geography) assumed less importance than such subjects as science, mathematics, and other technical subjects. History was treated as an academic subject that could be displaced in a crowded curriculum to make room for more important or useful courses (Lau 1992).

History education during the survival-driven phase was consequently unimaginative and subjected to careful control by curriculum planners. At the primary level, the subject was partly nonexaminable and, by 1972, it was no longer offered in the Primary School Leaving Examination, the national examination taken by all primary six students. At the secondary level, Malayan history was offered as an optional subject and then only at upper secondary levels.[1] This was a carryover from an earlier period when Singapore, as part of the Straits Settlements, was included in accounts of Malaysian history, and was also due to the requirements of the major examining authority, the Cambridge Local Examinations Syndicate.

By the later 1970s, Singapore had achieved full employment and had enjoyed several years of double-digit economic growth. Along with the phenomenal rise of postwar industrial Japan, the city-state's success was viewed as an economic miracle. In tandem with its new economic restructuring strategy of shedding its sweat-shop factory image and moving toward higher skills and valued added industries, Singapore's education system was revamped in 1978.

Reflecting the importance given to technical and engineering education, a team of systems engineers and analysts (and not professional educators), under Education Minister Goh Keng Swee, was appointed to review the education system. The Report on the Ministry of Education, or the Goh Report, as it came to be popularly known, introduced widespread changes, targeted at reducing attrition rates and attaining high literacy and numeracy in languages and mathematics via streaming. The period from 1978 to 1997 is regarded as the efficiency-driven phase in education in Singapore.

Significant changes were made to the curriculum during this period, with history education serving the political agenda of promoting nationalism among the multiethnic Singaporean youth. Defined succinctly by Stein and Hans (1996) as "an ideological movement for attaining or maintaining a nation-state," there was a concerted move to strengthen the relationship between citizens and the state, emphasizing the importance of forging ahead with the government as one people, one nation. In line with wider state policies, young Singaporeans were to be more explicitly instructed on how to think and act as national subjects. As in the case of many contemporary societies, schools and history textbooks in Singapore were now seen as important vehicles through which these ideas of identity and citizenship could be transmitted to the young. To ensure that changes were carried out uniformly in all schools, the Curriculum Development Institute of Singapore (CDIS) was established in 1981 at the Ministry of Education (MOE). Whereas the previous practice was for the MOE to develop the syllabus and for commercial publishers to approach writers, usually history teachers, to write the texts (still the practice followed in Hong Kong), the establishment of the CDIS turned text production into a state-dominated activity (as it then was in Taiwan and South Korea). Textbooks and teaching aids were centrally written to be user-proof, so that even an untrained and inexperienced relief teacher could teach a lesson well following the given content and instructions. As noted earlier, because textbooks are MOE-approved or state-authored before they can gain ready acceptance by schools and because, directly or indirectly, they carry the imprimatur of the state, history textbooks contain the niches or sites of memory of Singapore's modern history. They contain the authoritative chronological narratives (or official version) of Singapore's colonial history as the "Clapham Junction of the Eastern Seas," recount its fall to imperial Japan, and set out how its citizens are to view the turbulent decades of the 1950s and 1960s and take pride in the city's phenomenal rise as a newly industrializing economy in the 1970s.

Beyond Survival: 1978–1995

The 1980s represent a period of important socioeconomic change in Singapore. The fears and anxiety of the Separation Period, beginning in the midsixties, were replaced by growing confidence in Singapore's prospects as a result of vibrant economic growth. Thus, while the political issues appeared resolved, a growing consumerism and individualism unsettled the political elite and raised questions about the desired moral-cultural order (although the two were by no means unconnected).

On the political front, in 1981, the PAP lost an important by-election in Anson to J. B. Jeyaratnam, suggesting the beginnings of an erosion of support for the ruling party. This was all the more galling in that it happened in a constituency that should have been particularly safe territory for the PAP. The "Anson loss" convinced the PAP leadership that Western materialistic values were threatening the hearts and minds of young Singaporeans who had no memory or understanding of the tumultuous years leading to Singapore's independence; they seemed, in the government's eyes, to have forgotten the lessons of the survival phase. Their relatively comfortable lifestyles — a result of hard work and sacrifice by the older generation — and their indifferent attitudes toward political matters were seen by the PAP as strong indications of an erosion of important elements of Singapore's Asian values. In short, the leadership was worried that the younger generation would undermine both Singapore's impressive legacy of economic growth and the political hegemony of the PAP. The party's response to this situation was, according to Loh, to "reconceptualise its strategy for hegemony" (1998, 4). Education was to be utilized as a powerful channel to cultivate a strong ideological affinity between the population and the PAP.

This period also witnessed a growing recognition of the economic success of Japan and the emergence of the "little dragons," which seemed to suggest the possibility of a distinctively Asian model of governance, termed by some as "neo-traditional modernity" (Wee 2003). In contrast to the earlier period, when reference to the more traditional ethnic-cultures-rooted past was seen as problematic, primordialist, and tending to foster chauvinism, this period marked the start of the Asian values discourse and a positive view of ancient and ancestral civilizations. The ruling elites were now convinced that the ethnic cultures of Singaporeans had been largely sanitized by the state and were no longer necessarily sources of division, and it was considered timely to inculcate a new sense of Singaporeanness that stressed the emergence of a consensual culture based on Asian values. As in Japan, many among the elite felt that the nation should adopt a more organic, communitarian, and corporatist culture that, as the Japanese experience seemed to show, promoted economic prosperity and national cohesion.

As a consequence, significant changes were made to the curriculum. In February 1982, the MOE announced the introduction of a "Religious Knowledge" syllabus that included Confucian ethics (Gopinathan 1995). As explained by Goh Keng Swee, "Confucius believed that unless the government is in the hands of upright men, disaster will befall the country." The introduction of Confucian ethics and religious knowledge more broadly into the school curriculum was aimed at countering the "less desirable aspects of Western culture"

(*Straits Times*, February 4, 1982, and October 7, 1982).[2] Additionally, the history curriculum shifted significantly to the teaching and learning of Singapore's own history, now seen as a useful medium for nation-building (Gan 1997). From 1984 onward, the lower secondary history syllabus covered the period from the founding of Singapore in 1819 to 1965, when Singapore became an independent nation. A two-volume, state-authored text entitled *Social and Economic History of Modern Singapore* was developed for use in all schools.[3] For upper secondary students, a broader, more regional history syllabus covering Singapore, Malaya, and Southeast Asia was introduced.[4] These remained in use until a decade later when, as part of the MOE's cyclical review of the school curriculum, the history syllabus was reviewed once again.

History and National Education: 1996–2003

Even this coverage came to be deemed inadequate by the mid-1990s and, in July 1996, the government expressed its dissatisfaction and the need to review once again the teaching and learning of the history subject. Lee Hsien Loong, the deputy prime minister (son of Lee Kuan Yew and, as of 2004, Singapore's new prime minister), identified the need to inculcate a sense of history as a key task of the local education system because "[i]f we do not know what happened 30 or 40 years ago which made us an independent country, or worse, if we believe that the past is irrelevant to the present, then Singapore cannot hold together" (*Straits Times*, July 27, 1996). His remarks signaled the beginning of another milestone in educational change in Singapore — and in the teaching of history. National Education (NE) initiatives were introduced into schools in 1997. The intended outcome of NE is to develop a sense of national identity and social responsibility in young Singaporeans. In line with the objectives of NE, in June 1997, Prime Minister Goh Chok Tong launched his Thinking Schools, Learning Nation (TSLN) vision, aimed at setting new directions for Singapore education and preparing the young for the challenges of the twenty-first century. The aim of TSLN was to encourage the younger generation to think critically and, in the process, to stimulate them to contribute ideas and suggestions for the further development of the nation. Schools were entrusted with the responsibility of developing future generations of thinking and committed citizens, capable of making good decisions to keep the city-state vibrant and successful.

What precipitated the desire to teach students "what happened 30 or 40 years ago" in Singapore's modern history? This can be attributed to Singapore's often uneasy and, at times, tense relations with its immediate neighbor, Malaysia. In a speech made on June 8, 1996, Lee Kuan Yew, now senior minister, commented that Singaporeans must not rule out the possibility of a remerger with Malaysia. This was more of a wake-up call regarding the danger of reliving the experience of the Merger-Separation Era (1963–1965), when the island-republic was reluctantly accepted into the Malaysian federation and, within 2 years, unceremoniously booted out.[5] It was obvious to Lee that young Singaporeans were generally ignorant of what had happened in Singapore's recent past. He and other political leaders had noted that when contentious issues emerged between Malaysia and Singapore, Malaysian youths were more nationalistic while Singapore youths tended to be relatively apathetic. It was felt that this could in part be due to the reluctance to use history deliberately for purposes of identity formation. A month later, the senior minister's observation was reiterated by Lee Hsien Loong, who stated succinctly that "the circumstances of Merger and Separation being fundamental to Singapore's nationhood, ignorance of, or lack of interest in, those momentous events is a gap in 'national education'" (*Straits Times*, July 18, 1996).

The MOE responded swiftly with a review of the history (and social studies, civics, and moral education) curriculum so that, in the words of Prime Minister Goh Chok Tong, "students will have a deeper knowledge of Singapore's past by the time they leave school" (*Straits Times*, July 22, 1996). NE's key messages were infused in both the formal and nonformal curriculum from the primary level to the preuniversity level to sensitize students to NE values both inside and outside the classroom.[6] In the formal curriculum, NE is woven into various subjects to bring in the "head" knowledge so that at the end of their schooling, students will have a clear understanding of the official NE perspective on Singapore's governing principles and way of life. In addition, a new, compulsory subject, combined humanities, was introduced for all upper secondary pupils in 2001. This has two components — a compulsory social studies component and an elective component of either history, geography, or literature. The social studies syllabus was designed to instill a sense of national identity and its content revolves around the six key NE messages. In the informal curriculum, NE activities were introduced to create an environment that allows values to germinate and take root in order to take care of the effective part of NE. Thus, uniquely, historical knowledge is imparted not via a history syllabus or textbooks, as per the conventional practice in East Asia and elsewhere, but through a schoolwide and systemwide set of activities and experiences.

As a compulsory subject for all lower secondary pupils, the new history syllabus (implemented in 2000) aims to provide them with (1) an understanding of their cultural roots and heritage through the learning of the ancient history of Southeast Asia, India, and China and (2) a "sound knowledge of and lessons from our nation's history, especially the political developments in the postwar years leading to self-government and independence and how Singapore succeeded against all odds to become a thriving nation" (MOE 1999). The textbook *Understanding Our Past. Singapore: From Colony to Nation* (Curriculum Planning and Development Division [CPDD] 1999) is widely used in Singapore schools.[7] The ancestral civilizations model, propagated in the 1980s through a study of Confucian ethics and religious knowledge, was revived and given greater emphasis in the first four chapters of the book. The textbook also includes discussions of the factors that led to the rise of civilizations in India, Southeast Asia, and China; their achievements in science and the arts; and how these great civilizations were sustained by responding to internal and external threats. In contrast to the immediate postindependence years, when the concept of an immigrant society was not expounded in textbooks, much space is devoted in *Understanding Our Past* to the role of early immigrants (mainly Malays, Indians, Chinese, and Europeans) in laying the foundation of modern Singapore. All the races are equitably represented as playing key occupational roles, from the rich compradors and European trading houses, to the Chinese "coolies" and Indian convicts and laborers, in the development of the British colony. The success stories of three forefathers who "extended a helping hand to others in need and contributed generously to society" — Syed Sharif Omar Aljunied, Seah Eu Chin, and P. Govindasamy Pillai — are highlighted (33–34). [8]

The ideal of community service as exemplified by pioneer community leaders is strongly emphasized in the textbook. Pupils learn that during the colonial period, "people from various races came forward and took it upon themselves to provide social services like hospitals and schools for their community and the society" (28). The message is reinforced in the later chapters (12 to 14), which highlight the role of "upright men" in nation-building — Goh Keng Swee, who pioneered the transformation of an area of jungle and swamp at Jurong into Singapore's industrial heartland and "masterminded the creation of a citizens' army"; the late Dutchman, Dr. Albert Winsemius, who contributed greatly to Singapore's economic planning and development in the 1960s and 1970s; and Lim Kim San, who played a key role in the development of public housing. [9]

At the Ordinary (as at the Advanced) level, history is seen as a key subject for developing in young Singaporeans a "knowledge of important international affairs so that they will gain a broader perspective of the world and understand the interdependence between Singapore and other nations ... [and, more specifically,] to know the relationship with our nearest neighbor, Malaysia, which has shared a similar colonial experience with us." A whole year is devoted to topics that cover postwar nationalism in Southeast Asia, constitutional developments in Malaya and Singapore, the Communist Emergency, Singapore's struggle for full self-government, Indonesian confrontation, formation of Malaysia, the merger and separation of Singapore from Malaysia, and the building of the independent Republic. Another year of study is devoted to modern world history from 1910 to 1980. This covers both the World Wars, the formation of the United Nations, the Cold War in the West, China from 1949 until the period of economic modernization policy in the 1980s, and the disintegration of the Iron Curtain and the failure of Communism in Eastern Europe. The political motivation is clear — Singaporeans should know and understand the historical events and personalities surrounding the relationship between Singapore and Malaysia. At a broader level, they are expected to develop an empathy for and sensitivity toward different political experiences and to appreciate that different societies hold different beliefs, values, and attitudes at different times.

Going beyond the Textbook

While the government and its leaders view history (and social studies) as a significant school subject for imparting national values, the subject is still not a popular choice for upper-secondary pupils, as compared to geography.[10] Until recently, history teaching and learning was often branded as boring and uninspiring, with little emphasis on investigative and thinking processes. It was seen as mostly involving rote learning and regurgitation of facts and figures. Pedagogic approaches amounted to nothing more than drilling pupils to answer essays and structured examination questions. Teaching was didactic and emphasized the acquisition of received knowledge by pupils, rather than the skills involved in enquiry and investigation. It was uncommon for the history teacher to teach beyond the textbook and to engage pupils in historical thinking because the examinations basically encouraged pupils (and teachers) to spot questions and to present model answers. The outcome of this traditional approach was that teachers and pupils alike tended to view history as an unimportant subject that did not serve to impart any sense of national heritage or any heightened sense of community awareness.

The TSLN initiative introduced in 1997 provided a framework for changing the way that history was taught and assessed. The aim of the initiative was to promote higher-order thinking skills and creativity. In history, interpretation and evaluation of historical sources was introduced into the syllabus at all levels and pupils were expected to tackle, in addition to structured essay questions, source-based questions. In terms of its pedagogy and content, history is now seen as an investigative and scientific subject with the potential for stimulating conceptual understanding and critical thinking in pupils. This is because it is likely that pupils who use historical content in creative ways learn the content well and they also learn strategies for identifying problems, making appropriate judgments and providing reasons for their decisions.

History teaching has now shifted toward the development of the craft of the historian in the history teacher and the students. Two main approaches are emphasized — interpretation of historical events and use of source materials. The key obviously lies in the ability of history teachers to engage pupils in the interpretation of historical events and personalities. The pupils are expected to evaluate the significance of events and to develop insights into the social and moral values that led to the unfolding of events within particular historical circumstances. In the words of the historian Chris Husbands, "if they [the pupils] cannot explain why some historical periods and events have a significance and resonance *for* them … then knowing about the past is reduced to a sort of quiz game" (1996).

An interesting example is the views on British imperialism and the impact of British colonialism. Hitherto, coverage of this phase of Singapore's modern history focused mainly on the role of the British government in the provision of law and order and policies to develop the colony into one of its key nodal trading entrepôts. With the new emphasis on historical thinking, the relationship between the British rulers and the ruled has been made more central and critical. Pupils read statements like:

> [T]he (British) government generally did not treat Asians serving in the government very fairly. The officials in control of the government departments were all Europeans. Many government officials believed that Europeans were superior to Asians. The British did not reward people according to their talents or contributions, but according to their race … Furthermore, young European officials who had just come to Singapore were told not to mix freely with Asians. This shows that certain European officials looked down on Asians. (*Singapore: From Colony to Nation* 1999, 45–46)

Teachers are expected to bring up the color bar and attitudes and beliefs of British colonialists. Source material based on a speech made by Tommy Koh, a distinguished Singapore diplomat, is also included in the teachers' resource file to illustrate the Asian-European connection in Singapore's past and present:

> Asians and Europeans both suffer from the several hundred years of domination in Asia. Asians still have less interest in, and respect for, Asian arts than they do for European arts. … Asians need to liberate themselves from the legacy of colonialism. Europeans still sometimes accord an attitude towards Asia which is not in accord with the contemporary world, which should be one of treating each other with mutual respect. (*Straits Times*, April 6, 1998, cited Singapore: From Colony to Nation–teachers' resource file, 29)

Hence, one fundamental teaching objective for history and social studies teachers is to ensure that pupils are clear about the importance or significance of what they study and how this contributes to their understanding of moral, social, and cultural issues relevant to their own and other societies. Pupils are expected to reflect more deeply on the value and relevance of learning about the past and its relationship with contemporary events.

Curriculum planners hope that the source-based approach will be an effective pedagogical tool for training young Singaporeans to develop a certain level of understanding and appreciation of human motivations. As they mature, the training provided in the learning of history and social studies will, it is expected, enable them to distinguish between facts and opinions, between means and ends, with a view to promoting a consensus among divergent perspectives, or arriving at a wise choice of alternative views based on rational judgment and sound arguments supported by ample evidence. In short, the policymakers now hope that history education will help young citizens to participate more actively and responsibly in nation-building as the government creates more political space for the electorate.

Two Sensitive Issues in the History Curriculum

One outstanding issue in the textbook narrative of the national past is the account of the years 1942 to 1945, during which Singapore was under the control of the Japanese Imperial Administration. The Japanese occupation was one of the most significant turning points in the modern history of the Asia-Pacific. This period and its place in the social studies and history syllabi illustrates the utilitarian value of education in Singapore. As mentioned earlier, prior to 1984, the war and occupation years — and the lessons to be learned — were not emphasized in history textbooks. With the revamping of the lower secondary history syllabus and the introduction of social studies in the primary schools, the study of the Japanese occupation period became more explicit. Indeed, all pupils are taught the lessons of the war years three times — in primary social studies, lower secondary history, and upper secondary social studies (and four times for those who opt to take upper secondary history).[11] Teachers, too, were guided by the textbooks and resource books published by the CDIS, in particular regarding the lessons to be imparted to students studying each chapter. Pupils were reminded that Singapore had been lost to the Japanese "partly because [the British] had not been well prepared for it [and] one can learn the lesson that the government and people of a country should always be well prepared to defend the country against its enemy" (CDIS 1985, 116). This lesson was more explicitly reinforced in another textbook written about 10 years later (in 1994) — "[T]he government and people of a country should always be prepared to defend the country against any enemy [and the lesson of war] also taught the people to see the need to get rid of their foreign masters" (CDIS 1994, 153). The explicit reminder of the need to evict all foreign masters illustrates the nationalistic messages embedded in the textbook narratives. This was strongly reinforced by the quotation from Lee Kuan Yew that was used in several textbooks:

> My colleagues and I are of that generation of young men who went through the Second World War and the Japanese Occupation and became determined that no one — neither the Japanese nor the British — had the right to push and kick us around. We were determined that we could govern ourselves and bring up our children in a country where we can be a self-respecting people. (CDIS 1994, 153)

It was obvious to the politicians that, within the short modern history of Singapore, only the events of the war years could be used to rally Singaporeans for the creation of a collective memory that could serve to reinforce the nation-building process.[12] In all textbooks, the period was consistently described in emotive words, such as, "The Dark Years," "Nightmare under the Japanese," "The Beginning of a Nightmare," "The Syonan Years: Surviving the Horrors of War," and "Living the Days of Darkness." The narratives also consistently claim that all living in Singapore experienced the horrors. For example, in *Understanding Our Past. Singapore: From Colony to Nation*, published in 1999 for use in lower secondary level, it was stated that "large numbers of local civilians of all races lost their lives during the Japanese Occupation" (CPPD, 93). A firsthand account by a Malay war survivor was included to support this account: "The Japanese didn't care whether you were a Chinese or a Malay. At roadblocks, if you didn't bow to them properly, or if you couldn't answer their question, they would slap you" (CDIS 1999, 93). The textbook also paid tribute to "people of courage and resilience" to illustrate the role of Singapore's patriots. Two individuals often cited in history texts are Adnan bin Saidi and Lim Bo Seng (CPPD 1999, 78, 106–107). Adnan led one of the Malay Regiments to defend Bukit Chandu in the battle of Pasir Panjang and was captured and burned to death. Hussein Mutalib (1992, 85) has attributed this inclusion of the account of the bravery of Adnan and his Malay soldiers to a desire to counter an increasing sense of political alienation felt by the Singapore's Malay community during the 1990s.[13] In the case of Lim Bo Seng, there was no mention of his affiliation (as a soldier) to the Chinese Kuomintang. Lim joined the British-formed Force 136 after seeking permission from the Kuomintang. Hence, one could argue that his loyalty, like that of many Nanyang Chinese at this time, was still to China.

The perpetuation of the memory of war and occupation in history textbooks (and in the commemoration in all schools of Total Defence Day on February 15, the day when the British surrendered the "Invincible Fortress") is intended to convey a sense of common history and common suffering amongst the disparate people who migrated to the island to seek their fortunes. Teachers are instructed to stress the lessons to be taught and the values and attitudes that are deemed nationally desirable by the Singapore Government.

Textbook writers (many of whom are teachers themselves) and history teachers face a daunting task when confronted with writing about and teaching the Japanese Occupation of Singapore.[14] Should textbooks and teachers stress the brutality of the conquerors and, in the process, reinforce an impression in the minds of the young that the Japanese of today are also of warlike mentality? Or should they condemn the muddling and uncoordinated efforts of the Allied forces, who actually outnumbered the Japanese forces? Should they praise the Japanese for liberating Asia, and Southeast Asia in particular, from the yoke of European imperialism? Was the military occupation by a fellow

Asian power a blessing in disguise in that it hastened the rise of nationalism in the hearts and minds of the indigenous population? What about the relationship between the conquerors and the Chinese, Malays, Eurasians, and Indians? Why did the Chinese suffer tremendously while the Malays and Indians were perceived to be favored by the Japanese? Many of these questions are left unanswered in the textbooks and are likely to remain so in the near future. And, as mentioned earlier, in terms of foreign direct investment, Japan has contributed much to the economic growth of postwar Singapore. Indeed, in the current social studies syllabus for upper secondary schools, a whole chapter is devoted to learning about Japan's rapid modernization and industrialization efforts since 1868 and the lessons to be derived for Singapore. Should Japan then be seen as a friend or foe? Many of these questions are left unanswered in the textbooks.

Interestingly, over the years, the approach adopted by history textbooks toward the Japanese Occupation of Singapore has continued to be bland and noncontroversial. More often than not, the history teacher has to refrain from debating issues in order to achieve the official learning outcome. Similarly, the writing of history textbooks is required to carefully follow the government-developed syllabus regulated by curriculum officials. For the students, since there is a tendency for textbooks to dominate the learning of a subject, it is not surprising that many view the textbook information as an accurate and complete narrative chronology of the past and hence a valid presentation of knowledge (Kumar 2002). Kumar (2002) asserts that history and social studies textbooks are written with the intention of sanitizing the country's past for Singapore's younger generation.

The second major problematic issue in Singapore's historiography is how to deal with the earlier strident nationalism of some elements among the Chinese-educated and how this should be represented in textbooks. The root of the problem lies in the growth of a plural and fragmented society under colonial rule, a process aided by occupational, housing, and educational segregation. Within the Chinese community, dialect and other differences were an additional factor. Perhaps most significant was educational experience. The vast majority of Chinese youths until the early seventies studied in Chinese-medium schools, most of them outside government control as they had been set up by individuals and clan associations. A legacy of neglect and crude attempts to control such schools created mistrust (Gopinathan 1974). But in the 1950s, the proposals of the Rendel commission drastically changed political and cultural dynamics as vast numbers of Chinese-educated people became eligible to vote. This stirring to consciousness of the Chinese-educated was influenced by the victory of the Communists in mainland China, the rising tide of anticolonialism, and a largely Chinese-led Communist insurgency in Malaya. On the education front, the publication of the All Party Report on Chinese Education in 1956, following upon the establishment of Nanyang University in 1955, signaled a new, more positive turn of events for this group. However, later differences with the English-educated group in the PAP, especially over the terms of merger with Malaya led to a split. Characterization of the former group as leftist-inclined and chauvinist still rankles. Recent work by historians and others (Sai Siew Min and Huang Jianli 1999; Hong Lysa and Huang Jianli 2003; Wee 2003; Goh Sin Hwee 2003) call into question established (and textbook) versions of the tumultuous fifties and sixties, especially the nature of the political and cultural orientations of the Chinese-educated. By utilizing different perspectives and allowing the voices of these minorities to be heard, the possibility of a more open, complex history of Singapore's development could be realized.

Conclusion

How are Singapore's citizens to face the challenges of internationalization and globalization? As stated by the MOE: "In the 21st century, Singapore will face vigorous challenges resulting from globalisation, the accelerating pace of technological development and the expansion of the Asian economies. The history syllabus has been revised to meet the needs of Singapore in the 21st century. It seeks to provide a balance between international and local history as well as between the acquisition of values, skills and content." For many countries, it could be argued that no single subject in the curriculum has stronger implications for citizenship and values education than history. In the case of Singapore, history as a school subject was marginalized from 1945 until the late 1970s. In the early years of nationhood, the main concern was to survive through export-oriented industrialization and to impart the necessary technical skills to prepare the young to support the rapid industrialization of the economy. By the end of the 1980s, when Singapore had established itself as a sustainable, newly industrializing economy, a corporatist Singaporean national identity was actively promoted. History education was now to serve the political agenda of promoting patriotism within the context of interethnic solidarity. History was pushed further into the limelight from 1997 onward with the introduction of NE in the school curriculum.

Though NE deals with issues such as loyalty and religious harmony, the key thrust centers around the ongoing construction of a politically expedient narrative of the past. The key message relates to the successful transformation of an island engulfed by ethnic and religious strife into an independent city-state that enjoys unprecedented and sustainable economic and social progress. The quality of leadership, vision, and incorruptibility of the PAP is portrayed as having been indispensable to this transformation. This drive to educate young Singaporeans regarding the historical "truth" of the "Singapore Story" coexists with the shift toward source-based teaching in history. The textbooks include a range of extracts from primary documents that, though ostensibly meant to stimulate students' critical and analytical skills, have in fact been selected to support the official interpretation of the Singapore Story.

As Singapore enters into a new phase of its economic and social development, new curricular challenges have emerged. The successful economic transformation of Singapore has strengthened the PAP's political legitimacy and made possible a hegemonic rendering of the Singapore Story. The postindustrial economy however requires more creativity, innovation, and risk taking among citizens, a shift acknowledged by the TSLN initiative and the use of source-based teaching in history. However, for now the selection of sources as well as the production of history texts remains firmly in government hands. Even though various alternative historical interpretations are now emerging, it is likely to be a while yet before a genuine contestation of ideas is possible in Singapore's history classrooms.

Endnotes

1. One of the main texts used was P. C. Kon, *The Certificate History of Malaya, 1900–1965* (Preston Publication, Singapore, 1971; reprinted 1980).

2. Within a few years, the teaching of religious knowledge was replaced by civics, which was designed to develop "aspects of nation-building, awareness of shared values and an appreciation of Singapore's major religions and races." The fear was that religious knowledge could contribute to a religious revivalism which, in turn, could threaten ethnic harmony — as exemplified by the Maria Hertogh riots of December 1950.

3. Curriculum Development Institute of Singapore, *Social and Economic History of Modern Singapore* (Singapore: Longman, 1984).

4. The popular texts for upper secondary history were Tan Ding Eing, *A Portrait of Malaysia and Singapore* (Singapore: Oxford University Press, 1983); Kok Koun Chin, *Malaya and Singapore, 1400–1963* (Singapore: Oxford University Press, 1988); and Nigel Kelly, *History of Modern Malaya and Southeast Asia* (Singapore: Heinemann Asia, 1993).

5. Talk organized by the Singapore Press Club and the Foreign Correspondents' Association on June 7, 1996. The short period when Singapore was part of Malaysia was fraught with racial tension between the Chinese and Malays in Singapore.

6. The six key NE messages are: (1) Singapore is our homeland, (2) we must preserve racial and religious harmony, (3) we must uphold meritocracy and prevent corruption, (4) no one owes Singapore a living, (5) we must ourselves defend Singapore, and (6) we have confidence in our future.

7. This textbook was written by the curriculum specialists from Curriculum Planning and Development Division (CPDD) which was formed in December 1996. Its functions included those of the previous CDIS.

8. It is interesting to note that the study of ancient civilizations harked back to the late 1960s, when lower secondary pupils had to learn the heritage of great civilizations, including the Renaissance in Europe. See, for example, Lim Chin Tok and Muzaffar Tate, *Oxford Progressive History for Singapore: The Growth of Civilisation* (Singapore: Oxford University Press, 1969).

9. This notion of "upright men" as exemplars of incorruptibility in serving the nation is encapsulated in one of the NE's messages, "We must uphold meritocracy and prevent corruption." Singapore is often rated as one of the least corrupted countries in the world.

10. Paradoxically, as the city-state forges ahead in strengthening its place in the world economy and constantly revamps its educational system to match changing political and developmental needs, the assessment of history in schools (and other key subjects, such as English language, geography, and the sciences) is still influenced by colonial legacies. The Cambridge Local Examinations Syndicate continues to operate as a clearing house for the setting and marking of Ordinary and Advanced level papers. It also advises and recommends content changes to Singapore's MOE.

11. Within the content of the *Upper Secondary Social Studies*, published by the CDIS, MOE, in 2001, 44 pages out of 177 were devoted to historical developments presented in two chapters, entitled "Southeast Asia: From Colonies to Nations" and "Singapore: From Colony to Independent Nation." Hence, pupils have a double dose of history since these topics were also covered in the history textbooks at upper secondary level.

12. See K. Blackburn, "The Collective Memory of the Sook Ching Massacre and the Creation of the Civilian War Memorial of Singapore," *Journal of the Malayan Branch of the Royal Asiatic Society* 73, 2 (2000):71–90. The other significant events in Singapore's history, such as the riots of the 1950s and 1960s, merger, and separation, had strong racial overtones.

13. Adnan bin Saidi was born in Selangor, Malaya. His place in history became a contentious issue between Singapore and Malaysia, both giving him a well-deserved profile in their national histories. In 1999, Malaysia produced a film shot entirely in the country that portrayed him as a national hero. For Singapore, Adnan was prominently featured in a new war interpretive museum, situated at the site where he fought against the Japanese and opened to the public on February 15, 2002.

14. For a more detailed discussion on the implications for NE in Singapore, see Goh Chor Boon, "Things Japanese in Our History Syllabus: Implications for National Education," in Steven Tan Kwang San and Goh Chor Boon (eds.), *Securing Our Future: Sourcebook for National Education Ideas and Strategies for Secondary Schools and Junior Colleges* (Singapore: Pearson

Prentice Hall, 2003), ch. 18. See also, Lee Lay Hong, *Forgive But Not Forget: The Japanese Occupation in Singapore Textbooks, 1965–2003*. (Unpublished paper. Department of History, National University of Singapore).

References

Abu Talib Ahmad and Tan Liok Ee, eds. 2003. *New Terrains in Southeast Asian History.* Singapore: Centre for International Studies, Ohio University and Singapore University Press.

Apple, M. and Smith, L. C. 1991. *The Politics of the Textbook.* London: Routledge.

Blackburn, K. 2000. "The Collective Memory of the Sook Ching Massacre and the Creation of the Civilian War Memorial of Singapore." *Journal of the Malayan Branch of the Royal Asiatic Society* 73, 2:71–90.

Bloodworth, D. 1986. *The Tiger and the Trojan Horse.*

Crawford, K. 2003. "Revisiting Hiroshima: The Role of US and Japanese History Textbooks in the Construction of National Memory." *Asia Pacific Education Review* 4, 1:108–117.

Curriculum Development Institute of Singapore. 1985. *Social and Economic History of Modern Singapore.* Singapore: Longman.

———. 1994. *History of Modern Singapore.* Singapore: Longman.

Curriculum Planning and Development Division. 1999. *Understanding Our Past. Singapore: From Colony to Nation.* Singapore: Federal Publications.

———. 1999. *Understanding Our Past. Singapore: From Colony to Nation. Teacher's Resource.* Singapore: Federal Publications.

———. 2001. *Upper Secondary Social Studies.* Singapore: Longman.

Drysdale, J. 1984. *Singapore: Struggle for Success.* Singapore: Times Books International.

Gan, Dennis Eunne-Ru. 1997. "Public History in Singapore in the 1990s: The Second World War." Unpublished B.A. thesis, Department of History, National University of Singapore.

Goh Chor Boon. 2003. "Things Japanese in Our History Syllabus: Implications for National Education," in Steven Tan Kwang San and Goh Chor Boon, eds., *Securing Our Future: Sourcebook for National Education Ideas and Strategies for Secondary Schools and Junior Colleges.* Singapore: Pearson Prentice Hall.

Goh Sin Hwee. 2003. Revisiting the 1950s and 1960s: Deconstructing the Political Discourse and Structure of Singapore's History." *Tangent* 6:50–60.

Gopinathan, S. 1974. *Toward a National System of Education in Singapore 1945–1973.* Singapore: Oxford University Press.

———. 1995. "Religious Education in a Secular State: The Singapore Experience." *Asian Journal of Political Science* 3, 2.

Harper, T. N. 2001. "Lim Chin Siong and the 'Singapore Story,'" in Tang Jing Quce and K. S. Jomo, eds., *Comet in Our Sky: Lim Chin Siong in History.* Kuala Lumpur: INSAN.

Hein, L. and Selden M. 1998. "Learning Citizenship from the Past: Textbook Nationalism, Global Context, and Social Change." *Bulletin of Concerned Asian Scholars* 30, 2:3–15.

Hong Lysa and Huang Jianli. 2003. "The Scripting of Singapore's National Heroes: Toying with Pandora's Box" in Ahmad and Ee.

Husbands, C. 1996. *What Is History? Language, Ideas and Meaning in Learning about the Past.* London: Open University Press.

Kumar, A. 2002. "The Role of History Textbooks in the Learning of History: A Secondary School Pupils' Perspective in Singapore." Unpublished M. Ed. thesis, National Institute of Education, Nanyang Technological University [Singapore].

Lam Peng Er and Tan, Y.L. Kevin, eds. 1999. *Lee's Lieutenants: Singapore's Old Guard.* Sydney: Allen & Unwin.

Lau, A. 1992. "The National Past and the Writing of the History of Singapore," in Ban Kah Choon, A. Pakir, and Tong Chee Kiong, eds., *Imagining Singapore.* Singapore: Times Academic Press.

Lee Kuan Yew. 1998. *The Singapore Story.* Singapore: Times Editions.

———. 2000. *From Third World to First.* Singapore: Times Editions.

Lee Lay Hong. 2003. Forgive but Not Forget: The Japanese Occupation in Singapore Textbooks, 1965–2003. Unpublished paper, Department of History, National University of Singapore.

Lim Chin Tok and Tate, M. 1969. *Oxford Progressive History for Singapore: The Growth of Civilisation.* Oxford: Oxford University Press.

Loh Kah Seng. 1998. "Within the Singapore Story: The Use and Narrative of History in Singapore." *Crossroads* 12, 2.

Ludmilla J. 2000. *History in Practice.* London: Arnold.

Ministry of Education. 1999. *History Syllabus, Lower Secondary.* Singapore: Curriculum Planning and Development Division.

———. 2002. *GCE 'O' Level Revised History Syllabus.* Singapore: Curriculum Planning and Development Division.

Moore, D. and Moore, J. 1969. *The First 150 Years of Singapore.* Singapore: Donald Moore Press.

Mutalib, H. 1992. "Singapore's Quest for a National Identity," in Ban Kah Choon, A. Pakir, and Tong Chee Kiong, eds., *Imagining Singapore.* Singapore: Times Academic Press.

Nazareth, P. N. 1961. *The Story of Malaya and Her Neighbours.* Singapore: Peter Chong Publications.

Sai Siew Min and Huang Jianli. 1999. "The Chinese-Educated Political Vanguards," in Lam Peng Er and Kevin Y. L. Tan, eds., *Lee's Lieutenants: Singapore's Old Guard.* Sydney: Allen and Unwin.

Tan Jing Quee and Jomo, K. S., eds. 2001. *Comet in Our Sky: Lim Chin Siong in History.* Kuala Lumpur: INSAN.

Tonnesson, S. and Hans A. 1996. *Asian Forms of the Nation.* Surrey, Richmond: Curzon Press.

Turnbull, M. (1989) *A History of Singapore, 1819–1988, 2nd ed.* Singapore: Oxford University Press.

Wee, C. J. W. L. 1999. "The Vanquished: Lim Chin Siong and a Progressivist National Narrative," in Lam Peng Er and Y.L. Tan, *Lee's Lieutenants.*

———. 2003. *Our Island Story: Economic Development and the National Narrative in Singapore.* In Abu Talib Ahmad and Tan Liok Ee, eds., *New Terrains in Southeast Asian History.*

7

The History Text: Framing Ethno-Cultural and Civic Nationalism in the Divided Koreas

CHRIS WILSON, DANTON FORD, AND ALISA JONES

Perhaps by no one in East Asia has the cry of distress over altered historical content been more loudly voiced than by the Korean people (Nozaki and Inokuchi 2000). Elements included, omitted, or perceived as having been misrepresented in the various national and global histories produced in Japan, China, the USSR/Russia, and the United States have often been angrily challenged by North and South Koreans. School textbooks, in particular, have been denounced for purveying distorted history and deliberately misleading impressionable children about the truth of the past; indeed, disputes (principally with Japan) over textbook content have led on more than one occasion to official protests from both North and South Korea and calls for the offending textbooks to be withdrawn or revised. Even seemingly apolitical cultural imports have been dragged into the melee. As reported by Louis in 2001:

> The music industry is one of the latest casualties in the ongoing dispute between Japan and South Korea over Tokyo's much-publicised refusal to make changes to the controversial new history textbooks that, the Korean Government claims, gloss over Japanese World War II atrocities.
>
> In April, South Korea recalled its ambassador to Japan in protest at Tokyo's approval of the textbooks. Now, in an escalation of the dispute, the South Korean government has indefinitely put off plans to further open its markets to Japanese cultural imports. (41)

Clearly, both Koreas have been dissatisfied with the portrayal of their history in foreign textbooks, but how has Korean history been written, contested, and rewritten in Korean school textbooks since the end of the 1910 to 1945 Japanese occupation and the subsequent division of the peninsular into two separate states? Has a unified history evolved across both countries, rooting Northern and Southern identities in a shared past that sustains the possibility of future reconciliation and even reunification? Or have divergent views of the past created an insurmountable divide through positing entirely different ideas about what constitutes the Korean nation(s) and who should rule over it (or them)? According to Baker (1998), difference has hitherto largely prevailed over commonality, with textbooks having long been treated by both sides as a vehicle for reinforcing their own legitimacy and denouncing their opponents. "Education officials on the two sides of the heavily armoured border between the capitalist South and the communist North," he observes, "still employ textbooks in an ongoing war of words over the divided peninsula's future" (ibid., 7). So sensitive and so deeply implicated in regime legitimation is history that any acknowledgment of the other Korea that is not purely negative has tended to be viewed as almost treasonous. In South Korea, the author of a recent primary school textbook that took a more lenient view of the North was even charged with breaching the National Security Law (ibid., 7).

In such a climate, it seems a foregone conclusion that history textbooks would cause the same kind of hindrance to the reestablishment of harmonious relations between the two Koreas as they have in their relations with other states. It is undoubtedly true that textbooks have been constantly embroiled in ideological warfare and have remained a major source of friction between North and South. Korean students on both sides of the border have learned in their history classes that their state is superior and the true representative of the nation, and that the other Korea is the enemy, desecrating the memory of a once great kingdom with wrong-headed values and political ideologies. At the same time, however, they have learned that the people of the Korean peninsula share a common ethnic and cultural ancestry that unites them physically and spiritually as a nation, even though they are now politically divided into two states. Thus, while the promotion of patriotism has remained a consistent objective of the history curriculum in both North and South Korea, the nature of the sentiment students are supposed to feel has varied widely and often contradictorily.

The purpose of this chapter is to examine why and how the nature of the patriotic imperative has changed over the past half-century, analyzing two types of nationalism that we argue have been propagated — often simultaneously — through the history curriculum, North and South, and evaluating their implications for future relations between the two sides. On the one hand is a civic nationalism that emphasizes the rights and duties of citizenship and identification with the political state; on the other is an ethno-cultural nationalism that highlights the inherent unity of the Korean national people (*minjok*). We undertake this study through an exploration of the contexts in which history education policies have been designed and implemented since the division of the two Koreas and through an analysis of history syllabus and textbook content in both North and South. Before embarking on this discussion, it is worth remembering that any analysis of North Korea is limited by the nonavailability and inaccuracy of much information about the Democratic People's Republic of Korea (DPRK), as the North is officially known. Although international concern over its nuclear weapons program ensures that it makes the headlines more frequently today than it did 20 years ago, the DPRK is still a nation shrouded in mystery and secrecy, and much contradictory information circulates concerning all aspects of its domestic conditions. Although we believe the data presented here to be generally accurate and broadly representative, it should not be taken as holy writ. In the case of South Korea, officially entitled the Republic of Korea (ROK), liberalization over the past decade and much greater openness have made a far wider range of materials available. This liberalization has also permitted diversification in education, while — as in other parts of East Asia and elsewhere — efforts to compete in the global knowledge economy have led to calls for history to promote creativity and critical thinking skills. As shown below, this has entailed a number of curricular changes, including recent legislation to allow limited textbook pluralism. We argue, nonetheless, that despite the political chasm between the ROK and DPRK, the history curriculum on both sides remains heavily politicized and continues to act as a vehicle for official attempts to claim ownership over the definition and redefinition of Korean identity.

The Historical Context: Historiography and Nationalism in Colonial Korea

As shown in chapter 1, the Confucian tradition was dominant throughout much of East Asia until the late nineteenth century, particularly in the areas of education and historiography. Perhaps nowhere was this more so than in Choson Korea, where administrators were recruited on the basis of their knowledge of the Confucian canon and where court historians compiled official records and histories until the fall of the dynasty in 1910, when Korea was annexed by Japan. With Japanese rule came Japanese-style modernization in all spheres, including education and historiography. Modern schools were established and Rankean historiography flourished under Japanese patronage. At the same time, however, Japanese rule was bitterly resented by the majority of the population. Some activists fled the peninsula, setting up a government-in-exile in China; others braved Japanese reprisals at home, most notably in the March 1st Movement of 1919, in which more than half a million Koreans participated in demonstrations across the country, protesting against Japanese rule; but most Koreans passively resisted, sending their children to classical academies and attempting to preserve Korean tradition in the face of an enforced Japanese modernity. By the late 1930s, however, the colonial authorities were attempting to subdue even passive resistance through the Japanization policy, which sought to transform Koreans into Japanese subjects, loyal to the Japanese empire now engaged in a war of conquest across East Asia. Japanese troops removed Korean history books and biographies of illustrious Koreans from homes, libraries, and schools and frequently destroyed them (Brudnoy 1970), actions that served only to reinforce a growing anti-Japanese nationalism.

As fast as the Japanese authorities destroyed old Korean histories, however, Korean nationalist historians produced new ones. Works such as Shin Ch'ae-ho's *Toksa Shillon* (*A New Way of Reading History*) and Pak Unsik's *Hanguk t'ongsa* (*The Tragic History of Korea*) and *Hanguk tongnip undong chi hylsa* (*The Bloody History of Korea's Independence Movement*) demonstrated how a once glorious nation had been victimized and oppressed, especially by Japan, and called for a strengthening of the national spirit (*kukhon*) to reinvigorate and liberate the nation. Nationalist historians fell by and large into two camps, conventionally described as liberal and Marxian; although, as we shall see, there were many ideological differences between them, both exhorted the Korean people to remember and strengthen their Korean identity and oppose foreign domination. Liberal nationalist historians such as Yi Kwangsu, Yi Tonhwa, Ch'oe Namsŏn, and Chŏng In-bo saw cultural development and the infusion of modern Western values into Korean society as the means to this end. Rather than confronting the colonial occupation, therefore, liberal nationalists concentrated on purifying[1] and reconstructing Korean cultural identity. Meanwhile, Marxian nationalist historians, such as Paek Nam-un and Yi Chŏng-wŏn, wrote new Korean histories using Marx's historical materialism to interpret Korea's past (Kwon 2000). While the two camps disagreed on theory and in their visions for Korea's postcolonial future, they wholeheartedly converged in taking a primordial ethno-cultural nation "both as the subject of history and as the object for historical research" (Em 1999, 289). Most of these nationalist histories were published abroad by exiles and circulated in Korea only underground, but the two schools of historical thought that emerged at this time were later to form the basis of historiography in the divided Koreas.

The end of World War II liberated Korea from Japanese colonial rule and exposed it to the reality of a strange new polarized world order. The Korean peninsula was divided into Northern and Southern zones along the thirty-eighth parallel and governed by the ill-fated Four Power Trusteeship (the U.S., USSR, U.K., and China). The powers that had defeated the Japanese, however, now distrusted each other's future intentions in the region, and under superpower influence, the fractures present in the nationalist movement before World War II deepened. By 1948, the nation was divided and the hopes of a rapid move toward a united, independent and sovereign Korea were never realized. Over the past half-century, both sides have existed in a state of constant tension, and despite the recent post–Cold War thaw under Kim Dae-jung's "Sunshine policy," to this day neither trusts the other. The threat from the other Korea has also been used to justify authoritarian government and repressive domestic policies in each state. As we shall see below, these many tensions and unresolved issues have been directly reflected in the curriculum and textbooks for history in both North and South Korea.

North Korea

State Formation and Soviet Influence in the DPRK

After surrendering to the Allied forces in August 1945, the Japanese withdrew from Korea. While Koreans were virtually unanimous in their desire to eradicate the influence of colonialism, to restore their nationhood and, as it were, to make Korea Korean again, rival political groups with competing visions for the peninsula's postcolonial future vied for credibility, legitimacy, and popular support. The Communists regarded history as an indispensable part of their campaign. They thus sought to establish their superiority and supremacy over their rivals and demonstrate their rightful inheritance of the ruling mandate through the laws of historical materialism and the championing of the "advanced" ideology of Marxism-Leninism, as well as through claims to have resisted the Japanese more fiercely than their opponents and by extension to be the true Korean patriots — much as the Communist Party in China was doing at this time in its struggle with the Kuomintang (KMT; see chapter 2). No time was wasted as a twenty-five member Provisional History Compilation Committee was appointed in February of 1947 within the Provisional People's Committee and entrusted with the task of reinterpreting Korean history from a historical materialist perspective that demonstrated the inevitable progress of Korea from primitive society through slave, feudal, and capitalist socioeconomic formations to the highest form of society, Communism (Jeon 2002; Petrov 2002). When the DPRK was established in 1948, Marxism and historical materialism became official orthodoxy. Considerable resources were directed toward historical research and the publication of new histories that made the laboring people the subject and agents of history and proved historical materialist laws and the inevitable rise to power of the Communist regime.

Dissemination of the new national narrative was attempted largely through the education system and through the history curriculum in particular. Under Soviet tutelage, a highly centralized education system was introduced based on the USSR model of a system of 10-year primary, junior, and senior secondary education (divided 4-3-3). In addition, with the help of Soviet Koreans (many of whom were former teachers)[2] sent by Moscow between 1945 and 1950 to aid North Korea's development and promote USSR influence, Soviet pedagogical theories and practices were widely implemented. Russian was introduced as a second language in North Korean schools and early curricula were closely modeled on Soviet versions with many textbooks, especially in sciences and technical areas, often translated directly from the Russian (Lankov 2000; Armstrong 2003). Gradually, however, the North Korean authorities took over supervision of the curriculum, establishing a centralized system of curriculum development and government control over the drafting, publication, and distribution of textbooks. In this way, the DPRK government was able to retain a monopoly over the historical narrative transmitted to the country's children.

As in academic historiography, history textbooks for schoolchildren during the early years of the DPRK were dominated by the historical materialist interpretation of the national past, albeit simplified for younger minds.

From Marxism to Chuch'e

Until the mid-1950s, Moscow remained an important influence on the fledgling DPRK, with the slogan "Learn from the Soviet Union!" frequently invoked (Buzo 2002) to exhort the people to strive for the rapid industrialization apparently achieved by the USSR. By the end of the Korean War in 1953, this influence was still prevalent in both historiography and education. Studying Marxism-Leninism was emphasized to provide a solid ideological foundation, while the Soviet "principle of combining the theoretical with the practical" was invoked to highlight the corresponding importance of developing technical skills to serve the needs of reconstruction after the devastating war years. The 1950s also saw the beginnings of North Korean leader Kim Il Sung's personality cult as he began to solidify his power. Students began to learn about Kim's unparalleled revolutionary activities as he was promoted to the people as an idol to be unquestioningly emulated (Kim 1990). The most important development of the period, however, was the gradual formulation of the theory of *chuch'e*, which by the end of the 1960s would come to supplant Marxism-Leninism as the basic ideology of the DPRK.

Often translated as "self-reliance" or "self-determination," *chuch'e* (also spelled *juche*)[3] remains the official ideology of the DPRK today and continues to provide an ideological basis for North Korea's isolation from the rest of the world. *Chuch'e* is championed as a purely Korean ideology created and developed by Kim Il Sung and further elaborated upon by his son, Kim Jong Il. *Chuch'e* is predicated on the concept of *chajusong*, meaning "independence" or "self-sufficiency," and is based upon a conviction that Koreans must manage all political economic and military affairs free from reliance on foreign intervention or assistance. The formulation of *chuch'e* was clearly a reaction to Korea's past history of being dominated — if not necessarily ruled — by imperial China and assorted "barbarians" from the central Asian steppes (Jurchen, Mongols, Manchus), as well as being conquered by the Japanese and subsequently becoming reliant on the USSR and China to defend DPRK statehood. It thus aimed to affirm national independence through staunchly rejecting any form of *sadaejui* (flunkeyism), a term derived from the terms of the traditional relationship with imperial China, according to which Korea recognized the Middle Kingdom as the senior state.

Much as in Communist China, where balancing ideological orthodoxy with ethnic and cultural pride quickly led to a reworking of Marxism (see chapter 2), the evidently nationalist impulse underpinning *chuch'e* had to be squared with the Marxist-Leninist ideological basis of Kim Il Sung's ruling Korean Workers' Party (KWP). *Chuch'e* was thus portrayed as a creative application of universal

Marxism-Leninism to the particular, indeed unique, situation of Korea. According to the theory of *chuch'e*, humans are the masters of the world, with the ability to control and manipulate the environment through the power of their will in order to serve their own needs, whereas all other creatures are subordinate and must adapt to the objective world (Kim 1985). The revolutionary transformation of the world, therefore, will be accomplished by the collective will of the people. At the same time, however, *chuch'e* was formulated as a leader-centered idea, which averred that the revolutionary transformation of the world may be driven by the people but that their will can only be harnessed to the task under the leadership of a superior man; Kim Il Sung and later Kim Jong Il thus became as important as the *chuch'e* idea itself. Clearly *chuch'e* drew not only on Marxism but also on traditional Confucian ideas of the virtuous hegemon ruling by example with wisdom, justice, and benevolence, leading the people back (or in this case forward) to utopia. Drawing also on Confucian notions of the family and its related virtues of filial piety and obedience, the nation was depicted as one large family with Kim Il Sung as the benevolent Father at its head (Cummings, 1993). Kim's sacrifices for the people were thus emphasized while the people were enjoined to follow his stellar moral example and display their loyalty to and love for him. In addition to regular publications and speeches by the great leader, education was to be the main method of instilling the *chuch'e* ideology in the nation's youth, and history was to be one of the most important subjects in this endeavor.

Chuch'e in the History Curriculum

In the 1950s and 60s, North Korean secondary students learned both ancient and modern Korean history through a set of textbooks entitled *Chosŏn Ryŏksa* (*History of Korea*).[4] While it was important for the Marxist DPRK authorities to continue to emphasize Marxism-Leninism in the national narrative, even in the early years, a prototype of the *chuch'e* perspective was evident in school history texts. A 1957 *Chosŏn Ryŏksa* textbook, for example, although closely adhering to Marxist terminology and historical materialist laws, displayed a distinct tendency toward merging Marxism-Leninism with traditional Confucian ideas and asserting a more nationalist position. It also sought to demonstrate the superiority of North Korea, both morally and politically, over the South, primarily through the modern component of the curriculum. Thus, the formation of the Korean People's Army (KPA) in 1948 was presented as born of the legacy of the heroic leader Kim Il Sung's patriotic credentials as a partisan fighter against the Japanese, as well as of the superior morality of Communism. The communist KPA, by extension, was morally superior to the capitalist armies of the South, which were said to be characterized by political and moral corruption (Chŏson Ryŏksa 1957, 200). Ways were found, however, to trace DPRK legitimacy back to ancient times, to show that the North represented the true Korea and that the KWP had the mandate to unite the whole nation under the *chuch'e* form of Communism (Petrov 2003). Both professional historians and history textbooks thus displayed partiality toward the ancient northern states of Old Chosn, Kogury, and Palhae as the source of Korean tradition and sought to downplay the kingdoms of the South (Paekche, Silla) to justify the historical inferiority of the southern part of the peninsula and its unsuitability to rule the nation.

During the 1960s, *chuch'e* was increasingly promoted as the official ideology and, at the same time, the authorities emphasized an indigenous revolutionary tradition and began to distance themselves from Soviet influence (Kim 1990). The drive to "learn from the Soviet Union" was now replaced by a slogan calling for Koreans to "learn from the glorious revolutionary tradition founded by Kim Il Sung and his anti-Japanese partisans!" (Buzo 2002). This was reflected in modern history texts by increasing emphasis on Kim's heroic revolutionary exploits and the importance of his *chuch'e* idea, with its creative application of Marxism-Leninism to Korea's unique circumstances. Although *chuch'e* became increasingly prominent in history texts, Marxism-Leninism was not eradicated. A 1964 *Chosŏn Ryŏksa* text, for example, emphasized the basic requirement of leadership by a party based on Marxist-Leninist principles in order to secure the freedom and happiness of the workers and guarantee success in the revolution (Chŏson Ryŏksa, 1964, 133). However, the creativity of the Korean brand of Marxism-Leninism was also strongly emphasized. In one passage in the 1964 text it was noted that after the Korean War, the KWP carried out a policy of class cooperation (rather than all-out class struggle), especially between poor farmers and middle-class farmers, while merely limiting rather than seizing all the assets of wealthy farmers. This was said to be a creative application of Marxism-Leninism to the solution of farmers' problems (ibid., 247). In another example of the creativity of Kim's thinking, his instructions in 1958 had reportedly led to the acquisition of the funds and materials needed to build seven thousand homes, yet within 9 months, twenty-six thousand homes and various cultural facilities had been built in Pyongyang (ibid., 264). Kim's creative teachings were also said to be revered by artists, whose work had thus reflected the heroic struggles of the KPA and the people. Meanwhile, in continued efforts to denigrate the South, it was asserted that the imperialists had suppressed the native culture of Koreans who lived under U.S. forces during the Four Power Trusteeship. A Yankee-style culture had been imposed on them and South Korea had thus become a living hell for the people there. No longer able to tolerate this hell and inspired by the democratic reforms taking place in the North, workers in the South were preparing to rise up against the American imperialists and Syngman Rhee's puppet government (ibid., 149). In the North, by contrast, free as it was from the yoke of foreign imperialism under the glorious *chuch'e* policy, pure Koreanness had been preserved. When the North conquered the South, as it inevitably would, it would restore authentic nationhood to its Southern compatriots.

By the late 1960s and 1970s, Marxism-Leninism was being further down-played and *chuch'e* highlighted as the dominant, if not quite yet the sole, ideol-ogy of the state. The personality cult of Kim was taken to new heights and Kim became not only a great political and military leader and loving father of the nation, but the *suryŏng* (leader or head) who played an almost godlike role as the ultimate or supreme leader and the brain guiding the body of the people in the revolutionary struggle for independence. In this conception, just as the brain controls and regulates all functions of the human body, so the *suryŏng* controlled and regulated all functions of the state. The *suryŏng* was seen to embody the interests of the masses and every thought and intention of the leader represented the will of the popular masses. The masses, meanwhile, could only make their intentions and will manifest by acting in accordance with the directions of the leader (Kim 1984).

The government advancement of the *chuch'e* ideology in the 1970s required an intense process of indoctrination that could best be carried out through the education system. In his 1977 *Theses on Socialist Education*, Kim Il Sung stated, "Political and ideological education is the most important part of social-ist education. Only through a proper political and ideological education is it possible to rear students as revolutionaries, equipped with a revolutionary world outlook and the ideological and moral qualities of a communist" (Kim 1988, 357). Throughout the 1970s, therefore, North Korean authorities intensified the process of political indoctrination through the education system, empha-sizing the Korean way and the importance of knowing only things Korean (U.S. Library of Congress: Country Studies, Online). Children were thereby to be molded by *chuch'e* to become a new kind of revolutionary human being (Kim 1990). Historiography was also extremely important for promoting the *chuch'e* ethos, and Pyongyang's historians, such as the Moscow-trained Hwang Chang-yp, began to depict the national past less from the Marxian standpoint of class and economic determinism and more from the voluntarist perspective of "the people as the subject of history," emphasizing the themes of national-ism, self-reliance, loyalty to Kim Il Sung, and boundless commitment to the nation. It is hardly surprising then that the history curriculum was signifi-cantly revised to accommodate the demands of *chuch'e*.

In accordance with Kim Il Sung's status and personality cult, two new texts appeared as part of the history curriculum. *Chosŏn Ryŏksa* was retained, but it now covered Korea's history only to about 1920, ending abruptly to clear the stage for Kim Il Sung to make his grand entrance. Born in 1912 and suppos-edly an active Communist from an extremely young age, Kim's life story became the pivot around which the unfolding of the next 70 years of DPRK history revolved. His story and that of modern Korea were thus recounted in a text entitled, *The Revolutionary Activities of the Leader Kim Il Sung*, which was later followed by the *Revolutionary History of the Leader Kim Il Sung*. Both were to be taught throughout the period of secondary education (see chapter appendix, table 7.1 for class hour allocation). While the *Chosŏn Ryŏksa* texts continued to use historical materialism to explain the general trajectory of Korean history, they continued to emphasize many *chuch'e* concerns such as the need to eschew all forms of *sadaejui*. The texts devoted to Kim's revolutionary exploits, however, were directly and explicitly focused on the *chuch'e* ideology and made little mention of Marxism, even though Kim was described as the ideal Communist. In the 1972, 1974, and 1975 editions of *The Revolutionary Activities of the Leader Kim Il Sung*, *chuch'e*-related terms, such as *chaju* (independence) were frequently mentioned and, in the 1972 text, *chuch'e* was highlighted as a means of inspiring revolution in the South and reuniting the nation (220). Kim's importance to the masses and their unswerving loyalty to the *chuch'e* idea and its source, Kim himself, were also given increasing prominence. Additionally, Confucian elements were evident; Kim was repeatedly described as a benevolent and loving father. The 1974 text, for example, has a section entitled "The Great Leader of the Revolution Kim Il Sung Shows His Deep Care through Raising up the Livelihood of the People;" in the same text there is a picture with a caption stating "The Great Leader Kim Il Sung Watches over the Young Revolutionaries Like a True Father" (113, 195). Likewise, the 1975 text states that with his wise leadership and warm care, he was able quickly to bring stability to the lives of the people even during the difficult time of the Korean War (134). His personal sacrifices were also noted as he was said to have created and implemented *chuch'e* with his own flesh and bones (190). This text also devoted much attention to Kim Il Sung's ideological activities and the development of the *chuch'e* philosophy itself. It is clear that the political and civic nationalist elements of *chuch'e* overlapped here with a more ethno-cultural nationalism, as *chuch'e* was also shown as a means of helping the working masses to understand their own politics, natural environment, geography, culture, and customs for the purpose of raising national dignity and pride (189).

One Ideology, Two Leaders

Educational developments in the 1980s and 1990s were characterized by a marked strengthening of the *chuch'e* ideology and an increasing deemphasis of Marxism-Leninism. A 1981 text of *The Revolutionary History of the Leader Kim Il Sung*, for example, provided only one mention of Marxism-Leninism, although it still referred to the efforts of "communists" involved in resistance movements against Japanese colonisers (74). Not only were *chuch'e* and its related terms and concepts ubiquitous throughout history textbooks, but the word "great" began to appear frequently before the word *chuch'e*. The above-mentioned 1981 text stated that, more than anything else, Kim's establishment of the "great *chuch'e* idea" had been the basis for victory in the revolution and national construction (14). While *chuch'e* predominated as the primary objective of history education, some other goals were also added. These included encouraging the masses to strive for the Three Revolutions (in ideology, culture, and technology) and to display loyalty not only toward their paramount leader Kim Il Sung but also toward his son Kim Jong Il, who was now being openly groomed as his father's successor. In 1985, a book was published that outlined a theory and method for "recreating the revolutionary human," the means by which to manifest the *chuch'e* idea. In the book, the theory was explained not only through Kim Il Sung's instructions but also through "things pointed out by" Kim Jong Il. Quotes from both Kims became increasingly prevalent and were a noticeable characteristic of textbooks during this time, with frequent use of such phrases as "The Great Leader Kim Il Sung teaches ..." or "The Dear Leader Kim Jong Il has pointed out ..."(Kim 1990). The elevation of Kim Jong Il was most significant in the history curriculum, which added two new texts — *The Revolutionary History of the Leader Kim Jong Il* and the *Revolutionary Activities of the Leader Kim Jong Il* — to stress the importance of the younger Kim both in the past and to the future. A third text, *The Revolutionary History of the Communist Revolutionary Leader Mother Kim Jong Suk*, Kim Il Sung's wife and mother to Kim Jong Il, was also added to the curriculum.

The 1990s were a turbulent time for the Communist world. North Korea suffered from economic crisis and it was painfully obvious that the South's vision for the national future had borne more fruit than the revolutionary and isolationist path taken by the North. Further complications resulted from the unexpected passing of Kim Il Sung in 1994. However, rather than opening to the outside world and engaging in economic or political reform, as China and other Communist countries had done, the DPRK regime remained isolationist, seeking to maintain the steadfast devotion and loyalty of the masses with continued emphasis on political and ideological education to create revolutionaries faithful both to the late Kim Il Sung and to the new leader, Kim Jong Il (Cho and Zang 2002). History was a key element of ideological education and, as shown below, the tensions of the time resulted in an increased curricular emphasis on the centrality of leadership, on Confucian virtues, and on ethno-cultural nationalism rather than on socialism as the guiding ethos of the national narrative.

History Textbooks in Contemporary North Korea

Currently, secondary school students in North Korea devote a considerable amount of time to the study of the ancient Koguryŏ and Koryŏ kingdoms. Although DPRK authorities have long displayed a bias toward those kingdoms once located in the northern half of the peninsula, such as Old Chosŏn, Koguryŏ, Koryŏ, and Palhae, this bias was intensified during the 1990s and into the twenty-first century. Vehement criticism of Korea's Silla Kingdom, located in the South, was correspondingly increased. The *Chosŏn Ryŏksa* texts published in the 1990s and 2000s for third- or fourth-year (depending on the year published) secondary history deal solely with the period leading up to Korea's unification under the Koryŏ Kingdom. In perfect *chuch'e* fashion, Koguryŏ is shown to have ended Chinese domination of Korea in 313 A.D. and thereafter to have continued to ward off foreign invasions, defeating Sui China in 618 and the Tang Dynasty in 645. However, by 668, the three kingdoms of Koguryŏ, Silla, and Paekchae were unified by military means under the Silla Dynasty. Historically, the Silla period was a prosperous time for Korea, but it receives a less than glorious mention in the North's recent history textbooks as the behavior of Silla was completely contrary to *chuch'e*. Silla relied on the help of a foreign power, Tang China, to bring down Koguryŏ and Paekchae and, moreover, later imported Tang culture and blended it with local culture. Reliance on a foreign power and the adoption of foreign culture are the hallmarks of "Silla's Traitorous Behaviour against the Nation" *Chosŏn Ryŏksa* as one section of the 2001 textbook is headed, "proving" the illegitimacy of the southern half of the peninsula, which is heir to these Silla traditions. After all, is not contemporary South Korea a puppet of the United States? As an inferior state, Silla inevitably fell to the northern state of Koryŏ, which established a unified kingdom lasting more than four centuries. North Korean history texts accordingly emphasize the independence of Koryŏ, which continued to struggle (not always successfully, although this is downplayed) with foreign aggressors near its Northern borders. (That Koguryŏ and Koryŏ were also culturally influenced by their powerful Chinese neighbor is not acknowledged.) Finding yet another genetic link between the great Koryŏ and the great DPRK, students are shown that socialist traditions are in their blood; Koryŏ, after all, showed some proto-socialist good will in establishing public welfare systems for the people, despite being an aristocratic, hierarchical society (Nahm 1994).

The focus on ancient history and the rival kingdoms of north and south may have provided a means of elevating the North and denigrating the South (and as we shall see below, vice versa in South Korea's narratives), but in the early 1990s the DPRK trumped the South in its claims to be the source of the true Korea, asserting that its archaeologists had discovered the remains of the legendary founder of the Korean nation, Tan'gun, near Pyongyang. This "discovery" was incorporated into the *Chosŏn Ryŏksa* texts after 1993, which emphasize that Tan'gun is the founding father of the Korean nation, both North and South. Tan'gun's links to Old Chosŏn and Pyongyang proved Pyongyang to be the true and eternal capital of the nation and its people. Reunification of the Korean people, who had all originated from this common ancestor, was thus to be accomplished by the North under Kim Il Sung's formula for a confederated Korean state to be called *Koryŏ Yŏnbang Konghwaguk* (Federation of the Kory Republic) (Oh and Hassig 2000). While this discovery was loudly trumpeted by the regime and many academic papers on the subject were subsequently delivered by North Korean archaeologists, little is really known about it. It is hard to escape the suspicion, therefore, that it was a last ditch effort by Kim Il Sung and his floundering regime to recoup some national pride in the face of the harsh reality of having been far surpassed by the prosperous South and to reinvigorate a sense of patriotism and loyalty to the North among its own citizens. The Tan'gun myth does, after all, tend to resurface primarily when the state is facing a political crisis or when ethnic or national identity seems threatened (Jorganson 1996).

Although ancient history has tended to be highlighted in recent years, this does not mean that modern history has been sidelined. In the twenty-first century, *The Revolutionary Activities* and *The Revolutionary Histories* (of Kim Il Sung, Kim Jong Il, and Kim Jong Suk) remain core texts in the history curriculum. *The Revolutionary Activities* texts of both Kim Il Sung and Kim Jong Il are largely filled with anecdotal stories illustrating the moral excellence of the two Kims, imbuing them with the aura of virtuous Confucian rulers. The *Revolutionary History* texts, meanwhile, are chronological accounts charting their revolutionary activities from childhood to the present. The texts on both Kims continue to stress *chuch'e* and to emphasize the two great revolutionaries' shining example of sacrifice and devotion to the nation. These and other Confucian qualities are particularly evident in the texts on Kim Jong Il. As shown in the 1999 *Revolutionary History of the Dear Leader Kim Jong Il*, the younger Kim has always been a model of loyalty and filial piety toward his father (5). The text on his mother, Kim Jong Suk, meanwhile, shows her as a great revolutionary who raised her son in the image of his father. Kim Jong Il is thereby shown to be the product of two great revolutionaries and thus a worthy successor to his father as the standard-bearer for *chuch'e* or Kim Il Sung'ism as a 1999 text has renamed it. In this same text, *chuch'e* is also referred to as "Our style" of socialism, a way to demonstrate both the uniqueness of *chuch'e* and its continued relevance despite the demise of socialism in other parts of the world.

Clearly the ethno-cultural vision of the nation has come to supersede the civic and political nationalism propounded in the early DPRK years. It is interesting to note, however, that despite the evidently long-standing nationalist orientation of DPRK historiography and history textbooks, "nationalism" is a very recent term in the North, having previously been viewed negatively as an idea that allowed the bourgeoisie to defend its rule and continue the practice of exploitation. Prior to 1991, the terms "nationalism" and "nationalist" were actually banned in the DPRK (Cho 1996). In 1986, however, Kim Jong Il referred for the first time to the notion of *chosŏn minjok cheil chŭi* meaning "the supremacy of the Korean nation" or "our-nation-first idea." A few years later, in 1991, he referred to *chinjŏnghan minjok chŭui* (genuine nationalism) and defined *minjok* (the nation or national people) as a "unit of social life and a solid group of people which has been developed and established historically"(Cho 1996). These references indicate how important nationalism became to the regime in the late 1980s and 1990s, for having lost the battle with

South Korea to create a civic identity that could unify the nation, Pyongyang began to emphasize cultural connections as a basis for reunification with South Korea. Some recent newspaper and magazine publications in North Korea have consequently included such headlines as "National Identity Basis for National Unity, Korean Nation with a Single Culture" and "The Supremacy of Our Nation Is the Banner of National Unification." Yet, in a continuing game of one-upmanship with its rival across the border, the center and focus of this cultural connection, according to DPRK historians and school history textbooks, remains in the North, rooted in the Tan'gun legend and the glorious and true Korean legacy of the Northern kingdoms of Koguyrŏ and Koryŏ. And the present regime appears to be entertaining no thoughts of rewriting this narrative of the national past in the immediate future.

South Korea

Education in the Republic of Korea

The North and South Korean regimes have been at a stand-off on either side of the demilitarised zone (DMZ) for the past half-century. Each has consistently sought to depict itself as the one true Korea and its regime as the one legitimate national authority and to disparage the other Korea as having betrayed the glorious heritage of the nation. Yet, despite their vastly different worldviews and tendencies to portray themselves as diametrically opposed to one another, North and South Korea have far more similarities than nationalists on either side have been wont to claim. This is especially true with regard to education, where on both sides a highly centralized system exists over which their respective governments have tremendous influence. Furthermore, during the past 50 years, successive South Korean governments and two North Korean dictators have attempted to use these highly centralized education systems to reclaim and define a coherent national identity, establish the legitimacy of their respective governments, defend their states, and rebuild their economies, all the while hoping eventually to unify the two sides as a single nation-state with themselves at its head.

Like the DPRK, the fledgling South Korean government was greatly influenced in its education policies during the immediate postcolonial period by its patron superpower, the United States. Between 1945 and the start of the Korean War, joint commissions and educational missions were organized and the American 6-3-3-4 structure (of primary, junior, and senior secondary schooling and undergraduate tertiary education) was adopted (Lee 2001). Other features of American-style schooling, such as decentralized administration, were also planned in the South, but the pressures of the Korean War and a series of military dictatorships with other priorities halted the progress of this trend. Once the war was over, however, the South Korean authorities, like their Northern counterparts, turned to the process of reconstruction and especially to education, which soon came to be seen as vital to the task of economic development. Indeed, a major part of the economic development plan was the massive expansion of the South's educational system to improve both the quality and the quantity of educational provision. Under Rhee's presidency, the Ministry of Education (MOE) began laying the groundwork for making economic development and modernization the central aim of education, and during the decade of the 1950s, the number of schools, teachers, and students at all levels nearly doubled (MOE 2000).

As shown in appendix table 7.1, different objectives have been highlighted with each of the seven revisions of the national curriculum between 1954 and 2001, but education has consistently been viewed as a functional means of serving the political state or the ethnic nation, much as it was in premodern and colonial Korea and continues to be in the DPRK. Accordingly, a highly centralized system of curriculum and textbook development has existed under direct control of the MOE. Only very recently, as we show in the final section, has limited textbook pluralism been legislated and education come to be seen as an instrument of personal development. As in the past, and in other states, history has been seen as a crucial component of the curriculum for transmitting ideological goals and has been inextricably tied to the development of South Korean national identity. As the following discussion demonstrates, however, using history both as a source of identification with an ethno-cultural nation and as a means to promote the civic values and legitimacy of the ruling regime, as well as to denigrate the North, has — as in the DPRK — involved something of a balancing act. Exactly what kind of identity was intended to be promoted through the history curriculum, therefore, has often been rather unclear.

History Education in the Aftermath of War

The first South Korean government under Syngman Rhee wasted little time in enlisting liberal nationalist historians to help define South Korean identity, much as the KMT had done after its retreat to Taiwan in 1949 (see chapter 3). As in the DPRK, historians working under the strict control of the national government, specifically the MOE,[5] began the process of defining a civic layer of national identity to accompany the existing ethno-nationalist consciousness that had developed during the colonial period and that had been articulated by thinkers such as Shin Ch'ae-ho. This brand of nationalism aimed chiefly to legitimize the Southern regime vis-à-vis the Communist North and involved extolling the political system and democracy of the South and lauding its economic policies and the rapidity of its industrial development. This, it was hoped, would remind ROK citizens to remain loyal and grateful to their state and its ruling regime. Education was central to this project and subjects such as moral education and ethics (*Todŏk, Kungmin Yulli, Yulli*)[6] and general society courses (*Ilban Sahoe*[7] and *Kongt'ong Sahoe*) were harnessed to convey the nationalist, democratic, and capitalist message (The Korean National Curriculum

Information Service, June 24, 2004, www.kncis.or.kr). Thus, for example, in the national curriculum guidelines for the second revision of general society, one of the seven major areas of study listed in the syllabus was *Kongsanjuŭiŭi Pip'an* (Criticism of Communism) (1963, 23). In addition, in the objectives section of the ethics curriculum guidelines (*Kungmin Yulli*), "understanding the superiority of Korean Democracy along with internalzing an anti-communist, pro-democracy outlook" was listed as a primary teaching and learning goal (The Korean National Curriculum Information Service, June 24, 2004, www. kncis.or.kr 3 ch'a *kodnŭggyoyuk kwajŏng*, 4). While these subjects were — and have largely remained — the key to promoting civic values from a practical and theoretical standpoint, history was to provide the veridical evidence that would incontrovertibly demonstrate the legitimacy of the regime and the political system. It would also demonstrate how the past had shaped the present and help students to place current issues in perspective. Most importantly, it would stimulate students' love of and pride in their nation and culture giving them an understanding of their glorious traditions and of the struggles of their forebears to defend their nation and its heritage against all comers. Korean history was thus to be the chief focus of study.

In the 1963 Korean History (*Kuksa*) textbook, under the heading *South Korea's Responsibility*, students were taught that the democracy of the present was a direct continuation of democratization movements in the past. They were therefore to recognize "the historical responsibility of South Korea to successfully fulfil the dreams of the March 1st 1919 Independence Movement by securing freedom and equality through establishing a democratic culture" (195). Anticommunism was promoted, but there was no mention of North Korea except in the conclusion of the second edition, where in one of the only places touching on the topic of unification, students were instructed that "We have to achieve unification between South and North Korea as soon as possible and relieve the economic suffering of the Korean people" (196). The national drive for economic development that education was directed to promote was also linked to the past and, in textbooks of the period the number of illustrations and sections recounting economic and developmental achievement were increased. Perhaps the most important theme in these early history textbooks, however, was the focus on the hardships Korea had suffered at the hands of foreign powers, most notably Japan, although relations with the Soviet Union, China, and the United States were also discussed. Denouncing Japanese imperialism was ideologically satisfying and aimed to increase patriotism and the desire to defend the nation. The colonial period accordingly received extensive treatment, emphasizing the brutality of the colonial regime and demonstrating its devastating impact on the livelihood of ordinary Koreans. In the 1963 textbook, under the heading, "Japanese Military Rule and Exploitation" (*Ilbonŭi mundanjŏngch'iwa kŭch'akch'wi*) students read that the Japanese eliminated private ownership of farms and bought farm products and raw materials at cheap prices and sold manufactured goods at high prices causing the Korean people to suffer. They also failed to develop Korea's manufacturing sector in favour of using the peninsula as the breadbasket for their expanding empire. Consequently, this Japanese policy failed to increase the nation's productivity while exporting wealth and benefits to Japan (186).

History and National Development

The third major curriculum revision under President Park Chung-hee in 1973 marked the implementation of "developmental education." This was not the developmental education normally associated with child development but was education oriented to economic growth. As shown above, this direction in education policy had begun under Rhee's presidency, but under Park it was consolidated and the curriculum revised accordingly. As Kim has described, "Educational content that was considered to be helpful to economic growth was greatly increased. 'Education that produces' was a slogan that could be found on the wall of any school during this period" (1987, 13). The South Korean economy did experience incredible growth during this period, and this growth is often attributed to the explicit emphasis on the use of education for economic development. Indeed, South Korea and other East Asian nations are commonly held up in the development literature as successful examples of human capital theory and the role of education therein. Yet, economic growth did not prevent criticisms being leveled at Park's government and, in 1971, both to silence his critics and to harness all the resources of the state for the economic development drive, Park declared a state of national emergency, suspended the constitution, and dissolved the legislature. Ten months later, he instituted the *Yushin* reforms, which allowed the president to be elected to an unlimited number of 6-year terms by the newly formed Conference for Unification (NCU), thereby subverting democratic political processes and protecting his authoritarian regime. In addition to using force and promoting economic development to legitimize his authoritarian policies, Park also sought to create an ideological foundation for military rule and accordingly promoted a Koreanized democracy. As Wang (1997) described

> [According to Park, the] western democracy which the previous regime had briefly adopted was not fitted to Korean politics and culture. Korea [needed to] find its own style of democracy.[8] Later the junta proclaimed the establishment of a 'liberal democratic society' as an ongoing political project. Again in 1963 the regime offered another halting definition for implementation, saying, 'a democratic political order, based on individual self-discipline and responsibility, should be established.'[9] ... *Koreanised* democracy, allows the regime to practice authoritarian politics ... Introduced to salve people's demand for democracy, '*Koreanised* democracy' was authoritarianism with only the veneer of democracy. The rhetoric of the regime for a '*Koreanised* democracy' persuaded the

> Korean people to accept democracy as a norm and a universal principle to be realized in their country. (152–153, 174)

Undemocratic though Koreanised democracy may have been, it was nevertheless promoted heavily through the school curriculum until the late 1980s. Ethics and common society were, of course, heavily used to teach the new ideology, but history was also used to present Koreanised democracy as a logical extension of the democratic movements of the past. In the third to fifth textbook revisions, under headings such as "Democracy's Growth/Progress" (*Minjujŭi Sŏngjang/paljŏn*), students found historical events that demonstrated a heritage of democratic achievement. Events such as the revolution protesting against the illegal elections of 1960 that led to the end of Syngman Rhee's first republic and the events surrounding the brief second republic were detailed. In the third revision (and only in the third revision), students were also shown the Public Pledge of the Revolution and its six major points.

As in the past, anticommunism remained an important element of the history curriculum, although this began to wane by the time of the fifth curriculum revision. In the third revision, however, the first article of the Public Pledge, which stated "We will repair and strengthen anticommunism by having anticommunism as the most important national consciousness," was emphasized (MOE 1980, 297). The other Korea, however, barely featured in the narrative, and it was not until the fifth curriculum revision that any attention was devoted to its history. Until then, the North was only discussed within the context of the events leading up to the Korean War and the war itself. A passage from the fourth edition exemplifies the North's treatment. Under the heading of "North Korea's Communization" (*Puk'anŭi Kongsanhwa*), students read that "North Korea's communists established the U.S.S.R's puppet government led by Kim Il Sung. North Korean communists have established one of the strongest dictatorships in the world" (163). It appears that South Korea purposefully omitted from textbooks references to events in the North as a passive component of the larger anticommunist campaign. By not including information about the North, the South attempted to reduce its importance as a subject in the minds of high school students and effectively deny its existence, much in the same way as the KMT in Taiwan (a close ally of South Korea during this period) excluded the People's Rebulic of China from their narrative of Chinese history (see chapters 3 and 4). Yet, at the same time as downplaying the existence of the DPRK, the textbooks encouraged students to look forward to and strive for national reunification. In both the third and fourth editions students were taught of the July 4, 1972, joint declaration, the aims of which were frustrated because, as the textbook explained, North Korea would not abandon the possibility of using force to achieve reunification. This served to reinforce the notion of the North and Communism as barbarous and cruel and to confirm the self-image of the South as benevolent and peace loving.

In the concluding paragraph, the true (South Korean) way to unification was shown. Students were to "embrace a scientific spirit in the fields of economics, society, and culture," and this would "eventually strengthen the national spirit and realize our dream of unification" (300).

While the ROK's enemy on the other side of the DMZ received scant coverage, Japanese colonialism and economic imperialism remained heavily emphasized. In the third edition, much more concrete evidence was given to students concerning the vast monopolies Japan had established during the occupation. Under the heading "Colonized Economy" (*Shingminji Kyŏngje*), students were taught that 40 percent of farms had been taken from their private Korean owners and resold to Japanese immigrants at cheap prices. Also, students learned that other sectors of the economy such as communications, transportation, finance, lumber, fishing, and mining industries had also been monopolized and Koreans excluded. In the concluding paragraphs of this section, the effects of Japanese economic policy were summarized as the root cause for the failure of national industry to develop (267). The final paragraph closes by explaining that over 50 percent of Korean farmers survived by eating the roots of plants and bark from trees. This final paragraph appeared again in the fourth edition but was later revised to state simply that many Korean farmers suffered from starvation.

In the fourth edition, the new subtitle "Japan's Economic Invasion" (*Ilboniŭ kyŏngjejŏk ch'imt'u*) appeared as an expansion of the discussion of the 1894 Tonghak rebellion, which went on to explain that even before the Japanese protectorate was in place, Japanese merchants had set up large trading ventures in the country, pushing out Korean business interests. The "Colonized Economy" section was also renamed "The Nation's Ordeal during the Invasion of Japanese Imperialism" (*Ilje ch'imnyak' ai minjoksunan*) and was expanded to include two new subheadings: "Exploitation of Land" and "Exploitation of Industry" (*T'ojiŭi sut'al, sanŏbŭi ch'imt'al*). The fifth edition added to this list the subheading "Exploitation of Food" (*Shingnyang-i ch'imt'al*). Under these headings, further data regarding the fishing, mining, and lumber industries were given, providing still more evidence of Korea's economic subjugation under Japanese colonization. Students also learned that the Japanese military had used Korean land as bases for the expansion of the empire onto the continent (for example, for the occupation of Manchuria and the invasion of China in the 1930s).

Democratization and Educational Reform

In 1988, with the first peaceful transfer of power from Chun Doo-hwan to Roh Tae-woo,[10] a gradual process of democratization began in South Korea. Along with these changes, attempts were made at a gradual decentralization of the administration, and by 1990 this had come to encompass education. The MOE "streamlined its organization with the clarification of its role. New laws for the promotion of local autonomy were legislated in March 1991, and district offices of education were inaugurated at the provincial level, setting a new benchmark in the democratisation and localisation of education" (MOE 2000, 37). Under Presidents Kim Young-sam and Kim Dae Jung, who were both opponents of the earlier authoritarian regimes, the pace of democratization accelerated, and curricular content was reformed to reflect this. The sixth and seventh curriculum revisions completed under their presidencies accordingly demonstrate a marked departure from earlier curricula, attempting to define democracy not simply as a set of social norms for good citizens but to assign responsibility for defending liberal democratic rights and freedoms to the government. Their regimes have deemphasized the role of education in economic development and made democracy the primary focus. Most recently, there have also been moves toward a more child-centered and less text- and examination-centered education. As in the rest of East Asia, such goals have not been easily achieved, and curriculum developers and educators are still struggling to devise an education system that they deem useful both to the nation and the individual.

Even with democratization and the decentralization of educational institutions, however, it was not until the adoption and implementation of the seventh and most recent curriculum guidelines in 2000 that textbook publication was opened to tender by private companies. Under the Seventh National Curriculum, there are three types of textbooks:

> Textbooks of the first type are ones whose copyrights are held by the MOE. The textbooks that are published by private publishers and authorized by the MOE pertain to the second type. Textbooks of the third type are recognized by the MOE or superintendents as relevant and usable. For the textbooks of the second and third types, individual schools may select textbooks to best fit the characteristics and the needs of the students. (MOE 2000, 57)

The history curriculum includes all three types; however, according to Sung Kyung-hee of the Korea Institute of Curriculum and Evaluation "much work is left to be done in creating quality Type II and Type III texts" (2002). Many of the Type II and III history textbooks are still under development at the time of writing (2004) and in the majority of schools, therefore, the standard MOE textbooks have remained the bulwark of teaching and learning.

History and Democracy

The history curriculum in the fifth revision began to include more data pertaining to the democratization process, but it was the sixth revision of the history text, developed under President Kim Young-sam, that most clearly illustrated this change. History was to demonstrate the tradition of democratic thought in Korea, and students were to learn how democratic citizenship is inextricably bound to the maintenance of democratic government. The sixth and seventh textbook editions accordingly paid particular attention to the democratization process of the twentieth century, from the anticolonial March 1st Movement to the antiauthoritarian protests of the 1980s. The sixth edition was the first high school history text to include pictures of individuals at the polls. It is significant also that the individuals shown in photographs in the textbook were females, voting in the general election of 1948. The sixth and seventh editions also explicitly criticized the former military regime and showed explicit images of the oppression by the junta of its own citizens, such as incidents of civil unrest in 1960 and 1964. By presenting internal oppression by a past government as unjust, history textbooks implicitly held the current regime accountable for protecting basic liberal democratic freedoms.

In addition to emphasizing democracy and repudiating authoritarianism, the sixth and especially the seventh editions also reflected the gradual rapprochement with Japan and the DPRK. Although anticolonialism remained an important feature of the textbooks, and the sixth revision added further details on the militarization of Korea as a forward base for Japan's expansion into the continent, the seventh revision made dramatic alterations, summarizing this hitherto expansive anti-Japanese discourse in two pages, down from six in the sixth edition. North Korea, by contrast, received far more extensive coverage than heretofore. This had begun in the fifth edition with the addition of a new section (*Puk'anŭi pyŏnch'ŏn/pyŏnhwa*) that briefly discussed changes in the North decade by decade. In the opening sentence of the North Korean section in the fifth edition, Kim Il Sung was held solely accountable for removing all opposition to his rule by imprisoning or killing other Communists who criticized him. In the sixth edition, Kim was no longer held personally responsible and the purges were said to have been carried out by his supporters. By the seventh edition, however, mention of the purges was completely deleted and the discussion on the rise of Kim Il Sung focused on the growth of the North Korean economy during the 1960s. Students went on to learn of the growing isolation of North Korea stemming from the breakup of the USSR and the opening of China to the capitalist world. It further explained how this isolation has been linked to the economic decline of North Korea since 1980. Why current information regarding the North did not appear in textbooks until the late 1980s seems fairly self-explanatory since it was not until then that a gradual thaw between the two sides began, but what purpose the removal of important references to Kim Il Sung's consolidation of power serves is unclear. In line with the tentative and wary détente between North and South, references to anticommunism have begun to disappear from history texts and the seventh edition, even contains a photograph of Kim Dae Jung and Kim Jong Il taken at the North/South Normalization Summit.

With a softening of the anticommunist/anti-DPRK stance, the history curriculum has also increasingly highlighted the theme of reunification. As with the introduction of the history of the DPRK, reunification was first seriously addressed in the history textbooks in the fifth edition under the section on "Efforts toward Unification" (*T'ong-irŭrwihan noryŏk*). In this section, which has been retained in the sixth and seventh revisions, art and cultural exchanges are noted and diplomatic efforts in the area of reuniting divided families are highlighted, a metaphor perhaps for the future hopes of reuniting the great national family. In one passage of the sixth edition, students also read that the South gained national confidence from holding the Olympic Games in 1988 and that this confidence has encouraged positive policies toward unification. In the seventh and latest revision the June 15, 2000, joint declaration has also been highlighted, teaching students that problems relating to the roadmap for unification (1) must be solved by the Koreans themselves; (2) require that the two countries reach a common understanding regarding the choice between "one country two systems" (*Yŏnbangje*) and "one country one system" (*Yŏnhapche*) models; (3) require continued efforts to reunite families and a resolution of issues regarding long-term political prisoners; and (4) the establishment of balanced economic growth and the encouragement of exchanges in the social, cultural, athletic, health, and environmental protection arenas. The fact that students are increasingly not only being told of diplomatic contacts between the North and South but also being presented with the basic plan for unification illustrates the growing confidence of South Korea. Relations with the North in the sixth and seventh editions of the history texts have thus been presented as constantly improving, increasing the likelihood of eventual reunification.

Conclusion

In the introduction to this chapter, it was asked whether the history curriculum has brought the two Koreas closer together through narrating the shared past of a national people, joined in ethnicity and cultural heritage, or whether it has driven them further apart through the construction of distinct identities rooted in the political systems and ideologies of their respective states. As this chapter has demonstrated, the promotion of both ethno-cultural and civic configurations of national identity has been a core feature of history curricula and textbooks in both the ROK and DPRK, as each side has constructed and harnessed national narratives to prove its own legitimacy and superiority to the other. In the North, the post–Cold War demise of Communism around the world and its own economic crises have seriously undermined its political ideology and any civic construction of identity it might once have attempted has been superseded by an increasing emphasis on ethnic identity and cultural traditions as the basis for continued KWP rule and the DPRK's claims to superiority over the South. In the South, by contrast, economic strength and political pluralism have given ROK citizens increasing confidence in their civic nationalism and allowed them to extend some sympathy and magnanimity toward their impoverished brethren across the DMZ and to take tentative steps toward reunification.

While we would argue that ethno-cultural identities reproduced and sustained through the education system in general and the history curriculum in particular have kept the two Koreas linked across the minefield over the past 50 years, they have also provided a source of rivalry, as each side claims to be more purely or truly Korean than the other. It would also seem that it is South Korea's confident political identity and economic superiority over the North that have finally allowed it to break the ice in relations with the North, even if the desire to do so has been underpinned by a sense of shared ethnic and cultural identity. However, although tentative dialogue has begun, the North remains unpredictable and the South wary. Furthermore, the long separation between the two, exacerbated by the dictatorial regimes under which both societies have suffered, has led to many significant differences and even language barriers. Add to this mix North Korea's ongoing nuclear program and South Korea's recent confession that it has enriched uranium far beyond levels needed for atomic energy production, and it appears that fears of an arms race on the peninsula are not unwarranted. Thus, while reunification may eventually come about, there are still too many tensions between the two for such an event to be imminent.

The Koreas' relations with one another clearly remain the fundamental concern in each side's construction of national identity, but the other Korea is not, of course, either Korea's only "Other." The scope of this paper has not permitted an analysis of world history teaching in either Korea but, as we have seen through our analysis of Korean history, relations with other states have also played an important role in identity formation. Most notable has been the historical relationship with Japan and the anticolonial, anti-imperialist movement engendered by the Japanese occupation from 1910 until 1945, which both sides have appropriated as part of their national and political identity. Here, a powerful ethno-nationalism rooted in anti-Japanese sentiment is common to both sides, yet this discourse is also divisive, for despite the shared historical struggle for independence, each side claims to have resisted colonialism more determinedly than the other. It would appear, therefore, that just as nationalism can be used both as a means to overcome oppression (as in resistance to colonialism) and as an instrument of social and ideological repression (Em 1999), it may have as much power to divide as it does to unite.

Nationalism and national identity are multifaceted, multilayered, and fluid, influenced by countless environmental factors but rooted almost invariably in historical experience and historical narratives. Shared ethnicity, as shown in previous chapters, does not necessarily entail shared identity, although it may constitute a potential basis for it. In Taiwan and Hong Kong, for example, many ethnic Chinese have formulated conceptions of their nationness that, to a greater or lesser extent, set them apart from mainlanders. Reunification, particularly for many Taiwanese, has come to be regarded as a far from desirable objective. In the politically divided, ethnically united context of North and South Korea, however, the dream of reunification remains alive and well. However, the realization of this dream will require not only patience and trust but also the formulation of a national identity in which both sides can participate. Such an identity must be rooted in historical narratives that acknowledge both sides as true Koreans and that allot both North and South an equal stake in the past, present, and future.

Endnotes

1. See Wells, K. M. (1990).
2. Ethnic Koreans raised in the Soviet Union were a valuable tool for the authorities in Moscow as they were able to act in a variety of capacities in North Korea during the occupation. Many of them were bilingual and helped the Soviet Union carry out its policies and exert its influence on the newly developing communist nation with great facility. For more information on the Soviet Koreans and their contribution to the formation of the DPRK see Lankov, (2000).
3. For a thorough treatment of *chuch'e* in English, see Park (2002).
4. Some of the texts examined here were published in Tokyo by pro-DPRK Koreans living in Japan known as Chongsunryun. It is assumed that the content of these texts is the same as those published in Pyongyang.
5. In 2001, the Ministry of Education was renamed the Ministry of Education & Human Resource Development.
6. *Todŏk* is the title used under the first curriculum guidelines; *Kungmin Yulli* is the title used during the second through fifth editions of the national curriculum and is translated as national ethics. In the latest two revisions, the *Kungkmin* (or national) part is dropped.
7. *Ilban Sahoe* is the title used for the under the first curriculum guidelines. In subsequent revisions it became *Kongt'ong Sahoe*, meaning "common society."
8. See "Kwangbokchŏl che 16 chunyŏn" [The 1961 Liberation Day Speech], in Park Chung-hee tae t'ong-ryng, che 1chip, ch'oego hoe-i p'yn, 28.
9. "Inaugural Address on December 17, 1963," *in Major Speeches by Koreans*, 287–88.
10. There are many factors that contributed to the decentralization of South Korea in the 1980s: resistance to dictatorship through the establishment of well-organized and disciplined democratic movements within the country, economic stabilization and modernization, Cold War tensions beginning to relax, and successful acceptance by the world community through hosting the Olympics in 1988.

References

A Handbook on North Korea. 1998. Seoul: Naewoe Press.
Armstrong, C. 2003. The North Korean Revolution 1945–1950. Ithaca, NY: Cornell University Press.
Baker, M. 1998. "Teaching of 'kinder, gentler' N. Korea Stirs Wrath." The Christian Science Monitor 90:7.
Brudnoy, D. 1970. "Japan's Experiment in Korea." Monumenta Nipponica 25:155–195.
Buzo, A. 1999. The Guerilla Dynasty: Politics and Leadership in North Korea. Sydney: Allen & Unwin.
———. 2002. The Making of Modern Korea. London: Routledge.
Ch'oe, Y.H. 1981. "Reinterpreting Traditional History in North Korea." The Journal of Asian Studies 40:503–523.
Cho, M.C. and Zang, H.S. 2002. "North Korea's Educational Policy and System, and External Cooperation with International Organisations." Journal of Asia Pacific Affairs 3, 2:73–111.
Cho, Y.H. 1996. "Unification in the 1990's: Historiographical Prospects." Korea Observer 27, 1:85–114.
Em, H. 1993. "Overcoming Korea's Division: Narrative Strategies in Recent South Korean Historiography." Positions 1:450–485.
———. 1999. "Nationalism, Post-Nationalism, and Shin Ch'ae-Ho." Korea Journal 39, 2:283–317.
Freire, P. 1970. Pedagogy of the Oppressed. New York: Herder and Herder.
Hagusŏbang Publishing. 1957. Chosŏn Ryŏksa 3 (Korean History). Tokyo.
———. 1964. Chosŏn Ryŏksa 2-3 (Korean History). Tokyo.
———. 1972. Kim Il Sung Wonsu Hyŏngmyŏng Hwaldong 3 (The Revolutionary Activities of the Leader Kim Il Sung). Tokyo.
———. 1974. Kim Il Sung Wonsu Hyŏngmyŏng Hwaldong 3 (The Revolutionary Activities of the Leader Kim Il Sung). Tokyo.
———. 1975. Kim Il Sung Wonsu Hyŏngmyŏng Hwaldong 2 (The Revolutionary Activities of the Leader Kim Il Sung). Tokyo.
———. 1981. Kim Il Sung Wonsu Hyŏngmyŏng Ryŏksa 2 (The Revolutionary History of the Leader Kim Il Sung). Tokyo.
Ilyon. 1283. Samguk yusa.
Jeon, J. 2002. "Nambuk'an Minjokchuŭi Pigyo Yngu:Yksai Iyong-l Chungshimro (Comparative Research on South and North Korean Nationalism: With a Focus on History)." Han-gukkwa Kukche jngch'i [Korea and World Politics] 18, 1:135–166.
Jorganson, J. 1996. "Tan'gun and the Legitimisation of a Threatened Dynasty: North Korea's Rediscovery of Tan'gun." Korea Observer 27, 2:273–306.
Kim, C. H. 1984. The Immortal Chuch'e Idea. Pyongyang: Foreign Languages Publishing House.
Kim, I. S. 1988. "Theses on Socialist Education," in Kim Il Sung Works, v. 32, Jan.–Dec., 1977. Pyongyang: Foreign Language Publishing House.
Kim, J. I. 1985. On the Chuch'e Idea of Our Party. Pyongyang: Foreign Languages Publishing House.
Kim, P. S. and Yi, C. H. 1145. Samguk sagi (Historical Record of the Three Kingdoms).
Kim, S. I. 1987. "Korean Education Past and Present." Korea Journal 27, 4:4–20.
Kim, T. K. 1990. "Puk'an Kyoyuk'agŭi Sŏngnip Kŭn-gŏwa Hakkyo Kyoyugi Chn-gae kwajng (The Foundation for the Establishment of Education in North Korea and Developments in School Education)," in H. C., Kim ed., Puk'ani Kyoyuk (North Korean Education). Seoul: Ryumunhwasa.
Kwon, Y. 2000. "Korean Historiography in the 20th Century: A Configuration of Paradigms." Korea Journal 40, 1:33.
Kyoyuktosŏ Publishing (1998). Chosŏn Ryŏksa 1 [Korean History]. Pyongyang.
———. 1998. Chosŏn Ryŏksa 2 (Korean History). Pyongyang.
———. 1998. Widaehan Suryng Kim Il Sung Taewonsunim HyŎngmyŎng RyŎksa 5 (The Revolutionary History of the Great Leader Comrade Kim Il Sung). Pyongyang.
———. 1999. Chosŏn Ryŏksa 3 (Korean History). Pyongyang.
———. 1999. Widaehan Suryŏng Kim Il Sung Taewonsunim Hyŏngmyŏng Ryŏksa 5 (The Revolutionary History of the Great Leader Comrade Kim Il Sung). Pyongyang.
———. 1999. Widaehan Suryŏng Kim Il Sung Taewonsunim Hyŏngmyŏng Ryŏksa 6 (The Revolutionary History of the Great Leader Comrade Kim Il Sung). Pyongyang.
———. 1999. Widaehan Ryŏngdoja Kim Jong Il Wonsunim Hyŏngmyŏng Ryŏksa 4 (The Revolutionary History of the Dear Leader Comrade Kim Jong Il). Pyongyang.
———. 1999. Widaehan Ryŏngdoja Kim Jong Il Wonsunim Hyŏngmyŏng Ryŏksa 5 (The Revolutionary History of the Dear Leader Comrade Kim Jong Il). Pyongyang.

———. 1999. *Widaehan Ryŏngdoja Kim Jong Il Wonsunim Hyŏngmyŏng Ryŏksa 6 (The Revolutionary History of the Dear Leader Comrade Kim Jong Il)*. Pyongyang.

———. 1999. *Widaehan Kongsanjui Hyŏngmyŏngt'usa Kim Jong Suk mni Hyŏngmyŏng Ryŏksa 4 (The Revolutionary History of the Communist Revolution Leader Mother Kim Jong Suk)*. Pyongyang.

———. 2000. *Chosŏn Ryŏksa 4 (Korean History)*. Pyongyang.

———. 2001. *Chosŏn Ryŏksa 3 (Korean History)*. Pyongyang.

Lee, G.S. 2001. *A Comparative Understanding of American Educational Missions to Korea and Japan after World War II*. Paper presented at the 11th World Congress of Comparative Education, Choonbuk, South Korea, July 2–6.

Lee, Tae-Y., 1999. "Problems in the Writing of Korean History Textbooks." *Korea Journal* 38, 1:323.

Louis, H. 2001. "World War II Dispute Hits Japanese Music in Korea." *Billboard Magazine* 113:41.

Ministry of Education (MOE). 1963. *Kuksa (National History)*. Seoul: Korean Textbook Publishing Co.

———. 1980. *Kuksa (National History)*. Seoul: Korean Textbook Publishing Co.

———. 1986. *Kuksa (National History)*. Seoul: Korean Textbook Publishing Co.

———. 1991. *Kuksa (National History)*. Seoul: Korean Textbook Publishing Co.

———. 1996. *Kuksa (National History)*. Seoul: Korean Textbook Publishing Co.

———. 2000. *Education in Korea 1999–2000*. Seoul: South Korea.

———. 2004. *Kuksa (National History)*. Seoul: Korean Textbook Publishing Co.

Ministry of Unification. 2004. Puk'an Kaeyo (North Korea Briefing). Seoul, Republic of Korea.

Nahm, A.C. 1994. *A Panorama of 5000 Years: Korean History*. Elizabeth, NJ: Hollym.

Oh, K. and Hassig, R. C. 2000. *North Korea through the Looking Glass*. Washington D.C.: Brookings Institution Press.

Park, C.S., 1999. "Should Korean Historians Abandon Nationalism?" *Korea Journal* 39, 2:318.

Petrov, L.A. 2002. *North Korean Historians at the Helm of Power*. Paper presented at the 1st World Congress of Korean Studies in Seoul, Republic of Korea: Academy of Korean Studies.

———. 2003. Restoring the Glorious Past: Chuch'e in Korean Historiography. Paper presented at the Third Biennial KSAA Conference "Korea: Language, Knowledge and Society." The Australian National University, Canberra. Online at http://north-korea.narod.ru/glorious_past.htm.

Sung, K.-H. 2002. A New School Curriculum for a New Age — A Korean Perspective. Paper presented at the Invitational Curriculum Policy Seminary School Based Curriculum Policy Renewal for the Knowledge Society: Developing Capacity for New Times in Hong Kong, November 14–16.

Wang, 1997. Persistence of Authoritarian Regimes in South Korea, 1948–1987. Unpublished dissertation, Claremont Graduate University, Claremont.

Nazoki, Y. and Inokuchi, H. 2000. "Japanese Education, Nationalism," in L. Hein and M. Selden, eds., *Censoring History: Citizenship and Memory in Japan, Germany, and the United States*. Armonk, NY: M. E. Sharpe.

APPENDIX

Appendix Table 7.1 Summary of Chief Objectives of South Korean Curriculum Guideline Revisions

Year	President	Focus
1954	Syngman Rhee	Nationalism, anticommunism, and anti-Japanese Imperialist legacy
1963	Syngman Rhee	Nationalism, anticommunism, and anti-Japanese Imperialist legacy
1973	Park Chung-hee	Nationalism and developmental education
1981	Chun Doo-hwan	Nationalism and autonomous development
1987	Chun Doo-hwan	Nationalism, autonomous development, and reduction of anti-Japanese sentiment
1997	Kim Young-sam	Nationalism and democratization
2001	Kim Dae Jung	Democratic international citizenship and decentralization

Appendix Table 7.2 Class Hours for Secondary History in North Korea, by Subject, Grade, and Hours Studied per Week

Text	Hours Studied Per Week For The Six Years of Secondary Schooling					
	1	2	3	4	5	6
The Revolutionary Activities of the Great Leader Kim Il Sung	1	1	1			
The Revolutionary History of the Great Leader Comrade Kim Il Sung				2	2	2
The Revolutionary Activities of the Dear Leader General Kim Jong Il	1	1	1			
The Revolutionary History of the Dear Leader Comrade Kim Jong Il				2	2	2
The Revolutionary History of the Communist Revolution Leader Mother Kim Jong Suk				1		
Chosn Ryksa/World History	1	1	2	2	2	2

Source: Puk'an Kaeyo (North Korea Briefing). Seoul, Republic of Korea, Ministry of Unification, 2004.

Appendix Table 7.3 A Summary of Nationalist Themes in the DPRK History Curriculum by Period and by Type of Nationalism They Are Designed to Promote

Type of Nationalism	Ethno-Cultural	Civic
1950s	Moral integrity and superiority of Communists as opposed to capitalists	Marxism-Leninism, historical materialism view
1960s	The heroic struggle of the people; teachings and instructions of Kim Il Sung	Creative applications of Marxism-Leninism
1970s	Kim Il Sung as benevolent "Father," Kim's sacrifices	*chuch'e, chaju* (independence or self-sufficiency) in politics, economics, and defense; national unification through *chuch'e*
1980s	Filial piety and devotion of Kim Jong Il toward his father, Kim Il Sung	Great *chuch'e* idea
1990s	Increased emphasis on kingdom of Koguryŏ and criticism of kingdom of Silla, Tan-gun as father of the Korean nation, moral example of Kim Il Sung and Kim Jong Il	Great *chuch'e* idea/Kim Il Sungism "Our style of socialism"

8

The Stability of Postwar Japanese History Education amid Global Changes

JULIAN DIERKES

According to John Meyer and his collaborators, the substantive orientation of university history education has undergone significant change in the course of the twentieth century (Frank et al. 2000). They argue that this change has its roots in global conceptualizations of the nation-state that have increasingly focused on arguments for the modern nation-state as an organizational form. Meyer and his collaborators locate the transmission of this trend in international organizations that bring professionals and experts into contact with each other and thus offer opportunities for the diffusion of global standards. Given Japan's ties to the world polity through various international bodies and Japanese activism in and enthusiasm for United Nations activities, particularly since the 1970s, Meyer's "world polity" thesis would suggest that developments in Japanese history education would be likely to follow global developments closely. As I show in this chapter, however, the content of junior high school history education in Japan has in fact remained remarkably stable over the postwar period. I turn to prominent theories of Japanese policymaking in search of an explanation for this departure from global trends.[1]

Leonard Schoppa (1991) described educational policymaking in Japan during the 1980s as a stalemate between various policymaking actors in politics: the national bureaucracy, academia, and the teaching profession. Schoppa ultimately blamed these countervailing forces for the lack of success in the implementation of educational policy reforms (ibid.). Below I consider a specific element of educational policy, the substantive content of junior high school history education, to examine whether Schoppa's conclusions hold for such specific elements of the school curriculum as well as they do for education policy in general. Although the content of history education has been very stable over the postwar period, it is not simply a stalemate between forces that has been responsible for this situation, but rather the dominance of one actor, the bureaucracy of the Ministry of Education Monbusho, or MOE (now Monbukagakusho or MOES) over the educational policymaking regime. Although the Ministry had initially been forced to share some control over the content of the school curriculum in the early period of the U.S. occupation, Monbusho bureaucrats quickly succeeded in recentralizing such control through the drafting of curricula and the textbook approval mechanism. They thus eliminated the formal possibility of participation by other actors and any immediate potential for a policymaking stalemate.

Given that immobilism seems to prevail despite the absence of any such stalemate, I call into doubt the assertion that such a stalemate is responsible for the immobilism in Japanese educational policy. Instead, I point to institutional factors that have favored the reproduction of the status quo in history education since the late 1950s. Based on my account of the lack of change in the content of secondary school history education in Japan, I develop an institutional perspective that focuses on the construction of the policymaking regime in the early postwar years and the subsequent perpetuation of this regime. Bureaucrats of the Ministry were endowed with control over educational content following a simmering battle with occupation authorities in the immediate postwar years. They laid claim to their authority on the basis of their supposedly neutral role in the administration of government policy. They replicated this claim to neutrality through an uncritically empiricist conception of historiography that was then persistently adhered to throughout the postwar period. The dominance of a narrow focus on domestic politics on the part of the MOE's bureaucrats, along with their claim to neutral objectivity and their opposition to attempts to reform the status quo in ways that might have undermined their authority, help to account for the minimal impact of global trends in history education on Japanese policymaking during the postwar period.

Global Trends in History Education

The world polity approach involves the claim that the worldwide content of education is determined to a large degree by prevalent models of nationhood within a global polity (Meyer, Kamens, and Benavot 1992; Meyer et al. 1997). As the nation-state has become the exclusive form of collective organization recognized by the international community, states around the world have tended to adhere closely to evolving criteria of nationhood. The status of the nation has changed, it is claimed, from a natural form of social organization to one that is grounded in rational arguments for its existence. Nation-states have "come to be organized around universally available rational-legal principles, rather than a distinctive high cultural heritage" (Frank et al. 2000, 33). In the postwar era in particular, standardized definitions of nationhood have expanded to encompass areas that were previously considered subject to cultural variation. In the process of this development of definitions of nationhood, structural differences between nation-states have eroded and today much of the basic structure of nation-states is characterized by substantive and structural isomorphism. These inter-state similarities extend from state symbols to educational policies such as mass compulsory primary education (Meyer, Kamens, and Benavot 1992; Meyer, Ramirez, and Soysal 1992).

According to world polity theorists, nation-states today have thus become largely disembedded from their culturally specific roots as they have increasingly sought to justify their legitimacy in terms of universal standards of rationality. Historical narratives founded upon theories of ethnic, racial, or cultural homogeneity have thus tended to be superseded in official discourse by narratives emphasizing causal interrelations between aspects of social systems and historical developments, thereby presenting an increasingly rationalized view of the nation. "With the rise of more open and rationalized forms of society ... legitimacy came to reside in functional operations of the empirical present ... Focus shifted from the glorious past to the operational present" (Frank et al. 2000, 34). On the basis of this shift, Frank and colleagues hypothesize that history curricula have tended to focus increasingly on subnational groups and that attention to "more social scientific and contemporary depictions of 'society'" (38) (as opposed to more ethno-culturally determinist and primordialist depictions) has increased in the course of the twentieth century. They have investigated these hypotheses by analyzing university history curricula from 1895 to 1994. They coded the course titles of a large, cross-national sample and investigated the proportion of the curriculum devoted to particular subjects across cases and over time. Using this methodology, they found strong support for an increase in attention to subnational groups (an elevenfold rise of the proportion of the curriculum) and also some support for the rise of more social-scientific depictions of history. Among various other measures, Frank and colleagues coded the share of the university curriculum that was devoted to contemporary history as one indication of an increasingly rationalized historiography. The share of contemporary history rose in the global sample from roughly a quarter (29 percent) to over a third (38 percent) of the curricula for the periods 1949 to 1969 and 1970 to 1994. For Japan in particular, this share rose from 17 percent to 27 percent in university curricula.[2] While Japan trailed the global trend somewhat, the direction and magnitude of change in the two postwar periods included in the data used by Frank and colleagues for Japan does appear to correspond to the worldwide shift they observe.

Clearly, higher education curricula are subject to different influences from those affecting secondary education. For one, the decentralized nature of curriculum writing at the university level implies that piecemeal changes might occur more readily, while the unified nature of most lower school curricula means that changes might be expected to come in spurts. However, following Frank and colleagues' argument that the changes they observe are rooted in shifts in global conceptualizations of nationhood, it seems reasonable to expect shifts in a similar direction at various levels of education over an extended period of time.

Given its emphasis on broad worldwide trends and developments, the world polity approach has been less concerned with explaining some of the variation that occurs within the general, internationally parallel trend. This lack of attention has resulted partly from a strategic choice (in other words, the desire to make a stronger case for structural and cultural isomorphism), and partly from methodology. Most of the research projects taking the world polity approach have involved statistical analyses of data (usually officially generated data relating to curriculum content, such as official syllabi or curricular guidelines) from a large number of countries around the world. Though this has yielded findings that appear to substantiate global developments, it makes a deeper understanding of reform processes in individual countries difficult and also precludes the exploration of the meaning of some of the specific changes observed. This chapter therefore sets out to examine portrayals of the Japanese nation in postwar history curricula and textbooks and to explain how such portrayals have reflected or negated the sorts of global trends identified by Frank et al. (2000).

Portrayals of the Nation in Postwar Japanese History Education Materials

To trace changes in educational policy regarding the content of Japanese junior high school history education, a sample of thirty-three textbooks approved for use in junior high schools between 1950 and 2000 was analyzed (see the chapter appendix for a list of the textbooks). The examination focused on portrayals of the nation in accounts of six historical episodes (the origins of human life in Japan, the Kaga Uprising [*Ikko Ikki*], the Meiji Restoration, Taisho Democracy, the Asia Pacific War, and the Postwar Reconstruction). In analyzing coverage of these six episodes, I have shown elsewhere that the narratives changed very little over time (Dierkes 2003). No entirely new areas for discussion were introduced nor were any eliminated, and the episodes included appeared very much in the same light throughout the postwar era. As Nozaki's chapter in this volume demonstrates, most debate over history curricula and textbooks in postwar Japan has focused on relatively minor changes to existing narratives and on terminological disputes such as that over whether the term "aggression" or "advance" should be used when describing the Japanese invasion of China. These may be important issues in themselves, but such disputes as these have generally taken place within a context of broad acceptance of the established narrative.

The most obvious substantive characteristic of Japanese textbook portrayals of the nation has been a strict focus on chronological sequences of events. Looking at the four modern episodes among the six selected for analysis (from the Meiji Restoration through the Postwar Reconstruction), this focus has tended to appear even narrower, in that it is the chronological sequences of *political* events that have formed the dominant theme of the narrative, at the expense of socioeconomic or cultural developments. The narrative concentrated on decisions by rulers and their bureaucratic implementation, with these decisions constituting the dynamic of the nation's historical development. Moreover, the motives underlying these decisions on the part of rulers or their ministers are generally subjected to little or no critical discussion in the texts, seldom, for example, being explained in relation to the broader contemporary intellectual or social context. Textbook narratives of the development of the nation were thus not obviously teleological, in that no continuous idea of the nation or thinking about the nation was discussed, but they certainly presented an unproblematized version of national history that saw the nation as having been the natural form of organization for Japanese society from time immemorial.

The Unreflective Empiricism of Textbook Historiography

No textbook departed from the chronological approach during the postwar era, and this chronological timeline was further subdivided through a periodization that usually took political events as the defining moments of the national story.

These periodizations were not entirely uniform across the range of textbooks and were sometimes revised in the course of the postwar era. Some textbooks, for example, chose to group the events immediately preceding the Meiji Restoration together with the Restoration itself and the modernization of Japan in the late nineteenth and early twentieth centuries, while others included these preceding events in a chapter on Tokugawa society. There were also shifts within chapters on modern periods when authors broke up the chronology somewhat to report on parallel developments in political, social, and artistic life. These shifts were not systematic, however, and within such reconfigured subchapters, narratives remained strictly chronological.

Changes that appeared in textbook narratives were subsumed under this dominant chronological paradigm and therefore came as omissions, additions, or the correction of previous information (see Chapter 9). The lack of discussion of the broader meaning of particularly sensitive topics in the textbooks illustrates the focus on chronology and "factual" narrative in textbook accounts. This pattern was strikingly visible in the treatment of Asia-Pacific War atrocities.

Given the dominant portrayals of the Asia-Pacific War in terms of the sequence of political events that led to the war and that constituted its course, coverage of atrocities tended to come as additions to narratives that in other respects remained essentially unaltered. For example, as existing narratives of the course of the war usually involved little consideration of responsibility for its outbreak, the insertion of brief footnotes referring to the Nanjing Massacre in the early 1980s did little to prompt discussion of such responsibility but instead appeared as an additional data point on an otherwise unchanging timeline. During the 1980s, these footnotes were then gradually expanded to include more detail, then promoted to the status of parenthetical statements, before finally being incorporated in the main text in the 1990s. Although this sequence was paralleled by similar shifts in the coverage of other controversial historical episodes, the inclusion of such additional data points seldom fundamentally altered the thrust of the overall narrative, which remained uncritically and unreflectively empirical, monolithic, and chronological.

Actors and Agency

Historical actors have generally played a prominent role in textbook historiography, with narratives of the national past focusing on the doings of Great Men. The importance of these individuals has been communicated to examination-conscious students through the frequent use of a bold typeface for their names, as well as for the names of the prominent events or episodes they were involved in and the dates when these took place.

Although individual and collective actors were portrayed as important features of the chronology of events emphasized by textbooks, the motivation of actors accorded responsibility for particular events was rarely discussed, and likewise the relative significance of individual agency in historical causation was rarely if ever critically assessed. Among the periods examined, the Meiji Restoration is perhaps the most obviously susceptible to an assessment of the importance of agency as it involved a conflict among fairly well-defined (or, at least, potentially well-defined) individual and collective actors. The conflict between individuals and domains supporting the Shogunate through the 1850s and 60s and those opposing it constituted the most significant element in narratives of the events leading up to the Restoration itself. Not only were collective actors mentioned frequently, but many accounts also featured a standardized gallery of individual actors deemed to have played a prominent role in Tokugawa politics, the Restoration, and Meiji-era politics. As compared with accounts of earlier periods in history, this gallery of mid-to-late nineteenth century figures included many individuals other than the dynastic leaders themselves, particularly since neither the last two Shoguns nor the young Meiji Emperor were a particular focus of narratives. Instead, active shapers of developments, such as Tokugawa regent Ii Naosuke or Meiji leader Ito Hirobumi, were associated with particular policy decisions and events. However, accounts of their doings did not extend to a discussion of the motivation for particular courses of action and thus offered no explanation for the ways individuals used their power to achieve particular aims. Although agency was attributed to individuals, it remained unclear whether anything other than unspecified personal preferences, loyalties, or circumstances accounted for their use of power.

If accounts of the Meiji period tended to play host to an unusually dense population of Great Men (even if discussion of individual agency was generally rather superficial), then narratives of the Asia-Pacific War were more notable for the absence of such figures. Other than the occasional mention of

Prime Minister Tojo in sections covering the attack on Pearl Harbor, the only individual who invariably warranted a mention in the textbooks was General Douglas MacArthur, who was cited for his leadership of the postwar occupation regime. Actors who might be deemed responsible for the outbreak of the Asia-Pacific War were mentioned only as undefined collectivities (such as "militarists" or "ultranationalist young officers") or were simply referred to without any explanation of what their actual role may have been (as for example in the case of convicted war criminals). Emporer Hirohito's role was never discussed.

Although many individual and collective actors thus populated the textbook narratives, little agency was attributed to either. This distinguishes the Japanese textbook narratives both from a dynastic historiography of the type that dominated the historiographical perspectives of the nineteenth century in Europe and from the traditional didactic-moralistic Confucian historiography of East Asia, with its galleries of moral exemplars.

Definitions of the Nation

The six episodes selected for analysis were deliberately chosen for the important roles they are generally considered to have played in Japanese history. These episodes were implicitly portrayed as crucial milestones in the development of the nation, but neither official curricula nor textbook narratives offered any explicit definition of the nation, nationhood, or national belonging. While the trend in some parts of the world in recent years has been toward a growing acknowledgment of the problematic nature of the nation as a historical category (a trend seen by some as a Western-led rationalization of accounts of the nation), Japanese history textbooks have persisted in portraying nationhood as an unproblematic given.

Textbook narratives have thus assumed a direct progression from prehistoric Japan to the "natural" (re)emergence of the nation-state in the postwar era, with the development of the united, homogenous, eternal Japanese nation providing the clear, if implicit, teleological subtext. While the rather simplistic connections that textbooks draw between prehistoric humans and today's Japanese may have been deemed appropriate for the age of students at which the textbooks are aimed, the lack of any discussion of the precise nature of the nation in the context of its modern foundation, the Meiji Restoration, or its modern catastrophe in the 1930s and 40s, has invariably characterized Japanese narratives and reflected the persistent dominance of an unreflectively empiricist historiography.

The only other terms used to refer to the nation were various expressions for the Japanese population, but especially *kokumin* (national people). As with treatment of the nation more generally, such terms were seldom defined or qualified even when minority populations were topics of discussion; instead, the implication of the continuous existence of the nation and its people was emphasized by the lack of any problematized discussion. The "people" thus occasionally appeared in narratives as actors, but only in the same way as the nation did, that is, without any discussion of the nature or implications of their agency.

Textbook references to Japan through the mid-1970s used terminology that encouraged identification on the part of students with their country. Although this was most obvious in various aspects of the narratives of prehistory, the 1974 edition of *Chugakko Shakai* (273)[3] was the latest textbook sampled to use the term "our country" (*waga kuni*) in reference to Japan, a term that had been commonly used as recently as the late 1960s (*Nihon no Ayumi*, 1969). After the mid-1970s, references to Japan generally relied on the more neutral Japan (Nihon) without a possessive modifier (although the Chinese equivalent for the possessive term *waga kuni* [*woguo*] is still used frequently in history textbooks and in official discourse generally in China).

Beyond identification with the nation as a seemingly natural unit, students were encouraged to identify with their Japanese predecessors from various eras of national history. Apart from the use of possessive modifiers, more recent textbooks frequently highlighted the situation of junior high school children in different periods of modern history. Narratives of educational reforms in the late nineteenth and early twentieth centuries, as well as accounts of the postwar reforms, specifically mentioned the ways these affected junior high school education.

Although particular subnational populations like the Burakumin, Ainu, Ryukyu Islanders, or Korean-Japanese were mentioned at various points in the narratives, their mention did not lead to a further discussion of who the presumed majority they joined might have been or of what implications the act of their incorporation into the majority population held for the nation as a whole. Even the existence of regional variations among the majority population was not mentioned or was glossed over, reflecting an overall perspective on the nation that assumed unity and homogeneity from time immemorial. National identity and the borders and shape of the nation were taken as given and not discussed further in teaching materials. While Japanese materials thus reflected global trends toward the increased inclusion of subnational groups in the history curricula, they did so in only very limited fashion and without in any way challenging the assumption of Japan's essential ethno-cultural homogeneity.

Indications of the Stability of Japanese Content vis-à-vis Global Trends

The preceding section outlined the perspective adopted in portrayals of the nation in teaching materials and, on the basis of qualitative analyses of textbook content, has demonstrated the lack of change in this perspective over the postwar period. The empirical work conducted by Meyer and his associates from their world polity perspective, by contrast, focused on quantitative measures of change in curricula. Although my focus here is on secondary rather than higher education, the teaching materials I have gathered do allow for a limited replication of Meyer's methods. Japanese textbooks for use in junior high schools do not distinguish many of the themes examined by Meyer and his collaborators in the same clear fashion that would allow for a coding of course titles but, given their chronological organization, the tables of content of textbooks do offer an opportunity for analysis of the share of the curriculum devoted to particular historical periods.

Based on Frank and colleagues' findings (2000) concerning global trends toward the demise of the prominence of antiquity in historiography and of the corresponding rise in the amount of attention devoted to discussions of universalizable aspects of modern nation-states, one would expect an increasing share of the textbooks to focus on more recent history. I have tested the validity of this expectation by examining the tables of contents of the thirty-three books sampled for this study.

To construct a measure that corresponds to Frank and associates' (ibid.) analysis of the rise of contemporary history, I recorded the page on which a given textbook lists the Meiji Restoration and the Japanese surrender in the Asia-Pacific War. As the sections on the Meiji Restoration typically occupied several pages, I recorded the first mention of the Restoration as tied to a specific date (rather than any mentions made in the introduction to the section on modern Japan, for example). I then standardized the measure of the proportion of coverage devoted to these events by showing the results as a percentage of the total number of pages in a textbook. Although more recent textbooks are less dense in terms of the amount of information offered per page due to the addition of such features as graphic elements and sidebars, I am assuming that this shift occurs across individual textbooks and is not specific to certain sections, implying that standardization by the percentage of pages provides a comparable measure across the entire period. I then averaged the proportions of the textbook devoted to pre-Meiji history across the three textbooks sampled for a given 5-year time period. Table 8.1 thus represents the share of the curriculum devoted to premodern (pre-Meiji) and contemporary history.

As is clear from the table, shifts in the weighting of different historical periods do not surpass 10 percent overall (with premodern history dropping from

Table 8.1 Percentage Shares of Historical Periods in Textbook Tables of Contents

	1950	1955	1960	1965	1970	1975	1980	1985	1990	1995	2000
Premodern History	70.5	67.8	67.2	66.5	66.8	66.5	65.4	62.6	62.6	62.6	62.5
Contemporary History	4.4	5	6.1	7.4	5.7	9.1	8.2	9.7	9.8	10.3	8.9

Based on sample of textbooks listed in chapter appendix.

70.5 percent of the curriculum in 1950 to 62.5 percent in the 2001 editions of textbooks. Even though 50 years of postwar history could potentially have been added to textbook narratives between 1950 and 2000, the share of contemporary history only expanded from 4.5 percent in 1950 to 9 percent in 2000. This contrasts with developments at the university level, cited in the opening section of this chapter, where even Japanese university curricula devoted over a quarter of the course of study to contemporary history. Seen in this light, history education at high school level in Japan appears to be bucking global trends.

The lack of change in the substantive orientation of portrayals of the nation in school textbooks is remarkable in light of the alternatives offered, for example, by the fashion for socialist historiography in Japan during the 1960s and by the nationalist discourse since the 1970s. However, the tight control of bureaucrats over educational policymaking has prevented either of these forces from having a major impact on history teaching materials. If anything, the uncritical, unreflective acts and facts empiricism that has characterized teaching materials has involved a scrupulous avoidance of some of the principal questions that have animated public, academic, and political discussions of Japanese history. Instead, history textbooks have reproduced a seemingly neutral, bureaucratic historiography that has embodied and reflected Monbusho's claim to legitimated power over educational content. Frank and colleagues' (2000) findings with regards to higher education history curricula are thus not reflected in the content of secondary history curricula in Japan.

The Educational Policymaking Regime for Postwar Junior High School History Education

In the immediate postwar years, Monbusho bureaucrats were on the defensive vis-à-vis occupation authorities as well as progressive domestic forces who advocated substantive changes to school curricula. Ultimately, bureaucrats succeeded in thwarting reforms that would have devolved authority over education to local levels by stalling during the occupation and immediately reasserting their authority after its end (see chapter 9). Occupation authorities in the period following the "Reverse Course"[4] and, later, conservative governing coalitions were only too happy to return power to the Ministry as some of the obvious alternatives, the Japanese Teachers' Union (*Nihon Kyoshokuin Kumiai*, abbreviated as Nikkyoso, or JTU) or academics, were politically unappealing because of their socialist sympathies. Particularly with regard to the drafting and implementation of curricula and of textbook approval based on these curricula, Monbusho bureaucrats were able to wrest control over educational content back from some of the actors who had earlier been deliberately empowered by occupation policies. The decision to make official curricula the mandatory basis of textbook approval from 1958 onward formalized this dominance of Monbusho bureaucrats over the educational policymaking regime.

(Chapter 9 offers a very detailed and careful analysis of policy decisions relating to textbooks and illustrates the high degree of ministerial power over the content of education.)

This educational policymaking regime remained in place for the duration of the period covered in this analysis and remains largely in place today in Japan. Although there were some challenges to Monbusho's dominance, these challenges either failed to wrest control over educational content from the bureaucracy or were largely directed at other elements of educational policymaking. A single actor — the ministry itself — thus in fact dominated policymaking in relation to the content of secondary history education.

In the early postwar period, ministerial bureaucrats were on the defensive against reform proposals for education advanced by the U.S. occupation authorities (SCAP) and Japanese progressives. Thakur (1990) has described the seesawing between U.S. occupation officials and ministerial bureaucrats in great detail. In the case of history education specifically, bureaucrats eventually responded to reform proposals with a seemingly neutral historiography that focused on the empirical facts of chronological developments. This followed repeated rounds into 1947 of requests for drafts of teaching materials by SCAP and their subsequent rejection for failing to fully meet American requirements. Bureaucrats consciously steered a middle course between some of the alternative conceptualizations of history that were current at the time in conservative circles, on the one hand, and among progressive educators and academics on the other. This historiographical perspective was then institutionalized following the end of the occupation — a period that witnessed a recentralization of power in bureaucratic hands as well as the setting of precedents for the dominance of Monbusho power over history curriculum content.

In their skirmishes with occupation officials and in subsequent statements on the importance of bureaucratic control over education, Monbusho bureaucrats asserted the legitimacy of their actions based on their ostensibly neutral position as administrators of political decisions. Particularly in response to Ienaga Saburo's criticisms of the textbook approval system (Nozaki and Inokuchi 1998; see also chapter 9), the official position was that part of the bureaucracy's role was to guard against the intrusion of value judgments into history education. McVeigh (1998, 128) has shown the extent to which this paralleled more general Monbusho concerns with the legitimacy of bureaucratic decision-making in postwar Japan.

Following the successful reestablishment of ministerial control over educational content in 1958, Monbusho bureaucrats maintained the status quo and their power over education policies. Examinations of Japanese education policy by political scientists have tended to characterize Monbusho's activities as very much akin to what organizational sociologists call "paleo-institutionalism" or "old institutionalism." Scholars such as Schoppa (1991), Kato (1994), and Aspinall (2001) have concluded that Monbusho bureaucrats have primarily been interested in the preservation of their power and control over educational content. Aspinall (2001, 98–99) approvingly cites two factors highlighted by Schoppa (1991, 92–94) to explain the continuity in ministerial bureaucrats' attempts to maintain power: (1) pride in past accomplishments, and (2) a proximity to schools as a locus of the implementation of educational policies, together contributing to a strong bias against bureaucratic or policy upheaval.

To these two factors could be added several others drawn from historical accounts of the development of Monbusho and from organizational theory. Particularly in the early postwar period, the Ministry was staffed primarily by bureaucrats who had entered government service before 1945, and while providing administrative continuity, many of these men also harbored a certain nostalgia for the even greater powers to determine curricular content previously wielded by government officials. Conservative politicians also repeatedly referred to aspects of the pre-1945 educational system that exhibited what they regarded as desirable qualities (the pre-1945 normal schools were mentioned particularly frequently in this context). Prime Minister Yasuhiro Nakasone's reform proposals in the 1980s were clearly motivated in part by such a pining for a romanticized past, and it appears that this nostalgia was as prevalent among most bureaucrats as it was among many conservative politicians.

To understand some of the continuity from the prewar and wartime Ministry, it is important to remember a number of organizational features of the Japanese national bureaucracy in general, as well as some aspects of Monbusho's history in particular. Japanese ministerial bureaucracies, including Monbusho, have been characterized by seniority promotion systems. Powerful bureaucrats post to several sections within the Ministry during their career and slowly ascend the hierarchy. Those who reach the apex of the bureaucratic pyramid occupy it only for a very brief stint, at the level just below that of the politically appointed minister. The rigid adherence to this system of seniority promotion meant that Monbusho was administered as late as the 1970s by bureaucrats who had been socialized into their bureaucratic habitus before 1945. As this socialization occurred in the context of strict hierarchical relations among bureaucrats, the influence of pre-1945 experience may be assumed to have lasted even longer through the power of senior bureaucrats over their juniors. In the postwar period, the Ministry's running conflict with the teachers' union also reinforced its reputation for conservatism. Given this reputation, self-selection tended to bring cohorts of conservative bureaucrats into the postwar Ministry who were particularly susceptible to some of the nostalgia among older bureaucrats.

Aspinall (2001, ch. 4) discussed previous models of educational policymaking specifically with regard to the realignment of political forces after the schism of the Nikkyoso and after the end of Liberal Democratic Party (LDP)–dominance in parliamentary politics. Despite the disappearance of a bipolar view of policymaking following the demise of the main opposition force with the split of Nikkyoso, bureaucrats have largely continued on their previous path. This continuity has been reinforced by Monbusho's success in defending its turf from unusual LDP interest in educational policymaking, particularly under Prime Minister Nakasone.

Monbusho officials thus emerged in control of history curriculum development following their effective resistance to reformist pressure during the period of U.S. occupation. While the formation of educational policy more broadly has been affected by a stalemate between various stakeholders, of which Monbusho was only one (Schoppa, 1991), history education specifically has been under tight bureaucratic control for the duration of the postwar period.

Challenges to Monbusho Dominance of the Educational Policymaking Regime

Two groups — the progressive opposition, particularly Nikkyoso, and activist, conservative politicians, most notably Prime Minister Nakasone during the 1980s — have posed the most significant threats to bureaucratic power over the content of history education. On specific questions concerning the representation of the Asia-Pacific War, the bureaucracy was also subject to pressure from the historian and textbook author Ienaga Saburo and other Japanese academics throughout the period from the 1960s onwards, as well as from foreign victims' groups and their governments and, increasingly during the 1990s, from Japanese groups supporting the aims of these victims' groups.

Nikkyoso constituted the most visible and vociferous opposition to Monbusho policies throughout the 1950s and into the 60s. The union scrutinized every policy proposed by the bureaucracy and responded with statements of the union's position and, not infrequently, open hostility and threats of industrial action on the part of the union leadership. In their political positions, the union leadership remained closely allied with the Japanese Socialist Party, and the high rate of mobilization of secondary teachers allowed the leadership to speak with some authority despite apparent gaps between its political orientation and that of the less radical general membership.

Among the most visible issues that led to conflict between the bureaucracy and the union were conservative proposals to reintroduce ethics instruction into the social studies curriculum in the mid-1950s. Eventually, an ethics class was reintroduced into upper secondary schools in 1958, but this class did not resemble the pre-1945 ethics curriculum that had been such a central element of wartime indoctrination, even though Prime Minister Yoshida Shigeru, who had introduced the call for moral education, clearly had something akin to the prewar curriculum in mind. Nikkyoso opposed the reintroduction of ethics classes and the proposals were amended to produce the more moderate and general version of moral education that emerged in 1958 (Takakura and Murata 1997, 211–213).

After these important and very visible battles with the Ministry, however, the long decline of Nikkyoso as a unified voice for teachers and as a prominent element among the opposition forces began.[5] Increasing tensions between a less radical membership and their socialist leadership led to a decline in the mobilization of members for union drives and campaigns during the 1960s. After a generational shift brought less radical union members into leadership positions in the 1970s, Nikkyoso factionalism increased and finally resulted in the union's split in 1989 into the moderate Nikkyoso and the more radical Zenkyo (Aspinall 2001). Because of its decline, Nikkyoso has not significantly challenged bureaucrats' authority over educational content since the 1960s. It remained one of the forces ranged in opposition to the LDP and to the bureaucracy through its alignment with the JSP and supported various initiatives on history textbooks, but this opposition was fairly ineffectual and did not lead to any realignment of the policymaking regime.

The government of Prime Minister Nakasone in the 1980s was the one exception to the general rule, following the debates about ethics education in the 1950s, that the governing LDP did not involve itself in bureaucratic decisions over educational content. Nakasone was unusual among LDP prime ministers in that he came to the position with a clearly stated education policy agenda and attempted to implement these policies during his premiership. His term as prime minister was also unusually long (1982–1987) compared with those of the various occupants of this office since the establishment of the LDP in 1955. His attempts at effecting structural and substantive reforms in the Japanese educational system have inspired three book-length studies in the English language alone (Schoppa 1991; Roesgaard 1998; Hood 2001) and continue to fuel educational policy debates within Japan itself. In 1984, Nakasone set up the Ad Hoc Council on Education (*Rinkyoshin*) to advise him on the policy changes he wanted to implement in education and as an attempt "to bypass the Ministry of Education, which [Nakasone] decided was too tradition-minded to share his vision" (Pyle 1992, 95–96). The Ad Hoc Council existed for the duration of Nakasone's premiership and offered a number of recommendations that were implemented in the late 1980s round of curricular reform. In contrast to the long-standing Central Council on Education (*Chukyoshin*) that advised the Minister of Education, the Rinkyoshin reported directly to the prime minister. As might be expected, most of the members were closely allied with Prime Minister Nakasone. Only two of the initial members were identified specifically as teachers. Among the main reforms that were considered by the Rinkyoshin were a revision of the 6-3-3 system for primary and secondary education, changes to the administration of education, and a rethinking of moral education. Schoppa (1991, 36) identifies Prime Minister Nakasone's (and other conservatives') resentment of certain post-1945 occupation measures as underlying this push for reform. Of particular relevance to the questions at hand, Nakasone's objection to the abolition of the Imperial

Rescript on Education as the foundation of educational policy and to the devolution of control over education from the Ministry to local authorities. The Rescript, issued in 1879, was one of the key documents of the Meiji Era and embodied a highly essentialist view of Japanese culture and identity while upholding a conservative, authoritarian interpretation of Confucian morality and warning against excessive borrowing from the West. Nakasone made these proposals at a time in the 1980s when Japanese self-confidence was resurgent and the Nihonjinron-boom had hit full stride. (*Nihonjinron* — the theory of Japaneseness — refers to a trend in intellectual, media, and political circles for celebrating what was seen as the superior essence of the Japanese race and/or their culture.)

Given the nature of the educational policymaking regime in the postwar era, however, the reforms introduced by Nakasone on the basis of the recommendations of the Rinkyoshin changed neither the existing framework for the drafting and promulgation of curricula nor the textbook authorization system. Regarding his desire to instill a more positive sense of national identity in students, the 1989 curriculum actually introduced very few substantive changes in this regard. Even though Nakasone's specific reform proposals came in the context of a general shift toward the political right in politics and of the increasing popularity and prominence of Nihonjinron literature in the 1970s and 80s, their direct impact on the curriculum for junior high school history was very limited. His more substantive agenda was also undermined by a series of political gaffes. In 1986, Prime Minister Nakasone himself had to dismiss Minister of Education Fujio Masayuki after the minister argued for the legitimacy of the colonization of Korea and of the Nanjing Massacre.

The most prominent and controversial change to the school curriculum at this time (the reintroduction of the Japanese national anthem and flag into schools) did not greatly affect textbooks, although it inspired some of the more vociferous opposition to Monbusho policies during the 1990s. This was an extremely contentious issue throughout the 1990s but was contested in relative independence from debates about textbook content, though some of the same actors have been involved in both controversies. Despite Nakasone's unusually activist agenda and his ability to implement some of his policy goals, his reforms to education policy had relatively little impact on the content of the school curriculum or on history education specifically, regardless of whether one follows Schoppa's (1991) fairly negative assessment of the efficacy of the Nakasone reforms or Hood's (2001) contention that the reforms were somewhat successful in the long run.

Apart from general criticism of the government's educational policies, Monbusho bureaucrats faced more specific opposition over their selection of the content of history education. From the 1960s onward, the historian Ienaga Saburo waged a long-running court battle with the Ministry after his textbooks were rejected during the Monbusho approval process. In the 1980s and 1990s, bureaucrats also faced increasing pressure from associations and individual victims of Japanese aggression in East Asia as well as from neighboring governments who supported their citizens in a quest for retribution and for changes to the portrayal of the Asia-Pacific War in school textbook. In the 1990s, nascent Japanese nongovernmental organizations increasingly supported the victims' agenda.

Ienaga had been one of the authors of the first Ministry-commissioned postwar textbook, *Kuni no Ayumi*. He remained one of the authors of several textbooks after that and also retained his position as a professor of history at Chuo University. According to my analysis of textbooks published during that period, the early postwar textbooks he coauthored or edited did not seem to be notably distinguishable from other contemporary textbooks. However, Ienaga later emerged as a very visible critic of Monbusho, with his lawsuits charging that his high school textbook drafts had been unlawfully rejected during the textbook approval process.[6] Ienaga brought the first of several lawsuits to the courts in 1965. These lawsuits continued through the 1970s and 1980s with Ienaga winning a partial victory in 1974 but appealing other parts of the decision. Ministerial bureaucrats attempted to insist on the correction of what they saw as factual mistakes in Ienaga's manuscripts but lost their case on this front. However, where Ienaga and his supporters attacked the broader issue of Monbusho's right to approve textbooks in the first place, they were rebuffed by the courts. Ienaga's various suits culminated in a Supreme Court decision in 1997 that granted his claim that his phrases and his inclusion of Unit 731[7] had been illegally rejected but turned down the larger claim that the Ministry was engaging in illegal censorship (Nozaki and Inokuchi 2000; see also chapter 9).

In the 1980s and 1990s, a number of victims of Japanese atrocities in Asian countries went public with their own memories and accounts of their victimization, leading to some broad-based movements to pressure the Japanese government to change textbook portrayals of the Asia Pacific War and atrocities committed in its course. Testimony by victims and continued dissatisfaction among Japan's East Asian neighbors over the official response to criticism of Japanese textbooks led to a series of foreign policy crises for Japanese governments.

In the 1990s, Japanese citizens' groups became increasingly involved in the issue of the portrayal of the Asia-Pacific War (Ducke 2002). Rallying around Ienaga or victims of Japanese aggression, these groups generally concentrated their efforts on the publication of historical research and the promotion of greater public understanding of the war, although some specifically targeted history education as well. During the same period, ministerial bureaucracies in Japan lost some of their power because their claims to administrative efficiency became less convincing after 1991, with the bursting of the high-growth bubble and the apparent inability of politicians and the bureaucracy to restore economic growth. Although this loss of prestige has been most obvious with regard to the status of the Ministry of International Trade and Industry (renamed the Ministry of Economy, Trade, and Industry in 2001), the other ministerial bureaucracies have also suffered. It still remains to be seen whether this loss of prestige and power constitutes a long-term shift in the educational policymaking regime.

The Immobility of Japanese Portrayals of the Nation

Bureaucrats' control of postwar Japanese curricula and textbooks led to a portrayal of the nation as the natural unit of analysis in their narratives. Before the tightening of the textbook approval process in 1958, some textbooks included suggestions of causal accounts for historical events like the Meiji Restoration or the Kaga Uprising, but bureaucrats excised these in the approval process for subsequent materials. Textbooks did not offer definitions of the Japanese nation or people, and the role of particular individuals in shaping the fate of the nation was not subjected to any critical examination. Instead, textbook authors reproduced the bureaucrats' historiographical perspective in presenting national history as a series of chronologically organized events that were set in motion by individual or collective actors whose motives were seen, by and large, as unproblematic. The historiographical perspective of these narratives was thus overwhelmingly uncritical and empiricist, emphasizing the "facts" of history and their chronological sequence to the exclusion of all other considerations. Through the promotion of this perspective on the national past, bureaucrats sought to reinforce a view of Japanese history and identity that portrayed the status quo as the natural order of things — a view that had served to bolster their power and legitimacy vis-à-vis U.S. occupation forces and the domestic opposition.

While my analysis of the content of teaching materials for Japanese junior high schools shows that this content remained very stable over the postwar period despite global trends in history curriculum development, my analysis of the educational policymaking process showed that this stability cannot be attributed simply to a stalemate among competing policy actors. Monbusho bureaucrats have continuously worked to maintain almost exclusive control over the content of history education. While this control was countered to some extent by a very vociferous opposition spearheaded by Nikkyoso up to and during the 1960s, the union's influence clearly began to wane from the early 1960s onwards, and it ceased to be a significant force influencing policymaking in the 1970s. I have also shown that politicians have been largely absent from policymaking debates over the curriculum for junior high schools, usually preferring to leave such matters to the bureaucratic "experts."

While Monbusho bureaucrats have thus had almost complete control over educational policy regarding the content of teaching materials, their policies have been highly immobile and the content of the junior high school history curriculum has changed very little since 1950. Factors other than the dominance of Monbusho bureaucrats have played a role in this stability, such as the fact-oriented nature of university entrance examinations and the ramifications of these examinations, but even many of these factors can be related to the influence of the Ministry over all aspects of education policy.

I have pointed to a number of organizational features of the Ministry in arguing that it is the institutionalization of a specific policymaking regime — and the historiographical perspective that emerged out of this institutionalization — that have played a central role in the immobilism of Japanese history education. While Schoppa's (1991) analysis of a policymaking stalemate of various actors may hold for educational policy generally, the similar lack of change observable in the history curriculum appears to have been due to somewhat different factors. Principal among these is the dominance of the Monbusho bureaucracy over the curriculum development and textbook screening processes — a dominance that has consciously worked to legitimate and reinforce a homogenous, monolithic vision of Japaneseness and a narrative of the national past that encourages uncritical acceptance of the political status quo (in the maintenance of which the Monbusho bureaucrats have a vested interest). The kind of institutional explanation offered here is better able to account for the variety of conditions under which immobilism can be observed in Japanese policymaking.

In addition to refuting claims that immobility in policymaking obtains only under conditions of political stalemate, I have also suggested that the course adopted by the Japanese educational policymaking regime casts doubt on the arguments of world polity theorists concerning the diffusion of global trends in education from a hegemonic (Western) center to a passive (non-Western) periphery. While at a very general level the content of history education around the world, and to some extent in Japanese higher education as well, does appear to have become increasingly rationalized in recent decades, teaching materials for Japanese high schools evince no such trends, but rather reflect bureaucratic concerns relating to the domestic political context. Elsewhere (Dierkes 2003) I have argued that the nature of the educational policymaking regime — the degree to which the curriculum development process has been centralized or decentralized, closed or open, inclusive or exclusive, bureaucratically directed or politically accountable — has been similarly crucial to explanations of the differences between the content and pedagogy of East and West German history education during the same postwar period. National education policymaking regimes do not simply transmit educational trends from the center to the periphery of a global polity; instead, even when there are superficial similarities in policy rhetoric and jargon, these more often than not belie substantial and fundamental differences in the actual meaning attached to specific policies and the ways these policies are implemented. These differences in turn need to be explained primarily in terms of motivations arising from the political, cultural, and social context in which curriculum development takes place and through which any external influences are mediated — and not on the basis of inferences drawn from grandiose universal theories.

Endnotes

1. Research for this paper was supported by the German Institute for Japanese Studies (Tokyo) and the Centre for Japanese Research at the University of British Columbia. Many thanks to Robert Aspinall, John Campbell, Peter Cave, Brian McVeigh, Leonard Schoppa, and the audience at the 2004 meetings of the Association for Asian Studies, San Diego, for comments on earlier versions and to Anna Turinov for research assistance.
2. I am grateful to David Frank for providing me with country-level data from their dataset.
3. I cite textbooks with reference to their titles, rather than the authors, given the collective nature of textbook authorship and the continuation of specific textbook titles under different lead authors.
4. This is the term used to describe the moderation of American reform plans for Japan from 1947 onward due to the onset of the Cold War. Fears of the spread of Communism there as elsewhere in East Asia, leading to the coopting of former militarists and imperialists as partners in an anticommunist united front.
5. The history of Nikkyoso and its conflicts with Mombusho bureaucrats is particularly well documented, even in English-language sources such as Duke (1973), Thurston (1973), Roesgaard (1998), and Aspinall (2001).
6. The recent prominence of Ienaga and his lawsuits have led to a large body of literature in English and Japanese. Here, I rely on the good overview and chronology of the lawsuits provided by Nozaki and Inokuchi (2000).
7. Unit 731 was the infamous unit of the Imperial Army that conducted medical experiments on prisoners of war and civilians. In Manchuria (Manchukuo) during World War II.

References

Aspinall, R. 2001. *Teachers' Unions and the Politics of Education in Japan*. Albany: State University of New York Press.

Dierkes, J. 2003. "Teaching Portrayals of the Nation: Postwar History Education in Japan and the Germanys." Ph.D. dissertation, Princeton University.

Ducke, I. 2002. "The History Textbook Issue 2001: A Successful Citizens' Movement or Foreign Intervention?" DIJ Working Paper 02/6. Tokyo: German Institute for Japanese Studies.

Duke, B. 1973. *Japan's Militant Teachers: A History of the Left-Wing Teachers' Movement*. Honolulu: University of Hawaii Press.

Frank, D., et al. 2000. "What Counts as History: A Cross-National and Longitudinal Study of University Curricula." *Comparative Education Review* 44:29–53.

Hood, C. 2001. *Japanese Education Reform: Nakasone's Legacy*. London: Routledge.

Johnson, C. 1982. *MITI and the Japanese Miracle*. Stanford: Stanford University Press.

Kato, J. 1994. *The Problem of Bureaucratic Rationality: Tax Politics in Japan*. Princeton: Princeton University Press.

McVeigh, B. 1998. *The Nature of the Japanese State: Rationality and Rituality.* New York: Routledge.

Meyer, J., et al., eds. 1992. *School Knowledge for the Masses: World Models and National Primary Curricular Categories in the Twentieth Century.* Washington, D.C.: Falmer Press.

Meyer, J., et al. 1992. "World Expansion of Mass Education." *Sociology of Education* 65:128–149.

Nozaki, Y. and Inokuchi H. 1998. "Japanese Education, Nationalism, and Ienaga Saburo's Court Challenges." *Bulletin of Concerned Asian Scholars* 30, 2:37–46.

Pyle, K. 1992. *The Japanese Question: Power and Purpose in a New Era.* Washington, D.C.: AEI Press.

Roesgaard, M. 1998. *Moving Mountains: Japanese Education Reform.* Aarhus: Aarhus University Press.

Schoppa, L. 1991. *Education Reform in Japan: A Case of Immobilist Politics.* London: Routledge.

Takakura, S. and Murata Y. 1997. *Education in Japan.* Tokyo: Gakushu Kenkyusha.

Thakur, Y. 1990. "Textbook Reform in Allied Occupied Japan, 1945–1952." Ph.D. dissertation, University of Maryland.

Thurston, D. 1973. *Teachers and Politics in Japan.* Princeton: Princeton University Press.

Textbooks Analyzed (In Chronological Order)

Fujii, J. 1952. *Sodachi yuku Nihon.* Tokyo: Phoenix Shoin.

Kobata, J. 1952. *Watashitachi no Nihonshi.* Tokyo: Kyoikusha.

Tokyo University Historiographical Institute. 1952. *Nihon no Ayumi.* Tokyo: Yamakawa Shuppansha.

Ienaga, S. 1954. *Atarashii Nihonshi.* Tokyo: Tokyo Shoin.

———. 1954. *Chugaku Nihonshi.* Tokyo: Gakko Tosho.

Konishi, S. 1954. *Chuto Rekishi.* Tokyo: Sanshodo.

Kotake, F. 1954. *Shakai no Shinpo.* Tokyo: Koima Shoin.

Toyoda, T. 1956. *Nihon no Ayumi.* Tokyo: Chukyo Shuppan.

Nishida, N. 1958. *Nihon to Sekai.* Tokyo: Teikoku Shoin.

Arisawa, H. 1962. *Atarashii Shakai.* Tokyo: Tokyo Shoseki.

Kobata, A. 1962. *Nihon no Rekishi to Sekai.* Tokyo: Shimizu Shoin.

Toyoda, T. 1962. *Nihon no Ayumi to Sekai.* Tokyo: Chukyo Shuppan.

Kawasaki, T. 1965. *Rekishi no Nagare.* Tokyo: Kyoiku Shuppan.

Kodama, K. 1968. *Chugaku Shakai.* Tokyo: Nihon Shoseki.

Toyoda, T. 1969. *Nihon no Ayumi to Sekai.* Tokyo: Chukyo Shuppan.

Arizawa, H. 1975. *Atarashii Shakai.* Tokyo: Tokyo Shoseki.

Inoue, C. 1975. *Chugaku Shakai.* Osaka: Osaka Shoseki.

Kasahara, K. 1975. *Chugakko Shakai.* Tokyo: Gakko Tosho.

Nomura, M. 1977. *Chugaku Shakai.* Tokyo: Kyoiku Shuppan.

Aoki, K. 1978. *Nihon no Ayumi to Sekai.* Tokyo: Chukyo Shuppan.

Ukai, N. 1978. *Atarashii Shakai.* Tokyo: Tokyo Shoseki.

———. 1981. *Atarashii Shakai.* Tokyo: Tokyo Shoseki.

Aoki, K. 1983. *Nihon no Ayumi to Sekai.* Tokyo: Chukyo Shuppan.

Nagahara, K. 1984. *Chugakko Shakai.* Tokyo: Gakko Tosho.

Mori, M. 1986. *Nihon no Rekishi to Sekai.* Tokyo: Shimizu Shoin.

Tokinoya, M. 1989. *Chugaku Shakai.* Osaka: Osaka Shoseki.

Kawada, K. 1990. *Atarashii Shakai.* Tokyo: Tokyo Shoseki.

———. 1992. *Atarashii Shakai.* Tokyo: Tokyo Shoseki.

Sasayama, H. 1992. *Chugaku Shakai.* Tokyo: Kyoiku Shuppan.

Teruya, Y. 1995. *Nihon no Ayumi to Sekai no Ugoki.* Tokyo: Teikoku Shoin.

Sasayama, H. 2001. *Chugaku Shakai.* Tokyo: Kyoiku Shuppan.

Kuroda, H. 2003. *Nihon no Ayumi to Sekai no Ugoki.* Tokyo: Teikoku Shoin.

Tanabe, H. 2003. *Atarashii Shakai.* Tokyo: Tokyo Shoseki.

9

Japanese Politics and the History Textbook Controversy, 1945–2001

YOSHIKO NOZAKI

The Democratization of the Curriculum Halted: Education and the Allied Occupation

A modern democratic nation with a universal (state) education system always faces a curriculum question concerning the knowledge taught in its schools: Whose knowledge ought to be presented to students, who ought to decide it, and by what processes? Political struggles over textbook portrayals of Japan's wartime past stretch back over half a century, with roots grounded in the contradictory process of Japan's postwar democratization of education, curriculum policy, and official knowledge and in the subsequent process whereby the early democratization policies were reversed.

From the beginning of the Allied occupation, the governing structure of wartime Japanese education, which had enthusiastically promoted ultranationalist ideologies and practices, remained solidly intact. Occupation forces chose to use this established governing structure as the instrument for democratizing the nation and its education system, thus creating a fundamental contradiction within the reform process. Moreover, with the onset of the Cold War in the late 1940s and the outbreak of the Korean War (1950–1953), the United States prioritized the maintenance of an anticommunist united front over policies aimed at a throroughgoing democratization of Japan. This shift allowed the political and educational leaders of the presurrender period to remain in power, or to return to power, and resulted in a curriculum policy embodying decidedly mixed messages. Meanwhile, after two short-lived socialist-oriented administrations, formed after the first election under the 1946 (Peace) Constitution, Yoshida Shigeru and his fellow conservatives were allowed to recapture the levers of state authority in 1948.[1]

In 1947, the Ministry of Education (Monbusho or MOE) published a series of instructional guidelines (a volume of general guidelines followed by volumes of subject guidelines). The titles of these volumes included the term *shian* (tentative plan), meaning that schools and teachers at the local level, not the MOE, would develop the final plans — a radical break from past curriculum policy. For example, "Instruction Guidelines: General Guidelines (A Tentative Plan)" criticized presurrender education for having brought uniformity to schools and stated that a curriculum (*kyoka katei*) "should be determined at each school." The guidelines were designed as a sort of reference book, "written as a guide for teachers" (Monbusho 1947a, 2), and as such tended to present the results of curriculum research rather than seeking to impose mandatory goals and standards (Nagao 1989; Yokoyama 1998).

Importantly, one volume of social studies guidelines directly referred to Japan's war responsibility and its mistake in adopting an ideology of ultranationalism:

> Japan, as the major bearer of the responsibility for the Pacific War, ... is in the process of nation-state rebuilding. In the past ten years or so, the extreme nationalist tendency was dominant. It regarded the state and the [Japanese] race as absolute, and closed the normal paths of international relations. As a result, [Japan] fell into isolation and invited the current wretched circumstance. (Monbusho 1947b, 278)

The text also plainly stated that Japan's "aggressive" (*shiryaku-teki*) policies of the past had brought much misery to the world and to Japan.

When it came to textbook policy, however, the state was unprepared, or reluctant, to give up its control over educational content (as textbooks were by and large the basis of the actual daily curriculum). The School Education Law, proclaimed on March 31, 1947, stipulated that elementary school textbooks were to be screened, approved, or authored by "competent authorities," with similar procedures stipulated for secondary school textbooks. At first, these competent authorities were assumed to encompass not only the MOE but also the prefectural education boards (made up of elected board members) that were to be created. However, a few months later, in the School Education Law Enforcement Regulations — which were not an actual piece of legislation but rather a set of supplementary regulations developed by the ministry on the basis of its reading of the law — the MOE defined "competent authorities" as referring to the ministry itself, at least "for the time being" (though in subsequent developments, "for the time being" became permanent).

The MOE then announced the introduction of a state screening system for textbooks, in place of the short-lived system of loose guidelines, and formed several preparatory committees for this purpose. Nevertheless, the preparatory process did not involve a complete negation of the earlier more democratic spirit, as the Japan Teacher's Union (JTU) was allowed to participate through its representatives and the screening, which began in 1948, was not excessively controlling (though the occupation forces did exercise some forms of censorship). The ministry did not have its own staff examining textbooks; instead, it delegated this task to several groups of textbook examiners (*kyokasho chosakan*) who then reported on assigned textbooks.[2] The Textbook Screening Council (*Kyokayotosho Kentei Chosa Shingikai*) then read the examiners' reports and made its decisions.[3] Concerning the issue of textbook adoption, the ministry suggested that the schools, in consultation with their teachers, would be expected to select textbooks appropriate to their own educational needs. It even suggested that each classroom could adopt different textbooks, though who was to have the right to select the textbooks was not legally defined (Kimijima 1996; Tokutake 1995; Nakauchi et al. 1987).

Interestingly, many of the Japanese history textbooks that successfully passed through these early years of textbook screening and were published in the early 1950s used the term "aggression" (*shinryaku*) in one way or another to describe Japanese military activities in China, and its conflicts with China, in the early 1930s. Several textbooks also included descriptions of the Nanjing Massacre of 1937. For example, *Gendai Nihon no Naritachi* (*The History of Contemporary Japan*), a high school textbook published in 1952, contained the line, "The Japanese Army's manner of pillaging and assault, including 'the violent incident of Nanjing,' brought it worldwide notoriety" (Wakamori 1952, 105).[4]

However, as early as 1950, the Japanese government (supported by a strong U.S. anticommunist policy) began to undermine the democratic spirit of early postwar education/curriculum reforms. For example, in 1950, the Education Minister argued for a reintroduction of curricular content associated with the old imperial system of schooling, such as the teaching of Shushin (the moral education of the presurrender period) and the hoisting of the Hinomaru (Rising Sun) flag and singing of the Kimigayo (Our Emperor's Reign) anthem at school events. The MOE also began to develop a series of regulations, procedures, and (sometimes unwritten) rules, in which faits accompli and ministerial regulations would play a more powerful role than formal statutory provisions.[5]

The First Right-Wing Textbooks Campaign and the Birth of the Liberal Democratic Party in 1955

Japan regained its sovereignty in 1952 and reentered an international arena in which the Cold War had become the dominant framework of a new world order. (It is important to note that the continuing military conflicts in Asia were intimately related to this global political context.) Japan's educational policy took an overtly conservative turn after the Ikeda-Robertson talks of October 1953. Ikeda Hayato, Prime Minister Yoshida's right-hand man, was then the head of the Policy Research Committee of the Liberal Party (Jiyuto, hereafter LP); Walter Robertson was the U.S. assistant secretary of state. At their meeting, the United States demanded the remilitarization of Japan. Both the LP and the U.S. government saw Japanese education as one of the major obstacles to Japan's remilitarization and agreed that the Japanese government would make sure that education and the media would propagate the spirit of patriotism and self-defense. In 1954, the Self-Defense Force (*Jieitai*) was established. It was a substantial military force consisting of an army, navy, and air force — and its constitutionality would be disputed for years to come.

Conservative politicians began to attack peace education curricula, accusing the JTU of promoting a communist agenda. At the same time the Yoshida administration succeeded in passing a series of new laws: the first, passed in 1953, gave the Education Minister the authority to screen textbooks; another, in 1954, limited the political activities of public school teachers; and a third, also in 1954, ensured the "political neutrality" of compulsory education. (It is worth noting that this push to "depoliticize" the Japanese school curriculum was contemporaneous with similar drives elsewhere in noncommunist East Asia, for example in Hong Kong, where fears likewise existed concerning the potential of communist agitators to subvert the existing political order (see chapter 5).

In December 1954, however, the Yoshida administration collapsed after a corruption scandal involving Sato Esaku (then the LP's secretary general) and a number of prominent business leaders,[6] allowing Hatoyama Ichiro of the Democratic Party (Minshuto, formed in the fall 1954, hereafter DP), then the second largest party in the Diet, to form a temporary administration.[7] In the general election of February 1955, the revision of the 1947 constitution — especially its Pacifist Clause renouncing war (Article 9) — was at stake. Textbook policy also became a major issue, as Nakasone Yasuhiro of the DP advocated a more centralized system of publishing and adopting textbooks. The election results marked a clear political division: out of 467 seats, the DP won 185, the LP 112, and the Socialist Party (Shakaito, hereafter SP) won 156 (the Left Faction SP winning 89 and the Right Faction SP winning 67).[8] In control of one-third of the Lower House seats, the SP as a whole held enough votes to block the initiation of any amendment to the 1947 constitution that it considered undesirable. Thus, the battle over the constitution was over (at least for the time being), but not the battle over the textbooks.

The first major political controversy over textbooks during the postwar period began when the Diet opened in June 1955, as right-wing politicians invited Ishii Kazutomo, a former official of the JTU, to the Diet to testify on a case of alleged bribery of local school officials in charge of textbook adoption.[9] Ishii's main topic, however, turned out to be biased textbooks, particularly social studies and history textbooks. Ishii claimed that these textbooks promoted a left-wing, anticapitalist agenda. He was soon working secretly with the DP on a series of brochures criticizing textbook narratives written by authors close to the JTU.

However, not all conservative politicians supported the right-wing campaign to revise school textbooks. For example, Education Minister Matsumura Kenzo, a respected conservative, was not in favor of the attack. However, Matsumura did not call a halt to the attack mounted by other members of his party (the DP) because, at the time, he was involved in talks over the merger of the DP and LP, the most significant political maneuver of the time. With the reunification of the progressive camp (consisting of the SP's Right and Left Factions), the demands by business and industry for a consolidation of conservative forces through a merger of the DP and LP grew stronger than ever, despite the fact that the two parties had been on bad terms. The attack on textbooks offered an opportunity for the two to be united ideologically. Finally, in November, the two merged and formed the Liberal Democratic Party (Jiyuminshuto, hereafter LDP), which would remain in power without interruption until 1993 (Kyoiku no Sengoshi Henshu Iinkai 1986).

After the merger, Hatoyama continued as the prime minister and, in 1956, his administration submitted three education bills: the first would halt the local election of school boards, allowing the MOE to appoint them; the second would establish a special council for educational reform (to change the Fundamental Law of Education); and the third would enforce stricter policies for screening and adopting textbooks. The protest against these proposed measures was immediate and strong, and it arose not only from intellectuals and educators but also from the public, in what was, to date, the biggest protest concerning education. The administration brought a police force into the Diet, and it succeeded in pushing the first measure through, although it could not save the second and third.

The System of Regulatory Control over Textbooks

After the 1956 Diet session, the LDP administration did not venture to resubmit the second and the third bills but instead took an alternative path toward achieving its goals through the use of extralegal administrative measures. In other words, the LDP strategy for controlling textbooks shifted from legislative methods to regulating the existing textbook system — and this was, in fact, in line with the approach already being taken by the bureaucrats in the MOE. By 1956, the MOE had already tightened its criteria for screening textbooks and brought more right-wingers into the Textbook Screening Council. In 1956, while increasing the number of Textbook Screening Council members (to include more right-wing members), the MOE made the Textbook Examiners full-time ministry employees.[10] In addition, in 1957, the ministry stopped sharing with authors certain key documents produced during the screening process — namely those documents listing and explaining the reasons for disapproval of a text. Instead, it gave out only informal, verbal comments (*iken*).

These changes took place as part of a broader "reverse course" in curriculum policy. In 1952, when amending the Law of Establishment of the Ministry of Education, the government made the MOE the only body with authority for developing instructional guidelines.[11] In 1955, the MOE removed the term "Tentative Plan" from the titles of its Instruction Guidelines. In 1958, a ministerial ordinance was issued, stating that the Instruction Guidelines were now official pronouncements and that they would have legal force. In the same year, the ministry published a revised set of the Instruction Guidelines, which stipulated that schools, not teachers, would be regarded as being in charge of "organizing the appropriate curriculum" by "following ... the laws and regulations" (Monbusho 1958, 1; Nagao 1989; Yokoyama 1998).

It should be noted that the most powerful means the MOE deployed to control textbooks in this period was the textbook screening process, which took place behind closed doors. In the late 1950s, the MOE rejected many textbooks for their bias and required authors to make revisions that included eliminating negative references to Japan's wartime conduct. It also implicitly pressured some textbook companies to remove or exclude certain authors from their textbook preparation projects. The Textbook Examiners not only checked textbooks for accuracy but also evaluated the level of patriotism of each text.[12] One reported example of a critical comment on a textbook by an MOE official reflected this concern for the image of the presurrender imperial state:

> Do not write bad things about Japan in [describing] the Pacific War. Even though they are facts, represent them in romantic [language]. (MOE comment quoted in Tawara 1998, 120)

The MOE rejected eight social studies textbooks in 1956 and one-third of textbook manuscripts in 1958; in the following years, more than a few publishers decided to discontinue some of their textbook series. In 1955, for example, thirty-three junior high school social studies textbook series were competing for the market, but by 1965 the number had been reduced to fourteen, and in 1969 to eight (Nagayoshi, Nakamura, and Kato 1969). The books discontinued included some that contained descriptions of the Nanjing Massacre.

The discontinuation of some texts was also due to the change in the textbook adoption system in the early 1960s. While making textbooks free to all compulsory education students (grades 1–9), the state consolidated the textbook adoption processes for those grades. In the new arrangement, county-level school boards, instead of local schools and districts, were to select the textbooks. As a result, junior high school teachers lost a significant amount of control over the adoption of textbooks, and a trend toward greater concentration of the textbook industry was set in progress, as the county-level adoption procedure tended to be disadvantageous to small publishers.[13]

Even those textbooks that survived the screening process showed the scars of their struggle to get through. For example, Atarashii Shakai (New Social Studies), a junior high school social studies textbook series published by Tokyo Shoseki, was one of the two series enjoying the bulk of market share during these years.[14] The series survived the new screening regime, but only by making major changes to the terminology used in relation to sensitive events. Among such changes was the abandonment of the term "aggression" (shinryaku) in relation to the conduct of the Japanese army during the Pacific War. The 1955 edition of *Atarashii Shakai* had used the term to describe the 1937 Japanese invasion of Northern China (Nishioka et al. 1955, 170–171); however, in the 1962 edition, the term "advance[ment]" (*shinshutsu*) was used (Nishioka et al. 1962, 291–292). Also, the description of the atomic bomb damage to Hiroshima and Nagasaki was radically reduced in the 1962 version by comparison with the 1955 version. There was, however, a new line in the 1962 edition concerning Emperor Hirohito's role in accepting the Potsdam Declaration; in the 1969 version this was further expanded to stress the emperor's exercise of "decisive judgment" (*saidan*) at this critical juncture (Nishioka et al. 1969, 294).

The Progressive Challenge in the 1970s

The late 1960s and 1970s witnessed increasingly determined and outspoken attempts by elements on the political left to challenge the right-wing dominance over education policy, especially with regard to the sensitive area of history education. Ienaga Saburo, a well-respected historian and textbook author, initiated his marathon series of lawsuits against the Japanese government — the first suit was filed in 1965 and the second in 1967. These two lawsuits brought the state textbook screening system, which had been hidden from public scrutiny, out into the open. In particular, in the first lawsuit, the MOE was ordered to submit its official file on Ienaga's textbook. Up to this point, the state had been able to dismiss criticisms from textbook authors and publishing houses regarding the undemocratic nature of the state textbook screening system as rumors. However, but now the ministry's own documents confirmed the allegations of its critics.

During the 1970s, Ienaga won some victories in the lower courts. Most importantly, in 1970, the Sugimoto decision in the Tokyo District Court awarded him a clear-cut victory over the ministry. The decision found that state textbook screening, as applied to Ienaga's textbook, violated his freedom of expression (though it fell short of declaring that the state textbook screening process in general was unconstitutional). It proclaimed the need for "truthful education" (*shinjitsu kyoiku*), holding that teachers were guaranteed academic freedom to decide their daily curriculum and that the state could only set the general standards for educational content. In other words, the decision expressly limited the power of the state to impose its official knowledge upon teachers and students. Although the state appealed the Sugimoto decision to the higher courts, the MOE was compelled to relax its criteria for textbook screening.

The timing of the Sugimoto decision coincided with a broader shift in Japanese views regarding the Asia-Pacific War. In the late 1960s and throughout the 1970s, Japanese began to recognize the suffering and damage the Asia-Pacific War had caused to Asian countries and peoples. This was due largely to a reappraisal by some Japanese of their own wartime experiences in light of the Vietnam War. The U.S. war planes and bombers flying from Okinawa to Southeast Asia, and the U.S. military presence in other Japanese cities, reminded some Japanese of their own past aggression in Asia, and media reports of Vietnamese civilian sufferings, often with vivid photos, reminded them of their own wartime sufferings (Yoshida 1995). In addition, in 1972, Japan established diplomatic relations with the People's Republic of China, and this heightened the sense among some Japanese of the need for greater critical reflection on Japan's against China.

In this context, counternarratives of the Asia-Pacific War began to emerge to challenge the official narratives promoted by the state since the early 1950s. Various grassroots oral history projects — some of which received funding from municipal governments — recorded accounts by ordinary Japanese of their wartime experiences (involving, for example, U.S. air raids on many cities, the atomic bombs dropped on Hiroshima and Nagasaki, and the Battle of Okinawa).[15] In 1971, the journalist Honda Katsuichi, having been impressed by U.S. media coverage of the Vietnam War and the atrocities committed by the U.S. forces, began to report in a similar manner on Japan's wartime wrongdoings in China (Honda 1972). Similarly, Emperor Hirohito's visit to Europe (September to October 1971), which was met in many places with resentment, triggered historian Inoue Kiyoshi's interest in conducting serious scholarly research into the emperor's active role in the conduct of the war (Inoue 1975).

The new research on the Asia-Pacific War inspired a number of textbook authors, who became more willing to include in their texts a wider range of war-related topics — including those concerning Japanese wartime atrocities — a task made easier by the softening of the MOE's textbook screening policy in the wake of Ienaga's early court successes. By the late 1970s, some textbooks containing more details about the Nanjing Massacre appeared on the market, and by the early 1980s, almost all Japanese history textbooks came to include some description of the massacre. For example, the 1974 edition of *Atarashii Shakai* contained a line stating "[The Japanese Army] captured Nanjing, and caused terrible damage to the lives of Chinese people in various places" (Ukai et al. 1978, 283). The 1978 edition of the same text expanded the line to read: "[The Japanese Army] captured Nanjing, took the lives of numerous Chinese civilians throughout China, and caused enormous damage to their daily lives (Ukai et al. 1978, 272). Moreover, the line was footnoted as follows:

> Immediately after entering the city of Nanjing, the Japanese Army killed and wounded an enormous number of Chinese people, including women, children, and soldiers who were either no longer armed or wearing civilian clothes. For its actions in this incident, [Japan] met with criticism from various foreign countries, which denounced [the incident] as the Nanjing Massacre, but ordinary Japanese were not informed of the facts [of the event]. (ibid., 272)

The Right-Wing Backlash of the Late 1970s and the Early 1980s

The late 1970s brought a right-wing backlash, however, as the battle over text-books formed part of a larger cultural and political struggle. While Japan felt the effects of the so-called Nixon shock[16] and the worldwide oil crisis, a spate of corruption scandals hit the ruling LDP. Prime Minister Tanaka Kakuei, once extremely popular as a nonelite prime minister,[17] resigned in 1974 after being criticized for raising enormous political funds through paper companies dealing in real estate. In 1976, after he was arrested for accepting a bribe from Lockheed, a U.S. aircraft company, Tanaka left the party but remained its king-maker (even while serving his jail term). The LDP lost a significant number of seats in the 1976 and 1979 elections, while Tanaka's confidants and rivals in the LDP fought over the premiership, and for a time, it looked as if the party might disintegrate. What saved the LDP was the sudden death of Prime Minister Ohira Masayoshi, Tanaka's most trusted friend, during the 1980 election cam-paign. Ironically, Ohira's death helped mobilize LDP support in urban areas (where it had generally had a hard fight). The LDP won the election by a wide margin and the factional leaders called a truce (Ishikawa 1995).

After the election, young hawks in the LDP began to argue vociferously that most of the textbooks published in the 1970s were biased and/or communist inspired, and they attempted to enact stricter legislation for controlling teaching materials for schools. The textbook issue was a populist one that appealed to a significant number of LDP activists and was thus a useful vehicle for young politicians eager to enhance their influence. A campaign was launched in the LDP's weekly newspaper, criticizing some textbooks, particularly Japanese lan-guage and social studies textbooks, on the grounds that many of the textbook authors had supported the JTU, the Communist Party, or various nongovern-mental democratic education movements.

The campaign for textbook revision also helped conservatives to form a united front. Right-wing intellectuals (including a group of scholars based at Tsukuba University), along with business groups (such as Keidanren [in full the Keizai Dantai Rengo-kai], or the Federation of Economic Organizations), all joined the campaign and lobbied the MOE for textbook revision. Soon the Science and Technology Agency, an organization within the prime minister's office, lent its support by requesting that negative descriptions of atomic power plants be removed from the new junior high school civics textbooks. The descriptions had in fact already been approved, so the MOE could not affect such a change (doing so would have violated its own regulations). How-ever, the agency gained backing from an unusual quarter, as the Minshato, an opposition party supported by small-business owners, joined the calls for text-book revision. Eventually the MOE succeeded in getting the publishers to change the descriptions by means of informal pressure (Shakaika Kyokasho Shippitsusha Kondankai [hereafter SKSK] 1984).

While keeping some distance from the highly charged political attacks on textbooks, from the late 1970s, the MOE proceeded to steadily tighten its control over school curriculum and textbooks. This is evident in its revised Instructional Guidelines of 1977 and 1978.[18] While using catch phrases such as *yutori* education (reduction of curriculum content), the ministry strengthened nationalist orientations in some subject areas, including the curriculum for social studies. The guidelines stressed moral education through extracurricular activities and strongly suggested that the Hinomaru flag be hoisted and the Kimigayo anthem be sung at school events.[19]

The MOE was also using the textbook screening process to reassert official authority over narratives of the national past. In 1977, the ministry rejected five high school textbooks (one on ethics, two on Japanese history, and two on world history). At about the same time, it changed its regulations to require textbooks to follow the Instruction Guidelines more closely and raised the bar for textbook approval. For example, in the 1980–1981 textbook screening, it ordered Ienaga Saburo to change various passages in his textbook, including descriptions of the Nanjing Massacre.[20] The censorship of history texts did not receive a great deal of mass media attention at the time, however, because the media was more interested in textbooks for a new high school subject called contemporary society (*Gendai Shakai*). In the Contemporary Society textbooks, the MOE was accused of conducting excessive censorship of the descriptions of the 1946 (Peace) Constitution, the Self-Defense Forces (Jieitai, hereafter SDF), the Northern Territories problem with the USSR, and issues of human rights and industrial pollution (Mainichi Shinbunsha Kyoiku Shuzaihan 1981). Widely reported in the summer of 1981, this censorship aroused public dismay and prompted heightened media vigilance concerning the outcome of the 1981–1982 textbook screening (see Nozaki and Inokuchi 2000).

The 1982 History Textbook Controversy

In the summer of 1982, when the MOE announced the 1981–1982 textbook screening results, leading articles in the major newspapers declared that state control over education had been strengthened and that the descriptions of Japanese wartime atrocities in Asian countries and Okinawa had been watered down. While some of the sensational reporting was not entirely accurate (the uproar seems to have been a response partly to the cumulative tightening of official control over previous years and partly to particular instances of censorship during the 1981–1982 textbook screening round),[21] the grounds for concern were real, and strong domestic and international protests followed.

As soon as the stories were reported abroad, they were greeted by widespread international censure of Japanese revisionism, especially in East and Southeast Asia. In July, both the Republic of Korea (South Korea) and the People's Republic of China lodged official protests with the Japanese government, and some labor unions and social action groups in Hong Kong sent a letter of complaint to the Japanese Consulate there (as noted in chapter 5, anti-Japanese Chinese nationalism has long played a particularly significant role in Hong Kong's identity politics). The official party newspaper of the Democratic Republic of Korea (North Korea) criticized the Japanese government over this issue, and the Vietnamese government asked the Japanese ambassador for corrections concerning textbook accounts relating to that country (Tokutake 1995).

Protests from Okinawa also flared up instantly (though media attention was directed for the most part to the international protests). In July, two major Okinawan newspapers ran a series of articles criticizing the MOE's censorship of some accounts of the Battle of Okinawa (principally passages describing the killing of Okinawan civilians by Japanese troops through forced group suicides as American troops were advancing across the island), and Okinawan citizens initiated movements demanding the restoration of the original descriptions. In September, the Okinawan Assembly held an extraordinary session and unanimously adopted "A Letter of Opinion Concerning Textbook Screening" and sent it to the MOE. Stating that the murder of Okinawans by Japanese military forces was "an undeniable fact as clear as day," the letter demanded that "the restoration of the description be achieved in short order" (Eguchi 1987, 232–233). These international and domestic developments clearly indicated that in both arenas the political context surrounding the history textbook controversy had changed and that the right-wing nationalists had apparently underestimated the extent of this change.

The Japanese government was especially anxious to limit the diplomatic damage caused by this issue. In August 1982, while the protests were still growing, Chief Cabinet Secretary Miyazawa Kiichi (of the Suzuki administration) stated that the Japanese government would consider fully the criticisms of its Asian neighbors in order to promote friendship with them and then referred to "making a correction on government responsibility" ("Seifu Kenkai" Aug. 27, 1982).[22] The Miyazawa statement was not clear about what specific measures the government would take, but the South Korean government essentially accepted the proposal. The Chinese government initially insisted that it was insufficient as a guarantee against future revisionism in textbook screening but eventually agreed to trust the Japanese government.

Divisions within the Government and the Improvement of Textbooks

The government nevertheless still faced problems in resolving the textbook crisis. First, it did not (and still does not) possess the power to actually dictate what textbook authors should or should not include in their textbooks. Of course, the MOE had to a large extent done so in practice — but it had done so behind closed doors. Technically, it was authors alone, not the government, who could correct textbooks. Secondly, MOE officials disagreed with Miyazawa. Before giving his statement, Miyazawa called a senior MOE official to question him about the legal basis of the official textbook screening process. He wanted the MOE to immediately begin another round of screening of the same text-books in order to make corrections (in other words, to allow the authors to restore the original phrases), because there was no law preventing it. The official was unable to give a convincing answer, primarily because most of the text-book screening procedures were governed by ministerial regulations, rather than by actual statutory requirements. The official insisted, however, that to give in to foreign pressure and allow an immediate correction by authors would result in the collapse of the textbook screening system. The LDP hawks backed the MOE's position ("Kyokasho Mondai" October 6, 1982).

Predictably, the MOE was unwilling to admit that it had done anything wrong in regard to textbook screening. In the autumn, publishers and authors applied for a correction procedure to restore descriptions they had been com-pelled to modify during the 1980–1981 and 1981–1982 textbook screening rounds. If allowed, the procedure would have corrected textbooks more quickly than another round of screening. However, the MOE refused to accept the applications, stating that the procedure was for "correction of errors," not for "restoration of passages previously dropped." A senior official even criticized the Miyazawa statement as obscure because it "lack[ed] both grammatical subject and object" (SKSK 1984, 375).

From late October to November, however, the MOE issued official announce-ments concerning its new screening arrangements. It added a new clause (the so-called Neighboring Countries Clause) to the textbook screening criteria, requiring textbooks to give "necessary consideration, in the interests of interna-tional friendship and cooperation," to the modern and contemporary history of relations between Japan and its Asian neighbors. The MOE also noted that it would not ask authors to replace the term "aggression" with "advance" or to add phrasing suggesting that the Nanjing Massacre occurred as the result of a moment of chaos (issues that had aroused particular outrage in China). With respect to authors' references to the number of victims of the Nanjing Massacre, the MOE announced that it would only ask authors to provide citations.

At this juncture, in view of the MOE's moves to effect a compromise, the government unilaterally declared the textbook controversy settled. The Educa-tion Minister held a press conference to "[officially] close the textbook contro-versy" and expressed his desire that schools and teachers should cultivate a spirit of international understanding and cooperation among students until the spring of 1985, when new textbooks would become available. However, his statement did not refer to the ministry's own responsibility in this regard, indicating that the MOE basically would not take an active or leading role ("Rekishi Kyokasho" Nov. 24, 1982).[23] The settlement left the bureaucratic structure of the MOE and its right-wing nationalist orientation untouched. It was, therefore, superficial at best and did not eliminate the cause of the prob-lems for the future.

Nevertheless, the textbook screening policy change did have an impact on history textbooks — however reluctant the MOE was about enforcing it. In particular, the Neighboring Countries Clause gave textbook authors a basis upon which they were able to write about Japanese war atrocities from the victims' perspectives. For example, descriptions of the Nanjing Massacre in textbooks continued to become more commonplace, more detailed, and more explicit. Textbooks referring to the number of Nanjing Massacre victims as exceeding two hundred thousand (the number of victims is one of the most controversial issues relating to the massacre [see Fogel 2000]) passed the textbook screening. All of the 1984 editions of junior high history textbooks, all 1985 editions of high school Japanese history textbooks, and six out of seven of the 1986 editions of elementary school social studies textbooks included some description of the Nanjing Massacre (Tawara 1998).[24]

Some of the textbooks also expanded their descriptions of Japanese tyranny in the occupied territories in Asia. For example, the 1984 edition of one junior-high history textbook included the following passage:

> In [the parts of] Southeast Asia that Japan occupied, independent governments were established, but Japan held the reins. In the occupied territories, ordinary people's lives became very hard, as materials and rice that were needed for the pursuit of war were collected by force. On top of that, the Japanese military ruled highhandedly, taking the lives of more than 6,000 resident Chinese in occupied Singapore and severely punishing people who opposed its policies in the Philippines and other regions. As a result of this kind of occupation policy, resistance to Japan spread to various regions. (The 1984 edition of *Chugakko Shakaika Rekishi Bunya,* cited in Tokutake 1995, 207)

Some textbooks also came to include — though not entirely without restriction — descriptions of the massacre of Okinawans by Japanese forces. For example, the 1985 edition of Ienaga's text added a reference to this event, though he had to change his original phrasing in order to pass the screening (Ienaga 1991). In another example, one of the 1987 junior-high school texts stated:

> In April [1945] U.S. forces landed on Okinawa, intense battles unfolded … and Okinawa residents were dragged into the conflict. In that situation, some lost their lives because of the forced group suicides and massacres of residents [by the Japanese forces]. In June, after more than 120,000 of [the total population of] 570,000 Okinawans had become the victims [of the war], Okinawa was conquered [by U.S. forces]. (Kodama et al. 1987, 267)

The late 1980s and early 1990s saw continuing improvement in the content of Japanese history textbooks.[25] This did not mean that the MOE halted its censorship or abandoned its nationalist bias. For example, it strongly pressed local schools to implement nationalistic policies, including the hoisting of the Hinomaru flag and the singing of the Kimigayo anthem at school ceremonies. The improvements to textbooks were possible because a number of textbook authors made efforts to incorporate the viewpoints of Asian and Okinawan war victims, even though the MOE was not actively supportive of this.

A Continuation of the Right-Wing Nationalist Educational Policy

Meanwhile, the MOE's efforts to censor descriptions of Japan's aggression and war crimes continued, but in ways that did not obviously break bureaucratic regulations (including the new arrangements announced in the autumn of 1982). For example, while allowing the use of the term "aggression," officials continued to suggest to authors and publishers that they refer to smaller numbers of victims for the massacres that took place in Nanjing, Singapore, and Okinawa during the war (SKSK 1984).[26]

Moreover, Prime Minister Nakasone Yasuhiro, who took office in November 1982, was strongly in favour of a right-wing nationalist reform of education aimed at the "reconstruction of a Japanese identity." He called for neoconservatism and expressed open admiration for Ronald Reagan and Margaret Thatcher. Having found that use of militant rhetoric, or suggestions that he favored reforms to the Peace Constitution, harmed his popularity, he turned his attention more to softer issues such as educational reform.

Nakasone created the Ad Hoc Council on Education (Rinji Kyoiku Shingikai) and handpicked its members. The council's role was to recommend new policies, shape public opinion, and bring about rapid change in the school system, while bypassing the bureaucracy and the Diet politicians (Hood 2001). He also challenged the bureaucratic structure of the MOE, and some MOE officials did not welcome his top-down approach to reform. However, in terms of textbook policy, there was no essential disagreement between Nakasone and the MOE because he had campaigned for nationalist textbooks and tight state control of education since the 1950s.[27]

During the 1980s, the right-wing nationalists also expanded their activities. In their view, the revisions to history textbooks since the 1970s represented a change for the worse. First, they attacked the media as having falsely reported the MOE's order to change the term "aggression" to "advance" in lines referring to the Japanese invasion of northern China in the 1981–1982 round of textbook screening. It was true that no such exact orders were made in that round (because the term had been altered previously), but similar changes in terminology in sections referring to the Japanese invasion of Southeast Asia and southern China were indeed the result of direct and indirect pressure from the ministry (Kimijima 1996, Tawara 1997). Despite the general accuracy of media portrayals of MOE policies, the nationalists attempted to use this minor inaccuracy to discredit all the media reports concerning this issue. (Since the 1970s, right-wing nationalists have often used similar tactics to discredit their opponents and confuse the public).

There was also nationalist criticism of the government's management of the international dimension of the controversy. In their view, it was for each nation to decide the content of its own school curriculum, and it was diplomatically humiliating for Japan to have to apologize for its textbooks to countries such as China and South Korea. In the fall of 1982, one of the major right-wing organizations, the National Conference to Defend Japan (Nihon o Mamoru Kokumin Kaigi, established in 1981), therefore announced that it would develop its own Japanese history textbook for high schools. This organization had as its main goal the revision of Japan's 1946 Peace Constitution, which pledged Japan to a pacifist role in international affairs and forbade her to maintain her own armed forces. The organization's chair was a former Japanese ambassador to the United Nations and a member of Nakasone's informal brain trust. (Its membership to date has consisted of some affiliated religious organizations, business leaders such as the former CEOs of Sony and Sankei Shinbunsha [publisher of the right-wing daily newspaper Sankei Shinbun], and several prominent right-wing scholars.)

A Nationalist History Textbook in 1987

The right-wing textbook project began in the spring of 1984, with Hara Shobo selected as the publisher, and a draft was submitted to the MOE in the summer of 1985. However, it was not easy even for the MOE to pass the text. To begin with, it contained numerous factual errors as well as misprints, in part because the authors had rushed to complete it in time for the 1985 celebration of Emperor Hirohito's sixtieth year on the throne. It also clearly challenged the spirit of the 1946 Peace Constitution. Although the MOE's Textbook Screening Council approved the text conditionally in January 1986, it had to convene an extra session in May, because some members of the council felt the revised manuscript was still "distasteful," "biased," and "lacking in consideration for neighboring countries." Nonetheless, the council passed it, essentially because of political pressure (Prime Minister Nakasone was in favor of the text, though he did not back it publicly). At this point, it thus became clear that *Shinpen Nihonshi*, the first nationalist school textbook in postwar Japan, would be published in 1987 (Nagano 1998, "'Shinpen Nihonshi'" 1987).

There followed an extraordinary bureaucratic muddle that, according to some observers, consisted of "measures beyond laws and rules." Soon after approval of the text, the MOE requested further revisions (an extensive revision after approval had no precedent). Some speculated that the MOE was attempting to avoid media criticism over careless mistakes the text still contained, or that it needed to appease some Textbook Screening Council members. However, soon the South Korean media and the Chinese government voiced criticism of the new book, and the MOE decided to request another revision (for example recommending the use of the term "massacre" instead of "incident" to refer to the Nanjing Massacre). One of the MOE's senior officials, knowing it was against the ministry's own regulations, even asked the publisher to backdate the request so that it would appear to have been received before the approval of the text ("'Shinpen Nihonshi'" 1987).

Eventually, because diplomatic tensions did not abate, some cabinet members asked the MOE to withdraw its approval of the text, but the MOE (under Education Minister Kaifu Toshiki) rejected this, choosing instead to request a third revision at the end of June, this time with the informal involvement of the Ministry of Foreign Affairs. Nevertheless, a fourth revision was requested before the MOE went to a press conference at which the results of the textbook screening were announced. Officials maintained that in order to ensure the quality of textbooks, it was within the Education Minister's authority and responsibility to take extraordinary measures ("'Shinpen Nihonshi Naze'" 1987).

The text's authors (and their right-wing supporters) publicly criticized the government for ignoring its own laws and regulations, but they had achieved their primary goal. Progressives felt that the extraordinary measures would create a bad precedent and that the MOE should not have approved the textbook in the first place. Partly in order to address these criticisms, the Ad Hoc Council on Education deliberated on the textbook screening system and decided to enable the Education Minister to order revisions even after the formal approval of a textbook (the change was announced in 1988 and effected in 1990). In other words, the government changed its rules ex post facto (Kimijima 1996).

However, *Shinpen Nihonshi* did not sell well, in part because textbooks at high-school level were (and still are, as of 2004) adopted by each school. (Eventually, in 1993, Hara Shobo discontinued publication, and another publisher, Kokusho Kankokai, issued the book under the new title *Saishin Nihonshi*. However, the new publisher also ceased publication shortly afterwards, and yet another company, Meiseisha, took over the publication rights. The MOE approved its new edition in 2002.)

The Emergence of the Comfort Women Issue in the Early 1990s

The late 1980s saw no end to the struggle over history textbooks, and an event took place at the beginning of the 1990s that entirely recast the whole controversy — the eruption of the "comfort women" issue.[28] To many Japanese the existence of wartime military prostitution facilities and comfort women was no secret. A number of wartime reports, diaries, and memoirs published in Japan during and after the Asia-Pacific War referred to the existence of so-called comfort facilities. For example, in his memoirs, Prime Minister Nakasone himself mentioned his involvement in building comfort facilities on the island of Borneo when he was a young naval officer. In the 1970s and 1980s, in both Japan and South Korea, several publications appeared that took somewhat critical views of the issue, but in both countries, former comfort women remained silent — or ignored — and the issue was generally seen as marginal (Nozaki 2001).

The late 1980s and early 1990s witnessed a number of cultural and political changes, both within and outside Japan: Emperor Hirohito died in January 1989, signaling the possibility of a shift in Japan's cultural politics; South Korea became more democratic; the Berlin Wall collapsed; the Gulf War broke out (raising question marks over the future of Japan's Peace Constitution); and the Soviet Union collapsed. These developments heralded the end of the Cold War dispensation in East Asia, which had effectively kept the lid on discussions between Japan and its Asian neighbors of sensitive and potentially divisive issues relating to its wartime record. Meanwhile the emergence of women's movements in Korea, Japan, and other countries in the region gave added impetus to demands that the Japanese government should acknowledge and compensate the surviving comfort women (Nozaki 2001).

Japan now entered an era in which its policy concerning teaching about the Asia-Pacific War became a major focus of international as well as domestic debate.[29] The comfort women issue underlined the need for Japan to develop new policies both with respect to its relations with its Asian neighbors and to the education of its own youth. However, Japan was at the same time also experiencing an increasingly unstable political situation, along with growing economic uncertainty. In November 1987, Takeshita Noboru succeeded Nakasone as prime minister. The new administration was short-lived, with Takeshita resigning in January 1989 because of a corruption scandal, and for various similar reasons, none of his LDP successors managed more than a brief tenure in office (Ishikawa 1995). The LDP, in apparent decline, was reluctant and unable to form a clear, firm, and consistent line on the comfort women issue — or for that matter on any other unresolved issues relating to the war — because it could not afford to lose the support of right-wing nationalists inside and outside the Diet.

When the issue of comfort women first surfaced in the Japanese Diet in 1990, the Japanese government (under Prime Minister Kaifu) flatly denied a request for an investigation, maintaining that the wartime state and its military had had no involvement in this matter. However, in 1991, the first former Korean comfort woman came out in public, followed by others in various Asian countries, and they spoke openly of their terrible experiences. At the same time, research by Japanese historians such as Yoshimi Yoshiaki showed that the military had in fact been intimately involved in the running of comfort facilities during the war.

In 1993, the Japanese government (under Prime Minister Miyazawa) heard the testimonies of fifteen former comfort women in Seoul, and on August 4, Chief Cabinet Secretary Kono Yohei stated that the Imperial Japanese Forces were directly and indirectly involved in the establishment and administration of comfort facilities. Although the Kono statement remained somewhat

292 • History Education and National Identity in East Asia

ambiguous — perhaps deliberately — on several key points such as legal responsibility and compensation, it expressed "a firm determination" to remember the historical facts "through historical research and education" ("Jugun ianfu chosakekka" Aug. 5, 1993).[30]

These developments, particularly the Kono statement, gave textbook authors the justification they needed for including the topic in their textbooks. In all, twenty-two high school Japanese history textbooks referring to comfort women passed the MOE's 1992–1993 and 1993–1994 textbook screenings (in fact, the only textbook containing no reference was the right-wing nationalist textbook discussed above). In addition, all seven of the junior high social studies history textbooks that included it passed the 1995–1996 screening. By 1997, many textbooks in other social studies–related areas (such as geography, world history, and contemporary society) also included the topic. A paragraph in the 1997 edition of one junior high textbook of the period read as follows:

> In colonized Taiwan and Korea, the compulsory draft was implemented. There were also women who were forced to accompany the military to the front as comfort women. Because the labor force inside the country [Japan] was limited, approximately 700,000 people from Korea and 40,000 from China were taken by force and made to work in places such as coalmines (Ohama et al. 1997, 252).

However, this was only the beginning of the struggle over the depiction of comfort women in textbooks, since in the mid-1990s, right-wing nationalists launched a fierce revisionist campaign. They were able to exploit the uncertainty of Japanese politics during this period, taking the opportunity to consolidate their influence upon the LDP, Diet members, and public discourse more generally.

The Fluctuations of Japanese Politics and the Neo-Nationalist Movement

The year in which the Kono statement was made, 1993, also marked the end of almost 40 years of LDP single-party rule. In July, the LDP lost the election because of a split in which some factions and influential politicians broke away and established new parties. On August 6, only a few days after the Kono statement, a seven-party coalition government was formed under an anti-LDP banner. Upon taking office, Hosokawa Morihiro of the Japan New Party, the new Prime Minister, made several remarks on key aspects of Japan's wartime conduct. He said of the Asia-Pacific War: "I personally recognize it as a *shinryaku senso* (war of aggression), an *ayamatta senso* (wrong war)" ("Hosokawa Shusho" Aug. 11, 1993). In a subsequent speech, he called the colonization of Korea "colonial rule" instead of using the conventional euphemism "annexation" ("Shusho no Shoshin" Aug. 23, 1993). These were the first such clear-cut admissions by a postwar Japanese prime minister.

Hosokawa's statements were regarded as threatening by the right. In the autumn, a group of right-wing LDP politicians established the LDP Committee for the Examination of History. Approximately one hundred LDP Diet members joined, including the future prime ministers Hashimoto Ryutaro and Mori Yoshiro. They agreed to launch a campaign promoting views of history that held the Asia-Pacific War to be justifiable and denied the existence of the Nanjing Massacre and comfort women.[31]

Although Hosokawa was popular with the electorate, he resigned in April 1994 after being accused of corruption and was succeeded by Hata Tsutomu (of the Shinseito, a new party established by former LDP members). The political scene became increasingly tumultuous and uncertain, and right-wing politicians became ever more vocal. For example, in May 1994, Justice Minister Nagano Shigeto denied the factuality of the Nanjing Massacre and the validity of the use of the term "aggression" to describe Japan's wartime behavior. The Hata administration fired him almost immediately, only to collapse itself soon afterwards, when the Japan Socialist Party (JSP) left the coalition.

In June, the LDP returned to power by forming a three-party coalition government with the JSP and the Sakigake (another small new party). The new coalition was a compromise for both the JSP and the LDP, with both moving toward the center ground. Murayama Tomiichi of the JSP became prime minister, but real power lay with the LDP (with Kono as its party president). While Murayama soon announced the JSP's abandonment of many of its long-held leftist positions on major postwar political issues (e.g., its opposition to the U.S.-Japan Security Treaty, to the SDF, and to the Hinomaru flag and the Kimigayo anthem), the LDP agreed to issue a Diet resolution apologizing to Asian victims of Japan's past aggression — a general apology, not one specifically directed at the comfort women (Wada et al. 1996).

However, the right wing of the LDP, including some cabinet members, openly dissented from this move. In the following months of 1994 and 1995, several cabinet members and influential politicians made remarks denying Japan's wartime aggression. Some were dismissed, while others apologized in order to keep their posts. Also during these months, the right-wing politicians of the LDP (along with some opposition party members such as Nagano) worked hard to block the resolution of apology that was to be issued on the fiftieth anniversary of Japan's 1945 surrender. They strongly opposed the inclusion of key terms such as "Japan's war of aggression" and "Japan's colonial rule of Korea." The LDP leadership was not really able to control them but nonetheless decided to allow the terms to be included in somewhat indirect ways. The House of Representatives passed the resolution in June 1995, to the anger of the LDP right-wingers, and the LDP leadership then decided not to lay the resolution before the House of Councilors. This situation left both the left and the right extremely dissatisfied (Wada et al. 1996, Benfell 2002).

After this episode, right-wing politicians and organizations began increasingly to focus their attacks on history textbooks. In January 1996, Murayama resigned, and Hashimoto of the LDP became the prime minister, with the JSP remaining in the coalition but no longer holding any cabinet positions. The LDP thus returned to power in both name and reality, and the history textbook issue was one of the few issues that united a majority of LDP Diet members, who held differing views on other policy areas ranging from structural reform to gender equality. The textbook issue was also an avenue through which LDP hawks could work with hawks of other parties. Subsequently, right-wing elements repeatedly demanded the removal of textbook references to comfort women which, under its regulations and rules, the MOE could not do (see Nozaki 2001).

In the public arena, new faces joined the nationalist cause and energized its activities by attracting media interest. One such face was Fujioka Nobukatsu, an education professor at the University of Tokyo. He had originally been a leftist scholar; however, after taking a year's study leave in the United States around the time of the Gulf War, he converted to the right, and in early 1995, he started a group called the Liberal-View-of-History Study Group (*Jiyushugi Shikan Kenkyukai*).

Fujioka published many articles in journals for teachers, such as *Shakaika Kyoiku* (*Social Studies Education*) and *Gendai Kyoiku Kagaku* (*Contemporary Education Science*), as well as in the right-wing media, including *Sankei Shinbun*, criticizing history education in postwar Japan and current history textbooks as "masochistic" (*jigyakuteki*) and lacking "pride in the history of our nation" (see, for example, McCormack 2000). He also argued for a pedagogy called the "debate" approach, in which students would be encouraged to debate by taking opposing positions on controversial issues such as the Nanjing Massacre. In late 1996, he and others established the Japanese Society for History Textbook Reform (Atarashii Rekishi Kyokasho o Tsukurukai, hereafter the JSHTR), declaring that they would publish "a new history textbook" to be used in junior high schools in 2002. Later, Fusosha (a subsidiary company of Sankei Shinbunsha) was chosen to be the publisher.

Textbook Policy and Moves toward "Guided Self-Censorship"
In June 1998, Education Minister Machimura Nobutaka (of the Hashimoto administration), responding to a question raised by Diet member Nagano Shigeto (the justice minister fired in 1994) in a special committee session in the House of Councilors, stated that history textbooks "lacked balance" and that the MOE was deliberating over ways to improve the situation. In particular, Machimura referred to three possible means of improvement: first, through textbook screening; second, by "ensuring a good balance … at the stage of authoring" (i.e., before the submission of textbook drafts to the MOE); and third, through improvements at the stage of textbook adoption (Tawara 2000).

The MOE's censorship role in the textbook screening process was nothing new, but Machimura's response was novel in making explicit reference to the textbook authoring and adoption stages and in his implication that the MOE would seek ways to intervene at those stages.

In January 1999, the MOE asked publishers to make their textbook content more "balanced" and to reconsider their choice of authors. In the summer, although a few publishers made minor textbook corrections and replaced some authors in charge of writing sections that included the issue of comfort women, overall it appeared that they did not intend significantly to alter sections dealing with Japanese wartime atrocities. The contents of the earlier drafts of the textbook editions being prepared for publication in 2002 were little changed from previous editions. However, when the final drafts of the same books were actually submitted to the MOE in the spring of 2000, many descriptions concerning Japanese wartime atrocities had been cut back or removed altogether, the publishers having exercised self-censorship of the texts (Tawara 2000, 37).

The most striking development was the almost total erasure from textbooks of the comfort women issue. In the previous 1997 editions, all seven junior high history textbooks on the market had made some reference to this issue. In the new drafts for 2002, three of the seven textbooks removed all such references. Another draft textbook included only the sentence "many Korean and other women were sent to the front," whereas the previous edition had referred to the issue in three different sections and included a photo. Two other texts referred to it only briefly, using the term "comfort facilities." Only one text used the term "comfort women," and this was the only one that expanded its discussion as compared with the previous edition.

While the treatment of the comfort women issue best illustrates the degree of self-censorship exercised by the publishers, the new textbook drafts also altered or cut descriptions of other Japanese wartime atrocities. For example, in the 2002 editions, only one text referred to the Three-Alls Strategy (*Sanko Sakusen*, the Japanese wartime military strategy "kill all, burn all, and loot all"), whereas in the old editions five out of seven textbooks had referred to it. Other examples of self-censorship included the removal of the term "aggression"; the omission of any mention of Unit 731 (a biological warfare unit that conducted a series of experiments upon live civilians and POWs in Northern Manchuria [Harris 1994]) by all of the 2002 editions, after one 1997 edition textbook had referred to it; and fewer references to resistance to Japanese rule in Korea and other Asian countries.

Publishers did not disclose what had happened between the summer of 1999 and spring of 2000 to cause them to make these changes. Some Japanese experts such as Yoshifumi Tawara alleged, however, that high government officials had applied political pressure. According to Tawara (2000), in December 1999, as the deadline for the submission of textbook drafts neared, CEOs of the publishing houses received telephone calls from "a source in the Prime Minister's office" asking them to "use discretion" in dealing with the textbook reference to war comfort women (*jugun ianfu*)."[32]

Tawara (2001) speculated that Machimura (the education minister who spoke of "three ways to improve textbooks" in 1998) might have been involved because at that time he was working in the prime minister's office to develop an agenda for educational reform. Another theory was that publishers were extremely nervous about a potential loss of market share because of right-wing attacks on their textbooks as masochistic. The truth has not yet emerged (and perhaps never will, given the general reluctance in Japanese business circles to openly criticize the government). From the very beginning of the MOE's textbook screening process, however, it was clear that the 2002 edition of history textbooks would include fewer discussions of Japanese war atrocities. This was, of course, very much what the MOE desired, because it would forestall the sorts of diplomatic problems that tended to arise as a result of direct censorship. Indeed, this seems to be what Machimura had been proposing in his pronouncement a few years previously, indicating that what occurred subsequently might more accurately be described not simply as self-censorship but as "guided self-censorship." (This phenomenon is found in other Asian contexts that combine an authoritarian political culture with a relatively free press. As noted in chapter 5, publishers in Hong Kong also tend to second-guess the wishes of the local and national governments, thereby ensuring approval of their books, sparing themselves from criticism in the nationalist press, and sparing the government from the greater criticism that would arise if it engaged in cruder forms of censorship.)

The *New History Textbook*

While self-censorship was leading to a watering-down of accounts in mainstream textbooks of Japan's wartime atrocities, a draft history textbook authored by members of the right-wing JSHTR was also submitted for screening in April 2000.[33] Soon after the submission, Nishio Kanji, the lead author, appeared on a TV program to promote it. The publisher, Fusosha, also distributed promotional leaflets, and sometimes photocopies of the text, to schools and teachers, while the authors undertook a series of lectures and study meetings to inform politicians and local community leaders about the text. As the content of the new book became public knowledge, more and more people, including many historians and history teachers, began to express their dismay and concern at both the chauvinism and basic inaccuracy of the text. In addition, there were protests and criticism from South Korea, China, and other Asian countries (Uesugi 2001b).

However, right-wing forces within Japan were determined not to give way. In the autumn of 2000, when a member of the Textbook Screening Council (Noda Eijiro, a former ambassador to India) raised a serious question about the text and began to discuss rejecting it with other members (something that he was within his rights to do in his role as a council member), right-wing newspapers such as *Sankei Shinbun* reported that he was "engineering" disapproval of the text. The LDP's hawks demanded that the MOE remove him from his position and, after some hesitation, he was eventually transferred to another section. Similarly, when the LDP Secretary General Nonaka Hiromu, responded to Chinese protests by implying that the government would correct the text through the screening process, young LDP hawks and JSHTR members made him retract his statement, indicating the strength of nationalist influence within the LDP (Tawara 2000).

In the spring of 2001, after the authors of the text had made 137 corrections, the newly formed Ministry of Education and Science (hereafter MOES)[34] approved the text and declared that it would request no further revisions.[35] The South Korean and Chinese governments requested a further revision, but the MOES refused (even though technically it could still advise revisions because of the changes to textbook screening procedures introduced in 1990). Instead, it was argued that the local education boards, rather than the MOES itself, would be responsible for textbook adoption. The MOES's neutrality here was questionable at best, since its statement meant that the education boards could disregard teachers' opinions about the textbooks (teachers had tended to prefer progressive textbooks). In fact, right-wing forces had been working steadily to exclude teachers from the textbook adoption processes, with some local education boards having already changed their adoption procedures to lessen teacher influence.

The situation was hardly auspicious for those opposing the adoption of the *New History Textbook*. Concerned citizens and lobby groups, exchanging information through the Internet, organized study meetings and initiated local petitions. Many appeals — some reported by the media and others posted on web sites — were issued by different groups and individuals, including the novelist and Nobel laureate Oe Kenzaburo and renowned historians inside and outside Japan. Labor unions, including the JTU, made common cause, despite the fact that they had disagreements over other matters. International pressure was also stepped up, most notably with a petition signed by four hundred thousand South Koreans opposing the adoption of the text. In mid-July and August, as the deadline neared for the education boards to make their final decisions, grassroots progressives redoubled their efforts. Even so, it seemed as if the progressives were fighting an uphill battle.[36]

Among the public schools, the textbook adoption council of Shimotsuga District, a consolidated district of two cities and eight towns located in Shimotsuga County, Tochigi Prefecture, was the first body to decide to adopt the new right-wing text. Although each city or town in Shimotsuga had its own local education board, decisions on textbook adoptions were to be made at the level of the (consolidated) Shimotsuga District. However, shortly after the media reported the decision to adopt the *New History Textbook*, the council began to receive strong criticism from both inside and outside the region. For example, the mayor of a local town wrote to a newspaper:

> What I witnessed there on the Chinese front where I [fought during the war] was nothing but aggression. Who made the rule that imposes a textbook which is so internationally problematic … on towns and cities by a majority decision, and when? … The education board members of our town will not agree to vote [for it] since they understand well enough the will of the people in our town. I urge the [textbook adoption] council of the Shimotsuga District to reflect [on this matter] seriously. (Published in *Asahi Shinbun*, cited in Fujii 2001, 45)

In another case, a group of homemakers collected more than 1,500 signatures against the text within 5 days. By the end of July, all the education boards in Shimotsuga had reversed the decision. In a sense, therefore, the MOES's designation of local education boards as responsible for textbook adoption (which was also the position of JSHTR in the debate over textbook adoption) could be said to have backfired (Uesugi 2001a).

The events in Shimotsuga marked a turning point. The local education boards reported to have been in favor of the text did not win enough votes to adopt it after all. The only exceptions were the Tokyo Metropolitan Education Board, which selected the text for a few schools and classes for mentally and physically handicapped children, and the Ehime Prefectural Education Board, which chose it for its schools for handicapped and deaf children. In both cases, the board members were appointees owing their positions to governors strongly supportive of the text. Because several private schools adopted the text, the market share of the *New History Textbook* was approximately 0.04 percent (amounting to a total of 520 to 570 copies sold) in the spring of 2002. Thus local, national, and international pressure appeared to have prevented the text from acquiring a wider circulation.[37]

Concluding Thoughts

The Japanese history textbook controversy has been one front in a persistent cultural and political struggle at home, a struggle set in the wider context of Japan's postwar international relations. The controversy has been a symbolic battle with implications for the real world, as it has also been a war by proxy, the target of struggle being not merely textbooks per se but the founding principles of postwar pacifist Japan as embodied in documents such as the 1946 (Peace) Constitution. History lessons "[instruct] people how to think and act as national subjects and how to view relations with outsiders" (Hein and Selden 2001, 4). In the final analysis, therefore, the history textbook controversy can be seen as part of a larger struggle over Japan's national identity and security policy fought by progressives and right-wing nationalists, with the latter playing a leading role within the dominant power bloc, and thereby enjoying significant influence over state policy (Nozaki and Inokuchi 2000, Midford 2002).

However, it is critically important to note that the political struggles at home have also strongly influenced (and been influenced by) the history textbook controversy. Not only has there been a constant struggle between the progressive and nationalist camps, but in addition, the elements of the dominant bloc — different factions of the LDP, other political parties, and bureaucracies such as the MOE — have seldom been entirely in concert. In particular, the LDP has always been riven by factional conflicts, having originated in the 1950s in the merger of two rival conservative parties. Since the late 1970s, the LDP has been beset by internal power struggles, and since the early 1990s, it has been unable to maintain its single-party rule. In this context, the attacks on textbooks, particularly history textbooks, have served as a focal point around which to unite the various LDP factions and through which its young politicians have sought to gain more influence. Textbook campaigns have also served as a tool with which the LDP could forge alliances with right-wing elements of other parties. Right-wing nationalism, in other words, has served the LDP well as a kind of ideological glue.

The Japanese textbook controversy offers an empirical insight into the nature of the modern (governmental) state and its ways of wielding power. Michel Foucault states that "it is not through law that the aims of government are to be reached" but by "multiform tactic[al]" devices that are in essence regulatory and nonlegal in character (Foucault 1991, 95–96). The MOE (which became the MOES in 2001) has built up its control over textbooks and schools by developing and accumulating ministerial regulations, rules, and customs over several decades. In other words, it has gradually developed "the complex and multiple practices of a 'governmentality which presupposes ... rational forms, technical procedures, [and] instrumentations through which to operate'" (Foucault 1984, 338).

It should be noted here, however, that the MOE has developed these practices by maintaining close ties with right-wing nationalists. In this case, the power of the state, which is administrative in essence, has been linked to the existing power of right-wing nationalism over the nation. Although the MOE(S) has claimed that its regulations and procedures are neutral and that they are applied to everyone evenhandedly, the present study shows that it has clearly exercised discretion with regard to how those regulations are applied. It has often helped nationalists achieve their major goals by bending regulations (and in some cases by introducing a new regulation to justify a fait accompli), while generally rejecting — in the name of the same regulations — most requests from progressive textbook authors or from Japan's Asian neighbors.

Acknowledgments

This article is part of a larger study supported by a 2001–2002 (U.S.) National Academy of Education/Spencer Postdoctoral Fellowship. I would like to thank Peter Cave, Sylvan Esh, Hiromitsu Inokuchi, Richard Minear, Mark Selden, Chug Bo Shim, and Edward Vickers for their encouragement, criticism, and assistance.

Endnotes

1. Japanese names in this article follow the Japanese name order. In the pre-surrender period, Yoshida was a career diplomat, supporting Japan's aggression in northern China in the 1920s. During the early postwar years, Yoshida served as Prime Minster for more than 7 years in total.
2. Five textbook examiners (consisting of college professors and primary/secondary school teachers) formed one group.
3. This was (and is) a blue ribbon council appointed by the MOE, consisting of scholars, public intellectuals, and leaders of other occupations.
4. For the postwar history of the Japanese controversy over the Nanjing Massacre, see Yoshida (2000).
5. For a discussion of the present textbook screening and adoption system, see Hamada (2002) and Nozaki (2002).
6. The Yoshida administration stopped Sato's arrest by Justice Minister's supersedeas.
7. Hatoyama was the most popular politician around this time, though he had been purged because of his wartime militarist and ultranationalist positions from 1946 to 1951.
8. The SP had been divided into two parties (the so-called Left Faction SP and Right Faction SP) since 1951; however, the two were on the way to reunification (which eventually took place in October 1955).
9. Ishii was once a music teacher and one of the most influential members of the JTU in charge of textbook-related matters. He was then employed by the JTU as a public relations officer but was dismissed in disgrace in 1954 because of his corrupt relationships with some textbook companies.
10. These were part of Hatoyama's third education bill scrapped in 1956; however, the budget for these was approved, enabling the MOE to change the system without legislation.
11. One of the supplementary provisions for the law had originally read: "The [Ministry's] Division of Elementary and Secondary Education, for the time being, draws up the *Instruction Guidelines*. This, however, does not mean to stand in the way of [local] school boards making their own instructional guidelines." The second sentence was eliminated when the law was amended.
12. The Shuppan Roren, or Nihon Shuppan Rodo Kumiai Rengo in full (Publishing Industry Workers' Union), decided to make the rejection

comments public, publishing *Kyokasho Repoto* (*Annual Report on Textbooks*). To date, this report remains one of the best sources for information about Japanese textbooks.

13. The number of high school Japanese history textbooks remained more or less the same, mainly because the free textbook policy was not applied to them. Twenty-three high school Japanese history textbooks were on the market in 1957, twenty in 1966, and twenty-six in 1969 (Nakamura, Kato, and Hirotake 1970). Many high school textbooks with small market share, including Ienaga Saburo's *Shin Nihonshi*, were able to survive.

14. To date the series remains one of the most popular junior high school social studies textbook series.

15. For example, a research project funded by the Okinawa government was launched to publish two volumes containing the records of Okinawans' personal accounts regarding their experiences in the Battle of Okinawa, resulting in a series entitled *Okinawa Kenshi* (*Okinawa Prefectural History*).

16. In 1971, U.S. President Richard Nixon cut the link between gold and the U.S. dollar, thereby ending the post–World War II international monetary system. Japan, revaluing the yen, suffered an extreme rise in prices.

17. Tanaka, who only had primary school education, became the Prime Minister in 1972.

18. The guidelines for elementary schools were revised in 1977 and implemented in 1980, those for junior-high schools in 1977 and 1981, and those for high schools in 1978 and 1982.

19. The treatment of the flag and the anthem in schools has been one of the major fronts of struggle between the progressives and the nationalists. At this point, they were not legally the national flag and the national anthem, but the MOE forced the schools to treat them as if they were. The flag and the song become "national" by a law in 1999. In other words, the MOE's ministerial attempt preceded the legislation. Since the 1999 legislation, even though the Diet promised not to make it compulsory, the ministry made hoisting the flag and singing the anthem mandatory at school ceremonies and instructed local education boards to punish teachers who opposed it. In spring 2004, the Tokyo Prefectural Education Board (with its board members appointed by Governor Ishihara Shintaro) punished more than 200 teachers who acted against the policy at the graduation ceremony (Ikezoe, 2004). For further discussion of the strong measure taken recently against schools and teachers, see several articles posted at Japan Focus (www.japanfocus.org)

20. Eventually Ienaga brought the case to court in 1984, in his third textbook lawsuit.

21. Although the media reported that the term "aggression" was replaced with "advance" in the section of the textbooks treating Japanese invasion

of northern China, in fact the replacement had taken place previously, in the 1960s and 1970s.

22. Miyazawa's words appeared in the form of a danwa, an unwritten statement of the government position.

23. The Education Minister's statement took the form of a danwa.

24. The MOE, however, did not allow elementary school texts to refer to the number of victims because of the "developmental stage" of the children.

25. The recent textbooks still have some flaws. For example, Barnard (2001) finds problematic the language used to describe the Nanjing Massacre in the textbooks used in 1995.

26. To determine "correct" numbers for the victims of these massacres is difficult; however, some numbers more closely reflect the findings of latest historical research than others.

27. The author's assessment of Nakasane's education reform differs significantly from that of Hood (2001).

28. As many critics have pointed out, the term "military sexual slavery" would be more accurate than the term "comfort women"; however, I employ the latter in this article (hereafter, without quotes) because it is the one that has been most often used. For further discussion of the emergence of the issue in Japan as well as internationally, see, for example, Hein (1999).

29. The issue was international also. In the fall of 1990, LDP representatives visited the United States and held meetings with Dick Cheney, Robert S. Macnamara, and others, in which one of the major topics of their discussion was "Japan's international contribution," i.e., sending Japan's SDF overseas. They regarded "education" as the major obstacle to the overseas deployment of the SDF ("Jiminto Kokubo Sanbukai," 1991).

30. Kono stated this in the form of a danwa.

31. The committee reached its conclusion and disbanded itself in February 1995.

32. *Jugun* means "serving in the war" or "accompanying the military"; *jugun kangofu*, "war nurse"; *jugun kisha*, "war correspondent." The right-wing nationalists made the comfort women issue controversial in part by attacking the use of the term *jugun inanfu*, a term that had not existed during the war but was frequently used in the early 1990s. The nationalists argued that the textbooks taught students a lie by using a term that had not existed during the war. Some even argued that *jugun inanfu* had not existed because no such term had existed.

33. A draft civics textbook, whose content was as problematic as the history text, was also submitted at the same time (and later authorized by the MOE). The present article only discusses the history text.

34. The MOE became the Ministry of Education, Culture, Sports, Science, and Technology in 2001 due to a ministerial reorganisation. Its new

abbreviation has been Monbukagakusho, the Ministry of Education and Science.

35. For analysis of the text's description of modern Japanese history, see "Facts Sheet Concerning *New History Textbook* " posted at http://csf._colorado.edu/bcas/campaign/textbk3.htm. Also see Nelson (2002).

36. The extent to which the Internet helped enhance the community activism against the nationalist text varied in Japan as well as in Korea. See Ducke (2003). For some of the web sites, see Nozaki (2002).

37. It is beyond the scope of this chapter to examine the ways history has been taught in Japanese classrooms. For a historical case study on this topic, see Nozaki (2003). For a study of contemporary classrooms, see Cave (2002).

References

Barnard, C. 2001. "Isolating Knowledge of the Unpleasant: The Rape of Nanking in Japanese High-School Textbooks." *British Journal of Sociology of Education* 22, 4:520–529.

Benfell, S.T. 2002. "Why Can't Japan Apologize? Institutions and War Memory since 1945." *Harvard Asia Quarterly* 6, 1–21.

Cave, P. 2002. "Teaching the History of Empire in Japan and England." *International Journal of Educational Research* 37, 6–7:623–641.

Ducke, I. 2003. "Activism and the Internet: Japan's 2001 History Textbook Affair," in N. Gottlieb and M. McLelland, eds., *Japanese Cybercultures.* London: Routledge, 205–221.

Eguchi, K. 1987. "Kyokasho mondai to okinawasen: Nihongun niyoru kenmin satsugai o chushin'ni. (Textbook Controversy and the Battle of Okinawa: On the Issue of Murdering of Okinawan Residents by Japanese Forces)," In A. Fujiwara, ed., *Okinawasen to tennosei.* Tokyo: Rippu Shobo, 223–254.

Field, N. 1991. *In the Realm of a Dying Emperor: Japan at Century's End.* New York: Vintage Books.

Foucault, M. 1984. "Preface to the History of Sexuality, Volume 2," in P. Rabinow, ed., *Foucault Reader.* New York: Pantheon Books, 333–339.

———. 1991. "Governmentality," in G. Burchell, C. Gordon, and P. Miller, eds., *The Foucault Effect: Studies in Governmentality with Two Lectures by and an Interview with Michel Foucault.* Chicago: University of Chicago Press, 87–104.

Fujii, K. 2001. "'Tsukurukai' kyokasho saitaku no hoshin ga kogisatto de yuragu tochigiken shimotsuga" (Shimotsuga, Tochigi-Pref, Shaken by Protests against Its Decision to Adopt the Textbook Written by the JSHTR), *Shukan Kinyobi* 372:45.

Hamada, T. 2002. "Contested Memories of the Imperial Sun: History Textbook Controversy in Japan." *The American Asian Review: An International Journal on Modern and Contemporary Asia* 20, 4:1–37.

Harris, S.H. 1994. *Factories of Death: Japanese Biological Warfare, 1932–45, and the American Cover-Up.* London: Routledge.

Hein, L. 1999. "Savage Irony: The Imaginative Power of the Military Comfort Women in the 1990s." *Gender and History* 11, 2:336–372.

Hein, L. and Selden, M. 2001. "The Lessons of War, Global Power, and Social Change," in L. Hein and M. Selden, eds., *Censoring History: Citizenship and Memory in Japan, Germany, and the United States.* Armonk: M. E. Sharp, 3–50.

Honda, K. 1972. *Chugoku no tabi (A Journey in China).* Tokyo: Asahi Shinbunsha.

Hood, C.P. 2001. *Japanese Education Reform: Nakasone's Legacy.* London: Routledge.

"Hosokawa shusho kishakaiken no yoshi" (An outline of a press conference of Prime Minister Hosokawa). (1993, August 11). *Asahi Shinbun,* 3.

Ienaga, S. 1991. *Zoku "misshitsu" kentei no kiroku (The Record of Textbooks Screening behind "Closed Doors": The Second Volume).* Tokyo: Kyokasho Kentei Sosho o Shiensurukai.

Ikezoe, N. 2004. "Tokyoi no sessoku tairyo shobun ni hirogaru hamon" (A Growing Stir at the Large Scale, Quick Punishment by the Tokyo Education Board). *Shukan Kinyobi* 504 (April 16):22.

Inoue, K. 1975. *Tenno no senso sekinin (The Emperor's War Responsibility)*. Tokyo: Gendai Hyoronsha.

Ishikawa, M. 1995. *Sengo seijishi (History of Postwar Japanese Politics)*. Tokyo: Iwanami Shoten.

"Jiminto kokubo sanbukai hobei hokokusho: Jieitai kaigakihahei o aotta amerika no tainichi atsuryoku" (A Report Written by the Three Liberal Democratic Party's National Defense Committees that Visited the United States: The American Pressure to Send [Japan's] Self Defense Forces Overseas). 1991. *Bunka Hyoron* 360:62–83.

"Jugun ianfu chosakekka nikansuru kanbochokan danwa" (Chief Cabinet Secretary's Unwritten Statement on the Results of the Investigation into War Comfort Women). 1993. *Asahi Shinbun* (August 5):2.

Kimijima, K. 1996. *Kyokasho no shiso: Nihon to kankoku no kingendaishi (Perspectives in Textbooks: The Modern History of Japan and Korea)*. Tokyo: Suzusawa Shoten.

Kodama, K. et al. 1987. *Chugaku shakai: Rekishiteki bunya (Junior High Social Studies Historical Studies)*. Tokyo: Nihon Shoseki.

"Kyokasho mondai seifu kenkai no butaiura" (Behind the Scenes of the Announcement of the Government Position on Textbook Controversy). 1982. *Asahi Shinbun* (October 6):3.

Mainichi Shinbunsha Kyoiku Shuzaihan. 1981. *Kyokasho senso: Seiji to bijinesu no hazama (Textbook War: Between Politics and Business)*. Tokyo: San'ichi Shobo.

McCormack, G. 2000. "The Japanese Movement to 'Correct' History,'" in L. Hein and M. Selden, eds., *Censoring History: Citizenship and Memory in Japan, Germany, and the United States*. Armonk: M. E. Sharp, 53–73.

Midford, P. 2002. "The Logic of Reassurance and Japan's Grand Strategy." *Security Studies* 11, 3:1–43.

Monbusho [Ministry of Education]. 1947a. *Gakushu shido yoryo: Ippanhen (shian) (Instruction Guidelines: General Guidelines [tentative plan])*. Tokyo: Monbusho.

———. 1947b. *Gakushu shido yoryo: Shakaikahen II (dai 7 gakunen-dai 10 gakunen) (shian) (Instruction Guidelines: Social Studies Guidelines II [grades 7th to 10th] [Tentative Plan])*. Tokyo: Monbusho.

———. 1958. *Shogakko gakushu shido yoryo (Instruction Guidelines for Elementary Schools)*. Tokyo: Okurasho Insatsukyoku.

Nagano, T. 1998. "'Shinpen nihonshi' jiken nitsuite" (On the event of the *New History Textbook*), in M. Kakinuma and T. Nagano, eds., *Kyokasho ronso o koete*. Tokyo: Hihyosha, 133–146.

Nagao, A. 1989. *Shin Karikyuramuron (New Curriculum Theory)*. Tokyo: Yuhikaku.

Nagayoshi, H., Nakamura, K., and Kato S. 1969. *Kyokasho kentei soran: chugakkohen (A General List of Screened Textbooks: Junior High)*. Tokyo: Komiyayama Shoten.

Nakamura, K., Kato, S., and Hirotake, N. 1970. *Kyokasho kentei soran: Kotogakkohen jokan (A General List of Screened Textbooks: High School, the First Volume)*. Tokyo: Komiyayama Shoten.

Nakauchi, T. et al. 1987. *Nihon kyoiku no sengoshi (The Postwar History of Japanese Education)*. Tokyo: Sanseido.

Nelson, J.K. 2002. "Tempest in a Textbook: A Report on the New Middle-School History Textbook in Japan." *Critical Asian Studies* 34, 1:129–148.

Nishioka, T. et al. 1955. *Atarashii shakai 3 (New Social Studies, Vol. 3)*. Tokyo: Tokyo Shoseki.

———. 1962. *Atarashii shakai 2 (New Social Studies, Vol. 2)* Tokyo: Tokyo Shoseki.

———. 1969. *Shintei atarashii shakai 2 (New Social Studies: New Edition, Vol. 2)* Tokyo: Tokyo Shoseki.

Nozaki, Y. 2001. "Feminism, Nationalism, and the Japanese Textbook Controversy," in F.W. Twine and K.M. Blee, eds., *Feminism and Antiracism: International Struggles for Justice*. New York: New York University Press, 170–189.

———. 2002. "Japanese Politics and the History Textbook Controversy, 1982–2001." *International Journal of Educational Research* 37, 6–7:603–622.

———. 2003. "Japanese Critical Teaching about the Asia-Pacific War, 1960s and 1970s." Paper presented at the 2003 Spring Fellows' Retreat, National Academy of Education, Brown University, Providence, Rhode Island, March.

Nozaki, Y. and Inokuchi, H. 2000. "Japanese Education, Nationalism, and Ienaga Saburo's Textbook Lawsuits," in L. Hein and M. Selden, eds., *Censoring History: Citizenship and Memory in Japan, Germany, and the United States*. Armonk: M.E. Sharp, 96–126.

Ohama, T. et al. 1997. *Chugakusei no shakaika rekishi: Nihon no ayumi to sekai (Social Studies History for Junior High Students: Japan's Progress and the World)*. Tokyo: Nihonbunkyo Shuppan.

"Rekishi kyokasho nitsuiteno bunso danwa" (The education minister's unwritten statement on history textbooks). 1982. *Asahi Shinbun* (November 24):14.

"Seifu kenkai (kanbochokan danwa)" (The government position [the chief cabinet secretary's unwritten statement]). 1982. *Asahi Shinbun* (August 27):1.

Shakaika Kyokasho Shippitsusha Kondankai [SKSK], ed. 1984. *Kyokasho mondai towa nanika (What Is the Textbook Controversy?)*. Tokyo: Miraisha.

"'Shinpen nihonshi' naze gokakuka" (Why *Shinpen Nihonshi* Passed). 1987. *Kyokasho Repoto* 31:12–13.

"Shusho no shoshin hyomei enzetsu" (The prime minister's address on his positions). 1993. *Asahi Shinbun* (August 23):3

Tawara, Y. 1997. *Kyokasho kogeki no shinso: "Ianfu" mondai to "jiyushugishikan" no sajyutsu (The Truth of Textbook Attacks: The Swindling Technique of the "Comfort Women" Issue and "Liberal View of History")*. Tokyo: Gakushu no Tomosha.

———. 1998. "Nankin daigyakusatsu jiken to rekishi kyokasho mondai" (History Textbook Controversy and the Nanjing Massacre), in A. Fujiwara, ed., *Nankin jiken o domiruka: Ni chu bei kenkyusha niyoru kensho*. Tokyo: Aoki Shoten, 116–131.

———. 2000. "Kenpo ihan shinryaku senso kotei no 'abunai kyokasho' no jittai" [The Reality of Ideologically "Dangerous Textbook" that Affirms Aggressive War and that Breaches the Constitution]. *Senso Sekinin Kenkyu* 30:28–49.

———. 2001. *Abunai kyokasho: "Senso ga dekirukuni" o mezasu "tsukurukai" no jittai (Ideologically Dangerous Textbooks: The Reality of the JSHTR, which Wants to Have a "Country that Can Fight a War")*. Tokyo: Gakushu no Tomosha, 2001.

Tokutake, T. 1995. *Kyokasho no sengoshi (Postwar History of Textbooks)*. Tokyo: Shinnihon Shuppansha.

Uesugi, S. 2001a. "'Tsukurukai' no haiboku wa heiwa jinken ishiki no shori" (The Defeat of the JSHTR Is the Victory of Consciousness for Peace and Human Rights). *Senso Sekinin Kenkyu* 33:44–47.

———. 2001b. "Uyoku no seijiundo ga tsuini kyokasho o tsukutta" (Finally, the Right-Wing Politics Developed and Published School Textbooks], in S. Uesugi, K. Kimijima, T. Koshida, and N. Takashima, eds., *Iranai "Kaminokuni" Rekishi Komin Kyokasho*. Tokyo: Akashi Shoten.

Ukai, N. et al. 1975. *(Shintei) Atarashii Shakai (New Social Studies [new revision])*. Tokyo: Tokyo Shoseki.

———. 1978. *(Shinpen) Atarashii Shakai (New Social Studies [new edition])*. Tokyo: Tokyo Shoseki.

Wada, H., Ishizaki, K., and the Sengo Gojunen Kokkai Ketsugi o Motomerukai, eds. 1996. *Nihon wa shokuminchi shihai o do kangaetekitaka (How Japan Has Reflected on Its Colonialism)*. Tokyo: Nashinokisha.

Wakamori, T. 1952. *Gendai nihon no naritachi ge (The History of Contemporary Japan, Vol. 2)*. Tokyo: Jitsugyo no Nihonsha.

Yokoyama, Y. 1998. "Kyokasho saiban to gakushushido yoryo" (The Textbook Lawsuits and the Instructional Guidelines), in Kyokasho Kentei Sosho o Shiensuru Zenkokurenrakukai (The National League for Support of the School Textbook Screening Suit), in *Rekishi no hotei*. Tokyo: Otsuki Shoten, 107–122.

Yoshida, T. 2000. "A Battle over History: The Nanjing Massacre in Japan," in J.A. Fogel, ed., *The Nanjing Massacre in History and Historiography*. Berkley: University of California Press, 70–132.

Yoshida, Y. 1995. *Nihonjin no sensokan: Sengoshi no nakano henyo (The Japanese Views on the Asia-Pacific War: The Transformations in the Postwar History)*. Tokyo: Iwanami Shoten.

10

Learning to Live with the Imperial Past? History Teaching, Empire, and War in Japan and England

PETER CAVE

Japan's school education has been the object of much admiration abroad, particularly for its record in mathematics and science (e.g., Stevenson and Stigler 1992; Lewis 1996). One field of study, however, has received mostly criticism. Japan's history education has been attacked overseas (Rose 1999; Barnard 2003, 17) and within Japan (Nozaki and Inokuchi 2000; Nozaki 2003) for allegedly failing to give children an adequate understanding of the atrocities and oppression carried out during Japan's colonial period, especially during the wars of the 1930s and 1940s.

In an earlier article (Cave 2003b), I began a comparison of history education in contemporary Japan and England, attempting to ascertain in particular how education in these two former imperial powers deals with the topics of empire and imperialist war. As I argued there (ibid., 624), Japan and England have much in common in terms of their histories, polities, and educational structures. Moreover, a comparative approach has the advantage of illuminating common and contrasting features and explanatory factors.

In my earlier essay, I concentrated for reasons of space on a comparison of curricula, textbooks, and lesson observations, noting that despite some fundamental differences in the way history is taught in Japanese and English schools, neither system devotes much time to the study of empire and imperialist wars. In this essay, I shall use data from teacher and student interviews, as well as data I have presented earlier, to analyze more fully how these controversial topics are dealt with and why. I argue that the teaching of controversial historical topics must be understood in the context of the institutionalized purposes, structures, and practices of history education as a whole.

Methods

This study examines documents (curricula, examination syllabi, textbooks, and examination papers) and also draws on classroom observations and semistructured interviews[1] at secondary schools in Japan[2] and England.[3] Research in Japan was mainly conducted in June and July 2000, and, in England in January 2001. Details of the school visits conducted are provided in table 10.1 and table 10.2. My previous fieldwork in Japanese schools had included 12 months in a junior high school from 1996 to 1997, during which I observed many history lessons; this provided a useful contextual understanding for the present study.

History and the Curriculum in Japan and England

In both Japan and England, history ceases to be a compulsory subject in the midteens. In practice, students in Japan are likely to spend more time studying

Table 10.1 Schools visited in Japan (JHS = junior high school, HS = high school)

Pseudonym	Location	Type	Date of visit	Number of lessons observed	Number of teachers interviewed
Tokyo National	Tokyo (Urban)	Boys' National (JHS + HS)	13.6.2000	1 JHS + 1 HS	1
Tokyo Girls'	Tokyo (Urban)	Girls' Private (JHS + HS)	15.6.2000	1 JHS + 1 HS	1
Tokyo Boys'	Tokyo (Urban)	Boys' Private (JHS + HS)	20.6.2000	1 HS	1
Kansai Rural A	Kansai (Rural)	Public JHS	30.6.2000	2	1
Kansai Rural B	Kansai (Rural)	Public JHS	17.6.2001	2	1
Kansai Town	Kansai (Semi rural)	Public JHS	7.7.2000	2	1
Tokyo High	Tokyo (Urban)	Public HS	3.6.2000	2	1
Kanto High	Near Tokyo (Urban)	Public HS	14.6.2000	3	2
Kansai High A	Kansai (Rural)	Public HS	29.6.2000	4	1
Kansai High B	Kansai (Semi rural)	Public HS	3.7.2000	2	2
Kansai High C	Kansai (Semi rural)	Public HS	5.7.2000	0	1
Kansai High D	Kansai (Semi rural)	Public HS	6.7.2000	1	1
Kansai High E	Kansai (Rural)	Public HS	14.5.2001	2	2

Table 10.2 Schools Visited in England

Pseudonym	Location	Type	Date of visit	Number of lessons observed	Number of teachers interviewed
St. Ignatius	Birmingham	Catholic Aided Comprehensive	16.1.2001	2	1
Greenfields	Birmingham	Comprehensive	17.1.2001	1	2
Greathouse	Birmingham	Comprehensive	18.1.2001	2	2
Newbridge	London	Foundation Comprehensive	22-23.1.2001	2	2
Park Grammar	London	Boys' Grammar	24.1.2001	1	2
Kingsbury	London	Comprehensive	25.1.2001	2	1
Carpenters	London	Boys' Public	26.1.2001	1	2

history than students in England. However, the aims and design of the two countries' curricula[4] make for strikingly different educational experiences.

History and the Curriculum in the Compulsory Years

In Japan, history is compulsory until age 15, as part of the curricular subject of social studies. Children study Japanese history (along with some civics) during their final year at primary school and then study a mixture of Japanese and world history (predominantly the former) for three of their nine terms at junior high school. In each case, the approach is based on a linear chronology, covering a very long time span (in the junior high case, from prehistoric times to the present) but without in-depth study of any one period.[5]

In England, history is compulsory until age 14. Before age 11, children study selected periods of British history, along with ancient European and world history. The 11- to-14 curriculum prescribes 50 percent British history, 33 percent world history, and 17 percent European history. For this age-group, British history covers selected periods between 1066 and 1900, while world history comprises one study before 1900 and one after (Department for Education and Employment [DFEE] 1999, 17–23).[6] In contrast to the Japanese curriculum, limited chronological coverage is mixed with in-depth study of selected periods and topics.

History and the Curriculum in the Postcompulsory Years

At high school, Japanese children must study world history, as well as either Japanese history or geography. All these subjects have two alternative syllabi (A and B). A is for students in humanities streams and is more in-depth, and B is for students in science streams and is shorter (Monbushō 1989b, 5, 20–42).[7] The treatment of the subject is more detailed and complex than at junior high level. However, as at junior high school, the fundamental approach continues to be linear and chronological, covering a very long time span and with little time for in-depth study of particular periods.

In England, children between ages 14 and 16 study selected subjects for the General Certificate Secondary Education (GCSE) public examination. History is not compulsory; in 2002 and 2003, only 33 percent of students age 15 or older took GCSE history.[8] From ages 16 to 18, most students study only three or four subjects, albeit to a much higher level and in greater depth than for GCSE, and in 2001 and 2002, only 5 percent of the entire age cohort took the culminating History A Level examination.[9] GCSE and A Level courses cover shorter periods in more depth than the Japanese high school curricula.

The Japanese curriculum thus ensures that all students are taught a more comprehensive chronological overview of history than that in England, but it does not for allow the in-depth study of particular periods. More students continue to study history at age 16 or older in Japan than in England, but those in England study the subject in greater depth than their Japanese counterparts and at a higher analytical level.

Dominant Conceptualizations of History Education in Japan and England

My research indicated that dominant conceptualizations of history education differed significantly in Japan and England. These conceptualizations were institutionalized at the supraschool level in curricula, textbooks, and examinations and were also evident at the intraschool level, in teacher interviews and lesson observations. In England, there was strong agreement between the supraschool and intraschool levels. In Japan, teachers' views were more varied and ambivalent, divided between conceptualizations that conformed to those institutionalized at supraschool level and dissatisfaction with the constraints imposed. However, lesson observations largely conformed to the institutionalized conceptualizations.

Dominant Conceptualizations of History Education in Japan

School education in Japan is often seen as emphasizing knowledge and understanding, and this description certainly applies well to history education. Emphasis on having students understand historical events and processes dominates the Japanese history curriculum.[10] In contrast, there is no curricular injunction to develop the kind of critical intellectual skills that are mandated by the curriculum in England (Cave 2003b, 627).

History textbooks in Japan are consistent with the curriculum. They are written "in an impersonal narrative style which gives the impression of authoritative objectivity" (ibid., 631). In contrast to textbooks in England, exercises for students are few and rarely develop analytical skills. One important reason for this is the format of Japan's high school and university entrance examinations in history, which test knowledge of facts and short, prepackaged interpretations, mostly through multiple-choice and short-answer questions (ibid., 633–636). Skills of interpretation, analysis, and argument are hardly tested at all.

In my observations at Japanese schools, almost all lessons observed took the form of teacher exposition, often interspersed with simple questions to students about facts or reasons, with written exercises limited to note-taking and filling in blanks on handouts. The two exceptions[11] showed that teachers were not obliged to follow the dominant lesson format, but such exceptions seemed to be rare. This finding agreed with previous observations by Rohlen (1983, 241–245); Fukuzawa (1994, 64); and Booth, Sato, and Matthews (1995) and was supported by teachers, who confirmed that the lessons observed were representative. Teachers also almost invariably stated that the central goals of the lessons were transmission of knowledge and development of understanding. The teaching observed thus conformed to a conceptualization of history teaching consistent with the curriculum.

In the lessons observed, students were never required to do any textbook or other exercises for homework. Several high school teachers interviewed stated that they set little or no homework for history. The main reason they gave (aside from the burden that marking it would involve, with forty students in each class) was that the students were very busy studying for other subjects outside school hours,[12] and that since history was relatively unimportant in university entrance exams, homework would be resented. Examination structures thus seem to marginalize history as a subject of study in Japan and make it even harder for teachers to develop critical intellectual skills through study outside class.

When asked what they thought were the purposes of teaching history at junior high or high school, teachers' answers were diverse but often included either the transmission of knowledge, the development of understanding, or both and were thus broadly consonant with the curriculum. One teacher described the purpose of history teaching as to impart kyōyō (general cultural knowledge) and another said that his impression was that, whereas history teaching in England emphasized building theories (ronri o kumitateru), in Japan the stress was on enabling everyone to have the same kind of basic, taken-for-granted knowledge (jōshiki).

Among other answers, three teachers mentioned a specific moral/political purpose that they saw in history teaching: learning "not to repeat the mistakes of the past" or having students appreciate that Japan was the aggressor (kagaisha) in the wars of the 1930s and 1940s. In addition, several teachers expressed or implied some dissatisfaction at the present situation of history education in Japanese schools, commenting that there was too little stress on thinking, too much content, or not enough time for students to undertake investigative studies of their own. One commented that the textbooks were so boring that nobody felt like reading them. A teacher at one of Tokyo's most prestigious private schools complained that knowledge and information became important to students at high school because of exam pressure. It was problematic, he commented, that people thought that what the teacher taught was correct and should be memorized uncritically. Nonetheless, he himself admitted increasingly emphasizing exposition as students approached exams. It seemed that teachers did not or could not change their teaching practices, even when they felt dissatisfied with the present state of history teaching — evidence of the power of institutionalized constraints upon them (in particular the pressure of high-stakes public examinations that test factual recall).

Dominant Conceptualizations of History Teaching in England

The history curriculum in England differs sharply from its Japanese counterpart in its emphasis on the development of critical and intellectual skills (Cave 2003b, 627–628). It also differs in concentrating in-depth attention on selected historical periods or subjects in order to facilitate the development of these skills. Perhaps as a result, students' knowledge of historical events and chronology can be patchy (Booth, Sato, and Matthews 1995).

History textbooks used at the schools visited were consistent with the curriculum in containing many exercises aimed at developing analytical, explanatory, and argumentative skills, as well as historical source materials that students were supposed to analyze. These exercises were also designed to develop abilities needed in public examinations. GCSE textbooks contain sample exam questions that test such skills; for example:

> "President Hoover did not bring the USA out of the Depression because he did too little too late." Use the sources and your own knowledge to explain whether you agree with this view. (Chandler and Wright 2001, 69)

Whereas Japanese textbooks were organized chronologically and invariably written in an impersonal style, textbooks in England were usually organized by topic, with a broad chronological framework, and written in various styles (Cave 2003b, 631–632).

Observations at schools in England provided abundant evidence that topic- and skills-based teaching approaches were widespread. In particular, lessons tended to emphasize analysis, interpretation, and evaluation, especially through extended writing tasks of a kind rarely seen in the Japanese schools (Cave 2003b, 634). Homework of this type was also common.

Extended exposition by the teacher during the lesson became more frequent the older the students were. One GCSE lesson observed was dominated by teacher exposition interspersed with short-answer questions to students, a teaching style similar to many of the lessons observed at Japanese junior high schools. However, most GCSE lessons focused more on analytical questions than did lessons in Japan.

In A Level lessons, a mixture of teacher exposition and questioning of students was also very common. Nonetheless, these lessons differed from lessons in the Japanese schools in several important ways. The most fundamental of these was their intensive concentration on in-depth analysis and explanation of a narrowly focused topic. Lessons observed dealt in some detail with subjects ranging from an analytic review of four of the key domestic policies of Bismarck, an examination of how William the Conqueror secured the realm of England in the last 2 months of 1066, introduction and discussion of Thomas Babington Macaulay as a Whig historian, and the policies and problems of Peel as Prime Minister in 1841 and 1842. In one lesson, the students were reading and analyzing an eleventh century historical source with the teacher's help; in several others, the teacher referred the students either to contemporary sources, the views of one or more leading historians on the subject, or both. In contrast, most lessons in Japanese schools covered a much longer time period in one lesson, with less analysis of detail. It was also very rare for teachers in Japan to refer to contemporary sources or the arguments of prominent historians on the subject. Resemblances between the style of lessons in Japan and A Level lessons in England were thus only superficial.

Teachers in England were asked similar questions to their Japanese counterparts. Most British teachers also agreed that the lessons observed had been broadly representative of their teaching approaches, although many qualified this by saying that they used various methods and styles, depending on the topic and level being taught.[13] There was considerable consensus about the purposes of teaching history at school. Almost all teachers saw one major purpose as the development of critical and intellectual skills, with many mentioning specific skills such as analysis, source evaluation, or the formulation and justification of arguments. Other frequently mentioned purposes were learning to understand society and the world and developing self-understanding in terms of a sense of identity, or "where you've come from." Three teachers also mentioned history's potential connections to the teaching of citizenship, a government educational initiative much in the news at the time. None of the teachers stated that there were overt moral/political lessons to be learned from history, of the kind mentioned by some teachers in Japan, although several suggested or implied that what was learned in history had moral/political implications, either in terms of issues such as equality or multiculturalism or in terms of the application of critical thinking skills to political participation and to interpreting media representations of past or current affairs.

Explaining Differing Conceptualizations

The contrast between the dominant conceptualizations of history education in Japan and England can be understood as stemming primarily from differences in pedagogical traditions and the structure of educational institutions, with possible historiographical influences.

In terms of pedagogical tradition, history teaching in England has long emphasized the development of skills of written analysis and argumentation at the upper secondary level (age 14 and older), since public examinations in history for this age-group have been essay-based for at least a century. Increased emphasis on the development of analytic and interpretative skills at lower secondary level in England since 1970 can thus be seen as rooted in long-established practices within the secondary school institution (Cave 2003b, 635). In contrast, Japan has no such tradition even at upper secondary level, so most history teachers are unfamiliar with such pedagogical approaches and the techniques they demand. Introducing such approaches would demand innovation almost from scratch, and this is, not surprisingly, rare.

Greater flexibility in educational structures also explains why history teaching has seen more change in England than in Japan since 1970. One major catalyst for change in England seems to have been the Schools Council History Project (SCHP),[14] established in 1972, which produced new textbooks and examination syllabi that could be adopted in place of more traditional approaches by innovative teachers (Phillips 1998, 17–24). What allowed such innovative alternatives to become established and extend their influence from small beginnings was the fact that public examination boards in England offered so many alternative history syllabi, from which teachers could choose the one for which they intended to enter their students. In Japan, however, such diversity has never existed.[15] All junior high school teachers have to teach with a view to the public high school examination set by their prefecture, and all high school teachers with a view to the *Sentā Shiken*, the examination that is taken by all candidates for national universities and is also used by many private universities. In each case, these examinations have only one version, with no alternative choices. This institutional framework makes major pedagogical innovation extremely difficult, if not impossible. Primary responsibility for this enduring rigidity must lie with Japan's Ministry of Education, as the government body that oversees and exercises overall control over such educational structures (see chapters 8 and 9).

Finally, it is possible that Japanese history teaching is influenced by what some (e.g., Mehl 1998, 166; Ueno 1999) see as a dominant positivistic mode of historiography within the discipline of history in Japan (or what Dierkes in his chapter in this volume terms "uncritical empiricism"). If positivism is dominant, however, the origins and extent of its dominance are unclear; Mehl (1998, 166) sees it as a long-standing tradition, while Sand (1999, 123) sees positivism's rise as dating from the 1970s and the decline of historical materialism (Akita 1982). Moreover, positivism is hardly the only game in town, given the influence of older approaches like those of the Modernist School historians (*kindai-shugisha*), such as Ōtsuka Hisao (Conrad 1999), or alternatives such as the *minshushi* (people's history) school (Gluck 1978). Firm conclusions about historiographical influence therefore seem premature.

Empire, War, and History in Japan and England

Similarities exist in the curricular position of controversial historical topics in Japan and England. However, teachers' views about how to teach these topics differ significantly, influenced partly by the contrasting conceptualizations and practices of history teaching in the two countries and partly by the different contemporary significance of the topics in question.

Empire and Imperial Aggression in Curriculum and Textbooks

The topics of colonialism, empire, and imperial aggression occupy not dissimilar positions in the school curricula of Japan and England. In Japan, the compulsory junior high curriculum fully covers the period of Japanese colonial empire (1895–1945). In England, the compulsory curriculum for 11- to 14-year-olds covers British history from 1750 to 1900, the period when much of the British Empire was acquired. However, while both curricula allow for teaching on the subject of empire and imperialism, neither explicitly requires it (Cave 2003b, 628–629; Monbush 1989b, 20–35). In England at age 14 or older, only one of the nine GCSE syllabi on offer in 2003 dealt with the British Empire at all, and that was as an option.[16]

Secondary school textbooks in both Japan and England deal with the subjects of empire and colonialism to a limited extent. Japanese junior high textbooks' coverage of Japanese colonial oppression and wartime atrocities increased significantly between 1970 and 1997 (Cave 2003b, 630), reaching a peak in 1997 (Nozaki 2003, 613) before diminishing somewhat in the 2002 editions, allegedly as a result of political pressure and self-censorship associated with the furore over the subject of textbook content at the time (Nelson 2002, 144; Nozaki 2003, 616). Fish (forthcoming) reaches similar conclusions about increasing openness in high school textbooks. Key Stage 3[17] textbooks used at the schools visited in England contained limited coverage of the British Empire and British involvement in the slave trade, taking a particularly critical stance toward the latter. Material dealing with the impact of British colonization on the colonies themselves was critical, but scanty (Cave 2003b, 631). Only one 2001 GCSE textbook (Chandler and Wright 2001) contains (optional) material on the British Empire, in a chapter on "Nationalism and Independence in India: c. 1900–49" that covers twenty-nine pages and is highly critical of Britain, with very clear and forthright moral and political judgments.

Examination of textbooks in both countries thus suggests that without elaboration or supplementation by the teacher, they would give students important but nonetheless very limited information about their countries' imperial pasts, and especially the controversial aspects of those pasts. Besides the issue of content, moreover, presentation and approach must be considered. In the case of Japan, Barnard (2003) has forcibly argued that while today's history textbooks do cover controversial subjects such as the Nanking Massacre, the presentation of these subjects tends to leave it unclear who exactly acted and who caused such actions. Dierkes (this volume) adds that textbooks rarely explore actors' motivations in any depth. The lack of analytical or further study exercises encouraging Japanese students to go deeper into the issues can also be seen as problematic, though it must be noted that this deficiency runs through the entire textbook; it is not confined to controversial topics, but rather stems from the institutionalized practices of history teaching as a whole. In the case of the English textbooks, conversely, it can be noted that whereas pages on the slave trade sometimes present the issue in strongly moral terms and make an obvious appeal to humanitarian feelings, such an approach is much less evident in pages on the Empire. Here, a more coolly detached, analytical approach tends to prevail, with students being asked to consider issues such as whether the development of the Empire represented progress or not (Aylett 1993, 61).[18] In contrast, it is impossible to imagine a textbook asking students whether the abolition of the slave trade was an example of progress.

In both Japan and England, therefore, the history curriculum and textbooks give critical but limited coverage of the subjects of empire and imperial aggression, though there are important differences in presentational style. Significant differences were also apparent in teachers' views on how to teach these subjects, as we shall see.

Teachers' Views on the Teaching of Empire, Invasion, and War

Teachers interviewed in Japan and England were asked slightly different questions about teaching on the subjects of empire, invasion, and war. Japanese teachers were asked their views on the then-current debates over the teaching of the history of the Asia-Pacific War, sparked by the arguments of the so-called Liberal School of History (Kersten 1999) and were also asked what they thought was an appropriate way of teaching about the history of the period from 1926 through 1945 (the period of most intense militaristic nationalism and overseas aggression).

In Japanese teachers' replies, there was a strong emphasis on the teaching of facts (*jijitsu*), a word used by seven interviewees, with two of these also speaking of the desirability of teaching or allowing students to judge objectively (*kyakkan-teki ni*). This conformed to Japanese teachers' stress on knowledge and understanding as the purposes of history teaching in general. In addition, four teachers showed an explicit commitment to a moral/political view, in terms of antiwar teaching, teaching students to avoid repeating the same mistakes as were made in the past, or developing a self-critical consciousness (*hansei ninshiki*) about the past. Two others stated that the teacher should let students think for themselves or leave it to their judgment, and two teachers also referred to the need to teach in historical context, seen as the contemporary international situation or international Fascism. Some responses emphasized both moral/political and analytical approaches, combining antimilitaristic teaching with analysis of the causes of the 1930s situation or acknowledgment of how Japanese victories had stimulated Asian nationalist movements.

Teachers in England were asked what they saw as the main purposes of teaching about the British Empire and British imperialism, whether that coincided with their experience of the way the subjects were taught, how the teaching of the subjects had changed over the years, and how children responded to the topic. The British teachers differed from their Japanese counterparts in not emphasizing either facts or a moral/political view. Their views were also more diverse than those of teachers in Japan. Three thought that teaching about the Empire helped students to understand modern British society, specifically how various groups of people had come into Britain, and three others suggested that the topic dealt with the meeting of cultures, or was linked to education promoting understanding and acceptance within a multicultural society. Three others considered that the subject lent itself to debate, such as over the issue of the advantages and disadvantages of the Empire for the colonizers and colonized. As this suggests, there was little or no sense of outrage at the Empire as a perceivedly exploitative system or of a felt imperative to make students aware of the effects of the Empire on its peoples.

Nevertheless, teachers in England did see the subject of Empire as double-edged, offering both opportunities and potential problems. As noted above, several teachers suggested that students became engaged when debating the subject and also that it interested students whose families had originated in former colonies. However, involvement was also seen as the source of problems, if students found it impossible to stand on both sides of a debate. One teacher cited as an example his experience with students of Irish ancestry and a debate apportioning blame for the 1847 Irish Famine. Such partisan commitment conflicted with the teachers' desire to foster skills of liberal analysis and criticism. Involvement could also be a problem if it led to conflict among students, as two teachers who taught at an ethnically mixed London school both remarked independently — though one also expressed the view that teaching about the Empire was important to combat anti-immigrant prejudices. These issues of involvement and potential conflict were more obviously salient at the English schools, given their significant populations of students of South Asian or Afro-Caribbean origin, than at the relatively homogeneous Japanese schools.[19]

Explaining Differences between Japan and England

Why were the views of teachers in Japan and England so different? The answers probably lie in pedagogy, historiography, and the significance of the particular periods in question for the two societies today.

In the case of the Japanese teachers, the stress on facts and objectivity suggests the influence of the pedagogy of knowledge and understanding. It may also reflect positivist historiographical assumptions. However, teachers probably also feel that stressing facts is the most practical way to defend themselves from criticism about their teaching of this most controversial part of Japanese history. This is not to say that their belief in facts is insincere; rather, it is likely that for most, their pedagogical and historiographical understanding happily coincide with the best strategy for deflecting criticism.

In England, history pedagogy has moved radically away from a straightforwardly conceived transmission of knowledge (Larsson, Booth, and Matthews 1998; Phillips 1998; Cave 2003b, 635). It is therefore unsurprising that teachers in England did not mention facts at all and saw the Empire as a good subject for debate. As with the Japanese teachers' stress on facts, the English teachers' stress on debate conforms to institutionalized conceptualizations of history teaching.

Perhaps the most interesting difference between the two countries' teachers lay in the presence or absence of a felt imperative to teach according to a clear and strong moral/political view. The Japanese teachers who articulated such an imperative probably represented the views of a substantial minority nationwide. In contrast, no teachers in England articulated such an imperative with regard to teaching about the British Empire, even though several said that they thought that, in practice, teaching about the Empire tended to stress its negative aspects. This difference probably stems from the much greater sensitivity and centrality of the 1926 to 1945 (early Showa)[20] period to contemporary Japan and its debates about politics and identity, in comparison to the relatively marginal position of the imperial past to similar debates in contemporary Britain. Not only do the events of early Showa continue to exercise a major influence on Japan's international relations (Rose 1999; Kimijima 2000), but attitudes toward these events continue to be a key defining feature of contemporary Japanese politics. This is evidenced by outbursts from prominent right-of-center politicians; ongoing campaigns for "patriotic" history by significant figures in media, culture, and education; and the countercampaigns and media controversy that have followed (Kersten 1999; Barnard 2003, 1–17; Nozaki 2003). Some see such outbursts and campaigns on the right as evidence of a deep-seated refusal to accept and come to terms with events that sully a fantasized image of a pure and noble early Showa state (McCormack 1998, 7; Barnard 2003, 162–163).

In contrast, the British Empire seems not only gone but largely forgotten and unmourned. One reason may be that it was never connected with the kind of massive dislocations in domestic life and politics that accompanied the Japanese invasion of China in the 1930s; another, that while many on the Japanese right seem unable to stop identifying with the leaders of early Showa, the political right in Britain made a decisive break with imperialism from the late 1950s (Ramsden 1996, 146–151). Thus, few people in British public life have an interest in remembering what is generally regarded as a somewhat uneasy and embarrassing piece of history. Nor do Britain's former colonies make vociferous complaints about teaching (or nonteaching) about empire in British schools. As a result, teachers in England can feel a relative detachment from the issue that is difficult, and perhaps even improper, for their counterparts in Japan.

Empire, War, and History: Students' Views

I have examined the institutionalized content of history in Japan and England, as well as classroom teaching practices and the reflections of teachers. Ultimately, however, history teaching is supposed to educate students. What was the perspective of the students interviewed on their own experiences of learning history, and specifically the history of empire and imperialist war?

Views of University Students in Japan. Research on Japanese secondary teaching has generally depicted lecture-style lessons in which student activity is mainly confined to listening and taking notes (Rohlen 1983, 241–247; Fukuzawa 1994, 6466; Cave 2003b, 633). Researchers have seen such lessons as dull and uninvolving (Rohlen 1983, 241–247), and there is some evidence that students feel the same (Yoneyama 1999, 142–154). However, nine of the twenty-two university students I interviewed said unequivocally that their history education had been interesting, and another eight said that parts had been interesting, with only four saying categorically that it had not been interesting.[21]

No fewer than eight students connected interest to going beyond the textbook. This could range from the introduction of supplementary material by the teacher, to students' conducting personal investigations. Students particularly seemed to appreciate it when the teacher had explained background (*urabanashi, jidai haikei*):

> On the whole it wasn't interesting, but one of my world history teachers didn't make the textbook the main thing, he gave us lots of handouts and used books he'd read himself about history, and he was interesting. (Naomi, F)[22]
>
> At junior high school, the teacher let us do our own free research (*jiyū kenkyū*) and such like for homework and we found out about various things ourselves, about these characters in history and so on — it wasn't much to do with the lessons — and it was interesting. (Risa, F)

Rohlen (1983, 243) argued that in Japanese high schools, the teacher's pedagogical authority derives from the textbook. However, these students' comments suggest that while teachers may need to accept the textbook as a broad framework, their authority and influence can be enhanced if they go beyond it. It also seems that teachers may depart from the textbook more than previous research has indicated. Almost all lessons I observed were textbook-based, but two-fifths went significantly beyond the textbook, while a further fifth included short digressions.[23]

The Japanese students, like the Japanese teachers, tended to understand history education as a matter of gaining knowledge and understanding. Two said that the main thing they had learned through history education was "general knowledge" (*ippan jōshiki, ippan kyōyō*), and two others said that the basic knowledge they had acquired had been useful at university. Understanding of ways of thinking in the past or of the differences between Japanese and other cultures were also mentioned. One student said that she had learned a more critical attitude toward media information, and another drew a moral/political lesson, "not to repeat the mistakes of the past, the war and such like."

When asked what they had learned at school about the wars of the 1930s and 1940s, students' answers varied widely. Almost half said that what they had learned had been quite superficial, though it was usually unclear what exactly that learning had included. In a number of cases, these students indicated that they had simply learned basic factual knowledge.

> We just learned about what happened (*atta koto*), I mean learning names and so on … but I hardly know about anything beyond that (*naiyō wa hotondo shiranai*), what kind of things actually happened — I mean, what kind of cruel things happened, what kind of things were done to other countries, that kind of thing. (Erina, F)
>
> The lessons on this overlapped with the exam season, and we didn't do modern history or the Fifteen Years War[24] in much detail, just what was in the textbook, like, in this year this happened, just learn that, so to be honest I don't understand it in much detail. (Rui, F)
>
> At school I was just taught superficial things like what happened in which year, how miserable it was, about how many people died, did people die, and so on … At school, they didn't teach us much content (*naibu*), not the deeper things. (Yoko, F)
>
> At junior high and high school they just taught us what was necessary for the exams, they didn't teach us details (*komakai koto*). I was only taught stuff like how Japan fought, won, lost, and so on, and then that we mustn't go to war again and such like, that's often said, but those kind of things were all they taught us, and I still don't understand why we mustn't go to war again … what Japan did to Chinese people and Koreans and so on, I wasn't taught much about that, and I think that Japan did terrible things, too, and I think that a deep way of thinking comes from studying those kind of things in detail (*fukai kangae ni tsunagatteiru*). (Hisao, M)

Several interviewees shared the view that schoolchildren should learn in more depth and detail about the early Showa period, and especially its human significance. When I asked the third student quoted, Yoko, what she meant by the "deeper things" that hadn't been taught at school, she elaborated:

> What kind of conditions the people who went as soldiers were fighting in, the feelings they had — that teacher[25] told us about the letters that

the kamikaze pilots, these 15- or 16-year-old boys, wrote at the end to their parents, their families ... the kind of things they wrote and so on.

Other students emphasized the importance of teaching about issues such as the so-called comfort women, Korean, Chinese and other women forced into sex work with the military, or Unit 731, the unit of the Japanese Imperial Army that tested biological weapons on human subjects.

However, although many students thought they had learned too little about the war, several others said that what they had learned about this period at school had made an impact on them, including two who mentioned being taught about the comfort women:

> When I was in the third year of high school I learned from the teacher about the Nanking Massacre and the comfort women. The first time I knew about the comfort women was also from a film when I was in the third year at junior high. (Yuri, F)
>
> I was shown a lot of documentaries about the *Himeyuri Butai*[26] in Okinawa and about Hiroshima when I was at junior high, and that has really stayed with me. (Aya, F)

What was also clear, however, was the variety of occasions and channels through which interviewees had come to learn about aspects of war and aggression in early Showa. Besides history lessons, these included school trips to Hiroshima and China, films and television programs, a teacher at after-school tutorial college (*juku*), and a comic about Hiroshima:

> I watched *Shitteiru Tsumori?!*[27] when it was about that thing in Okinawa, the *Himeyuri Butai* — I'd heard of that, but I didn't know anything about it, and when I watched it, I was 17, and those girls who were sacrificed and died were just 16, 17, 18, so I was crying like anything as I was watching. (Yuri, F)
>
> Our high school went to China for its school trip (*shūgaku ryokō*). Before that, as kind of preparatory study, they handed out incredible (*sugoi*) photos. Lots of incredible, cruel things were in them. You felt a bit small when you met Chinese people. (Shoko, F)
>
> I learned about the atrocities (*gyakutai*) and so on. I don't think we did that too much in lessons, but I learned quite a bit about it from comics. The situation at the time of the atomic bomb in Hiroshima. (Kazuo, M)
>
> The *juku* teacher I mentioned did talk pretty seriously about things like the comfort women and the kamikaze pilots, in detail. (Yoko, F)

Two students also mentioned watching the film *Kike Wadatsumi no Koe* (*Listen to the Voices from the Sea*), a 1995 remake of an antiwar film about student soldiers, originally shown in 1950.[28]

The variety of ways students learned about the wars of early Showa does not diminish the importance of school history teaching, since as several writers (e.g., Igarashi 2000; Seraphim 2001) have shown, public representations of this historical period vary dramatically in political perspective and certainly cannot be seen as an adequate substitute for an in-depth and critical historical education. It does show, however, how live and present the history of the early Showa war remains in contemporary Japan and how likely it is to impinge upon the awareness of young people in one way or another.[29]

Views of High School Students in England

Students in England were asked what they had learned at school about the British Empire and British imperialism, as well as how they thought students at school in England ought to study these topics. As with students in Japan, the responses of students in England concerning their learning experiences varied. Many claimed to have learned little or nothing about the British Empire and British imperialism at school. In some cases, this claim was quite definite, as in the case of two boys at Greathouse who said that they had never learned about the Empire before their A Level course. Similarly, a group of students interviewed at Newbridge claimed that they didn't remember study-ing anything about the Empire. In other cases, students said that while they had studied something about the topic, it had not been in much depth or detail, and their recollections of it were sketchy. Sometimes students at the same school disagreed about what they had learned, with some saying they didn't remember studying about the Empire and others disagreeing. Such disagreements draw attention to potential differences between what is taught in schools and what students actually assimilate and remember, an important point that is sometimes overlooked when using students' recollections as evidence. Judging from textbook content and teachers' statements, it seemed to me that students in England should have learned more about the British Empire than many claimed to recall. This difference could be at least partly explained by some students' lack of engagement with the subject at the time. Nonetheless, evidence from student interviews generally confirmed the impres-sion gained from textbook content and teacher interviews that Empire and imperialism were not subjects to which much lesson time was devoted.

Students tended to feel that more should be taught about the Empire and imperialism, though these feelings did not seem to be particularly strong and were sometimes qualified by unwillingness to sacrifice other historical areas, such as world history, in order to make more time.[30] They gave various reasons for their views. Several said that, being British, they should know their own history or that it was good to know how Britain had treated other countries. These students included some of South Asian origin:

> I think we should, because it's like, our country, and ... we should know about our past history. (Newbridge, F)[31]

If we [meet students from other countries, then][32] we don't feel intimidated, like everybody else knows, other countries know what we've done, and we don't know what we've basically achieved. (Greenfields, F)

Other students agreed that studying the British Empire was desirable but thought that teaching in a way that encouraged simple or unbalanced moral judgments should be avoided. In some cases, this seemed to result from a belief that events had to be studied in their own historical context, and anachronistic value judgments avoided. For one student, the complexity of the subject made it difficult to teach to younger children, who might make oversimple moral judgments. As in Japan, there was also an appeal to facts:

[Students should study the British Empire and British imperialism,] but I don't think that they should be taught to be guilty about it (St. Ignatius, M) ... I think you should be taught the truth. (F)

What happened. Facts. And though a lot of it is classed as morally wrong today, at the time ... people saw things differently. (M)

While the appeal to historical contextualization was no doubt genuine, it may in some cases have gone alongside a sense of defensive self-exculpation. On the other hand, one student was explicitly critical of what she considered the unduly favorable view of British actions that she had been given:

I've never been examined in History on something where the English were portrayed, behaved, really, really badly. Year Nine we were taught about India, but ... we learned about the ancient Indian empire ... As soon as it came up to, "Oh yes, the English came into trade, then they took over and slaughtered everyone," ... we didn't learn about that, we just stopped. (Kingsbury, F)

This criticism was unusual, however. Whereas many of the Japanese university students seemed strongly aware of the 1926 to 1945 period as a live issue that had engaged them in some way and that required a moral response, the English high school students often seemed to feel that the British Empire was a topic on the fringes of their knowledge, and even the more well informed were generally ambivalent about taking a moral attitude toward the Empire.

One should be cautious about drawing large generalizations from this comparison, bearing in mind the differences between the two sets of interviewees. The higher awareness of the Japanese students may partly be explained by the fact that, coming from a leading private university, they probably represented a more academically successful group than the British students. However, it is also likely that, as with differences between teachers in Japan and England, these differences between students can be explained by the contrasting impact of early Showa and the British Empire on contemporary international relations and national life.

Conclusion

Teaching the History of Empire in Japan and England

Strong evidence exists that the teaching and learning of history is conceptualized and carried out very differently in Japan and England. In Japan, history is seen as centering on knowledge and understanding imparted by the teacher, with relatively little attention to the development of analytic or argumentative skills. This way of doing things is institutionalized nationally through the curriculum, textbooks, and examination structures and is accepted by teachers and students, though by no means uncritically. In fact, there is evidence that significant numbers of teachers supplement, elaborate on, or digress from the textbook and that students often appreciate these efforts. However, the inflexibility of examination structures has severely hindered major pedagogical innovation.

In England, history is seen as a means of developing intellectual skills of analysis and argument formation, as well as a subject that provides knowledge and understanding fundamental to adult life. As in Japan, this view is institutionalized in curriculum, textbooks, and examinations and is readily and enthusiastically articulated by teachers and students. The pedagogical development that has occurred in England appears to have been made possible by an examination system that allows more diversity than in Japan. Pedagogical development has also been grounded in long-standing traditions of analytical writing undeveloped in Japanese secondary schools.

The way that history teachers in Japan and England deal with the more sensitive and controversial aspects of their respective countries' imperial pasts is influenced by these dominant pedagogical conceptualizations and practices. In Japan, there is often a tendency to emphasize the teaching of "facts" about controversial issues. Although different teachers may vary considerably in their understanding of what it means to teach the facts, the appeal to the legitimacy of positivist historiography is widely shared. If the evidence of the students interviewed for this study is at all representative, however, the result is often a dry presentation that gives little or no in-depth understanding of the human significance of the factual events and, as a result, leaves many students dissatisfied. It also seems that a minority of teachers go into more depth about sensitive issues from early Showa and that some consider it imperative to give students a moral and political perspective on these issues.

In England, teachers often saw the topic of Empire as a way of helping students understand contemporary British society. It was notable that the topic tended to be seen as a way of understanding Britain rather than the countries colonized, though the latter perspective was not completely absent. Teachers also considered the Empire as potentially a good subject through which to develop skills of analysis and argument. As in Japan, therefore, the dominant pedagogical framework influenced the approach to a potentially sensitive subject.

In England, however, there was little or no sense that teachers felt a moral or political imperative to teach children about the Empire. The subject appeared to be a relatively peripheral one for teachers, and one that was at or beyond the margins of awareness for many of the students interviewed.

It was clear from interviews that teachers in England were well aware of the moral, political, and emotional significance of Empire as a subject. Nonetheless, for them it was not as highly charged and unavoidably problematic an issue as was the issue of how to teach early Showa for their Japanese counterparts. It was particularly noticeable that no teacher in England indicated any necessity to draw certain moral or political lessons from studying the Empire, in strong contrast to Japan, where four teachers explicitly advocated this way of teaching early Showa. It is unlikely that this contrast was due to the unwillingness of history teachers in England to make moral or political points in lessons. It is clear that strong implicit moral/political positions form part of the rationale for the history curriculum in England (Phillips 1998, 73; DFEE 1999, 8–9) and are often explicitly endorsed by teachers.[33]

The lack of a explicitly expressed imperative for a moral or political position on Empire and imperialism in England is more likely to result from two things: the topic's relatively low profile in the consciousness of the teaching community and the public at large as well as the controversy that a clear moral/political position would be likely to generate, given the lack of the kind of public moral/political consensus that makes it generally acceptable for history teachers to condemn other episodes such as the slave trade or express approval of nineteenth or even twentieth century political and social reforms. A similar lack of consensus exists in Japan about early Showa, and this probably leads many teachers to adopt as uncontroversial an approach as possible in their teaching. However, unlike the British Empire in England, in Japan, early Showa remains key to contemporary debates about national politics and identity as well as an ever-present issue in the sphere of international relations. Not only is the period difficult for teachers to avoid entirely, but it is likely that many feel a certain obligation to deal with it to some degree. Some feel a strong need to deal with the period in some depth and to confront students with the challenges it poses.

The Purposes of History Teaching

This comparison of the ways that Japan and England deal with the more sensitive aspects of their history raises wider issues about the purposes of teaching history in school and about what approaches are appropriate to achieve these purposes.

As Dierkes points out in chapter 8, John W. Meyer and others have argued that the last 50 years have seen education in many countries place increased emphasis on modern history, at the expense of ancient, medieval, or even premodern periods. This has certainly been the case in England, for reasons I would suggest are fourfold. First, history has to justify its place in the curriculum to educational policymakers, and one way of doing this in England has been to stress its role in socializing children into the values and competencies that are deemed desirable for citizens of a participatory democracy. It is hardly surprising, therefore, that increasing attention has been paid to periods of history during which some of the core values of contemporary British society were either developed (as in the nineteenth century) or threatened (as in twentieth-century Germany and Russia). Secondly, history in England has operated in a partially market-based system in which students have a choice of subjects to study from age 14 on, and it has been felt easier to interest students in modern periods. Thirdly, the diversity built into institutional structures has allowed experimentation and change to take place in response to the above pressures, as well as to new movements within pedagogy or within history as an academic discipline. Fourthly, syllabus designers, textbook writers, and teachers have enjoyed a relatively high degree of autonomy (Phillips 1998, 23–24, 133), certainly in comparison with Japan (Barnard 2003, 10–17; Cave 2003b, 629), and this has also made such change easier.

The issue of history teaching's socializing role is particularly important. History education in schools can never be a purely academic or intellectual activity, devoid of moral and political implications. It is integrally bound up with questions of what kind of knowledge, values, and competences are felt important for a society's members to acquire. Answers to these questions shape the history curriculum, as well as textbooks, examinations, and classroom teaching. For example, it has long been one of the main purposes of history education in many countries to develop a sense of national identity in children, even though, as in England, this is not always explicit (Cave 2003b, 627). However, in at least some countries, this purpose has undergone a relative decline in recent decades, as more emphasis has been placed on the development of other values and competences, such as international understanding or critical thinking. Result include the decline of history taught as a long and comprehensive chronology, and the increased concentration upon in-depth study of key periods that are considered particularly suitable for developing these understandings and competencies. England is an excellent example of this process at work.

In Japan, however, as Diekes observes in Chapter 8 the long chronology model of history education has continued to hold sway, and in-depth study of key periods has not developed. As the arguments made above imply, one reason for this is likely to be the strong persistence in Japan of a notion of history as a tool for developing national identity, especially in the governmental circles that control the curriculum (Buruma 1994, 195–196; Nozaki 2003, 615–618).[34] Another may be because these same governing powers are at best ambivalent about the desirability of developing in schoolchildren the kind of critical, autonomous thinking that could be fostered by in-depth study of key periods of modern history.[35] This is especially because one such key period would certainly be from 1926 to 1945, a period that continues to arouse intense political and public controversy.

A further reason for the immobilism of Japanese history education lies in the institutional structures of the examination system which, as noted above, lack the diversity built into the English system and thus hinder innovation. Of course, this is a political as well as structural issue. The maintenance of the structure is the responsibility of the Ministry of Education, which has shown little enthusiasm over the decades for loosening bureaucratic control over educational structures and allowing innovation from below.[36] Maintaining Japan's present history curriculum, along with the structures that prevent diversity and innovation, ensures that Japan's history education will continue to offer students a broad but shallow exposition of positivistic knowledge, without actively fostering either skills of analytic argument, or in-depth understanding of history's human significance.

However, even if this situation were to change, Japan's history educators would still be faced with dilemmas about how to deal with the modern history of Japan, especially the colonial period from 1895 to 1945, and in particular the highly controversial 1926 to 1945 period. In facing these dilemmas, they would probably not find it helpful to look for guidance at the way that the British Empire is taught in England. The Empire has simply become too marginal a topic in England's history curriculum and public consciousness to be compared with the significance of the 1895 to 1945 period for contemporary Japan. Instead, Japan's history educators would probably have to examine how German history from 1890 to 1945 is taught in European countries, such as England, or in Germany itself. There would, no doubt, be major disagreements about what sort of teaching approach would be most appropriate.

In the end, the question of how history should be taught cannot be evaded. I have little doubt that Japan's education needs to move toward more in-depth examination of key periods of history, including the first half of the twentieth century. In England, meanwhile, I believe there should be more time devoted to the study of the British Empire. Both of these courses of action would probably make life more difficult for teachers. However, both would be likely to improve the understanding that children have of their own country's history, to say nothing of international relations and the contemporary world. In a world of increasing international interaction among individuals as well as states, turning away from the controversial history of empire in all its forms surely means denying children an awareness of an aspect of the past that is fundamental to any understanding of the global society in which they live.

Endnotes

1. Interviews usually took between 30 and 60 minutes. In Japan, I interviewed two teachers whose lessons had not been observed, and in England,

three. In Japan, I interviewed twenty-two first-year students in the Education Faculty of a leading Tokyo private university in June 2000. Students were interviewed individually or in pairs (or, in one case, in a group of six), according to their preference. In England, a total of thirty-seven students were interviewed in small groups at their schools, except for one girl who was interviewed individually. All students in England were studying A Level History. Students were asked to participate by their teachers, the only practical approach given the brevity of my visits to England. It would therefore be unwise to draw firm conclusions about the representativeness of the views expressed. The interview data should be seen as material that generates suggestive hypotheses for further research.

2. Secondary schooling in Japan comprises 3 years of compulsory junior high school (ages 12–15) followed by three years of high school (ages 15–18), which is not compulsory but to which about 97 percent of children advance via an entrance examination (Monbushō 2000, 55). About 94 percent of children attend the local, public junior high school (ibid., 51), and most of the rest attend private schools. Less than 1 percent attend national schools, which are attached to universities and carry out practical research on pedagogical innovation. They are often selective. At high school level, about 30 percent of students attend private schools, and 0.2 percent national schools (ibid., 57).

3. All the secondary schools visited in England were for 11- to 18-year-olds. In England, education is compulsory between ages 5 and 16. Six schools visited were public (i.e., state-run), located in three different Local Education Authorities (LEAs), all of which contained state-run grammar schools that selected children by examination at 11+, along with nonselective comprehensive schools. The seventh school visited, Carpenters, is an old-established private school of the type usually called a public school in England. All of the schools visited were considered good schools, with examination results above the local average. All the state schools except Greathouse had high proportions of students from ethnic minority backgrounds, and there was also a significant proportion of such students at Carpenters.

4. The Japanese curricula referred to in this article are those in force 1992–2002, but there have been no material changes in the current curricula.

5. See the essay by Dierkes in this volume for further discussion of these features.

6. The National Curriculum for England is also available at www.nc.uk.net/home.html.

7. Students at Japanese academic high schools are often divided into arts and science streams from their second year.

8. Calculated from Department of Education and Skills, "GCSE/GNVQ Examination Results and Key Stage 3 to GCSE/GNVQ Value Added Measures for Young People in England, 2002–2003 (Revised)," www. dfes.gov.uk/rsgateway/DB/SFR/s000442/contents.shtml, accessed June 7, 2004.

9. Calculated from Department of Education and Skills, "GCE/VCE A/AS Examination Results for Young People in England, 2001/02 (Final Data)," www.dfes.gov.uk/rsgateway/DB/SFR/s000387/index.shtml, and "Participation in Education, Training and Employment by 16–18 Year Olds in England: 2001 and 2002," www.dfes.gov.uk/rsgateway/DB/SFR/s000426/index.shtml, accessed June 7, 2004.

10. For example, the phrase "have [students] understand" (*rikai saseru*) occurs four times, more than any other verb, in the goals of the junior high school history curriculum (Monbushō 1989a, 23).

11. For details, see Cave (2003b, 633–634).

12. Particularly mathematics, English, and Japanese, which the teachers claimed were the most important examination subjects.

13. This variation may arise because secondary school teachers in England face more diverse class groups. They teach across a wider age range (11 to 18 instead of 12 to 15 or 15 to 18) and often teach groups that are streamed according to academic performance. Most Japanese teachers teach a narrower age range and unstreamed mixed-ability classes.

14. Renamed the Schools History Project (SHP) in 1984.

15. There is diversity in the sense that each university (and each private high school) in Japan requires candidates to take its own entrance examination. However, students in one class will choose to aim for a great variety of universities, and it is impossible for teachers to teach with a view to such a diversity of examinations. In contrast, teachers in England can choose the examination that all their students take.

16. The Edexcel examination board's Specification [syllabus] A, Modern European and World History, was the only one of the nine GCSE History syllabi offered in 2004 to deal with the British Empire at all, offering "Nationalism and Independence in India, c1900–1949" as one of seven optional outline studies. The relative lack of interest in the Empire seems to be longstanding. An examination of the Annual Reports of the Joint Matriculation Board, a leading examination board for most of the twentieth century, for example, showed that of the GCE O Level History syllabi offered between 1965 and 1981, the syllabus on "The British Empire and Commonwealth from about 1750 to the present day" was always the least popular, attracting only 828 out of 42,263 candidates even in 1965, and a mere 52 out of 52,825 in 1981. The Examiners' Reports for the Associated Examining Board History A level between 1992 and 1996 also suggest that few students attempted questions to do with

empire and imperialism and that, in general, knowledge of the Empire was sketchy. On the 1995 question, "Account for the expansion of Britain's overseas Empire in the period 1815–1871," for example, the examiners commented, "Answers tended to focus on foreign policy in general terms. Little attention was paid to the overseas Empire."

17. Key Stage 3 refers to the curriculum for 11- to 14-year-olds.

18. Some textbooks of the recent past have confronted imperial violence more dramatically, for example, the coverage of the 1921 Amritsar Massacre in Fisher and Williams (1989).

19. I was not told of any substantial ethnic minority populations in the Japanese schools visited and unfortunately omitted to ask about this; however, based on my personal knowledge of the local area and the geographical distribution of ethnic minorities (mainly Koreans) in Japan, it is unlikely that any of the schools contained minority populations at all comparable to those of several of the English schools.

20. Emperor Hirohito came to the throne in 1926, and his reign (1926–1989) is referred to as the Showa period.

21. Of course, the fact that these students were among the best of their cohort (probably in the top 5 percent in Japan) may have made an important difference, though Yoneyama's sample was also weighted toward good high schools.

22. F indicates a female student, M a male student. Names are pseudonyms.

23. Here, I define going "beyond the textbook" as introducing teaching materials, explanations, illustrations, or stories that did not appear in the textbook. For example, one teacher gave students a photocopy of another book dealing with the same subject as the textbook, but with extra information; another spent 25 minutes discussing a handout about archaeological finds that was related but extraneous to the textbook, another spent 15 minutes talking about a particular historical character in the Tang Dynasty, and a fourth spent 10 minutes talking about the significance of certain numbers in China and Japan. In most cases, the extra material was connected to the subject of study and seemed intended to enhance students' understanding and/or arouse their interest. Teachers use the term *dassen* (digression) to describe this apparently common teaching technique.

24. The Fifteen Years War (*jūgonen sensō*) is a term sometimes used for the period between 1931 (the Manchurian Incident) and 1945. It is generally associated with historians critical of the pre-1945 regime.

25. A teacher at an afterschool tutorial college (*juku*).

26. The *Himeyuri Butai*, or Star Lily Corps, was a corps of 239 field hospital nurses, mostly students, assembled by the Japanese military authorities in 1945 and thrown into the Battle of Okinawa, of which only 98 survived. The story has been made into a film six times and is described

by Watanabe (2001, 144) as "a symbol of civilian tragic suffering in the war, and … the classic vehicle for carrying out well-intended antiwar messages."

27. A long-running program on cultural topics presented in a popular style, broadcast by Yomiuri Television in the Sunday 9 P.M. slot.

28. The two films, the extremely popular book on which they are based, and the antiwar *Wadatsumikai* organization from which the films and book spring are discussed in Seraphim (2001, 147–177) and Watanabe (2001, 143–146).

29. It should be noted that this particular cohort of students had been in their midteens at the time of the fiftieth anniversary of the end of World War II in 1995, an event that generated an unusually large amount of reflection on the war (Watanabe 2001). The students had also recently been learning about this period of Japanese history in their university courses, and several mentioned that they had learned more detail about Japanese military aggression and atrocities as a result. This might also have influenced at least some of the overwhelming majority who said that they thought that schoolchildren should be taught the honest facts about what happened during these wars — as, of course, might the fact that they were being interviewed by a foreigner whom they knew to be a friend of their own (left-wing) professor. I had hoped that interviewing students who were in their first term at university would ensure that they would not yet have been influenced by university education on the subject of the interview, but unfortunately this was not so. Nonetheless, I do not think that what the interviewees said about their preuniversity experiences would have been significantly affected by their recent lectures.

30. Though the study of the Empire might be considered world history, students seemed to think of it as British history, with world history referring to the study of areas such as China, Russia, or America.

31. Both statements quoted were made by girls who appeared to be of South Asian origin, though their accents suggested an upbringing in Britain. Unfortunately, the relatively brief nature of the interviews and school visits precluded deeper investigation of the possible complexities of their feelings of identity. One of the teachers interviewed at Greenfields did say to me that some students of Indian origin had told her that sometimes they felt more Indian, and sometimes more British.

32. Some students interviewed at Greenfields had been on an international exchange where they had been impressed by how much national and British history was known by the Irish and Australian students they met. They said that this had made them feel that they themselves should know more British history.

33. Teachers observed in England sometimes made moral or political statements, saying that the Chartists "tried to make things fairer," or giving

students the task of imaginatively going back to the "bigoted" days of the past to make a speech against the National Health Service. See also Kinloch (1998, 2001) on the teaching of the Holocaust, and the subsequent lively debate in letters to Teaching History Nos. 94–97 and 104–105.

34. The Japanese curricula are explicit that history should foster a sense of Japanese identity (e.g., Monbushō 1989a, 23).

35. For an example and analysis of such ambivalence, see Aspinall and Cave (2001).

36. However, there may be indications of change in this attitude in recent curriculum revisions; see Cave (2003a).

References

Akita, George. 1982. "Trends in Modern Japanese Political History: The 'Positivist' Studies." *Monumenta Nipponica* 73, 4:497–521.

Aspinall, Robert and Cave, Peter. 2001. "Lowering the Flag: Democracy, Authority and Rights at Tokorozawa High School." *Social Science Japan Journal* 4, 1:77–93.

Aylett, J. F. 1993. *Expansion, Trade and Industry 1750–1900*. London: Hodder and Stoughton.

Barnard, Christopher. 2003. *Language, Ideology, and Japanese History Textbooks*. London: Routledge Curzon.

Booth, Martin, Masayuki Sato, and Matthews, Richard. 1995. "Case Studies of History Teaching in Japanese Junior High Schools and English Comprehensive Secondary Schools." *Compare* 25, 3:279–301.

Buruma, Ian. 1994. *The Wages of Guilt: Memories of War in Germany and Japan*. New York: Farrar Straus Giroux.

Cave, Peter. 2003a. "Japanese Educational Reform: Developments and Prospects at Primary and Secondary Level," in Roger Goodman and David Phillips, eds., *Can the Japanese Change Their Education System?* Oxford: Symposium Books.

———. 2003b. "Teaching the History of Empire in Japan and England." *International Journal of Educational Research* 37:623–641.

Chandler, Malcolm, and Wright, John. 2001. *Modern World History for Edexcel Specification A: Core*. Oxford: Heinemann.

Conrad, Sebastian. 1999. "What Time Is Japan? Problems of Comparative (Intercultural) Historiography." *History and Theory* 38, 1:67–83.

Department for Education and Employment. 1999. *History: The National Curriculum for England*. Norwich: The Stationery Office.

Fish, Robert. (Forthcoming). "From the Manchurian Incident to Nagasaki in 20 Pages: The Pacific War as Seen in Postwar Japanese High School History Textbooks." In E.R. Beauchamp, ed., *Education in Modern Japan: Old Voices, New Voices*. Armonk, NY: M.E. Sharpe.

Fisher, Peter, and Williams, Nicholas. 1989. *Past into Present 3: 1700–Present Day*, Collins Lower School History. London: Collins Educational.

Fukuzawa, Rebecca E. 1994. "The Path to Adulthood According to Japanese Middle Schools." *Journal of Japanese Studies* 20, 1:61–86.

Gluck, Carol. 1978. "The People in History: Recent Trends in Japanese Historiography." *Journal of Asian Studies* 38, 1:25–50.

Igarashi, Yoshikuni. 2000. *Bodies of Memory: Narratives of War in Postwar Japanese Culture, 1945–1970*. Princeton: Princeton University Press.

Kersten, Rikki. 1999. "Neo-nationalism and the 'Liberal School of History.'" *Japan Forum* 11, 2:191–203.

Kimijima, Kazuhiko. 2000. "The Continuing Legacy of Japanese Colonialism: The Japan-South Korea Joint Study Group on History Textbooks," in Laura Hein and Mark Selden, eds., *Censoring History: Citizenship and Memory in Japan, Germany, and the United States*. Armonk, NY: M.E. Sharpe, 203–225.

Kinloch, Nicolas. 1998. "Learning About the Holocaust: Moral or Historical Question?" *Teaching History* 93:44–46.

———. 2001. "Parallel Catastophes? Uniqueness, Redemption and the Shoah." *Teaching History* 104:8–14.

Larsson, Yvonne, Booth, Martin, and Matthews, Richard. 1998. "Attitudes to the Teaching of History and the Use of Creative Skills in Japan and England: A Comparative Study." *Compare* 28, 3, 305–314.

Lewis, Catherine C. 1996. *Educating Hearts and Minds: Reflections on Japanese Preschool and Elementary Education.* Cambridge: Cambridge University Press.

McCormack, Gavan. 1998. "Japan's Uncomfortable Past." *History Today* 48, 5:5–7.

Mehl, Margaret. 1998. *History and the State in Nineteenth-Century Japan.* Basingstoke: Macmillan.

Monbushō. 1989a. *Chgakk Gakush Shid Yry (Junior High School Curriculum).* Tokyo: Kurash Insatsukyoku.

———. 1989b. *Kt Gakk Gakush Shid Yry (High School Curriculum).* Tokyo: Kurash Insatsukyoku.

———. 2000. *Monbu Tkei Yran (Digest of Educational Statistics).* Tokyo: Kurash Insatsukyoku.

Nelson, John K. 2002. "Tempest in a Textbook: A Report on the New Middle-School History Textbook in Japan." *Critical Asian Studies* 34, 1:129–148.

Nozaki, Yoshiko. 2003. "Japanese Politics and the History Textbook Controversy, 1982–2001." *International Journal of Educational Research* 37, 6–7:603–622.

Nozaki, Yoshiko and Inokuchi, Hiromitsu. 2000. "Japanese History, Nationalism, and Ienaga Saburo's Textbook Lawsuits," in Laura Hein and Mark Selden, eds., *Censoring History: Citizenship and Memory in Japan, Germany, and the United States.* Armonk, NY: M. E. Sharpe, 96–126.

Phillips, Robert. 1998. *History Teaching, Nationhood and the State: A Study in Educational Politics.* London: Cassell.

Ramsden, John. 1996. *The Winds of Change: Macmillan to Heath 1957–1975.* London: Longman.

Rohlen, Thomas P. 1983. *Japan's High Schools.* Berkeley: University of California Press.

Rose, Caroline. 1999. "The Textbook Issue: Domestic Sources of Japan's Foreign Policy." *Japan Forum* 11, 2:205–216.

Sand, Jordan. 1999. "Introduction." *History and Memory* 11, 2:117–126.

Seraphim, Franziska. 2001. "Negotiating the Post-War: Politics and Memory in Japan, 1945–1995." Ph.D. dissertation, Columbia University.

Stevenson, Harold W. and Stigler, James W. 1992. *The Learning Gap.* New York: Summit Books.

Ueno, Chizuko. 1999. "The Politics of Memory: Nation, Individual and Self." *History and Memory* 11, 2:129–152.

Watanabe, Morio. 2001. "Imagery and War in Japan: 1995," in Fujitani, T., Geoffrey M. White, and Lisa Yoneyama, eds., *Perilous Memories: The Asia-Pacific War(s).* Durham, NC: Duke University Press.

Yoneyama, Shoko. 1999. *The Japanese High School: Silence and Resistance.* London: Routledge.

Contributors

Goh Chor Boon is an associate professor at the National Institute of Education, Singapore. He completed his Ph.D. in 1995 at the University of New South Wales. His principal academic interests include the ancient and modern history of China and Japan, the ancient history of Greece and Rome, and the technological and economic development of the newly industrialising Asian economies. His current research interests include the impact of history and culture on the development of science and technology in Singapore and the use of political cartoons in the teaching and learning of history. He is also author of *Living Hell: Story of a WWII Survivor at the Death Railway* (Singapore: Asiapac, 1999).

Peter Cave is a lecturer in the Department of Japanese Studies at The University of Hong Kong. He completed a degree in English at St. Catherine's College, Oxford, before teaching English for 3 years in a Japanese high school. He then returned to Oxford to complete a second degree in Oriental Studies (Japanese), followed by masters and doctrate degrees in social anthropology. His thesis was an ethnographic study of upper primary and lower secondary schooling in Japan.

Stéphane Corcuff teaches Chinese politics and language at the University of La Rochelle and Taiwanese geopolitics at the Paris Institute of Political Studies. He is presently a visiting scholar at the Fairbank Center of East Asian Research, Harvard University. He is the editor of *Memories of the Future: National Identity Issues and the Search for a New Taiwan* (Armonk: M.E. Sharpe, 2002) and has published widely in French, English, and Chinese on identity issues in Taiwan.

Julian Dierkes is an assistant professor and Keidanren Chair in Japanese Research at the Institute of Asian Research of the University of British Columbia. In 2003, he completed a Ph.D. in sociology at the University of Princeton, writing a dissertation on *Teaching Portrayals of the Nation — Postwar History Education in the Germanys and Japan*. He has published a number of articles on history education and identity in Japan and Germany.

Danton Ford works in the research department at the Institute for Far Eastern Studies, Kyungnam University in Seoul, Korea. He completed a 1 year study of the Korean language at Sogang University from 1999 to 2000. He is currently doing graduate work at Kyungnam University's Graduate School of North Korean Studies, where his research focuses on educational issues related to Korean unification and comparative studies of North and South Korean nationalism. Mr. Ford has delivered papers on Korean issues at academic conferences in Korea and Australia.

Saravanan Gopinathan is dean of the School of Education, Nanyang Technological University, and head of the Centre for Educational Research at the National Institute of Education. He is also president of the Educational Research Association of Singapore. His primary research interests are education and development, higher education, language, and values education.

Alisa Jones is a Ph.D. candidate at the University of Leeds, U.K. In 1998, she completed a master's degree in Chinese history at the School of Oriental and African Studies in London, for which she wrote a dissertation on Chinese historiography. For her Ph.D., she is researching the development of China's history curriculum for junior secondary level from the 1980s to the present.

Flora Kan is assistant professor of the Department of Curriculum Studies, University of Hong Kong. She lectures on and researches history teaching in Hong Kong and is currently completing a Ph.D. on the postwar development of Chinese history as a school subject. She has published articles on history and civic education in Hong Kong in both Chinese- and English-language journals.

Li-Ching Hung received her master's degree at the Graduate Institute of Compulsory Education, National Hualien Teachers College, where she majored in social studies education. She is currently an elementary school teacher.

Liu Mei-Hui is Professor and Director of Academic Services at the National Hualien Teachers College, Hualien, Taiwan. She has made numerous presentations at international conferences on her work. Her publications include a chapter on civic education in Taiwan for a recent special issue of the *International Journal of Educational Research* (Volume 35, Number 1, 2001).

Edward Vickers is a lecturer in comparative education at the Institute of Education, University of London. He worked from 2000 to 2001 as a textbook writer at the People's Education Press, Beijing, and subsequently lived in Beijing as a freelance writer and independent scholar. From 1992 to 2000, he lived and worked in Hong Kong, first as a schoolteacher and later as a full-time Ph.D. student. He is the author of *In Search of an Identity: The Politics of History as a School Subject in Hong Kong, 1960s–2002* (New York: Routledge, 2003), a revised and updated second edition of which is shortly to be published by the Comparative Education Research Centre of the University of Hong Kong.

Chris Wilson, a Ph.D. candidate at Loyola University in Chicago, lived in South Korea for 2 years, worked for 4 years as a social studies teacher and department chairperson in a U.S. public school, and completed a master's degree in Comparative International Education at Brigham Young University, Idaho. He currently teaches in the secondary education department at Brigham Young University and is researching the role of history curriculum in the transition of educational systems for completion of his Ph.D. dissertation requirement.

Yoshiko Nozaki is currently an assistant professor at the Department of Educational Leadership and Policy, State University of New York (SUNY) at Buffalo. She earned her Ph.D. at the University of Wisconsin at Madison, where she studied curriculum history, educational anthropology, cultural studies, and critical and feminist theories. In her dissertation, she examined the Japanese textbook controversies in the years since 1945, particularly Saburo Ienaga's court challenges to the state's de facto censorship of school textbooks. She was a social studies teacher in Japan in the 1980s and has also had experience teaching in public schools in the United States and Australia. Before joining the staff at SUNY-Buffalo, she was a lecturer at Massey University in New Zealand.

Index

Lightning Source UK Ltd.
Milton Keynes UK
UKOW04n2000121213

222904UK00001B/64/P